THE

SARBANES-OXLEY ACT:

ANALYSIS AND PRACTICE

Cleary, Gottlieb, Steen & Hamilton

Edward F. Greene

Leslie N. Silverman

David M. Becker

Edward J. Rosen

Janet L. Fisher

Daniel A. Braverman

Sebastian R. Sperber

1185 Avenue of the Americas New York, NY 10036
www.aspenpublishers.com

This publication is designed to provide accurate and authoritative information in regard to the subject matter covered. It is sold with the understanding that the publisher is not engaged in rendering legal, accounting, or other professional services. If legal advice or other professional assistance is required, the services of a competent professional person should be sought.

—From a *Declaration of Principles* jointly adopted by
a Committee of the American Bar Association and a
Committee of Publishers and Associations

© 2003 Aspen Publishers, Inc.
www.aspenpublishers.com

All rights reserved. No part of this publication may be reproduced or transmitted in any form or by any means, electronic or mechanical, including photocopy, recording, or any information storage and retrieval system, without permission in writing from the publisher. Requests for permission to reproduce content should be directed to the Aspen Publishers website at *www.aspenpublishers.com*, or fax a letter of intent to the permissions department at 646-728-3048.

Printed in the United States of America

ISBN 0-7355-4492-1

About Aspen Publishers

Aspen Publishers, headquartered in New York City, is a leading information provider for attorneys, business professionals, and law students. Written by preeminent authorities, our products consist of analytical and practical information covering both U.S. and international topics. We publish in the full range of formats, including updated manuals, books, periodicals, CDs, and online products.

Our proprietary content is complemented by 2,500 legal databases, containing over 11 million documents, available through our Loislaw division. Aspen Publishers also offers a wide range of topical legal and business databases linked to Loislaw's primary material. Our mission is to provide accurate, timely, and authoritative content in easily accessible formats, supported by unmatched customer care.

To order any Aspen Publishers title, go to *www.aspenpublishers.com* or call 1-800-638-8437.

To reinstate your manual update service, call 1-800-638-8437.

For more information on Loislaw products, go to *www.loislaw.com* or call 1-800-364-2512.

For Customer Care issues, e-mail *CustomerCare@aspenpublishers.com*; call 1-800-234-1660; or fax 1-800-901-9075.

Aspen Publishers
A Wolters Kluwer Company

SUBSCRIPTION NOTICE

This Aspen Publishers product is updated on a periodic basis with supplements to reflect important changes in the subject matter. If you purchased this product directly from Aspen Publishers, we have already recorded your subscription for the update service.

If, however, you purchased this product from a bookstore and wish to receive future updates and revised or related volumes billed separately with a 30-day examination review, please contact our Customer Service Department at 1-800-234-1660, or send your name, company name (if applicable), address, and the title of the product to:

ASPEN PUBLISHERS
7201 McKinney Circle
Frederick, MD 21704

TABLE OF CONTENTS

	About the Authors	vii
	Introduction	xiii
I	Sarbanes-Oxley Act: Overview and Implementation	1
II	Considerations for Foreign Private Issuers	53
III	Audit Committee Responsibilities	59
IV	Listed Company Audit Committee Standards	85
V	NYSE and Nasdaq Governance Proposals	99
VI	Officer Certifications and Internal Control Reports	113
VII	Questions to Ask Before Certifying Periodic Reports	131
VIII	Designing Disclosure Controls and Procedures	141
IX	Practical Considerations for Earnings Releases	157
X	Attorney Professional Conduct Standards	165
Appendix A	Sarbanes-Oxley Act of 2002	191
Appendix B	Summary of New Disclosure Requirements	259
Appendix C	Additional Resources	277
Appendix D	Forms of Officer Certification	279

ABOUT THE AUTHORS

The authors of this publication are partners of Cleary, Gottlieb, Steen & Hamilton. Cleary Gottlieb is a leading U.S. and international law firm that is widely recognized for its expertise in finance and mergers and acquisitions and for its tax, regulatory and litigation practice. Named in 2001 as the inaugural "International Law Firm of the Year" by Chambers, the firm now has 11 offices located in New York, Washington, Paris, Brussels, London, Frankfurt, Rome, Milan, Moscow, Hong Kong and Tokyo.

Edward F. Greene

Edward F. Greene specializes in matters relating to U.S. regulation of capital markets and financial institutions. His practice involves the counseling and representation of corporate issuers, investment banks, merchant banks and commercial banks principally in connection with mergers and acquisitions, securitizations of assets, distributions of securities in domestic and international financings and enforcement proceedings before the Securities and Exchange Commission.

Mr. Greene is currently resident in the London office, but has also been resident in the Washington and Tokyo offices. Prior to joining the firm in 1983, he was General Counsel of the Securities and Exchange Commission, from 1981–1982, and Director of the Division of Corporation Finance, from 1979–1981. Prior to joining the SEC, he was engaged in private practice in New York.

Mr. Greene received an LL.B. degree from Harvard Law School in 1966 and an undergraduate degree from Amherst College in 1963. He is a member of the Bar of the State of New York.

He has published several articles in law reviews and other legal periodicals on federal securities and banking law and mergers and acquisitions, and is a co-author of *U.S. Regulation of the International Securities and Derivatives Markets* (Sixth Ed., Aspen Publishers). He is a Trustee of the SEC Historical Society and a member of the advisory and editorial boards of several legal education publications and institutes. Mr. Greene has been an Adjunct Professor of Law at the University of Pennsylvania and Georgetown University Law Center, was appointed to the Nomura Chair of International Securities Regulation (a part-time position) by the law faculty of the University of Tokyo for the 1989–1990 academic year, and was appointed Lecturer of the Harvard Law School for the 2003 Spring term. He was also Chairman of the Legal Advisory Board of the New York Stock Exchange from 1995 to 2001 and was a member of the SEC's Advisory Committee on Capital Formation and Regulatory Processes. He was a member of the Financial Accounting Standards Advisory Council from 1986 to 1987.

Leslie N. Silverman

Leslie N. Silverman specializes in domestic and international financial work and mergers and acquisitions. In recent years, he has been particularly active in cross-border financings, such as global public offerings and Rule 144A and other private placements, as well as securities repackaging, equity derivative and project financing transactions. He has extensive experience in advising Latin American private sector clients, having been responsible in particular for the firm's representation of a number of Mexican issuers in their initial public offerings. Mr. Silverman is a co-author of *U.S. Regulation of the International Securities and Derivatives Markets* (Sixth Ed., Aspen Publishers).

Mr. Silverman was resident in the firm's London office from 1985 to 1989 and is currently resident in the New York office. Prior to joining the firm, he served as law clerk to Chief Judge Irving R. Kaufman of the United States Court of Appeals for the Second Circuit.

Mr. Silverman received a J.D. degree from Yale Law School in 1973, where he was an editor of the *Law Journal*, and an undergraduate degree *summa cum laude* from the Wharton School of the University of Pennsylvania. He is a member of the Bar of the State of New York and the District of Columbia and is admitted to practice before the United States Court of Appeals, Second Circuit, and the United States District Court, Southern District of New York.

Mr. Silverman is a member of the American Bar Association, the Association of the Bar of the City of New York and the District of Columbia Bar Association.

David M. Becker

David M. Becker specializes in the full range of issues arising out of capital markets activities. He focuses on regulatory and other investigations, corporate governance issues and a broad range of regulatory matters. Mr. Becker has represented broker-dealers, financial institutions, issuers and individuals in enforcement investigations and proceedings before the Securities and Exchange Commission and the various self-regulatory organizations. He has also conducted corporate investigations and represented issuers and underwriters in securities class action and shareholder derivative lawsuits.

Mr. Becker is resident in the Washington, D.C. office. Prior to joining the firm in 2002, he served as General Counsel of the SEC. During his more than three years there, Mr. Becker counseled the SEC on virtually all of its enforcement, rule-

ABOUT THE AUTHORS

making and regulatory actions. He was particularly active in advising the SEC on matters related to corporate governance, accounting and disclosure. Mr. Becker was also responsible for representing the SEC in all appellate actions, including enforcement actions. Prior to joining the SEC, Mr. Becker was a partner of Wilmer, Cutler & Pickering.

Mr. Becker received a J.D. degree in 1973 from Columbia University Law School, where he was editor-in-chief of the *Columbia Law Review*, and an undergraduate degree from Columbia College in 1968. Following graduation, Mr. Becker served as law clerk to the Honorable Harold Leventhal of the U.S. Court of Appeals for the District of Columbia Circuit and a year later for the Honorable Stanley Reed (retired) of the U.S. Supreme Court. He is a member of the Bar of the District of Columbia and the State of New York.

Edward J. Rosen

Edward J. Rosen specializes in the structuring of complex securities and derivatives transactions, U.S. securities and commodities law regulation and derivative product development and documentation. Mr. Rosen also specializes in intellectual property and technology matters, particularly in relation to the financial sector.

Mr. Rosen advises a broad range of domestic and international market participants, including trade associations, exchanges, clearinghouses, e-commerce trading platforms, investment banks, commercial banks, brokers, money managers, traders, professional intermediaries and end-users in the United States and abroad. Mr. Rosen has advised a number of consortia of leading investment and commercial banks on legislative and regulatory initiatives relating to derivatives. Mr. Rosen also serves as counsel to the Derivative Products Committee and the Risk Management Committee of the U.S. Securities Industry Association. Mr. Rosen also acted as counsel to the Derivatives Policy Group and the Counterparty Risk Management Policy Group. Mr. Rosen is a co-author of *U.S. Regulation of the International Securities and Derivatives Markets* (Sixth Ed., Aspen Publishers).

Mr. Rosen is a member of the Board of Directors of the Futures Industry Association and the U.S. Regulatory Advisory Committee of the International Swaps and Derivatives Association. Mr. Rosen is also a member of the Commodity Futures Trading Commission Technology Advisory Committee. Mr. Rosen is a regular speaker on topics relating to derivatives and financial issues.

Mr. Rosen is resident in the New York office. He received a J.D. degree from Columbia University School of Law in 1982, where he was a Stone Scholar, and an undergraduate degree with honors from Balliol College, Oxford University, in 1975. He is admitted to the Bar of the State of New York and the U.S. Supreme Court.

THE SARBANES-OXLEY ACT: ANALYSIS AND PRACTICE

Janet L. Fisher

Janet L. Fisher specializes in corporate finance transactions and securities law matters, including public and private debt and equity offerings in the United States and elsewhere for domestic and foreign issuers, and financings related to corporate restructurings. Ms. Fisher represents both corporate issuers and investment banks and has extensive experience in the regulation of investment companies and investment advisers, as well as the creation and operation of private equity funds in the United States and abroad. Ms. Fisher lectures regularly and has published several articles on aspects of the U.S. securities laws and corporate governance.

From 1994 to 1997, Ms. Fisher was resident in the Hong Kong office, and she is currently resident in the New York office. She received a J.D. degree, *cum laude*, from the University of Chicago Law School in 1984, a Masters of Arts from Princeton University in 1981, and an undergraduate degree, *magna cum laude*, from Smith College in 1979.

Ms. Fisher is a member of the American Bar Association and the Bar of the State of New York.

Daniel A. Braverman

Daniel A. Braverman specializes in international finance, but he also does work in the areas of mergers and acquisitions, joint venture and restructuring, and he has assumed responsibility for a significant part of the firm's capital markets practice in Russia. Mr. Braverman is currently resident in the London office.

Mr. Braverman received a J.D. in 1985 from Yale Law School, an M.Sc. in Politics (with reference to China) in 1982 from the School of Oriental and African Studies of the University of London while on a Marshall Scholarship, and a Bachelor of Arts *summa cum laude* in East Asian Studies from Harvard College in 1980. He is a member of the Bar of the State of New York.

Mr. Braverman has published several articles on the U.S. securities laws as they relate to international financial transactions, including "U.S. Legal Considerations Affecting Global Offerings of Shares in Foreign Companies," *Journal of International Law and Business at Northwestern* (Fall 1996). Mr. Braverman is a co-author of *U.S. Regulation of the International Securities and Derivatives Markets* (Sixth Ed., Aspen Publishers).

Sebastian R. Sperber

Sebastian R. Sperber specializes in U.S. securities law and has extensive experience in international capital markets and mergers and acquisitions. Mr. Sperber has, in particular, devoted a substantial amount of time to working on global equity offerings, including privatization transactions in Denmark, Italy, Sweden and the United Kingdom. His experience in mergers and acquisitions in-

ABOUT THE AUTHORS

cludes both public and private transactions in various industries in Europe and Asia.

Mr. Sperber's practice also includes derivative products, and he regularly assists a number of clients in structuring over-the-counter and listed instruments. He has, for example, advised clients on the establishment of global warrant issuance programs.

Mr. Sperber is currently resident in the Hong Kong office, but has also been resident in the New York and London offices. He received a J.D. degree from Columbia University School of Law in 1988 and a B.A. degree in political science from Columbia College in 1985. Mr. Sperber was the Editor-in-Chief of the *Columbia Journal of Transnational Law* from 1987 to 1988. He is a member of the Bar of the State of New York.

Mr. Sperber is a member of the American Bar Association and the New York State Bar Association. He serves on the Board of Directors of the Columbia Journal of Transnational Law Association, Inc. and The Columbia Law School Center for European Legal Studies Advisory Board. Mr. Sperber is the co-author of numerous publications on U.S. securities law issues, and he regularly lectures on such issues at professional conferences. Recent publications co-authored by Mr. Sperber include "Important Disclosure Issues for Non-US Companies Seeking A US Listing," Chapter 6 of *A Practitioner's Guide to The EASDAQ Rules* (1999/2000 Edition). Mr. Sperber is a co-author of *U.S. Regulation of the International Securities and Derivatives Markets* (Sixth Ed., Aspen Publishers).

INTRODUCTION

The Sarbanes-Oxley Act is the most important securities legislation enacted by Congress since the 1930s. It affects all publicly-held companies—U.S. and foreign—and its provisions have influenced changes being considered and likely to be enacted in Europe and elsewhere. The Act effects major changes to the structure and oversight of the accounting profession and enhances disclosure requirements. Above all, however, the Act heightens the accountability of management for a company's public disclosures and the internal controls and processes necessary to the transparency and integrity of those disclosures. Equally central to these goals are the Act's provisions mandating increased oversight responsibility for audit committees and minimum independence and other requirements for audit committees of companies listed in the United States.

The purpose of this book is to provide guidance for boards of directors, audit committees and management as to best practices. The book starts with an overview of the key provisions of the Act, including a chart for quick reference indicating the status of rulemaking to date. In subsequent chapters, we address in more detail:

- special considerations for foreign private issuers;

- the changing role of the audit committee, including new independence requirements under SEC rules and proposed rules of the NYSE and Nasdaq;

- practical steps CEOs and CFOs should take before personally certifying the accuracy and completeness of a company's SEC filings;

- guidance when non-GAAP measures are used in earnings releases and related webcasts; and

- changes in disclosure for U.S. and foreign issuers that will be required as a result of the Act and subsequent rulemakings.

Other initiatives affecting corporate governance are being taken in light of the failures prompting the Act. Among them are the pending proposals of the NYSE and Nasdaq noted above, and we have included a chart comparing these

THE SARBANES-OXLEY ACT: ANALYSIS AND PRACTICE

proposals. Lawyers as a profession are also affected by the reforms. We have included a description of the SEC's new "up the ladder" reporting requirements that will apply to all lawyers who practice before the SEC.

The materials that follow reflect the status of the Act's implementation to date, but pending regulatory and enforcement initiatives both in the United States and abroad will certainly result in continuing evolution of governance reforms. Company directors and officers, as well as legal practitioners, must continue to remain alert to changes that will affect best practices. Additional memoranda addressing the changes effected by the Sarbanes-Oxley Act to date are listed at the end of these materials. Those materials and other practice resources are also available on our website: *www.clearygottlieb.com*.

This publication reflects the substantial effort of many of our colleagues at Cleary, Gottlieb, Steen & Hamilton. We owe special thanks to Barbara Gaffney and Tamara Sapilak, whose organizational and other skills were indispensable in bringing this book to press. We also thank our partners, Nicolas Grabar, Craig Brod, Arthur Kohn, Bob Raymond, Jeff Karpf and David Gottlieb, and our associates, Sandra Flow, Duane McLaughlin, Mark Adams, Jon Wallenberger, James McMullin, Melissa Johns, Pam Nadler, Marie Noble and Monica Kays, each of whom provided valuable insights and editorial assistance. We are indebted to them for their contribution and support in completing this project. Responsibility for any errors or omissions in these materials is of course ours alone.

* * *

The SEC and others are determined to restore investor confidence by vigorously reviewing and in some cases challenging financial reporting. Congress is overseeing these efforts. Compliance with both the letter and spirit of the new Sarbanes-Oxley regulatory regime is important for all companies, and we hope these materials will be helpful.

                                          Edward F. Greene
                                          Leslie N. Silverman
                                          David M. Becker
                                          Edward J. Rosen
                                          Janet L. Fisher
                                          Daniel A. Braverman
                                          Sebastian R. Sperber

June 23, 2003

I   SARBANES-OXLEY ACT: OVERVIEW AND IMPLEMENTATION

On July 30, 2002, President Bush signed into law the Sarbanes-Oxley Act of 2002 (the "Sarbanes-Oxley Act" or the "Act").[1] The Sarbanes-Oxley Act was approved by nearly unanimous votes[2] in the Congress in response to recent accounting scandals and corporate governance abuses. The Act was spurred by weak stock markets, voter anger and approaching Congressional elections and is the most sweeping legislation affecting public companies since the Depression-era laws that are the backbone of the U.S. securities laws. While some provisions of the Act were immediately effective, most required rulemaking by the Securities and Exchange Commission (the "SEC"), which is now substantially completed. Indeed, in some cases the SEC has already adopted amendments to its original rulemakings under the Act. Nevertheless, the application of the Act and many of the new regulations is unclear and may ultimately need to be decided by judicial proceedings or further SEC guidance. It is therefore difficult to predict the full consequences of the Sarbanes-Oxley Act.

I.   SUMMARY OF PRINCIPAL PROVISIONS

The following are the principal provisions of the Sarbanes-Oxley Act and related SEC rules.[3] Because the Act generally applies to all SEC-reporting companies,[4] and thus expands in critical ways the application of the U.S. securities laws to foreign issuers, we have highlighted its implications for foreign issuers in Section II below. Section III provides recommendations that all affected companies should consider. Section IV contains an analysis of the Act's principal provisions. A summary of the Sarbanes-Oxley Act, which sets out the effective date and/or required regulatory action for each of its provisions and a list of the various studies mandated by the Act, is included in the annexes to this Chapter.

---

[1] Sarbanes-Oxley Act of 2002, Pub. L. No. 107-204, 116 Stat. 745 (2002). The Act is reproduced in Appendix A.

[2] The House of Representatives approved the bill 423-3 (148 CONG. REC. H5480 (daily ed. July 25, 2002)); the Senate 99-0 (148 CONG. REC. 57365 (daily ed. July 25, 2002)).

[3] The staff of the SEC has provided responses to "frequently asked questions" about the Sarbanes-Oxley Act and related rules. *See* Division of Corporation Finance: Sarbanes-Oxley Act of 2002—Frequently Asked Questions (last revised Nov. 14, 2002); Frequently Asked Questions Regarding the Use of Non-GAAP Financial Measures (June 13, 2003).

[4] The following discussion does not address rules adopted by the SEC to implement the Sarbanes-Oxley Act in respect of small business issuers.

THE SARBANES-OXLEY ACT: ANALYSIS AND PRACTICE

- **CEO and CFO Certification Requirements.** As directed by the Sarbanes-Oxley Act, the SEC has adopted rules providing for various CEO and CFO certifications on an annual and quarterly basis.[5] A separate provision of the Sarbanes-Oxley Act imposes criminal liability, including in certain cases imprisonment for up to 20 years, for CEOs and CFOs who knowingly or willfully furnish inaccurate certifications.[6] These two certification requirements are phrased differently and are independent, and each differs from the SEC's original certification proposal.[7]

- **Disclosure Controls and Procedures/Internal Controls.** SEC rules now require each reporting company to maintain and provide disclosure with respect to "disclosure controls and procedures"—procedures designed to ensure that information required to be disclosed is processed and reported within the required time period.[8] Amendments to these rules adopted in 2003 expand this requirement and the related disclosure to "internal control over financial reporting."[9]

- **Report on Internal Control over Financial Reporting.** SEC rules will require that an issuer (other than a registered investment company) disclose management's assessment of the effectiveness of the issuer's internal control over financial reporting, among other matters. The issuer's independent auditor must issue an attestation report on management's assessment, which must itself be filed with the SEC.[10]

- **Audit Committee for Listed Companies.** The Sarbanes-Oxley Act and related SEC rules will require all listed companies, including foreign issuers and issuers that have only listed debt securities, to have fully independent audit committees.[11] The audit committee is now required to

---

[5] Section 302 of the Sarbanes-Oxley Act. SEC Release No. 33-8124 (Aug. 29, 2002); SEC Release No. 33-8238 (June 5, 2003) (amending the form of certification and manner of providing certifications to SEC).

[6] Section 906 of the Sarbanes-Oxley Act.

[7] *See* SEC Release No. 34-46079 (June 14, 2002).

[8] SEC Release No. 33-8124 (Aug. 29, 2002).

[9] SEC Release No. 33-8238 (June 5, 2003).

[10] Section 404 of the Sarbanes-Oxley Act; SEC Release No. 33-8238 (June 5, 2003).

[11] Section 301 of the Sarbanes-Oxley Act; SEC Release No. 33-8229 (Apr. 9, 2003). The New York Stock Exchange ("NYSE") and the NASD Inc. (the "NASD"), which regulates the Nasdaq Stock Market, Inc. ("Nasdaq"), have announced proposed changes to their corporate governance requirements, including changes relating to director independence and audit committees. *See* Amendment No. 1 to the NYSE's Corporate Governance Rule Proposals; SEC Release No. 34-47672 (Apr. 11, 2003). The most important of the SEC rules is Rule 10A-3 under the Exchange Act. The Nasdaq proposals are set out in Amendment No. 1: Rules 4200 and 4350 Regarding Board Independence and Independent Committees; SEC Release No. 34-47516 (Mar. 17, 2003). *See also* SEC Release No. 33-8220 (Apr. 9, 2003) implementing Section 301 of the Sarbanes-Oxley Act. The changes proposed by the NYSE and the

hire and supervise the company's independent auditor, and issuers must disclose whether their audit committee includes an "audit committee financial expert," and if not, explain why not.[12]

- **Disgorgement of CEO and CFO Compensation Following Restatement of Financial Statements.** Effective July 30, 2002, an issuer's CEO and CFO must disgorge all bonuses and incentive-based compensation, as well as profits from sales of the issuer's securities, if the issuer restates its financial statements due to material noncompliance with any financial reporting requirement as a result of misconduct.[13] This provision covers the foregoing sources of compensation earned in the 12-month period following the first public issuance or filing of the non-compliant report.

- **Prohibition on Insider Trades During Individual Account Plan Blackout Periods.** Effective January 26, 2003, the Sarbanes-Oxley Act prohibits executive officers and directors from purchasing or selling equity securities of an issuer during certain blackout periods imposed on 50% or more of the participants in an individual account plan, such as a 401(k) plan, maintained by the issuer (or its subsidiaries), if the director or officer acquired such securities in connection with his or her employment with the issuer.[14] Blackouts affecting mostly non-U.S. employees have been exempted.

- **Prohibition of Insider Loans.** Effective July 30, 2002, an issuer may not make, maintain or arrange for loans to executive officers and directors, subject to limited exceptions for loans on the effective date, home improvement loans, margin loans by a broker-dealer to its employees, loans by a depository institution subject to insider lending restrictions, and certain other credit transactions.[15]

- **Real Time Disclosure Requirements.** The Sarbanes-Oxley Act requires issuers to disclose "on a rapid and current basis" in plain English such information as the SEC may require concerning material changes in their financial condition and operations.[16] The Act does not establish

---

NASD do not appear to alter their traditional policy to allow foreign issuers to follow home country practices. The NYSE proposes, for example, that foreign issuers provide on either their websites or in their annual reports a brief, general summary of the material differences between the NYSE requirements and home country practices.

[12] Section 407 of the Sarbanes-Oxley Act. SEC Release No. 33-8177 (Jan. 23, 2003); SEC Release No. 33-8177A (Mar. 26, 2003) (technical corrections).

[13] Section 304 of the Sarbanes-Oxley Act.

[14] *Id.* Section 306. SEC Release No. 34-47225 (Jan. 22, 2003).

[15] Section 402 of the Sarbanes-Oxley Act.

[16] *Id.* Section 409.

a time frame for SEC rulemaking in this regard, and it remains unclear whether the rules to be adopted would establish a continuous reporting system (such as the ones that exist in many foreign jurisdictions) or take a more measured approach by expanding the list of events that give rise to a reporting obligation under existing SEC requirements (perhaps along the lines of an outstanding SEC proposed amendment to Form 8-K).[17] It also is unclear whether this will be applied to foreign issuers.

- **Additional Disclosure.** SEC rules require additional disclosure with respect to whether a reporting company has a code of ethics and whether its audit committee has a financial expert or, if not, why not. SEC rules also require more detailed disclosures about off-balance sheet transactions and restrict the use of financial measures that are not in accordance with generally accepted accounting principles ("GAAP"), notably by requiring that any non-GAAP financial measure in most public disclosures be quantitatively reconciled to the comparable GAAP measure.

- **Mandated Periodic SEC Review of Public Company Filings.** The Sarbanes-Oxley Act establishes criteria to be used by the SEC in determining the frequency with which a listed company's filings are reviewed and requires the review of each public company's disclosures at least once every three years.[18]

- **Accelerated Section 16 Reporting.** The Act amends § 16(a) of the Securities Exchange Act of 1934 (the "Exchange Act"), effective August 29, 2002, to require, among other things, reporting of insider transactions on Form 4 within two business days of the relevant transaction, and the SEC has adopted final rules under this provision.[19] Section 16 is not applicable to most foreign issuers.

- **New Accounting Oversight Board under SEC Supervision.** The Sarbanes-Oxley Act establishes the Public Company Accounting Oversight Board (the "PCAOB"), which has now been constituted and is responsible for establishing auditing, quality control, attestation and ethics standards for auditors of public companies.[20] The PCAOB is subject to SEC oversight.

- **Auditor Independence; Auditors Relationship with Audit Committee.** The Sarbanes-Oxley Act and related SEC rules prohibit auditors from providing eight types of non-audit services to their audit clients,

---

[17] *See* SEC Release No. 33-8106 (June 17, 2002).
[18] Section 408 of the Sarbanes-Oxley Act.
[19] *Id.* Section 403. SEC Release No. 34-46421 (Aug 27, 2002).
[20] Sections 101-107 of the Sarbanes-Oxley Act.

OVERVIEW AND IMPLEMENTATION

and require an issuer's audit committee to approve in advance any audit or permitted non-audit services provided by the issuer's auditors.[21] Auditors are required to report to the audit committee with respect to critical accounting policies, alternative treatments of financial information under GAAP that have been discussed with management and any other material written communications with management.[22] In addition, the Act requires that filings include all material adjustments that have been identified by an accounting firm.[23] The Act and SEC rules require rotation of lead and concurring audit partners every five years, rotation of other significant audit partners every seven years, and also impose new "time out" periods (five years for lead and concurring partners and two years for other significant audit partners).[24]

- **Enhanced Criminal and Civil Provisions.** The Sarbanes-Oxley Act significantly strengthens existing criminal provisions. Key provisions include (i) creation of a new crime for destruction or alteration of records in federal investigations or bankruptcy, subject to fines and imprisonment of up to 20 years;[25] (ii) creation of a new crime for destruction of audit records, which must be maintained under new SEC rules for seven years, subject to fines and imprisonment of up to ten years;[26] (iii) creation of a new securities fraud crime with respect to public companies, subject to fines and imprisonment of up to 25 years;[27] (iv) extension of the statute of limitations for securities fraud claims, which must be brought within two years of discovery and five years of the violation (previously, those periods were one and three years, respectively);[28] and (v) increases in the term of imprisonment for mail and wire fraud from five years to 20 years.[29] The effect of these provisions is that the U.S. Sentencing Commission is revising its guidelines for

---

[21] *Id.* Sections 201-202. SEC Release No. 33-8183 (Jan. 28, 2003); SEC Release No. 33-8183A (Mar. 26, 2003) (technical corrections). The Sarbanes-Oxley Act added the following definition of "audit committee" to the Exchange Act: "a committee (or equivalent body) established by and amongst the board of directors of an issuer for the purpose of overseeing the accounting and financial reporting processes of the issuer and audits of the financial statements of the issuer; and . . . if no such committee exists with respect to an issuer, the entire board of directors of the issuer." § 3(a)(58) of the Exchange Act.

[22] Section 204 of the Sarbanes-Oxley Act. SEC Release No. 33-8183 (Jan. 28, 2003); SEC Release No. 33-8183A (Mar. 26, 2003) (technical corrections).

[23] Section 401 of the Sarbanes-Oxley Act.

[24] *Id.* Section 203; SEC Release No. 33-8183 (Jan. 28, 2003); SEC Release No. 33-8183A (Mar. 26, 2003) (technical corrections).

[25] Section 802 of the Sarbanes-Oxley Act.

[26] *Id.* Section 802.

[27] *Id.* Section 807.

[28] *Id.* Section 804.

[29] *Id.* Section 903.

these crimes, resulting in stiffer sentences for defendants convicted of these crimes.

II. APPLICABILITY TO NON-U.S. ISSUERS

With one exception,[30] the provisions of the Sarbanes-Oxley Act apply to all "issuers," which is defined in the Act as a company:

- with securities registered under § 12 of the Exchange Act;

- that is required to file reports under § 15(d) of the Exchange Act; or

- that has filed a registration statement under the Securities Act of 1933 (the "Securities Act") that has not yet become effective and that it has not withdrawn.[31]

This includes all SEC-reporting companies, domestic or foreign.[32] It does not include a foreign issuer exempt from the reporting requirements of the Exchange Act pursuant to Rule 12g3-2(b).

The coverage of foreign issuers is surprising in light of policies of the SEC, the NYSE and the NASD to accommodate home country practices of foreign issuers.[33] In its rulemakings to date, the SEC has not exercised the exemptive au-

---

[30] The only exception is that the rules issued with respect to audit committees under Section 301 of the Sarbanes-Oxley Act apply only to listed companies, as discussed below. The Act also grants the SEC specific exemptive power and does not derogate from the SEC's general exemptive authority under § 36 of the Exchange Act.

[31] This last provision makes the Sarbanes-Oxley Act applicable to an issuer once it has filed its first registration statement with the SEC under the Securities Act. An issuer that cancels a proposed initial public offering would be required to withdraw its registration statement to remove itself from application of the requirements of the Sarbanes-Oxley Act. The Sarbanes-Oxley Act highlights the importance of the SEC's policy of reviewing the initial registration statement of a foreign issuer on a confidential basis, rather than requiring that it be publicly filed as would be required for domestic issuers. As a result of this policy, a foreign issuer making its initial U.S. public offering would not be subject to the Sarbanes-Oxley Act until after the SEC had reviewed and commented on its registration statement and the foreign issuer had made its first public filing of the registration statement.

[32] The definition includes foreign issuers organized in Canada, including those eligible to effect filings pursuant to the U.S.-Canadian multijurisdictional disclosure system (the "MJDS"). The definition of issuer would also appear inadvertently to include sovereign issuers with reporting obligations under § 12(b) of the Exchange Act with respect to listed debt securities, although it is not clear how a majority of the Sarbanes-Oxley Act's provisions could be applied to sovereigns.

[33] The SEC traditionally has made a number of accommodations for foreign issuers to avoid imposing undue burdens that might discourage them from accessing the U.S. capital markets. For example, foreign issuers generally are exempt from the proxy rules under § 14 of the Exchange Act and from the reporting and short swing profit provisions of § 16 of the Exchange Act. Foreign issuers also generally are not required to file quarterly reports on Form 10-Q or current reports on Form 8-K. As noted above, both the NYSE and the NASD have historically exempted foreign issuers from certain listing requirements in recognition of inconsistencies between home country practices and the standards ap-

OVERVIEW AND IMPLEMENTATION

thority granted to it under the Sarbanes-Oxley Act to exempt foreign private issuers, as a class, from the Act's application, although it has sought to accommodate significant differences between U.S. and foreign issuers, for example in relation to governance practices.

III. RECOMMENDATIONS

The Sarbanes-Oxley Act includes various far-reaching provisions that will have a significant impact on the corporate governance and management of all SEC-reporting companies, both domestic and foreign, and those planning on making a public offering in the United States. The Act's provisions and SEC rulemaking initiatives suggest a number of steps that domestic and foreign issuers should consider.

- **Monitor and Participate in Rule Adoption Process.** While substantially all of the Sarbanes-Oxley Act's required rulemaking is complete, issuers should continue to monitor the SEC's and the PCAOB's rulemaking process so that they can assess the potential impact of any further initiatives and be in a position to comment, either directly or through counsel.

- **Establish Appropriate Controls and Procedures for SEC Disclosures and Management's Internal Control Report.** The SEC's requirement that all issuers, domestic and foreign, maintain and evaluate their "disclosure controls and procedures" and "internal control over financial reporting" should be carefully considered by issuers in light of their existing practices. This is particularly important in light of management's required report on internal control over financial reporting. To permit an independent auditor to provide its attestation of the report, most issuers will likely need to heighten their focus on documentation of significant controls and to improve the quality and scope of those controls. Although

---

plicable to U.S. companies, and pending proposals by the NYSE and Nasdaq would maintain this approach except to the extent otherwise mandated by the Act.

The following comment by Sen. Michael Enzi during the Senate conference debate to approve the final version of the Sarbanes-Oxley Act suggests that the Act was not intended to apply equally to U.S. and non-U.S. issuers:

> In addition, I believe we need to be clear with respect to the area of foreign issuers and their coverage under the bill's broad definitions. While foreign issuers can be listed and traded in the U.S. if they agree to conform to GAAP and [NYSE] rules, the SEC historically has permitted the home country of the issuer to implement corporate governance standards. Foreign issuers are not part of the current problems being seen in the U.S. capital markets, and I do not believe it was the intent of the conferees to export U.S. standards, disregarding the sovereignty of other countries as well as their regulators.

148 CONG. REC. S7350-7365 (daily ed. July 25, 2002) (statement of Sen. Michael Enzi).

there is a lengthy transition period prior to effectiveness of this requirement, compliance is expected to be time-consuming and issuers should engage in early planning with their independent and internal auditors about necessary changes. Issuers should also evaluate the steps involved in the preparation of their disclosures filed or furnished to the SEC, including for purposes of providing a basis for the required CEO and CFO certifications.

- **Prepare for New Audit Committee Requirements.** Issuers should make an inventory of existing procedures, including a review of their audit committee charter and bylaw provisions pertaining to the composition and duties of their audit committees, to determine the changes that will be required to comply with the Sarbanes-Oxley Act and pending amendments to listing standards. Among other matters, issuers should consider whether their existing audit committee members are likely to be considered independent under the Act and the SEC's new rules applicable to listed companies in the United States and whether any member of their audit committee would likely qualify as an audit committee financial expert. Issuers should also plan the specific tasks to be assigned to their audit committees in light of the requirement that the committee hire and oversee their independent auditor and that it establish procedures to address complaints received from employees and third parties concerning accounting, internal controls and auditing matters. Foreign issuers listed on a U.S. exchange or Nasdaq that do not have audit committees should prepare to establish them by the required date.

- **Discuss the Act's Requirements with Auditors.** Issuers should meet with their independent auditors to discuss the requirements of the Sarbanes-Oxley Act and new SEC rules that affect them. For example, issuers should review the non-audit services historically provided by their auditors to determine which, if any, should continue to be provided by the auditors and which should be contracted out to other parties. Issuers should also adopt policies for the pre-approval of audit and permitted non-audit services, as well as policies for the employment of former personnel of the auditors. Issuers should consider asking their auditors to describe the changes they anticipate implementing in response to the Sarbanes-Oxley Act (*e.g.*, audit partner rotation and auditor attestations of management's internal control reports). Issuers and auditors should also formalize existing communication channels in light of new record-keeping requirements and requirements that independent auditors report to the audit committee on various matters.

OVERVIEW AND IMPLEMENTATION

- **Evaluate Compensation Arrangements to Ensure Compliance with the Act's Prohibitions on Loans to Executive Officers and Directors.** Because the Act's prohibition on loans to executive officers and directors became effective upon enactment, issuers should implement policies to verify compliance with the Act's broad prohibitions on loans to, and the arranging of financing for the benefit of, executive officers and directors. Split-dollar life insurance arrangements, after-tax leveraged co-investment programs and certain cashless exercises of options could, for example, run afoul of the Act's restrictions on the extension of credit.

- **Review Restrictions on Insider Transactions.** Issuers should review their policies covering stock sales by insiders and make the necessary modifications to comply with the Act's prohibition on insider transactions during blackout periods under 401(k) and other individual account plans, which became effective on January 26, 2003. Foreign issuers should be mindful that this restriction could apply to them if they or any of their subsidiaries have plans covered by the Sarbanes-Oxley Act.

- **IPO Participants Should Implement the Act's Corporate Governance Provisions Prior to First IPO Filing.** Issuers contemplating an initial public offering and their financial and legal advisors should revise their pre-IPO procedures to take account of corporate governance changes required to be implemented prior to an issuer's initial filing of its IPO registration statement with the SEC. These would include the need for audit committee pre-approval of audit and permitted non-audit services. Although some of the audit committee requirements of the Sarbanes-Oxley Act apply only upon listing, issuers should ensure that they are able to have a complying audit committee in place within the permitted transition periods under applicable listing standards. Private companies that extend credit or arrange financing for a director or executive officer after July 30, 2002 must ensure that the financing is repaid prior to that filing.

- **Review Document Retention Policies.** In view of the new criminal provisions concerning document destruction, particularly since they apply where proceedings are merely contemplated, issuers should review their existing document retention policies and programs to determine if they will assure compliance with the new provisions.

- **Anticipate Heightened SEC Review.** Issuers should expect that their registration statements and Exchange Act reports will be reviewed more frequently by the SEC. As a result of the SEC's expanded budget, issuers should anticipate that they will receive greater scrutiny in these reviews than they may have experienced in the past.[34]

---

[34] The SEC recently completed a review of the annual reports of all Fortune 500 companies. SEC, Summary by the Division of Corporation Finance of Significant Issues Addressed in the Review of the

THE SARBANES-OXLEY ACT: ANALYSIS AND PRACTICE

IV. ANALYSIS OF PRINCIPAL PROVISIONS

A. Corporate Governance and Management

1. CEO and CFO Certification Requirements. Section 302 of the Sarbanes-Oxley Act mandates that the SEC require CEOs and CFOs to make detailed certifications in each annual and quarterly report.[35] The new requirements are set out in Exchange Act Rules 13a-14 and 15d-14 and apply to annual reports on Forms 10-K, 20-F and 40-F, quarterly reports on Forms 10-Q, transition reports on any of these forms, and amendments to these reports.[36] They do not apply to reports on Form 6-K furnished by foreign private issuers, regardless of their content or timing, nor to materials furnished by foreign private issuers to the SEC pursuant to Rule 12g3-2(b) under the Exchange Act.

The form of required certification under Section 302 is reproduced in Appendix D.[37] An issuer's principal executive officer and principal financial officer (or persons performing similar functions) are each required to certify, based on his or her knowledge, that the report contains no material misstatements or omissions and that the financial statements and other financial information included in the report fairly present in all material respects the financial condition, results of operations and cash flows of the issuer as of and for the periods presented. The certification also effectively requires the certifying officers to disclose to the company's independent auditor and audit committee all significant deficiencies and material weaknesses in the design or operation of the issuer's internal control over financial reporting, and any fraud (regardless of materiality) involving management or other persons having a significant role in the issuer's internal control over financial reporting.[38] The relevant

---

Periodic Reports of the Fortune 500 Companies (Feb. 27, 2003), at http://www.sec.gov/divisions/corpfin/fortune500rep.htm. The SEC is also conducting a review of disclosure by foreign private issuers.

[35] A prior version of the Sarbanes-Oxley Act would also have required certification by the chairman of the board. Chapter VI includes a comprehensive discussion of the certification requirements of Sections 302 and 906 of the Sarbanes-Oxley Act, including the separate regime applicable to investment companies under the Investment Company Act of 1940 (the "Investment Company Act") and asset-backed issuers, as well as the companion requirements applicable to management's reports on internal control over financial reporting under Section 404 of the Act.

[36] In adopting rules under Section 302 of the Sarbanes-Oxley Act, the SEC requested comment on the possible extension of the certification requirement to other documents filed under the Exchange Act, but has not yet taken any action to do so. SEC Release No. 33-8124 (Aug. 29, 2002).

[37] Each certifying officer must provide a separate certification, and the certifications must be included in a separate section of the report immediately following the signatures. The SEC recently adopted rules to require that the Section 302 certifications be filed as exhibits to the related periodic report. SEC Release No. 33-8238 (June 5, 2003). This requirement will become effective on August 14, 2003.

[38] SEC Release No. 33-8238 (June 5, 2003). For guidance as to the definitions of "significant deficiency" (referred to in relevant accounting literature as a "reportable condition") and "material weakness," *see* Codification of Statements on Auditing Standards (AU) § 325, *Communication of Internal Control Related Matters Noted in an Audit. See also* text accompanying Note 94 *infra*.

OVERVIEW AND IMPLEMENTATION

report must include disclosure as to any material changes in the issuer's internal control over financial reporting.

The Section 302 certification also addresses a companion requirement imposed by the new rules, which is that all issuers, foreign and domestic, must maintain "disclosure controls and procedures." The term "disclosure controls and procedures" is defined as controls and other procedures of an issuer that are designed to ensure that information—both financial and non-financial—required to be disclosed in reports filed or submitted under the Exchange Act is recorded, processed, summarized and reported within the required time period.[39] Certifying officers must represent that they are responsible for establishing and maintaining these controls and procedures, have properly designed them (or supervised their design) and have presented in the related periodic report their conclusions as to the effectiveness of the controls and procedures.[40] The certification also requires that the officers conduct periodic evaluations of the issuer's disclosure controls and procedures.

As part of its rulemaking under Section 404 of the Act relating to management's internal control reports, the SEC has clarified the scope of the required controls and procedures, in part through the introduction of a new term, "internal control over financial reporting."[41] The SEC's rules extend the design, evaluation, disclosure and certification requirements to such control in a manner that is sub-

---

[39] Originally set out in Rules 13a-14 and 15d-14 under the Exchange Act, under recent amendments, the definition will be moved to new Rules 13a-15 and 15d-15. SEC Release No. 33-8238 (June 5, 2003).

[40] For a discussion of procedures to consider, *see* Chapter VIII. Questions that should be considered in connection with providing a certification and evaluating a company's controls and procedures are discussed in Chapter VII.

[41] SEC Release No. 33-8238 (June 5, 2003). The term "internal control over financial reporting" is defined as:

a process designed by, or under the supervision of, the registrant's principal executive and principal financial officers, or persons performing similar functions, and effected by the registrant's board of directors, management and other personnel, to provide reasonable assurance regarding the reliability of financial reporting and the preparation of financial statements for external purposes in accordance with generally accepted accounting principles and includes those policies and procedures that

- pertain to the maintenance of records that in reasonable detail accurately and fairly reflect the transactions and dispositions of the assets of the registrant;
- provide reasonable assurance that transactions are recorded as necessary to permit preparation of financial statements in accordance with GAAP, and receipts and expenditures of the registrant are being made only in accordance with authorizations of management and directors of the registrant; and
- provide reasonable assurance regarding prevention or timely detection of unauthorized acquisition, use or disposition of the registrant's assets that could have a material effect on the financial statements.

Rules 13a-15(f) and 15d-15(f) under the Exchange Act.

stantially parallel to those applicable to disclosure controls and procedures, subject to a lengthy transition period.[42] The amended text of the certification is reproduced in Appendix D.

Section 906 of the Sarbanes-Oxley Act separately requires that each "periodic report containing financial statements filed by an issuer with the [SEC]" be accompanied by a CEO and CFO certification that the report "fully complies with the requirements of § 13(a) or 15(d) of the [Exchange Act] and that information contained in the periodic report fairly presents, in all material respects, the financial condition and results of operations of the issuer." Section 906, which is enforceable by the Department of Justice and not the SEC, imposes criminal liability for inaccurate certifications knowingly or willfully furnished by a CEO or CFO.[43]

By its terms, Section 906 applies to annual reports on Forms 10-K, 20-F and 40-F and quarterly reports on Form 10-Q, because these are the only Exchange Act reports that require the filing of financial statements on a periodic basis.[44] Forms

---

[42] The transition period occurs in two stages. The changes in the first stage, effective August 14, 2003, primarily reorganize the certification and clarify the nature of the disclosures that must be made in an issuer's Exchange Act reports. U.S. companies must disclose quarterly "any change in the registrant's internal control over financial reporting that has occurred during the fiscal quarter covered by the quarterly report, or the last fiscal quarter in the case of an annual report, that has materially affected, or is reasonably likely to materially affect, the registrant's internal control over financial reporting." SEC Release No. 33-8238 (June 5, 2003). This requirement will be effective on an annual basis for foreign private issuers, since they are not required to file quarterly reports. The first stage of changes also clarifies the disclosures required to be made by the CEO and CFO to the issuer's independent auditor and audit committee.

The second stage of changes reflects the implementation of new requirements to maintain and evaluate internal control over financial reporting. These changes become effective for "accelerated filers" (generally U.S. issuers with an equity capitalization of more than $75 million that have filed an annual report with the SEC) beginning with the annual report for their first fiscal year ending on or after June 15, 2004 (April 15, 2005 for all other issuers, including foreign private issuers).

[43] The penalties include up to 20 years imprisonment for anyone who "willfully" certifies such statements, or up to ten years imprisonment for anyone who otherwise certifies such statements knowing that the report does not comport with all the relevant requirements. One peculiar aspect of the statute is that the penalties apply to non-compliance with the terms of the certification, but the statute does not explicitly provide that a failure to certify triggers liability. The Department of Justice has, however, clarified that it would "utilize [the criminal provisions of the Exchange Act, codified at 15 U.S.C. 78ff, to prosecute executives who violate the Sarbanes-Oxley Act by willfully failing to file Section 906's required certification." *See* Letter of Assistant Attorney General Daniel J. Bryant to the Honorable Joseph R. Biden, Jr. (Dec. 26, 2002); *see also* SEC Release No. 33-8238 (June 5, 2003) (requiring that Section 906 be furnished as an exhibit to relevant report, such that failure to file would result in a defective report).

[44] On its face, Section 906 would also appear to apply to annual reports by employee stock purchase plans on Form 11-K. While the SEC exempted such reports from certification under Section 302 of the Sarbanes-Oxley Act, it has taken note of a statement of Sen. Joseph R. Biden, Jr. introduced into the Congressional Record that indicates that such reports should be subject to certification under Section 906. 149 CONG. REC. S5325 (daily ed. Apr. 22, 2003). SEC Release No. 33-8238 (June 5, 2003). Al-

OVERVIEW AND IMPLEMENTATION

8-K and 6-K are event driven and not "periodic." In addition, the SEC rules require foreign issuers to "make" and "furnish" reports on Form 6-K rather than "file" them as is the case with Forms 10-K, 20-F, 10-Q and 8-K.[45] Despite some inconsistency in the SEC's rules and pronouncements in the use of the terms "periodic" and "filed,"[46] the better view is that Section 906 does not apply to reports on Form 8-K or 6-K that contain financial statements filed with (in the case of Form 8-K) or submitted to (in the case of Form 6-K) the SEC.[47] Issuers have to date generally followed this approach.

A form of certification satisfying Section 906 is reproduced in Appendix D.[48] As stated above, the Section 906 certification need only "accompany" the relevant report. As a result, companies have provided the certification in a variety of ways, including by filing it as an exhibit to the report or on a separate Form 8-K, or submitting it as non-public paper or electronic correspondence. Under recently adopted rules, companies will now be required to include the Section 906 certification as an exhibit to the relevant report, but the certifications would be deemed only to be "furnished," rather than "filed."[49] Accordingly, Section 906 certifica-

---

though the SEC has stated that it plans to consider the application of Section 906 further with the Department of Justice and has not amended Form 11-K to require officer certifications to be included as exhibits, it would be prudent for plans to comply with Section 906 pending further authoritative guidance.

[45] The rules applicable to Forms 10-K, 10-Q and 8-K all refer to "filing": (a) Rule 13a-1 requires each issuer with securities registered pursuant to § 12 of the Exchange Act to "file" an annual report on the appropriate form; (b) Rule 13a-13 requires a domestic issuer to "file" a quarterly report on Form 10-Q; and (c) Rule 13a-11 requires a domestic issuer to "file" a current report on Form 8-K. By contrast, Rule 13a-16 requires a foreign private issuer to "make" reports on Form 6-K, which reports are "transmitted" to the SEC. In addition, unlike Forms 10-K, 10-Q and 8-K, which all state they are to be "filed," Form 6-K provides it is to be "furnish[ed]."

[46] Neither the Exchange Act nor the rules thereunder define "periodic report" and the use of the term in SEC pronouncements (*e.g.*, in rule proposals, administrative proceedings and no-action letters) is not consistent as to the characterization of Form 8-K. In addition, Rule 13a-16(a)(3) under the Exchange Act refers to "periodic reports on Forms 10-K, 10-KSB, 10-Q, 10-QSB and 8-K." Moreover, the application of the Section 906 certifications to "periodic" reports (in contrast to Section 302, which refers to "annual and quarterly" reports) could be inferred to extend the Section 906 certifications to current reports on Form 8-K. The SEC's rules under the Exchange Act also are not consistent in their use of the term "file" in relation to Form 6-K. Rule 13a-3 uses "file" in addressing Forms 40-F and 6-K jointly.

[47] The SEC appeared to confirm this conclusion by stating that the Section 906 certification only applies to quarterly, semi-annual and annual reports that contain financial statements, making it comparable to the Section 302 requirement. SEC Release No. 33-8212 (Mar. 21, 2003). As noted above, in a subsequent release, the SEC has stated its intention to consider the application of Section 906 further in consultation with the Department of Justice. The SEC did, however, note that the application of Section 906 to Forms 8-K and 6-K "could potentially chill the disclosure of information by companies." SEC Release No. 33-8238 (June 5, 2003), 68 Fed. Reg. 36636, 36652 (June 18, 2003).

[48] The recommended form of certification includes a bracketed qualification relating to the "knowledge" of the certifying officer. While this language is not in the text of the Sarbanes-Oxley Act, we believe it is appropriate in light of similar qualifications included in the certification under Section 302 of the Sarbanes-Oxley Act and under the SEC's order and proposed rules requiring certifications. Knowledge also is a predicate requirement for the criminal penalties under Section 906 itself.

[49] SEC Release No. 33-8238 (June 5, 2003).

tions would not be subject to the civil anti-fraud provisions of § 18 of the Exchange Act, nor would they be automatically incorporated by reference into an issuer's Securities Act registration statements.[50]

2. Audit Committees for Listed Companies. The Sarbanes-Oxley Act amends § 10A of the Exchange Act by requiring the SEC to adopt rules (directly or through national securities exchanges and national securities associations ("SROs") such as the NYSE and Nasdaq) prohibiting the listing of any security of an issuer not in compliance with the audit committee provisions of the Act.[51] Under the Sarbanes-Oxley Act, each member of the audit committee must be a member of the board of directors and otherwise be "independent." The audit committee must also have the authority to engage independent advisors.

Audit committees must be directly responsible for:

- the appointment, compensation and oversight of the issuer's accounting firm, which is required to report directly to the audit committee; and

- the establishment of procedures for the (i) receipt, retention and treatment of complaints regarding accounting, internal accounting controls or auditing matters; and (ii) confidential, anonymous submission by employees of concerns regarding questionable accounting or auditing matters.

As noted elsewhere, the term "audit committee" is defined as the board of directors of the issuer if no audit committee exists. Although the Sarbanes-Oxley Act does not expressly mandate the establishment of an audit committee, as a practical matter it would be virtually impossible for the full board of most companies to satisfy the independence requirement.

The SEC's final rules implementing amended § 10A of the Exchange Act require issuers (other than foreign private issuers) to comply by the date of their first

---

[50] § 18 provides an express private right of action to any person who buys or sells securities in reliance on false or misleading statements in any application, report or document filed under the Exchange Act against any person responsible for such statements. Unlike actions under Rule 10b-5 under the Exchange Act, plaintiffs proceeding under § 18 do not have the burden of proving *scienter*, but defendants may avoid liability if they can establish that they acted in good faith and had no knowledge of the false or misleading statement. Pending effectiveness of the new rules, the SEC has encouraged issuers to submit Section 906 certifications as "additional exhibits" to the applicable report under Item 99 of Item 601(b) of Regulation S-K or, in the case of foreign private issuers, in accordance with the requirements of the applicable reporting form. Consistent with the effect of the new rules, Section 906 certifications so submitted will be treated as "accompanying" the related report, rather than as "filed" as part of the report. SEC Release No. 33-8212 (Mar. 21, 2003); SEC Release No. 33-8238 (June 5, 2003).

[51] These rules are discussed in greater detail in Chapter IV, and a summary comparison of the pending NYSE and Nasdaq proposals is included in Chapter V.

OVERVIEW AND IMPLEMENTATION

annual meeting following January 15, 2004, but no later than October 31, 2004.[52] Foreign private issuers will not be required to comply until July 31, 2005. Each SRO must file with the SEC proposed rules by July 15, 2003 and have in place final rules approved by the SEC by December 1, 2003.[53] The rules establish criteria for audit committee member independence. Apart from being a member of the board of directors and its committees, audit committee members may not accept any direct or indirect consulting, advisory or other compensatory payments from,[54] or be an affiliated person of,[55] the issuer or any subsidiary of the issuer. The SEC decided not to include a *de minimis* exception to the prohibition on these payments.

Although a number of commenters had sought broader exemptions, particularly for foreign private issuers, the final rules only contain the following specific exemptions:

- There are exemptions for foreign private issuers allowing (i) non-management employees to serve as audit committee members if the employee is elected to the audit committee or the board of directors pursuant to the issuer's governing law or documents, an employee collective bargaining agreement or other home country legal or listing requirements; (ii) a representative of an affiliate to sit on the audit committee as an observer; and (iii) a representative of a foreign government to sit on the audit committee if the representative is not an executive officer and does not receive any compensation prohibited by the independence requirements.[56] The final rules also permit a foreign private issuer

---

[52] SEC Release No. 33-8229 (Apr. 9, 2003).

[53] The adopting release specifically indicates that the SROs may adopt rules that are more specific or stringent than required by the Sarbanes-Oxley Act or the SEC's final rules.

[54] Indirect payments include payments made to certain family members, such as spouses, minor children, stepchildren or children or stepchildren sharing a home with the audit committee member, as well as payments to an entity in which the audit committee member is a partner, member, executive officer or officer such as managing director or occupies a similar position (except limited partners, non-managing members and those occupying similar positions who, in each case, have no active role in providing services to the entity) and which provides accounting, legal, investment banking or financial advisory services to the issuer or any subsidiary.

Compensatory fees do not include the receipt of fixed amounts of compensation under a retirement plan (including deferred compensation) for prior service with the listed issuer so long as such compensation is not contingent in any way on continued service.

[55] Under the final rules, the term "affiliate" of a specified person means a person that directly or indirectly controls, is controlled by or is under common control with, the person specified. The final rule includes a safe harbor for audit committee members who are neither executive officers nor beneficial owners of more than 10% of any class of voting equity securities, but also clarifies that the safe harbor is not intended to create any presumption that those outside the safe harbor are affiliates. Rather than creating a bright-line test, the final rule allows directors, issuers and their legal advisors to assess affiliate status based upon a traditional facts-and-circumstances analysis.

[56] There is also an exemption for foreign private issuers operating under a dual holding company structure that allows the two companies to establish a single audit committee.

- New issuers are only required to have one independent audit committee member at the time of initial listing, a majority within 90 days of the initial listing and a fully-independent audit committee within one year.

- To accommodate holding company structures, the final rule also includes an exemption from the independence requirements for an audit committee member that sits on the board of directors of both a listed issuer and an affiliate of the issuer, if such member is otherwise independent.

The SEC's rules do not provide any general relief, other than these specific exemptions, to foreign private issuers or other classes of issuers.[57] Any issuer relying on an exemption is required to provide disclosure in its annual reports filed with the SEC, as well as in any proxy statement or information statement for shareholders' meetings at which elections for directors are held. The rules also apply to issuers with only listed debt securities.[58] The Sarbanes-Oxley Act thus (presumably inadvertently) ignores the traditional corporate governance distinctions that are normally drawn between companies with listed debt securities and companies with listed equity securities.[59]

3. Prohibition on Personal Loans to Executive Officers and Directors. Section 402 of the Sarbanes-Oxley Act prohibits an issuer and its subsidiaries from directly or indirectly extending, maintaining, renewing or arranging for an extension of credit in the form of a personal loan to or for any executive officer[60] or director[61] of the issuer. This prohibition became effective July 30, 2002,

---

[57] Historically, the SEC has delegated the adoption of corporate governance standards to the national securities exchanges and national securities associations. As noted above, these SROs have exempted foreign issuers from many of their corporate governance requirements, including those relating to audit committees. The Sarbanes-Oxley Act and, in the light of the limited exceptions for foreign private issuers, the SEC's rules therefore represent a significant departure from prior practice.

[58] Under the final rules, additional listings of a company's securities are exempt from the audit committee requirements if the company is subject to the requirements as a result of listing any class of securities of the issuer on any market subject to the rules' requirements. This exemption extends to listing of non-equity securities by a direct or indirect subsidiary of a parent subject to the rules that is consolidated or at least 50% beneficially owned by a parent company.

[59] The NYSE, for example, limits its corporate governance requirements to companies listing common stock. NYSE LISTED COMPANY MANUAL Rule 303.00.

[60] "Executive officer" is used as defined in Rule 3b-7 under the Exchange Act and includes the president, any vice president in charge of a principal business unit, division or function and "any other officer who performs a policy making function, or any other person who performs similar policy making functions for the [issuer]."

[61] Many non-U.S. companies have a practice of designating alternate directors who may serve in the event of a director's absence. If an alternate director never in fact serves as a director, an argument could be made that the mere designation as an alternate does not trigger the Act's provisions ap-

OVERVIEW AND IMPLEMENTATION

but grandfathers loans outstanding on that date so long as no material modification to any term or renewal of those loans occurs.[62] Among the practices that may be prohibited are loans pursuant to split-dollar life insurance arrangements, after-tax leveraged co-investment programs and certain cashless exercises of options.

Section 402 does not require implementing regulations, and the SEC has informally indicated that interpretive guidance concerning Section 402 of the Sarbanes-Oxley Act is not likely to be issued. Some consistency of practice has developed with respect to certain issues arising under Section 402. For example, most issuers have not significantly changed their practices concerning the advancement of funds to pay business expenses. With respect to the cashless exercise of employee stock options, many issuers have looked closely at the mechanics of settlement under their programs in order to determine whether an extension of credit occurs; some issuers who settle cashless exercises on a "delivery-versus-payment" basis are concluding that there is no extension of credit from the issuer involved. On the other hand, many issuers have reconsidered the appropriateness of arrangements under which executive officers are provided with loans to pay taxes arising in connection with certain executive pay arrangements. Practices with respect to split-dollar life insurance arrangements have varied, with some issuers concluding that existing arrangements may be continued based on the grandfather provision referred to above.

The Sarbanes-Oxley Act provides limited exceptions for extensions of credit for home improvement, manufactured housing, consumer credit, open end credit, charge cards and margin loans by a broker or dealer to an employee of that broker or dealer (other than to acquire stock of the broker or dealer).[63] Extensions of credit pursuant to any of these exceptions must be (i) provided in the ordinary course of a "consumer credit" business; (ii) of a type generally made available by the issuer to the public; and (iii) made on market terms that are no more favorable than those offered by the issuer to the general public. There is no materiality exception in the Sarbanes-Oxley Act. These exceptions may not be available to most issuers, because, among other reasons, most issuers that are not financial institu-

---

plicable to directors. Due to the possibility that such persons will be called on to replace a director, it would nonetheless be prudent to treat such persons as directors for purposes of the key provisions of the Act that would be implicated. These would include the prohibition of Section 402 of the Act, as well as the independence requirements under Section 301 of the Act and related SEC rules.

[62] The provision applies to any "issuer" within the meaning of the Sarbanes-Oxley Act, which as noted above generally includes companies subject to the reporting requirements of the Exchange Act, but also includes any company that has filed (and not withdrawn) a registration statement under the Securities Act, even prior to that registration statement becoming effective. Although Section 402 grandfathers loans outstanding as of July 30, 2002, it does not provide a similar exception for loans made after that date but before a company seeks to go public by filing a registration statement under the Securities Act.

[63] Read literally, the exception does not apply to margin loans to employees of the parent of the broker or dealer.

tions cannot meet the ordinary course requirement. The Sarbanes-Oxley Act also exempts loans made by U.S. Federal Deposit Insurance Corporation ("FDIC") insured banks subject to certain existing U.S. insider lending restrictions.[64] This exemption does not extend to loans made by foreign banks, which are not permitted to be FDIC insured. The SEC has informally indicated that it is considering exemptive relief for foreign banks that is similar to that provided for FDIC insured banks.

4. Disgorgement of Incentive Compensation Received and Profits Realized by CEOs and CFOs Following Restatements. The Sarbanes-Oxley Act requires the CEO and CFO of an issuer (presumably the CEO and CFO during the relevant 12-month period described below) to reimburse it for all bonuses and other incentive-based or equity-based compensation received, as well as all profits realized from sales of issuer securities, in the 12-month period following the first public issuance or filing of reported financial statements that are later restated due to material noncompliance with any financial reporting requirement as a result of misconduct.[65] This provision of the Sarbanes-Oxley Act became effective July 30, 2002. It is still unclear, however, whether it applies to noncompliance on or after July 30, 2002, or to any restatement on or after July 30, 2002, regardless of when the noncompliance occurred.

The term "misconduct" is not defined in the Sarbanes-Oxley Act, and reimbursement is not limited to situations in which the CEO or the CFO engaged in the misconduct. The phrase "profits realized" is also not defined, so it is unclear how the cost basis of securities sold during the 12-month period will be determined (*e.g.*, using some artificial matching concept similar to § 16(b) of the Exchange Act or otherwise).[66] Similarly, the reference to compensation "received" during the 12-month period leaves unanswered questions regarding whether it is the grant of the compensation, its vesting or its payment that will control.

The Sarbanes-Oxley Act also does not specify the means of enforcement for the provision. The provision provides that the CEO and CFO "shall reimburse" the issuer, suggesting that the issuer itself is entitled to sue for reimbursement.[67] It

---

[64] § 5 of the Home Owners' Loan Act, 12 U.S.C.A. § 1464 (2002).

[65] Section 304 of the Sarbanes-Oxley Act.

[66] § 16(b) refers to "profit realized by him from any purchase and sale, or any sale and purchase." Under the short swing profit rules of § 16(b), multiple purchases and sales may be matched to create "profit" even where no net economic gain is realized.

[67] One company subject to criminal and SEC investigations for overstating its earnings has stated that it will invoke this provision against its CEO. In its letter dismissing CEO and Chairman Richard Scrushy, the Board of Directors of HealthSouth Corp. stated that, under the Sarbanes-Oxley Act, he would be required to forfeit bonuses or proceeds from HealthSouth stock sales if the company restates any of its financial results. Evan Perez *et al.*, *HealthSouth Fires CEO Scrushy*, WALL. ST. J., Apr. 1, 2003.

OVERVIEW AND IMPLEMENTATION

would appear that shareholders would not be entitled to sue the CEO and CFO directly to enforce this obligation, although they may be able to assert a derivative claim on behalf of the issuer, subject to the various restrictions on such claims provided by applicable state law.

5. Prohibition of Insider Trades During Certain Plan Blackout Periods. Effective January 26, 2003, Section 306 of the Sarbanes-Oxley Act makes it unlawful for any director or executive officer of an issuer of any equity security to purchase, sell or otherwise acquire or transfer any equity security of the issuer during any blackout period[68] with respect to that security if the director or executive officer acquired the equity security in connection with service to or employment by the issuer.[69] On January 22, 2003, the SEC issued Regulation BTR to implement Section 306.[70]

A person's profits realized in violation of this provision, regardless of his or her intent, are subject to disgorgement to the issuer. The Sarbanes-Oxley Act, however, once again provides no guidance as to how to calculate these profits. Under the Act, the issuer will have independent standing to bring a claim for disgorgement, but if the issuer fails to make a claim within 60 days of a request by a shareholder to do so, or fails to prosecute that claim diligently, the shareholder may bring a derivative claim, in either case no later than two years after the date such profits were realized.

---

[68] A blackout period means, with certain exceptions, a period longer than three consecutive business days during which 50% or more of the participants or beneficiaries under all individual account plans (such as 401(k) plans) maintained by the issuer are temporarily unable to purchase, sell or otherwise transfer their interests in the issuer's equity securities as a result of a suspension of such activities by the issuer or a plan fiduciary. Blackout periods generally do not include (i) a regularly scheduled period during which participants and beneficiaries may not transfer interests in equity securities of the issuer if such periods are incorporated into the plan and are timely disclosed to employees before they become participants or as a subsequent amendment to the plan; and (ii) any suspension imposed solely in connection with persons becoming or ceasing to be participants or beneficiaries by reason of a corporate event (*e.g.,* mergers, acquisitions and similar transactions). Blackout periods have been imposed most commonly in connection with a change in 401(k) plan administrators.

[69] Section 306 of the Sarbanes-Oxley Act. The issuer must timely notify affected directors and executive officers and the SEC of the above-described blackout periods. In addition, under the Employee Retirement Income Security Act of 1974 ("ERISA"), the plan administrator generally must notify participants and beneficiaries of "any period for which any ability of participants or beneficiaries under the plan, which is otherwise available under the terms of such plan, to direct or diversify assets credited to their account, to obtain loans from the plan, or to obtain distributions from the plan is temporarily suspended, limited, or restricted, if such suspension, limitation or restriction is for any period of more than three consecutive business days."

[70] SEC Release No. 34-47225 (Jan. 22, 2003). Regulation BTR, which was adopted substantially as proposed, is discussed more fully in our memorandum entitled "SEC Proposes Rules to Implement Section 306(A) of the Sarbanes-Oxley Act."

The prohibition precludes transactions by executive officers or directors during blackout periods resulting from events such as a change in record keeper, but does not do so in cases of events such as regularly scheduled periods during which employees are prohibited from trading in order to avoid the appearance of trading on the basis of material, non-public information or periods during which employees are prohibited from trading in connection with a corporate merger, acquisition, divestiture or similar transaction. Regulation BTR:

- clarifies that purchases made pursuant to automatic dividend reinvestment programs, as well as purchases or sales made pursuant to certain advance elections (such as, for example, elections under many broad-based employee stock purchase plans), will not violate the prohibition; and

- provides an exemption from the restrictions of Section 306 in circumstances in which the blackout affects mostly non-U.S. employees.[71]

6. Improper Influence on Audits. Section 303 of the Sarbanes-Oxley Act delegates to the SEC rulemaking to prohibit directors and officers of an issuer, and any person acting at their direction, from taking action to fraudulently influence, coerce, manipulate or mislead any public accountant in an audit for the purpose of rendering the issuer's financial statements materially misleading.[72] Violations are exclusively enforceable by the SEC.

The final SEC rules under Section 303 are effective on June 27, 2003.[73] In the release adopting the new rules, the SEC clarified several important points, including that a person acting "under the direction" of another person need not also be under the supervision or control of that other person. The rules are thus broad enough to cover third parties, such as lawyers or securities professionals whose actions are otherwise within the proscriptions of the rules.

The SEC also modified the rules as they were originally proposed to emphasize that only "influence" must be fraudulent, whereas coercion and manipulation imply only actions "compelling the auditor to act in a certain way through pressure, threats, trickery, intimidation or some other form of purposeful action."[74] The SEC retained its proposal that conduct is actionable if the relevant person

---

[71] Regulation BTR applies to equity securities transactions by directors and executive officers of a foreign private issuer only if (a) 50% or more of the participants or beneficiaries in pension plans maintained by the issuer who are located in the United States (including its territories and possessions) are subject to a blackout period; and (b) the affected employees represent (i) more than 15% of the issuer's individual account plan participants worldwide; or (ii) 50,000 participants worldwide.

[72] Section 303 of the Sarbanes-Oxley Act.

[73] SEC Release No. 34-47890 (May 20, 2003).

[74] *Id.*

OVERVIEW AND IMPLEMENTATION

"knew or should have known that such [conduct], if successful, could result in rendering the issuer's financial statements materially misleading," which the SEC acknowledged establishes a negligence standard. Assuming this standard is met, some of the types of conduct that the SEC believes may constitute improper influence are (i) the offer or payment of bribes or other incentives, including offers of future employment or engagements to provide non-audit services; (ii) misleading or inaccurate legal analysis; and (iii) threats to cancel or cancellation of existing engagements for audit or non-audit services if the auditor objects to the issuer's accounting.

Finally, while the rules apply to improper influence over an accountant "engaged in the performance of an audit," the SEC stated that it intends a broad interpretation of this phrase. For example, the rules would apply during negotiations of the accountant's retention as auditor and after the professional engagement when the auditor is asked to provide its consent to the use of prior year's audit report.[75]

7. Modifications to § 16 Disclosure Requirements for Officers, Directors and 10% Shareholders. Effective August 29, 2002, the Sarbanes-Oxley Act modifies disclosure requirements for officers, directors and 10% shareholders who are subject to reporting under § 16(a) of the Exchange Act.[76] These persons are now required to report certain changes in ownership of the issuer's equity securities generally within two business days of the transaction. These transactions were previously required to be reported, at the earliest, on Form 4 within ten days after the end of the month in which the change in beneficial ownership occurred, and, in some cases, on Form 5 within 45 days after the end of the issuer's fiscal year in which the change in beneficial ownership occurred.

The SEC has issued final amendments to its rules and forms effective for transactions executed on or after August 29, 2002.[77] The rules clarify that Form 4 is no longer a monthly form but instead must be filed within two business days of the date of execution of the reported transaction. The rules also require most transactions reportable on Form 5 to be reported within the two-day deadline.[78] The fi-

---

[75] *Id.*

[76] Section 403 of the Sarbanes-Oxley Act.

[77] SEC Release No. 34-46421 (Aug. 27, 2002).

[78] These transactions are generally exempt from § 16(b) short-swing profit recapture pursuant to Rule 16b-3 and include grants, awards and other acquisitions from the issuer, dispositions to the issuer and "discretionary transactions" (as defined in Rule 16b-3(b)(1)) pursuant to employee benefit plans. In addition, the SEC has provided that deferred reporting on Form 5 will not be available for small acquisitions from the issuer (including an employee benefit plan sponsored by the issuer) under Rule 16a-6. However, other transactions exempt from § 16(b) previously reportable on Form 5 will remain reportable on Form 5 (*e.g.*, small acquisitions not from the issuer and gifts) and transactions previously exempt from § 16(a) reporting will remain exempt from reporting (*e.g.*, transactions pursuant to cer-

THE SARBANES-OXLEY ACT: ANALYSIS AND PRACTICE

nal rules do, however, provide certain limited exceptions to the calculation of the two-day deadline in two specific cases where the insider does not select the date of execution of the transaction.[79]

Beginning not later than July 30, 2003, these filings must be made electronically, and issuers maintaining corporate websites will be required to post such filings on their websites. The SEC recently approved final rules regarding the electronic filing of all Forms 3, 4 and 5 under § 16(a).[80] The final rules require each issuer that maintains a corporate website to post all Forms 3, 4 and 5 on its website by the end of the business day after the filing. The SEC has also commenced a trial of an internet-based system for filing § 16 reports.[81]

The SEC's new rules in this area do not affect most foreign issuers, which generally continue to remain exempt from § 16.

8. Director and Officer Bars. The Sarbanes-Oxley Act amends § 21C of the Exchange Act and § 8A of the Securities Act to authorize the SEC, in connection with a cease-and-desist proceeding, to issue an order barring any person who has violated § 10(b) of the Exchange Act or § 17(a)(1) of the Securities Act, as applicable, from acting as a director or officer of any issuer "if the conduct of that person demonstrates unfitness to serve as an officer or director."[82] Previously, the SEC could only seek a bar in court. The Sarbanes-Oxley Act also amends § 21(d)(2) of the Exchange Act and § 20(e) of the Securities Act, which provide that a U.S. federal court may bar any person who violates § 10(b) of the Exchange Act or § 17(a)(1) of the Securities Act, respectively, from acting as an officer or director of any issuer in a proceeding initiated by the SEC.[83] Previously, a court could only bar a person whose "conduct demonstrates substantial unfitness to serve as an officer or director," and the amendment lowers the standard from "substantial unfitness" to simply "unfitness."

---

tain dividend reinvestment plans and non-discretionary transactions pursuant to certain broad-based employee benefit plans).

[79] The two exceptions are (i) transactions pursuant to a contract, instruction or written plan for the purchase or sale of issuer securities that satisfies the affirmative defense conditions of Rule 10b5-1(c) (including transactions pursuant to employee benefit plans and dividend and interest reinvestment plans that are not already exempt from § 16(a) reporting); and (ii) "discretionary transactions" (as defined in Rule 16b-3(b)(1)) involving an employee benefit plan, whether or not exempted by Rule 16b-3, in each case where the insider does not select the date of execution. In these cases, the date of execution (triggering the two-day reporting deadline) is deemed to be the earlier of the date the executing broker, dealer or plan administrator *notifies* the insider of the execution of the transaction and the third business day following the actual trade date of the transaction.

[80] SEC Release No. 34-47890 (May 20, 2003).
[81] *See* EDGAR, Online Forms Management, *at* http://www.onlineforms.edgarfiling.sec.gov.
[82] Section 1105 of the Sarbanes-Oxley Act.
[83] *Id.* Section 305.

OVERVIEW AND IMPLEMENTATION

9. SEC Authority to Seek Order Freezing Certain Assets of an Issuer During an Investigation Involving Possible Federal Securities Law Violations. The Sarbanes-Oxley Act authorizes the SEC to petition a U.S. federal court for a temporary order requiring an issuer of publicly traded securities to escrow any "extraordinary payments (whether compensation or otherwise)" that appear likely to the SEC to be made to any director, officer, partner, controlling person, agent or employee of the issuer, during an investigation of such issuer or individual involving possible violations of the federal securities laws.[84] A court may issue such an order after notice and an opportunity for a hearing, unless the court determines this requirement to be impracticable or contrary to the public interest.

A court order would take effect immediately and remain in effect for 45 days, unless set aside or modified by a court. The initial order may be extended by up to 45 additional days for "good cause shown." If, prior to the expiration of the order, the issuer or individual is "charged" with a federal securities law violation, the order will remain in effect until the conclusion of any related legal proceedings, subject to court approval and the right of the issuer or individual to petition the court. If no charges are brought prior to the order's expiration, the disputed payments (plus accrued interest) must be returned to the issuer or individual.

B. New Financial Disclosure Requirements

The Sarbanes-Oxley Act amends § 13 of the Exchange Act, which pertains to periodic and other reports, in the following three ways.[85]

1. Inclusion of All Material Adjustments in Financial Statements. The Sarbanes-Oxley Act adds § 13(i) to the Exchange Act mandating that all financial statements required to be prepared in accordance with, or reconciled to, U.S. GAAP and filed with the SEC reflect all material correcting adjustments that have been identified by a registered public accounting firm. Because new § 13(i) applies to "[e]ach financial report that contains financial statements" and not (as Section 906) only to periodic reports that contain financial statements, it may well apply to a Form 8-K that contains financial statements (*i.e.*, of acquired companies). This provision should not apply to submissions on Form 6-K because, as discussed above, these reports are not "filed."

2. Off-Balance Sheet Arrangements and Contractual Obligations. The Sarbanes-Oxley Act directs the SEC to require issuers to disclose all material off-balance sheet transactions and other relationships of the issuer with unconsolidated entities that may have a material effect on the issuer's financial condition.[86]

---

[84] *Id.* Section 1103.
[85] *Id.* Section 401.
[86] *Id.* Section 401(a).

THE SARBANES-OXLEY ACT: ANALYSIS AND PRACTICE

Final rules implementing this provision require, with limited exceptions, that issuers include specified disclosures regarding off-balance sheet arrangements and contractual obligations in a separately captioned section of the "Management's Discussion and Analysis," or "MD&A."[87] The rules regarding off-balance sheet arrangements apply to registration statements, annual reports and proxy or information statements that are required to include financial statements for fiscal years ending on or after June 15, 2003; the rules regarding contractual obligations apply to such documents that include financial statements for fiscal years ending on or after December 15, 2003.[88]

The new rules require a discussion of any off-balance sheet arrangements of an issuer that *have or are reasonably likely to have* a current or future effect on the issuer's financial condition, changes in financial condition, revenues or expenses, results of operations, liquidity, capital expenditures or capital resources that is material to investors. The probability threshold of "reasonably likely," which is consistent with existing MD&A rules, replaced the "not remote" threshold originally proposed. Several specific disclosures are required to the extent necessary to an understanding of the arrangements and their effects. These disclosures address, among other matters, the nature and business purpose of the arrangement, the importance of the arrangement to the issuer and the nature and amount of any other obligation or liability (including contingent obligations or liabilities) of the issuer arising from the arrangement that are or are reasonably likely to become material and the triggering events or circumstances that could cause them to arise.

The new rules provide that all forward-looking statements made in these disclosures have the benefit of the safe harbor under § 27A of the Securities Act and § 21E of the Exchange Act[89] to the same extent as other forward-looking statements, and that all information provided in response to the new rules, except for historical facts, will be deemed to constitute "forward-looking statements" within the meaning of the safe harbor. In addition, disclosure about off-balance sheet

---

[87] SEC Release No. 33-8182 (Jan. 28, 2003). These rules are discussed more fully in our memorandum entitled "SEC Adopts Rules Implementing § 401(a) of the Sarbanes-Oxley Act." While the new rules do apply to annual reports on Form 40-F filed by eligible Canadian companies under the MJDS, they do not apply to Securities Act registration statements filed thereunder.

[88] The staff of the SEC has confirmed informally that compliance with the new rules in quarterly reports on Form 10-Q is not mandatory until after the issuer has filed the first annual report on Form 10-K to which the rules apply. Thereafter, each quarterly report will be required to discuss material changes during the relevant period in previously disclosed off-balance sheet arrangements.

[89] This safe harbor, which does not apply in certain circumstances (including initial public offerings and tender offers), provides protection against liability in private actions for a forward-looking statement if, among other things, the statement is identified as such and accompanied by meaningful cautionary statements that identify important factors that could cause actual results to differ materially from those predicted by the forward-looking statement, or if the plaintiff fails to prove that the forward-looking statement was made by or with the approval of an executive officer of the company who had actual knowledge that it was false or misleading.

OVERVIEW AND IMPLEMENTATION

transactions is deemed to satisfy the "meaningful cautionary statements" element of the safe harbor if it satisfies all of the requirements of the new rules. On the other hand, forward-looking statements made in required disclosures about contractual obligations are not automatically deemed to satisfy the "meaningful cautionary statements" element of the safe harbors solely by reason of compliance with the requirements of the new rules. Issuers therefore must ensure that those disclosures otherwise contain "meaningful cautionary statements."

3. "Non-GAAP Financial Measures." The Sarbanes-Oxley Act directs the SEC to issue rules requiring that any *pro forma* financial information contained in any periodic or other report filed with the SEC or any public disclosure or press release not contain any material misstatement or omissions and be reconciled to GAAP. The rules implementing this Section consist of new Regulation G and amendments to the disclosure requirements applicable to Exchange Act reports that include so-called "non-GAAP financial measures."[90] Regulation G applies to disclosures as of March 28, 2003 by all U.S. and foreign issuers (other than registered investment companies).[91] The amendments to Exchange Act requirements apply to

---

[90] SEC Release No. 33-8176 (Jan. 22, 2003); *see also* Division of Corporation Finance: Frequently Asked Questions Regarding the Use of Non-GAAP Financial Measures (June 13, 2003). These rules are discussed more fully in our memorandum entitled "SEC Adopts Rules Implementing Section 401(b) of the Sarbanes-Oxley Act and to Require Furnishing of Earnings Releases on Form 8-K." Special issues raised by the use of non-GAAP financial measures in earnings press releases are discussed in Chapter IX. None of the rules relating to non-GAAP financial measures will apply to documents filed with the SEC by eligible Canadian issuers under the MJDS.

"Non-GAAP financial measure" is defined, subject to limited exceptions, as a numerical measure of a registrant's historical or future financial performance, financial position or cash flows that "excludes amounts, or is subject to adjustments that have the effect of excluding amounts, that are included in the most directly comparable measure calculated and presented in accordance with GAAP in the statement of income, balance sheet or statement of cash flows (or equivalent statements) of the issuer; or includes amounts, or is subject to adjustments that have the effect of including amounts, that are excluded from the most directly comparable measure so calculated and presented." *Pro forma* financial information presented pursuant to Article 11 of Regulation S-X (*e.g.*, required disclosures relating to certain acquisitions or divestitures) is not subject to the new rules.

"GAAP" refers to U.S. GAAP, except that (i) in the case of foreign private issuers whose primary financial statements are prepared in accordance with non-U.S. GAAP, it refers to the principles under which those primary financial statements are prepared; and (ii) in the case of foreign private issuers that include a non-GAAP financial measure derived from or based on a measure calculated in accordance with U.S. GAAP, it refers to U.S. GAAP for purposes of the application of the new rules to the disclosure of that measure.

[91] The new requirements seek to accommodate disclosure practices by foreign private issuers. Notably, Regulation G does not apply to disclosures of non-GAAP financial measures by foreign private issuers if (i) the securities of the issuer are listed or quoted on a securities exchange or inter-dealer quotation system outside the United States; (ii) the non-GAAP financial measure is not derived from or based on a measure calculated and presented in accordance with U.S. GAAP; and (iii) the disclosure is made by or on behalf of the issuer outside the United States, or is included in a written communication that is released by or on behalf of the issuer outside the United States. In the adopting release, the SEC stated that this exception should be available regardless of whether (a) a written communication is released contemporaneously or subsequently in the United States as well as outside the United States

any annual or quarterly report filed with respect to a fiscal period ending after March 28, 2003.

The new requirements impose a number of conditions on the ability to use non-GAAP financial measures, including principally that the measure must be accompanied by a presentation of the most comparable GAAP measure and a reconciliation, which must (with an exception applicable to forward-looking information) be quantitative, of the differences between the non-GAAP financial measure and the GAAP measure. In the case of Exchange Act reports[92] and Securities Act registration statements, the GAAP measure must be presented with equal or greater prominence and the disclosure must also be accompanied by an explanation of why the registrant's management believes that presentation of the non-GAAP financial measure provides useful information to investors.[93]

C. Other Disclosures

1. Report on Internal Control over Financial Reporting. The Sarbanes-Oxley Act directs the SEC to adopt rules requiring each annual report on Forms 10-K, 20-F and 40-F filed with the SEC to include an internal control report of the issuer's management.[94] The issuer's auditors also must issue an attestation regarding the internal control report. The SEC's final rules under Section 404 will require the report to contain:

- a statement of management's responsibilities for establishing and maintaining adequate internal control over financial reporting for the company;

- a statement identifying the framework used by management to evaluate the effectiveness of this internal control;[95]

---

so long as it is not otherwise targeted at persons located in the United States; (b) foreign journalists, U.S. journalists or other third parties have access to the information; (c) the information appears on one or more websites maintained by the registrant so long as they are not available exclusively to, or targeted at, persons located in the United States; or (d) the information is included in a submission to the SEC on Form 6-K. SEC Release No. 33-8176 (Jan. 22, 2003).

[92] These reports would include those, such as earnings press releases, made under Item 12 of Form 8-K with respect to a completed fiscal quarter.

[93] SEC Release No. 33-8176 (Jan. 22, 2003). The explanation need not be included if it was already included in the registrant's most recent annual report on Form 10-K (or a more recent Form 10-Q) or 20-F, except to the extent necessary to update it.

[94] Section 404 of the Sarbanes-Oxley Act. Management's report on internal control over financial reporting is discussed in greater detail in Chapter VI and in our memorandum entitled "SEC Adopts New Rules on CEO/CFO Certification and Internal Controls."

[95] The SEC staff has indicated that the evaluative framework set forth in the 1992 report of the Committee of Sponsoring Organizations (or "COSO") of the Treadway Commission on internal controls will qualify for this purpose. *See also* AU § 319, *Consideration of Internal Control in a Financial Statement Audit*. Foreign private issuers will be permitted to use the framework in effect in their home jurisdictions. The SEC identified *Guidance on Assessing Control*, published by the Canadian Institute of Chartered Accountants, and the *Turnbull Report*, published by the Institute of Chartered Accountants in England & Wales, as examples of appropriate frameworks. SEC Release No. 33-8238 (June 5, 2003), 68 Fed. Reg. 36636, 36642, n. 67 (June 18, 2003).

OVERVIEW AND IMPLEMENTATION

- management's assessment of the effectiveness of the company's internal control over financial reporting as of the end of the most recent fiscal year, including a statement as to whether or not internal control over financial reporting is effective and a discussion of any material weakness in such control;[96] and

- a statement that the independent auditor has issued an attestation report on management's assessment (which attestation report must itself be provided).[97]

The SEC has delayed the effectiveness of final rules under Section 404 to provide issuers with sufficient time to take steps necessary to enable compliance with the auditor attestation requirement. U.S. issuers that are "accelerated filers" under Exchange Act Rule 12b-2[98] must comply with the new rules commencing with the annual report for their first fiscal year ending on or after June 15, 2004. All other U.S. and foreign private issuers must comply beginning with the annual report for their first fiscal year ending on or after April 15, 2005.[99]

2. Code of Ethics and Audit Committee Financial Expert. The Sarbanes-Oxley Act directs the SEC to adopt rules requiring disclosure as to (i) whether or not each issuer has a code of ethics applicable to its senior financial officers (and if not, why not); and (ii) any changes to the code or waivers of its requirements.[100] The Sarbanes-Oxley Act also authorizes the SEC to adopt rules requiring issuers to disclose whether their audit committees have at least one member who is a "financial expert," as defined by the SEC. The final rules implementing these provisions require U.S. and foreign reporting companies to include

---

[96] The rules explicitly proscribe a conclusion that such control is effective where one or more material weaknesses exist. *See* Item 308 of Regulation S-K; *see also* Note 38 *supra*.

[97] The SEC has not otherwise prescribed detailed criteria for the content of management's report, with the intent that management should tailor the report to a company's particular circumstances.

The PCAOB has adopted interim professional auditing standards that include the existing standard on attestations on an entity's internal control over financial reporting, as addressed in Codification of Statements on Standards for Attestation Engagements (AT) § 501, *Reporting on an Entity's Internal Control Over Financial Reporting,* which have been approved by the SEC. *See* PCAOB Rel. No. 2003-006 (Apr. 18, 2003); SEC Release No. 33-8222 (Apr. 25, 2003). The PCAOB has also indicated that the adoption of a final standard for attestations is a priority and that it will consider the existing standard, an exposure draft issued by the American Institute of Certified Public Accountants ("AICPA") and the views of interested persons in discharging its duties under Sections 103 and 404(b) of the Act. *See* PCAOB Release No. 2003-005 (Apr. 18, 2003); AICPA Auditing Standards Board, Proposed Statements on Auditing Standards, *Auditing an Entity's Internal Control Over Financial Reporting in Conjunction with the Financial Statement Audit,* and Proposed Statement on Standards for Attestation Engagements, *Reporting on an Entity's Internal Control Over Financial Reporting* (Mar. 18, 2003).

[98] As previously noted, "accelerated filers" are generally those U.S. issuers with an equity capitalization of more than $75 million that have filed an annual report with the SEC.

[99] SEC Release No. 33-8238 (June 5, 2003).

[100] Section 406 of the Sarbanes-Oxley Act.

the new disclosures in their annual reports for fiscal years ending on or after July 15, 2003.[101]

The rules regarding the code of ethics expand the scope of the Sarbanes-Oxley Act by requiring that the code cover the CEO, CFO and principal accounting officer or controller, or persons performing similar functions, rather than just senior financial officers, and clarify that the disclosures are required to be made in each U.S. and non-U.S. reporting company's annual report on Form 10-K, Form 20-F or Form 40-F. The full text of the code of ethics is required to be made available to the public by a company by filing it as an exhibit to its annual report, posting it on its website or undertaking in its annual report to provide copies upon request. The rules also clarify that U.S. companies are required to file any amendment or waiver granted to a senior officer on a current basis on Form 8-K or by posting the relevant information on the company's website, while foreign issuers are only required to disclose amendments or waivers in their annual reports (or on their websites).

The rules create a new term, "audit committee financial expert," and specify several criteria that must be met by the expert as well as the permissible means for obtaining the necessary attributes. A U.S. or foreign company's annual report on Form 10-K, Form 20-F or Form 40-F must contain disclosure regarding whether its audit committee has at least one audit committee financial expert and, if not, why not. If the audit committee does have a qualifying financial expert, the disclosure must include the expert's name and whether he or she is independent.[102]

3. Mandated Periodic Review. The Sarbanes-Oxley Act sets out criteria for the SEC to use in determining the frequency of review of SEC filings by listed issuers and requires review of SEC filings by each reporting company at least once every three years.[103]

4. Current Reporting Requirement. The Sarbanes-Oxley Act adds § 13(1) to the Exchange Act, which requires issuers to disclose publicly in plain

---

[101] SEC Release No. 33-8177 (Jan. 23, 2003); SEC Release No. 33-8177A (Mar. 26, 2003) (technical corrections). These requirements are discussed more fully in our memorandum entitled "SEC Adopts Final Rules under Sections 406 and 407 of the Sarbanes-Oxley Act."

[102] For U.S. issuers, independence will initially be measured by existing listing standards that are expected to conform to the independence standards adopted by the SEC under Section 301 of the Sarbanes-Oxley Act. Foreign issuers are not initially required to provide any disclosure regarding independence but will subsequently be required to provide this disclosure based on the independence requirements adopted pursuant to Section 301.

[103] Section 408 of the Sarbanes-Oxley Act. The criteria include: whether an issuer has issued material restatements of its financial statements, the volatility of an issuer's stock price, an issuer's market capitalization, whether an issuer is an emerging company with a disparity in its price to earnings ratio and whether the issuer's operations significantly affect any material sector of the economy.

OVERVIEW AND IMPLEMENTATION

English "on a rapid and current basis" such information as the SEC may require concerning material changes in their financial condition or operations, including "trend and qualitative information and graphic presentations."[104] To date, the SEC has invoked its authority under Section 409 of the Sarbanes-Oxley Act only to require U.S. issuers to furnish their earnings releases with respect to completed fiscal periods on Form 8-K.[105]

The directive of Section 409 is also consistent with the SEC's approach in its pending proposal to expand the information that domestic issuers report on a "current" basis.[106] That proposal, for which the comment period expired on August 26, 2002, stops short of proposing a principles-based rule of continuous disclosure. The pending proposal mandates disclosure of specific categories of information that the SEC considers "unquestionably material." This approach is designed to make the proposed rules more definite and easier to apply, while still enhancing in a significant way the quality and quantity of information that is provided to the market on a prompt basis.[107] To date, the SEC has not issued final rules in respect of this proposal.

---

[104] *Id.* Section 409.

[105] SEC Release No. 33-8176 (Jan. 22, 2003). This requirement is discussed more fully in our memorandum entitled "SEC Adopts Rules to Implement Section 401(b) of the Sarbanes-Oxley Act and to Require Furnishing of Earnings Releases on Form 8-K." *See also* SEC Release No. 33-8128 (Sept. 5, 2002) (accelerating filing deadlines for SEC reports).

[106] Under the pending proposal, U.S. domestic issuers would be required to file a current report on Form 8-K within two business days of the occurrence of events falling within 19 categories (11 of which are proposed to be added): (i) entry into a material agreement not made in the ordinary course of business; (ii) termination of a material agreement not made in the ordinary course of business; (iii) termination or reduction of a business relationship with a customer that constitutes 10% or more of the company's revenues; (iv) completion of an acquisition or disposition of material assets; (v) bankruptcy or receivership; (vi) creation of a material direct or contingent financial obligation; (vii) events triggering a material direct or contingent financial obligation; (viii) "exit activities," including any material write-off or restructuring; (ix) any material impairment; (x) a change in a rating agency decision, issuance of a credit watch or change in company outlook; (xi) delisting, movement to a new exchange, or receipt of notice of failure to comply with listing standards; (xii) unregistered sales of equity securities; (xiii) material modifications of rights of security holders; (xiv) changes in certifying accountant; (xv) conclusion or notice that a previous audit report should no longer be relied upon; (xvi) changes in control; (xvii) election or departure of directors and appointment or departure of principal officers; (xviii) amendments to articles of incorporation or bylaws or change in fiscal year; and (xix) material limitations, restrictions or prohibitions regarding employee benefit, retirement and stock ownership plans. SEC Release No. 33-8106 (June 17, 2002).

[107] The current SEC proposal nonetheless raises a number of significant issues. Among other examples, the current SEC proposal would require companies to file a current report on Form 8-K whenever they enter into a "letter of intent or other non-binding agreement," a requirement that could significantly complicate merger negotiations and other types of negotiations where parties have traditionally awaited the signing of a definitive agreement before announcing a transaction.

Although the current reporting requirement called for by the Sarbanes-Oxley Act appears to endorse the SEC's pending proposal, and apparently to extend the proposal to foreign issuers, the language of the Act is sufficiently broad that it could be interpreted to authorize a more sweeping change to a principles-based continuous reporting regime that would generally require the disclosure of all material events and developments relating to an issuer. While the Act could be understood to authorize varying degrees of change to the existing Exchange Act reporting system, we believe the Act's use of the terms "rapid and current," rather than continuous, suggests that Congress did not intend to authorize a continuous reporting regime.

It is also unclear how the SEC will address the Act's apparent mandate to extend current reporting to foreign issuers. The SEC has already requested comment on whether it should extend its pending proposal to foreign private issuers. The Sarbanes-Oxley Act may place additional pressure on the SEC to do so. This would be a departure from the SEC's traditional deference to the home country requirements of foreign private issuers, and could raise significant issues. Although many foreign private issuers, particularly in Europe, are subject to stringent continuous reporting regimes imposed by listing requirements, harmonizing these requirements with any new SEC rules may prove difficult, and could expose foreign private issuers to greater liability for information reported under those rules.

Moving towards a current reporting regime may also increase the litigation exposure of reporting companies. First, requiring companies to report more information more quickly will decrease the time available for verification prior to filing and will require often difficult materiality decisions to be made much more quickly. This may lead to inaccurate or misleading disclosure, which may in turn provide the basis for increased litigation by private plaintiffs under Rule 10b-5 and, in the case of domestic companies, under § 18 of the Exchange Act.[108] New current reporting requirements may also lead to increased litigation from both the SEC and private plaintiffs over the timing of disclosure.[109] Failure to file reports

---

[108] Reports by foreign private issuers under Form 6-K currently are not deemed to be "filed" for purposes of § 18 of the Exchange Act. Rule 13a-16(c). If the SEC were to use its authority under the Sarbanes-Oxley Act to impose an affirmative current reporting obligation on foreign private issuers, it might also decide to treat those disclosures as "filed" for purposes of § 18.

[109] Under current law, companies generally have a significant amount of discretion over the timing of disclosure of material information when they are not offering securities or filing a required report with the SEC. "Silence, absent a duty to disclose, is not misleading under Rule 10b-5." *Basic, Inc v. Levinson*, 485 U.S. 224, 239 n.17 (1988). For this reason, most companies adopt a consistent "no comment" policy about certain matters, such as pending merger negotiations, to avoid triggering a duty to disclose. To the extent the Sarbanes-Oxley Act or the rules implementing it create a duty to disclose additional information as and when it arises, companies will no longer be able to adopt a "no comment" policy with respect to such matters, and failures to disclose such information on a timely basis when required may give rise to litigation.

OVERVIEW AND IMPLEMENTATION

on a timely basis may also cause companies to suffer other penalties, such as the loss of the ability to use short form registration.[110]

D. Oversight of Accounting Profession

1. Public Company Accounting Oversight Board. The Sarbanes-Oxley Act creates the PCAOB, a private non-profit corporation, to supervise public accounting firms that provide audit services.[111] The mandate of the PCAOB is to:

- register public accounting firms that prepare audit reports for issuers;

- establish "auditing, quality control, ethics, independence and other standards relating to the preparation of audit reports;"[112] and

- conduct inspections, investigations and disciplinary proceedings of, and take enforcement action against, public accounting firms.

The SEC is charged with the organization and oversight of the PCAOB, which it determined was appropriately organized on April 25, 2003.[113] Beginning 180 days from the date the PCAOB is fully organized, the Sarbanes-Oxley Act requires all public accounting firms to register with the PCAOB. It will be illegal to issue an audit report or participate in the preparation of an audit report with respect to any issuer without prior registration with the PCAOB.

Any foreign public accounting firm "that prepares or furnishes an audit report with respect to any issuer" is explicitly subject to the Sarbanes-Oxley Act. In addition, even foreign public accounting firms that do not furnish audit reports may be required to register if the public accounting firm "plays a substantial role"

---

[110] Under the SEC's current rule proposal, a company that fails to file a current report on Form 8-K when required will lose its eligibility for short-form registration, Form S-8 and Rule 144 resales for 12 months after the late filing.

[111] Sections 101–107 of the Sarbanes-Oxley Act.

[112] Although the Sarbanes-Oxley Act itself contains numerous provisions with respect to auditor independence, the PCAOB is entitled to create additional auditor independence rules.

[113] SEC Release No. 33-8223 (Apr. 25, 2003). The Sarbanes-Oxley Act provides that the PCAOB will be composed of five full-time members who will be prohibited from engaging in any other business or professional activity and will serve staggered, five-year terms up to a maximum of two terms. Two members (and only two members) of the PCAOB must be or have been certified public accountants, and the chairperson may only be a certified public accountant if he or she has not been a practicing certified public accountant in the preceding five years. Members of the PCAOB were initially appointed by the SEC in October 2002, after consultation with the Chairman of the Board of Governors of the Federal Reserve System and the Secretary of the Treasury. The SEC has also confirmed William McDonough, who previously served as President of the Federal Reserve Bank of New York, as the Chairman of the PCAOB.

THE SARBANES-OXLEY ACT: ANALYSIS AND PRACTICE

in the preparation of audit reports.[114] Furthermore, any foreign public accounting firm that "issues an opinion or otherwise performs material services" relied on by a registered public accounting firm is deemed to have consented to produce its workpapers to the PCAOB.[115]

The Sarbanes-Oxley Act largely delegates the adoption of auditing, quality control and ethics standards to the PCAOB, although the Act requires the PCAOB to adopt rules providing for the following:

- Auditors must maintain workpapers for seven years;[116]

- Audit reports must include additional disclosure about the auditors, testing of internal control procedures of the issuer and an evaluation of those procedures;

- The PCAOB may require testimony and production of documents from any public accounting firm. Noncompliance with this provision may result in a professional suspension or bar of the noncomplying person or firm; and

- The PCAOB may seek the issuance of a subpoena by the SEC to require testimony or document production from any third party, including issuers, to the PCAOB.

Except for the information required to be provided in the initial registration and subsequent annual reports filed with the PCAOB (including information regarding fees paid to the public accounting firms by each issuer client for audit and non-audit services), which will be publicly available,[117] other information received by the PCAOB is required to be maintained confidentially, although information with respect to an inspection or investigation may be shared with the SEC and, if deemed to be necessary by the PCAOB, with the U.S. Attorney General or other specified federal and state regulators.

---

[114] The PCAOB's rules require foreign public accounting forms to register if they audit companies listed on U.S. stock exchanges although such firms have an additional six months to register. PCAOB Release No. 2003-007 (May 6, 2003). The Sarbanes-Oxley Act specifically states that registration shall not provide a basis for subjecting a foreign public accounting firm to the jurisdiction of the federal or state courts, other than with respect to controversies with the PCAOB.

[115] The Sarbanes-Oxley Act states that any such foreign firms shall be deemed to have consented to the jurisdiction of the U.S. courts for purposes of enforcing such production of workpapers.

[116] Section 802 of the Sarbanes-Oxley Act, which criminalizes the destruction of corporate audit records, only requires maintenance of workpapers for a period of five years. The SEC's final rules under Section 802, however, increase this period to seven years. SEC Release No. 33-8180 (Jan. 24, 2003).

[117] The public availability of the registration application and subsequent annual reports is subject to the rules of the PCAOB or the SEC and applicable legal restrictions.

OVERVIEW AND IMPLEMENTATION

2. Accounting Standard Setting. The Sarbanes-Oxley Act adds § 19(b) to the Securities Act authorizing the SEC to recognize as GAAP any accounting principles established by a standard setting body meeting the requirements set forth in the Sarbanes-Oxley Act.[118] The SEC is given rulemaking authority to implement the provision and is charged with the responsibility of overseeing the standard setting board. The Sarbanes-Oxley Act requires the standard setting board to be organized as a private entity and to have a board of trustees, the majority of whom are not and have not been associated persons at a registered public accounting firm during the prior two years. The Act also requires the standard setting board to adopt procedures to ensure prompt consideration of necessary changes to accounting principles by a majority vote and to consider the need to keep standards current. The SEC has reaffirmed that it will continue to recognize pronouncements of the Financial Accounting Standards Board ("FASB") as being GAAP for purposes of filings with the SEC.[119]

3. Funding. The Sarbanes-Oxley Act provides for the funding of the PCAOB and the standard setting board from a fee to be assessed upon issuers calculated based on their market capitalization.[120]

E. Auditor Independence

Title II of the Sarbanes-Oxley Act amends § 10A of the Exchange Act to:

- ban specified non-audit services and require prior approval of audit and permitted non-audit services;

- require the auditors to report certain matters to the audit committee;

- require rotation of audit partners every five years; and

- seek to eliminate auditor conflicts of interest.

The SEC has issued final rules to implement these provisions.[121] The new rules became effective on May 6, 2003, subject in certain cases to transition periods.

---

[118] Section 108 of the Sarbanes-Oxley Act.

[119] SEC Release No. 33-8221 (Apr. 25, 2003). Although historically the vote of five out of FASB's seven trustees was required to set a new accounting standard, on April 24, 2002, FASB changed its voting process from a supermajority to a simple majority vote, which is consistent with the requirements of the Sarbanes-Oxley Act. FASB Press Release, Financial Accounting Foundation Changes Financial Accounting Standards Board's FASB Voting to Increase Efficiency (Apr. 24, 2002).

[120] Section 109 of the Sarbanes-Oxley Act. FASB was previously funded from sales of publications, licensing agreements, and voluntary contributions by accounting firms. Financial Accounting Foundation, 2001 Annual Report: High Quality Financial Reporting (2002). The PCAOB has issued final rules with respect to funding. PCAOB Release No. 2003-003 (Apr. 18, 2003).

[121] SEC Release No. 33-8183 (Jan. 28, 2003). These rules are discussed more fully in our memorandum entitled "SEC Adopts Final Rules under the Sarbanes-Oxley Act Regarding Auditor Independence and Retention of Audit Records."

The SEC's rules implementing Title II of the Sarbanes-Oxley Act amend and supplement the SEC's existing rules on auditor independence contained in Rule 2-01 of Regulation S-X, which were adopted in a major rulemaking in November 2000.[122] Consistent with the SEC's existing rules, the new rules apply to both U.S. and non-U.S. accountants performing audits of reporting company financial statements.

Paragraph (b) of Rule 2-01 sets forth the general standard that an accountant will not be considered independent if he or she is not "capable of exercising objective and impartial judgment on all issues encompassed within the accountant's engagement." In determining whether an accountant is independent, the SEC will consider "all relevant circumstances, including all relationships between the accountant and the audit client, and not just those relating to reports filed with the [SEC]." Neither the Sarbanes-Oxley Act nor the new rules modify this general standard.

Like the existing rules in Regulation S-X, the new rules are framed as requirements for an accountant to be considered "independent" for purposes of auditing financial statements filed with the SEC. The existing independence rules also identify a non-exclusive list of circumstances that are inconsistent with independence. Several of these are also unaffected by the Sarbanes-Oxley Act and the new rules—in particular, the prohibitions on certain financial relationships between the accountant and the audit client, on certain business relationships and on contingent fees. The new rules do, however, make significant changes to the list of circumstances that are inconsistent with independence. In order to clarify that a violation of the independence rules also constitutes a violation of the Exchange Act, the SEC has adopted a separate rule under § 10A of the Exchange Act that makes it unlawful for auditors not to be "independent" under the relevant Regulation S-X rules.[123]

1. Non-Audit Services. A centerpiece of the SEC's comprehensive November 2000 reformulation of its independence rules was the concept of listing specific non-audit services that auditors may not provide.[124] The November 2000 rules describe nine categories of prohibited services, and they set forth exemptions of varying kinds for many of the categories. Section 201 of the Sarbanes-Oxley Act requires the SEC to adopt rules prohibiting non-audit services, and it lists the following eight categories of services that correspond very closely to the titles of the subparagraphs in the November 2000 rules:[125]

---

[122] SEC Release No. 33-7919 (Nov. 21, 2000).
[123] This is consistent with Section 208(b) of the Sarbanes-Oxley Act, which frames the new independence requirements in terms of prohibited activities.
[124] *See* Rule 2-01(c)(4) of Regulation S-X.
[125] The only additions are references to "contribution-in-kind reports" and "expert services unrelated to the audit."

OVERVIEW AND IMPLEMENTATION

- bookkeeping or other services related to accounting records or financial statements;

- financial information systems design and implementation;

- appraisal or valuation services, fairness opinions or contribution-in-kind reports;

- actuarial services;

- internal audit outsourcing services;

- management functions or human resources;

- broker-dealer, investment adviser or investment banking services; and

- legal services or expert services unrelated to the audit.

To implement Section 201, the new rules amend the existing list to:

- remove the categorical exemptions contained in many of the existing rules;

- add expert services;

- add contribution-in-kind reports;

- expand the scope of prohibited actuarial services; and

- expand the scope of prohibited legal services to cover services under non-U.S. law.

In general, these changes make it increasingly difficult for public companies to engage their auditing firms for services other than auditing. The scope of permitted non-audit services, already narrow under the November 2000 rules, has become narrower still.[126]

---

[126] In accordance with Section 202, the new rules contain a *de minimis* exception, under which the pre-approval requirement for services other than audit, review and attest services would be waived if (i) the aggregate amount of all such services provided constitutes no more than 5% of the total amount of revenues paid by the company to its accountant during the fiscal year in which the services are provided; (ii) such services were not recognized by the company at the time of the engagement to be non-audit services; and (iii) such services are promptly brought to the attention of the audit committee and approved, prior to the completion of the audit, by the audit committee or by one or more members of the audit committee to whom authority to grant such approvals has been delegated. The audit committee's policies and procedures would have to describe, if applicable, the specific procedures that permit and monitor activities meeting the *de minimis* exception.

The SEC recognized in the release that audit clients may need a period of time to exit existing contracts in order to comply with the new rules on prohibited non-audit services. To that end, the new rules provide that until May 6, 2004 the provision of services described in the new rules will not impair an accountant's independence, provided that the services are pursuant to contracts in existence on May 6, 2003.

2. Audit Committee Administration of the Engagement. The new rules under Section 202 amend Regulation S-X to require that a reporting company's audit committee pre-approve all audit, review and attest engagements required under the securities laws and all engagements for permitted non-audit services. The rules require that either:

- the engagement is expressly approved by the audit committee before the accountant is engaged by the company or its subsidiaries to render audit or non-audit services; or

- the engagement is entered into pursuant to pre-approval policies and procedures established by the audit committee, provided the policies and procedures are detailed as to the particular service, the audit committee is informed of each service, and such policies and procedures do not include delegation of the audit committee's responsibilities to management.

Engagement pursuant to pre-approval policies and procedures could include delegation to an independent audit committee member, which is expressly provided for in Section 202 of the Sarbanes-Oxley Act,[127] but other approaches are also possible as long as they are carefully designed to ensure that they do not result in delegating the audit committee's responsibilities to management.

The new pre-approval requirements apply to all engagements for audit and non-audit services that are entered into after May 6, 2003. For non-audit engagements entered into prior to that date, regardless of whether they were pre-approved by the audit committee, the accounting firm will have 12 months from the effective date to complete the services.

The new rules apply to all reporting companies, including foreign companies and companies with only listed debt securities.[128] The new rules will also ap-

---

[127] The Sarbanes-Oxley Act does not define "independence" for purposes of delegation pursuant to Section 202. However, as discussed below, the SEC has issued final rules under Section 301 that will require that all audit committee members of listed companies in the United States meet specified independence criteria.

[128] The PCAOB is given explicit authority to exempt any issuer from the requirements of this provision, subject to SEC review. Section 201(b) of the Sarbanes-Oxley Act.

OVERVIEW AND IMPLEMENTATION

ply to a substantial number of companies that do not have audit committees. As noted above, if a company does not have an audit committee, the full board of directors is the audit committee under the definition of that term in the Sarbanes-Oxley Act. Because of the scope of the pre-approval requirement (for example, the provision of a comfort letter is specifically listed as an audit service), the new provision adds a significant procedural step to many ordinary course transactions, and these may be substantially more difficult to observe for issuers that do not have an audit committee.[129]

3. Audit Partner Rotation. Prior rules of the AICPA required the lead partner of U.S. auditing firms to rotate off an audit engagement after seven years, with a two-year "time out" period. Section 203 of the Sarbanes-Oxley Act imposes a five-year rotation requirement for both the lead partner and the partner responsible for reviewing the audit, without specifying any "time out" period. The new rules under Section 203 incorporate rotation and "time out" requirements into the auditor independence rules. They reach farther than Section 203 by covering additional members of the audit team and, unlike the AICPA rules, they also apply to non-U.S. auditing firms.

Under the new rules, an auditing firm is not independent if any "audit partner," as defined in the rules, performs:

- the services of a lead or concurring partner, for a period of more than five consecutive years;

- more than ten hours of audit, review or attest services in connection with the annual or interim consolidated financial statements of the reporting company, for a period of more than seven consecutive years; or

- the services of a lead partner in connection with certain subsidiary financial statements, for a period of more than seven consecutive years.[130]

In addition, the new rules require lead and concurring audit partners to observe a five-year "time out" period following any five-year period as part of an audit engagement team. Audit partners subject to the seven-year rotation requirement are required to observe a two-year "time out" period.

---

[129] Nonetheless, the potential burdens to an issuer without an audit committee under this provision are much less than those contemplated by the audit committee rules described above for listed companies.

[130] The rules apply to an audit or review related to the annual or interim financial statements of a subsidiary of the company whose assets or revenues constitute 20% or more of the consolidated assets or revenues of the parent company.

The new rules are subject to various transition periods established by the SEC. For a lead partner with a U.S. accounting firm, the rotation requirements are effective for the issuer's first fiscal year beginning after May 6, 2003. For a concurring partner with a U.S. accounting firm, the rules are effective for the issuer's first fiscal year beginning after May 6, 2004. For other U.S. audit partners and for all partners with foreign accounting firms, the rules are effective for the issuer's first fiscal year beginning after May 6, 2003. Because of a difference in the way in which time served is calculated, such other U.S. audit partners and foreign accounting firms have a longer transition period.[131]

4. Conflicts of Interest Resulting from Employment Relationships. The SEC's existing rules provide that an accounting firm is not independent of an audit client if a former partner, principal, shareholder or professional employee of the firm has accepted employment with the client and has a continuing financial interest in the accounting firm or is in a position to influence the firm's operations or financial policies.[132] The new rules are effective for employment relationships with issuers that commence after May 6, 2003.

The new rules under Section 206 of the Sarbanes-Oxley Act amend Regulation S-X to impose a further restriction on employment of former employees of an accounting firm by an issuer. The rules provide that an accounting firm is not independent of an issuer with respect to the audit for a given fiscal period if a former partner, principal, shareholder or professional employee of the accounting firm is in a "financial reporting oversight role" at the issuer and the individual was a member of the audit engagement team of the issuer during the one-year period preceding the date that audit procedures commenced for that fiscal period. Under the new rules, audit procedures are deemed to commence for a given fiscal period on the day following the filing with the SEC of the issuer's annual report on Form 10-K, Form 20-F or Form 40-F covering the previous fiscal period.

5. Prohibited Compensation. The SEC's new rules on auditor compensation add a requirement to Regulation S-X that is not mandated by the Sarbanes-Oxley Act. The rules provide that an accountant is not independent if, at any point during the audit and professional engagement period, any audit partner earns or receives compensation from the accountant based on the audit partners' procuring engagements with that audit client to provide any products or services other than audit, review or attest services. The new rules are effective beginning with the accounting firm's first fiscal year commencing after May 6, 2003.

---

[131] For lead and concurring partners with a U.S. accounting firm, time served in the capacity of lead or concurring partner prior to May 6, 2003 is counted. For other U.S. partners and *all* partners with foreign accounting firms, time served prior to May 6, 2003 is not counted and the first fiscal year beginning after May 6, 2003 constitutes the first year of service.

[132] *See* Rule 2-01(c)(2) of Regulation S-X.

OVERVIEW AND IMPLEMENTATION

6. Auditors Reports to Audit Committees. New rules under Section 204 of the Sarbanes-Oxley Act amend Regulation S-X to require each registered public accounting firm that performs for a reporting company an audit required under the securities laws to report to the company's audit committee, prior to the filing of its audit report with the SEC:

- all critical accounting policies and practices used by the company;

- all alternative treatments within GAAP for policies and practices related to material items that have been discussed with the company's management, including:

    — ramifications of the use of alternative disclosures and treatments; and

    — the treatment preferred by the accounting firm; and

- other material written communications between the accounting firm and the company's management, such as any "management letter" or schedule of unadjusted differences.

The new rules are effective May 6, 2003.

7. Expanded Disclosure. The new rules amend the SEC's existing requirements under the proxy rules regarding disclosure of fees paid to a company's principal accountant and introduce new disclosure requirements regarding the audit committee policies and procedures for pre-approval of non-audit fees. A U.S. reporting company must include the disclosures in its proxy statement and repeat or incorporate them by reference in its annual report on Form 10-K. Foreign private issuers, which were not previously required to provide this disclosure, must include the disclosures in their annual reports on Form 20-F or Form 40-F. The new disclosure provisions are effective for periodic annual filings for a reporting company's first fiscal year ending after December 15, 2003, but will require disclosure, broken down into four categories (audit fees, audit-related fees, tax fees and all other fees), for each of the two most recent fiscal years (*i.e.*, for 2002 and 2003 in the case of the first disclosure).

F. Analyst Conflicts of Interest

The Sarbanes-Oxley Act adds § 15D to the Exchange Act, which directs the SEC (or, as designated by the SEC, appropriate self-regulatory organizations) to adopt, within one year of the Act's enactment, rules designed to address equity research analyst conflicts of interest. Such rules, the stated objective of which is to "improve the objectivity of research and provide investors with more useful and reliable information," must include provisions that restrict investment banking department influence over research analysts and require disclosure by the analyst in research reports and public appearances of the existence of potential conflicts of interest.

The specific provisions cited in new § 15D by and large to track the rules regarding equity research analyst conflicts of interest recently adopted by the NYSE and the NASD, which were approved by the SEC on May 8, 2002.[133] This overlap between the previously approved rules and the scope of the rulemaking required by the Sarbanes-Oxley Act suggests that the Act is intended to encourage further rulemaking to ensure that the cited concerns are adequately addressed. This is not surprising, since the previously approved rules were widely understood to be only a first step in addressing analyst conflicts of interest.[134] The one area specifically identified in the Sarbanes-Oxley Act for new rulemaking that was not addressed in the previously approved equity research analyst conflict of interest rules concerns protections against retaliation by a broker-dealer against any analyst who issues a research report that may adversely affect the firm's current or potential investment banking relationship with the issuer covered by the report.[135]

G. Enhanced Civil Liability and Remedies

The Sarbanes-Oxley Act contains the following provisions relating to civil

---

[133] SEC Release No. 34-45908 (May 10, 2002). The new NYSE and NASD analyst conflicts of interest rules are discussed in our memorandum entitled, "SEC Approves Research Analyst Conflicts of Interest Rules; Merrill Settlement Agreement Reached."

[134] The NYSE and NASD have filed additional proposed rules with the SEC to further address analyst conflicts of interest. SEC Release No. 34-47110 (Dec. 31, 2002). The NASD has also proposed amendments to its rules requiring that the CEO and chief compliance officers of its members certify as to the adequacy of their compliance and supervisory policies and procedures. See NASD Notice to Members 03-29 (June 2003).

[135] As part of its continuing efforts to address analyst conflicts of interest, and perhaps in anticipation of the enactment of the Sarbanes-Oxley Act, the SEC proposed Regulation Analyst Certification ("Regulation AC") on July 24, 2002 (the proposal was released on August 2, 2002). SEC Release No. 33-8119 (Aug. 2, 2002). Final Regulation AC, which became effective on April 14, 2003, requires "clear and prominent" certifications addressed to analyst conflicts of interest in both debt and equity research reports, as well as the recording of similar statements following public appearances by research analysts. SEC Release No. 33-8193 (Feb. 20, 2003). Specifically, it requires analysts to certify in research reports that the views expressed "accurately reflect" the analyst's "personal views" about "any and all" of the subject securities or issuers and that no part of the analyst's compensation was, is or will be, directly or indirectly, related to the "specific" recommendations or views expressed or, if not, identifying the source, amount and purpose of the compensation and disclosing that it may influence the views expressed.

In addition, a settlement between ten investment firms and the SEC, the NYSE, the NASD, the New York Attorney General and other state regulators with respect to analyst conflicts of interest has been finalized. SEC Press Release, Ten of Nation's Top Investment Firms Settle Enforcement Actions Involving Conflicts of Interest Between Research and Investment Banking (Apr. 28, 2003).

litigation under the U.S. securities laws, each of which is applicable to all proceedings commenced on or after the date of the Act:

- **Statute of Limitations for Securities Fraud.** The Act creates a new statute of limitations for any private right of action involving a claim for fraud "in contravention of a regulatory requirement" under the securities laws of the earlier of two years from the date of discovery or five years from the date of the violation.[136] Although the Act is not explicit about the claims that it intends to cover, the likely interpretation of the provision is that it will supply the limitations period for securities claims only where the securities laws themselves do not expressly set out the limitations period. The new statute of limitations thus will not apply to causes of action pursuant to §§ 9 and 18 of the Exchange Act or §§ 11 and 12 of the Securities Act, but will likely apply to causes of action pursuant to §§ 10(b) and 14 of the Exchange Act. The statute of limitations for claims under §§ 10(b) and 14 had been the earlier of one year from the date of disclosure or three years from the date of violation.

- **Debts Nondischargeable if Incurred in Violation of Securities Fraud Laws.** The Act creates an additional exception to the discharge in bankruptcy of any individual debtor from any debt relating to any judgment, settlement or order from the violation of the federal or state securities laws or regulations or common law fraud in connection with the purchase or sale of a security.[137]

H. Enhanced Criminal Provisions

The Sarbanes-Oxley Act contains the following new crimes and criminal penalties:

- **Destruction, Alteration or Falsification of Records.** The Act adds § 1519 to Title 18, which makes it a crime to knowingly destroy, alter or falsify records with the intent to impede, obstruct or influence a federal investigation or bankruptcy or "in relation to or contemplation of any such matter," and amends existing § 1512 of Title 18 to apply to document destruction or alteration in any federal court or similar proceeding.[138] The maximum sentence is 20 years.

- **Destruction of Corporate Audit Records.** The Act adds § 1520 to Title 18, which requires (i) any accountant conducting an audit of an issuer to maintain workpapers for a period of five years; and (ii) the SEC to promulgate rules regarding the retention of workpapers and other documents

---

[136] Section 804 of the Sarbanes-Oxley Act.
[137] *Id.* Section 803.
[138] *Id.* Sections 802 and 1102.

within 180 days of the Act's enactment.[139] The SEC has adopted final rules under Section 802 that require an accounting firm to retain its records for a period of seven years following the completion of an audit or review of a reporting company's financial statements.[140] The maximum sentence for violation of the Act's requirement or the SEC's rules is ten years.

- **Securities Fraud.** The Act adds § 1348 to Title 18 making it a crime to defraud any person in connection with any security of an issuer.[141] This section does not contain the purchase or sale requirement in § 10(b) of the Exchange Act. The maximum sentence is 25 years.

- **Retaliation Against Informants.** The Act adds § 1513 to Title 18 making it a crime to retaliate against any person for providing information to a law enforcement officer.[142] The maximum sentence is ten years.

- **Increased Maximum Penalties.** The Act increases the maximum sentence for mail and wire fraud from five to 20 years.[143] The Sarbanes-Oxley Act also increases the maximum criminal penalties under the Exchange Act from $1 million to $5 million for individuals and from $2.5 million to $25 million for entities, and the maximum sentence from ten years to 20 years.[144] The Act increases the penalties for a willful violation of ERISA's reporting and disclosure provisions to a fine of up to $100,000 and imprisonment of up to ten years.[145]

- **Review by U.S. Sentencing Commission.** The Sarbanes-Oxley Act instructs the U.S. Sentencing Commission, which sets the sentencing guidelines used by U.S. federal courts, to review the guidelines for obstruction of justice, criminal fraud and securities and accounting fraud related offenses, and to ensure that the sentencing guidelines reflect the nature of the offenses and penalties set forth in the Act.[146] Pursuant to emergency power provided by the Act, the Sentencing Commission promulgated temporary amendments to the sentencing guidelines, which became effective on January 25, 2003 and will remain in effect only until November 1, 2003.[147] On April 18, 2003, the Sentencing Commission promulgated permanent amendments to reflect the provi-

---

[139] *Id.* Section 802.
[140] SEC Release No. 33-8180 (Jan. 24, 2003).
[141] Section 807 of the Sarbanes-Oxley Act.
[142] *Id.* Section 1107.
[143] *Id.* Section 903.
[144] *Id.* Section 1106.
[145] *Id.* Section 904.
[146] *Id.* Sections 805, 905 and 1104.
[147] U.S. Sentencing Guidelines Manual Supplement (Jan. 25, 2003).

sions of the Sarbanes-Oxley Act.[148] These amendments, which will become effective November 1, 2003, make permanent the temporary amendments and add several provisions. Together, the amendments have the effect of increasing the penalties and the scope of the current sentencing guidelines for corporate and serious white-collar frauds. Specifically, the amendments:

— significantly increase certain penalty enhancements for offenses affecting more than 50 victims;

— expand the scope of certain penalty enhancements to cover offenses that substantially endanger (i) the solvency or financial security of an organization that at the time was publicly traded or had 1,000 or more employees; or (ii) the solvency or financial security of 100 or more victims (prior to the amendments, the enhancements applied only if the offense substantially jeopardized the safety and soundness of a financial institution);

— create a new penalty enhancement to cover violations of securities laws by officers or directors of publicly traded companies, registered broker-dealers and investment advisers;

— significantly increase penalties for offenses such as wire fraud and mail fraud;

— significantly increase penalties for offenses in which the loss exceeds $200,000,000 (reduction in value of equity securities or other corporate assets is now a factor in measuring losses); and

— significantly increase penalties for obstruction of justice offenses, and create new penalty enhancements to cover alteration or fabrication of substantial numbers of documents or objects, destruction of particularly probative documents or objects, or offenses that were extensive in scope, planning or preparation.

I. Other Provisions

- **Lawyers' Professional Responsibility Rules.** Section 307 of the Sarbanes-Oxley Act requires the SEC to promulgate rules "setting forth minimum standards of professional conduct" for lawyers practicing be-

---

[148] U.S. Sentencing Guidelines Manual App. C (2003) (forthcoming Nov. 1, 2003).

fore it.[149] In recent years, the SEC generally has interpreted its Rules of Practice as housekeeping rules rather than a means to sanction lawyer misconduct. Rules adopted in response to the mandate in Section 307 could result in more frequent enforcement proceedings against lawyers. Section 307 also represents a departure from the traditional method of regulating attorney professional responsibility through state authorities, which in some jurisdictions already impose similar, though narrower, requirements (*e.g.,* DR 5-109 of New York's Code of Professional Responsibility).

The final rules issued by the SEC prescribe new reporting requirements for attorneys who become aware of evidence of misconduct by issuer clients.[150] The final rules apply to attorneys "appearing and practicing" before the SEC, which includes the full range of individuals who contribute, edit or prepare information contained in materials filed with the SEC, even if these individuals are not directly responsible for the actual filing. An attorney representing an issuer before the SEC who becomes aware of evidence that it is "reasonably likely" that a material violation of securities laws, breach of fiduciary duty or similar violation has occurred, is ongoing or is about to occur within the client issuer must report that evidence to the chief legal officer or to both the chief legal officer and CEO of the issuer. If the chief legal officer does not "appropriately respond" to the report within a reasonable time, the attorney must report the evidence further "up the ladder" to the audit committee, another committee made up solely of independent board members, or the issuer's board of directors itself. As an alternative, the final rules offer a second reporting procedure under which issuers may establish a qualified legal compliance committee to handle these reports.[151]

The SEC initially proposed to require reporting attorneys who do not receive an appropriate response to make, under certain circumstances, a "noisy withdrawal" from the representation of the issuer.[152] For outside counsel, noisy withdrawal would include resigning from the representa-

---

[149] Section 307 of the Sarbanes-Oxley Act. The SEC's final rules under Section 307 are discussed in Chapter X.

[150] SEC Release No. 33-8185 (Jan. 29, 2003).

[151] The final rules create an exemption from the reporting obligations for an attorney admitted to practice outside the United States that qualifies as a "non-appearing foreign attorney." To qualify as a "non-appearing foreign attorney," an attorney (i) must be admitted to practice in a foreign jurisdiction; (ii) cannot hold himself or herself out as practicing, or give legal advice regarding, U.S. federal or state securities or other laws; and (iii) must conduct activities that would constitute appearing and practicing before the SEC only (a) incidentally to, and in the ordinary course of, his or her foreign law practice; or (b) in consultation with U.S. counsel.

[152] SEC Release No. 33-8150 (Nov. 21, 2002).

tion, notifying the SEC that the withdrawal is based on "professional considerations" and disaffirming any submission to the SEC that the attorney helped prepare and believes is or may be materially false or misleading. In-house counsel also would be required to disaffirm any tainted submission, but would not be required to resign. This proposal was not incorporated into the final rule. Instead, at the time it adopted the final rule, the SEC extended the comment period on the "noisy withdrawal" proposal and proposed for comment an alternative "reporting out" proposal. Under this alternative, outside counsel would be required to withdraw from representation and notify the issuer of this withdrawal for "professional considerations" and in-house counsel would be required to cease participating in any matter relating to the violation and notify the issuer in writing. The issuer would be required to report the attorney's action to the SEC in an appropriate public filing. The comment period for both proposals ended on April 7, 2003.

- **SEC Resources.** The Sarbanes-Oxley Act authorizes additional funding of $776 million to the SEC for 2003.[153]

- **Whistleblower Protection.** The Sarbanes-Oxley Act prohibits retaliation by issuers or any representative thereof against employees assisting certain investigations and proceedings by federal agencies, Congress or persons with supervisory authority over the employee.[154]

---

[153] Section 601 of the Sarbanes-Oxley Act.

[154] *Id.* Section 806. President Bush has issued a statement that this provision protects whistleblowers that speak to a congressional committee in the course of an investigation, but not when evidence is provided to individual lawmakers or aides. This statement was criticized by Senators Leahy and Grassley as suggesting too narrow an application of this provision. Associated Press, *Bush Criticized on Whistle-Blowers*, WALL ST. J., Aug. 1, 2002.

ANNEX A

Provision of the Sarbanes-Oxley Act	Section	Effectiveness/Required Regulatory Action
PCAOB		
• PCAOB created to establish auditing standards and to oversee auditors.	§§ 101-107, 109	PCAOB members and Chairman have been appointed. SEC recognized PCAOB as organized on April 25, 2003. Registration of accounting firms required within 180 days of organization.
• Recognition of accounting standard setting board.	§§ 108, 109	SEC recognized FASB on April 25, 2003.
Auditor Independence		
• Prohibition on certain non-audit services and pre-approval requirement for audit and non-audit services.	§§ 201-202	SEC issued final rules on January 28, 2003. Rules effective May 6, 2003, though certain provisions have transition periods.
• Audit partner rotation.	§ 203	SEC issued final rules on January 28, 2003. Rules effective May 6, 2003, though certain provisions have transition periods.
• Auditors required to report to audit committees.	§ 204	SEC issued final rules on January 28, 2003. Rules effective May 6, 2003, though certain provisions have transition periods.
• Prohibition on officer's employment with auditors.	§ 206	SEC issued final rules on January 28, 2003. Rules effective May 6, 2003, though certain provisions have transition periods.
Corporate Responsibility		
• Listed companies required to have fully independent audit committees to hire and supervise the company's auditors.	§ 301	SEC issued final rules on April 9, 2003. Listed issuers required to comply by the earlier of their first annual meeting after January 15, 2004 or October 31, 2004, except that listed foreign private issuers are required to comply by July 31, 2005.

OVERVIEW AND IMPLEMENTATION

Provision of the Sarbanes-Oxley Act	Section	Effectiveness/Required Regulatory Action
• Certification by CEOs and CFOs of financial reports.	§ 302	SEC issued final rules on August 29, 2002, which were modified by rules adopted on May 27, 2003. These amendments, including a requirement to file the certifications as exhibits, but excluding certain amendments pertaining to internal control over financial reporting, are generally effective on August 14, 2003. Certain amendments pertaining to internal control over financial reporting apply to U.S. "accelerated filers" commencing with the annual report for their first fiscal year ending on or after June 15, 2004 and all subsequent periods. All other U.S. and foreign private issuers must comply beginning with the annual report for their first fiscal year ending on or after April 15, 2005.
• Directors and officers prohibited from fraudulently influencing any audit.	§ 303	SEC issued final rules on May 20, 2003 effective June 27, 2003.
• Disgorgement of CEO and CFO compensation following restatement of financial statements.	§ 304	Effective immediately.
• Lower standard for court officer and director bars.	§ 305	Effective immediately.
• Prohibition on certain insider transactions during blackout periods under individual account plans.	§ 306	SEC issued final rules on January 22, 2003 effective January 26, 2003.
• Attorney professional responsibility rulemaking that requires lawyer to report evidence of violations of laws	§ 307	SEC issued final rules on January 22, 2003. Rules effective beginning Au-

Provision of the Sarbanes-Oxley Act	Section	Effectiveness/Required Regulatory Action
and breaches of fiduciary duty to issuers.		gust 5, 2003. SEC has revised the proposed rules concerning and extended the comment period with respect to "noisy withdrawals" and issued an additional proposal for comment with respect to "reporting out."
• Restitution funds for victim of violations of securities laws.	§ 308	Effective immediately.
Enhanced Financial Disclosures		
• Disclosure of material correcting adjustments.	§ 401	SEC rulemaking required but no time period specified.
• Enhanced disclosure of *pro forma* (non-GAAP) financial measures.	§ 401	SEC issued final rules on January 22, 2003. Rules effective with respect to annual reports for fiscal years ended, and public disclosures made, on or after March 28, 2003.
• Enhanced disclosure of off-balance sheet arrangements and contractual obligations.	§ 401	SEC issued final rules on January 28, 2003. Rules effective with respect to annual reports for fiscal years ending on or after (i) June 15, 2003, with respect to off-balance sheet arrangements; and (ii) December 15, 2003, with respect to contractual obligations.
• Prohibition of loans to executive officers and directors, subject to limited exceptions.	§ 402	Effective immediately.
• Accelerated reporting of insider transactions on Form 4 under Section 16 of the Exchange Act (not applicable to foreign private issuers).	§ 403	Effective August 29, 2002. SEC final rules require electronic filing by July 30, 2003.
• Annual reports required to contain an internal control report.	§ 404	U.S. "accelerated filers" must comply with the new rules commencing with

OVERVIEW AND IMPLEMENTATION

Provision of the Sarbanes-Oxley Act	Section	Effectiveness/Required Regulatory Action
		the annual report for their first fiscal year ending on or after June 15, 2004. All other U.S. and foreign private issuers must comply beginning with the annual report for their first fiscal year ending on or after April 15, 2005.
• Required disclosure as to adoption of a code of ethics and whether the audit committee includes at least one audit committee financial expert.	§§ 406, 407	SEC issued final rules on January 23, 2003. Rules effective with respect to annual reports for fiscal years ending on or after July 15, 2003. Delayed effectiveness for foreign private issuers as to disclosure regarding independence.
• Mandated SEC review of public filings at least once every three years.	§ 408	Effective immediately.
• Issuers are required to disclose "on a rapid and current basis" information concerning material changes in their financial condition and operations.	§ 409	SEC issued final rules relating to filing of earnings press releases on Form 8-K on January 22, 2003. Rules effective immediately.
Analyst Conflict of Interest		
• Directs adoption of rules to address analyst conflicts of interest.	§ 501	SEC issued final rules on February 20, 2003. Rules effective beginning April 14, 2003.
Commission Resources and Authority		
• Additional funding for the SEC.	§ 601	Effective immediately.
Enhanced Criminal and Civil Provisions		
• New crimes for destruction or alteration of records in federal investigations, court proceedings or bankruptcy.	§§ 802, 1102	Effective immediately.

Provision of the Sarbanes-Oxley Act	Section	Effectiveness/Required Regulatory Action
• New crime for destruction of audit records.	§ 802	Effective immediately. SEC issued final rules for new 18 U.S.C. § 1520(a)(2) on January 24, 2003.
• Debts from violation of securities laws nondischargeable.	§ 803	Effective immediately.
• Extension of the statute of limitations for securities fraud claims.	§ 804	Effective immediately.
• Whistleblower protection.	§ 806	Effective immediately.
• New securities fraud crime.	§ 807	Effective immediately.
• Increase in the term of imprisonment possible in the case of mail and wire fraud from five years to 20 years.	§ 903	Effective immediately.
• Increased penalties for violation of ERISA.	§ 904	Effective immediately.
• Certification by CEOs and CFOs	§ 906	Effective immediately.
Corporate Fraud Accountability		
• SEC temporary freeze authority.	§ 1103	Effective immediately.
• SEC officer and director bars.	§ 1105	Effective immediately.
• Increased penalties under Exchange Act.	§ 1106	Effective immediately.
• New crime for retaliation against informants.	§ 1107	Effective immediately.

OVERVIEW AND IMPLEMENTATION

ANNEX B

Study	Responsible Agency	Date
Adoption of a Principles-Based Accounting System by the United States Financial Reporting System	SEC	Due by July 30, 2003
Potential Effects of Requiring Mandatory Rotation of Registered Public Accounting Firms as Auditors	GAO	Due by July 30, 2003
Historical Consolidation of Public Accounting Firms Since 1989	GAO	Due by July 30, 2003
Role and Function of Credit Rating Agencies in the Operation of the Securities Market, *available* at http://www.sec.gov/news/studies/credratingreport0103.pdf	SEC	Issued January 24, 2003
Study and Report on Violations by Securities Professionals from January 1, 1998 to December 31, 2001, *available* at http://www.sec.gov/news/studies/sox703report.pdf	SEC	Issued January 24, 2003
Report pursuant to Section 704 of the Sarbanes-Oxley Act of 2002 (Review of All SEC Enforcement Actions Involving Reporting Requirement Violations for Preceding Five Years) *available* at http://www.sec.gov/news/studies/sox704report.pdf	SEC	Issued January 24, 2003
The Role of Firms and their Analysts with Enron and Global Crossing, Report No. GAO-03-S11, *available* at http://www.gas.gov	GAO	Issued March 1, 2003

II CONSIDERATIONS FOR FOREIGN PRIVATE ISSUERS

The Sarbanes-Oxley Act applies to U.S. and foreign issuers alike. It consists largely of amendments to the Exchange Act to which a company becomes subject by either doing a U.S. public offering or listing its securities on an exchange in the United States. The coverage of foreign issuers is surprising in light of the customary policies of the SEC, the NYSE and Nasdaq to accommodate home country practices, including with respect to the frequency and content of periodic reports (foreign private issuers are not required to file quarterly reports on Form 10-Q or current reports on Form 8-K), proxy rules and corporate governance standards, including board composition.

This Chapter highlights provisions of the Sarbanes-Oxley Act that are of greatest significance to foreign private issuers and how—short of a "going private" or similar transaction or a share repurchase program—these issuers can exit the U.S. capital markets if they wish to avoid the Act's application. It is important to note that, although the SEC has felt constrained in its ability to exempt foreign private issuers from the Act, it has used its general and specific rulemaking and exemptive powers to address their concerns in certain limited respects.

KEY PROVISIONS

The provisions of particular relevance to foreign private issuers:

- require, in annual reports on Form 20-F, (i) an issuer's CEO and CFO to certify, among other things, the accuracy and fair presentation of the report and adequacy of the issuer's disclosure controls and internal control over financial reporting; and (ii) subject to a lengthy transition period, a report setting out management's conclusions about the effectiveness of an issuer's internal control over financial reporting, as attested to by the issuer's independent auditor;

- mandate disgorgement of certain CEO and CFO compensation following restatement of financial statements by reason of misconduct;

- require all issuers listed on a U.S. national securities exchange or Nasdaq to have an independent audit committee, with independence standards defined by reference to Section 301 of the Act; upon effectiveness of rules and listing standards implementing Section 301, committee members will be barred from receiving certain fees, directly or indirectly (*e.g.*, as a partner or managing director of a financial advisory firm or law firm), and being affiliates of an issuer or any of its subsidiaries;

- enhance standards for auditor independence by (i) broadening the list of services that an independent auditor may not provide; (ii) requiring that an issuer's audit committee administer the engagement of the accounting firm to provide audit and non-audit services; (iii) requiring that key partners on the audit engagement team rotate every five or seven years, depending on their role, and imposing "time out" periods on these partners (with favorable transition periods for foreign private issuers); (iv) making the audit client's employment of former auditor personnel in certain positions inconsistent with independence; and (v) prohibiting audit partners from receiving compensation from the accounting firm with respect to non-audit services provided to the audit client;

- expand existing requirements regarding the disclosure in Form 20-F of fees paid to an issuer's independent auditor and introduce new requirements, including disclosure, regarding audit committee pre-approval of audit and permitted non-audit services;

- require foreign accountants to (i) register with the PCAOB and consent to the production of their audit workpapers, whether or not the client consents; and (ii) retain audit workpapers for seven years following the conclusion of an audit or review of an issuer's financial statements;

- generally prohibit personal loans to executive officers and directors;

- establish standards of conduct for lawyers appearing and practicing before the SEC in the representation of an issuer, including required "up the ladder" reporting that imposes on an issuer's general counsel or other chief legal officer a duty to investigate alleged misconduct (there are special provisions for foreign lawyers not admitted to practice in the United States); and

- create a new crime, punishable by up to 20 years in prison, for the destruction, alteration or falsification of records with the intent to obstruct a federal investigation.

FOREIGN PRIVATE ISSUERS

DEREGISTRATION UNDER THE U.S. SECURITIES LAWS

In response to the increased burdens imposed by the Act, some foreign private issuers have sought to exit the U.S. markets by delisting and/or deregistering their securities under the Exchange Act.[1] It is important to note that a foreign issuer that has made a U.S. public offering of securities is subject to Exchange Act reporting obligations at least for the year in which the registration statement for the public offering became effective.[2] Thereafter, the issuer may only *suspend* its obligations under the Exchange Act (and thus the Act) and only if:

- the total number of holders of record of the class of offered securities is less than 300 worldwide; or

- the total number of beneficial owners of such securities who are resident in the United States is less than 300 (or 500, if the total assets of the foreign issuer have not exceeded $10 million on the last day of each of the issuer's three most recent fiscal years).[3]

If these shareholding thresholds are crossed in a subsequent year—no matter how much time has passed—the issuer would again be subject to the Exchange Act (and thus the Act). If the circumstances warranted the request, an issuer could apply to the SEC for an order effectively allowing it to terminate these obligations, although it is not yet clear what guidelines the SEC would apply in deciding whether or not to grant the request.

Obligations imposed by the Exchange Act (and thus the Act) on an issuer that has not made a U.S. public offering of securities but has listed its securities in the United States may generally be *terminated* if the total number of beneficial owners of such securities who are resident in the United States is less than 300 (or 500, if the total assets of the foreign issuer have not exceeded $10 million on the last day of each of the issuer's three most recent fiscal years).[4] Generally, to avoid application of the Act if this threshold is later crossed, the issuer must obtain an

---

[1] Issuers that only seek to delist their securities will remain subject to substantially all of the requirements of the Sarbanes-Oxley Act and the related SEC rules. The only requirements that would cease to be applicable are those mandated by Section 301 of the Act pertaining to a listed company's audit committee.

[2] § 15(d) of the Exchange Act. *See also* Rule 12h-3 under the Exchange Act.

[3] § 15(d) of the Exchange Act. Although suspension is automatic, the issuer must nevertheless so notify the SEC by filing a Form 15. *See* Rules 12h-3 and 15d-6 under the Exchange Act.

[4] § 12(g) of the Exchange Act. Pursuant to Rule 12g-4 under the Exchange Act, termination becomes effective 90 days following the issuer's filing of a Form 15 with the SEC certifying as to the number of holders of the relevant class of securities.

exemption from registration. The exemption, made on application under Rule 12g3-2(b) under the Exchange Act, must be obtained within 120 days of any year-end if at that date the issuer had more than the permitted number of U.S. shareholders. This relief would not, however, be available for 18 months following termination of the issuer's obligations under the Exchange Act, such that re-registration would be necessary if the issuer once again had more than the permitted number of resident U.S. holders during that period.[5]

DELISTING OR TERMINATING QUOTATION OF SECURITIES

Where applicable, deregistration is accompanied by delisting the securities from U.S. securities exchanges, such as the NYSE, or terminating their quotation by securities associations, such as the NASD, which regulates Nasdaq. To delist its common stock (including common stock traded in the form of American Depositary Receipts, or "ADRs") from the NYSE, a foreign private issuer must obtain the approval of its board of directors, publish a press release announcing the proposed delisting and provide written notice of the proposed delisting to its 35 largest U.S. shareholders of record and to the NYSE.[6] Delisting of debt securities from the NYSE requires only board approval.[7]

Delisting from a U.S. securities exchange also requires that the issuer file with the SEC an application with respect to the delisting and deregistration of the securities from the exchange.[8] The application must contain a description of the securities, a statement of the material facts relating to the reasons for the filing (presumably including a statement as to the number of beneficial owners of the securities) and the steps taken to comply with the NYSE's delisting requirements. Public notice of the application is required, together with a comment period during which interested persons may submit information relevant to the application and the appropriateness of granting relief.

The SEC has the authority to order a hearing and may approve delisting on a conditional basis. Where delisting arises in the context of deregistration under the Exchange Act, the SEC is unlikely to take these actions. Even where the issuer continued to have substantial public "float" and did not plan to list or quote its securities elsewhere in the United States, we believe that it would be unusual for the SEC to order a hearing or require the issuer to maintain its listing. The SEC's order on the application to delist is immediately effective on issuance.

---

[5] Rule 12g3-2(d) under the Exchange Act.
[6] NYSE LISTED COMPANY MANUAL, Rules 500 and 806.
[7] *Id.* Rule 500(c).
[8] Rule 12d2-2(d) under the Exchange Act.

FOREIGN PRIVATE ISSUERS

The rules applicable to Nasdaq are considerably less burdensome. A foreign private issuer may terminate the designation of its securities from Nasdaq (*i.e.*, delist) upon written notice to Nasdaq.[9] No additional procedures are required by the SEC to affirm the termination since Nasdaq is not registered as a national securities exchange. The Nasdaq has, however, applied to the SEC for registration as an exchange,[10] and if its application is granted, delisting from Nasdaq will also become subject to the SEC's procedures described above.

---

[9] NASD MANUAL, Rule 4480(b).
[10] SEC Release No. 34-44396 (June 7, 2001).

III AUDIT COMMITTEE RESPONSIBILITIES

The Sarbanes-Oxley Act has substantially recast governance practices of public companies in the United States, including the role of the audit committee of the board of directors. The Act and companion regulations mandate that the audit committee undertake many duties previously viewed only as best practices, and expand its duties in other areas. The reforms are also directed at audit committee effectiveness through heightened standards of independence and expertise. Service on an audit committee will now be more demanding than at any time in the past—and one consequence of this regulatory spotlight is of course the potential for increased personal liability.

We describe below the key reforms that will affect the audit committee of a company with listed equity securities on the NYSE.[1] Substantially similar requirements will be applicable to companies whose securities are listed elsewhere in the United States or are quoted on Nasdaq.[2] Many of the reforms are already effective while others will be effective by year-end 2003, subject to transition periods in some cases. Implementation of many of the reforms involving a company's independent auditor will also generally require further action by the PCAOB.

CONSIDERATIONS FOR FOREIGN PRIVATE ISSUERS

While the scope of the reforms is not surprising in light of recent corporate scandals in the United States, their application to non-U.S. issuers is a departure from long-standing efforts to accommodate home country governance practices. Foreign private issuers become subject to many of the new requirements that affect the role of the audit committee by virtue of being "issuers" under the Sarbanes-Oxley Act.[3] Among these are auditor independence requirements, including

---

[1] These reforms derive both from proposed changes to listing standards, as well as SEC rules implemented under the Sarbanes-Oxley Act. The NYSE proposals are set out in Amendment No. 1 to the NYSE's Corporate Governance Rule Proposals; SEC Release No. 34-47672 (Apr. 11, 2003). The most important of the SEC rules is Rule 10A-3 under the Exchange Act. *See* SEC Release No. 33-8220 (Apr. 9, 2003). Rule 10A-3 is discussed in greater detail in Chapter IV.

[2] The NASD proposals with respect to Nasdaq are set out in Amendment No. 1: Rules 4200 and 4350 Regarding Board Independence and Independent Committees; SEC Release No. 34-47516 (Mar. 17, 2003). A summary comparison of the NYSE and NASD proposals is included in Chapter V.

[3] The Act defines "issuer" as a company with securities registered under § 12 of the Exchange Act, that is required to file reports under § 15(d) of the Exchange Act or that has filed a registration statement under the Securities Act that has not yet become effective and that it has not withdrawn.

pre-approval of all audit and permitted non-audit services, and prescribed disclosures about "audit committee financial experts." U.S.-listed foreign private issuers must also comply with rules mandating a fully independent audit committee with ultimate responsibility for the engagement and work of the independent auditor and for whistleblowing procedures.

Foreign private issuers will face special issues in addressing the reforms. In particular, the Sarbanes-Oxley Act defines "audit committee" to be the entire board of directors where no audit committee exists. To avoid the burdens of this approach, foreign private issuers are now likely to appoint audit committees if they do not already have them. For issuers with a two-tiered board structure, the audit committee should be appointed as part of the supervisory board, rather than the management board.

Both the SEC and U.S. listing authorities have continued to accommodate home country practices in some respects. For example, certain company employees, foreign government representatives and controlling persons may serve on the audit committee of a foreign private issuer under exemptions from the independence standards. The SEC rules also exempt a foreign private issuer from all audit committee requirements if it has an alternative means (*e.g.*, a board of auditors or statutory auditors) to oversee the independent auditor. Aside from mandated listing standards under the Sarbanes-Oxley Act, foreign private issuers also need not comply with the NYSE's other audit committee requirements, although they would be required to disclose annually a brief summary of the differences between their governance practices and NYSE listing standards.[4]

MANDATORY PURPOSE OF AUDIT COMMITTEE

NYSE rules now require that the audit committee have a written charter, but provide limited guidance as to the content. NYSE proposals will change this approach by mandating both the committee's purpose and its minimum duties. The charter requirements apply only to listed U.S. companies, but we expect that many other companies, including foreign private issuers, will opt to comply with the requirements.

The committee's purpose must be to assist the board of directors in the oversight of:

- the integrity of the company's financial statements;

- the company's compliance with legal and regulatory requirements;

---

[4] The NYSE's accommodations also extend to U.S. companies that have listed only debt or preferred securities, which must comply with the new listing standards only in limited respects.

AUDIT COMMITTEE RESPONSIBILITIES

- the qualifications and independence of the independent auditor; and

- the performance of the company's internal audit function and independent auditor.

The charter must also specify the committee's responsibility to prepare the committee report required as part of a U.S. company's proxy statement, require regular reporting to the full board and acknowledge the committee's power to retain independent counsel and other advisors. Under SEC rules, listed U.S. and non-U.S. companies must provide funding to their audit committees for payment of auditor fees, fees of special advisors to the committee and administrative expenses.

The audit committee's required duties are discussed in the sections that follow.

HEIGHTENED OVERSIGHT OF INDEPENDENT AUDITOR

Direct Responsibility for Administration of Independent Auditor Engagement. The centerpiece of many of the reforms is the relationship of the audit committee with the independent auditor. Ultimate responsibility for the appointment, compensation, retention and oversight of the independent auditor will be mandatory for U.S. listed companies by the earlier of the first annual shareholders' meeting after January 15, 2004 or October 31, 2004. Foreign private issuers must comply by July 31, 2005. This requirement is noteworthy particularly because it extends the committee's oversight to the resolution of disagreements between management and the auditor regarding financial reporting. The reforms will demand more vigorous and unmediated participation by the committee in evaluating the company's accounting practices and financial presentation.

Monitoring Auditor Independence and Competence. Before engaging an accounting firm as its auditor, the audit committee of each issuer must determine that the firm is both independent and qualified under SEC rules. The SEC's independence standard—that an auditor be "capable of exercising objective and impartial judgment on all issues encompassed within the accountant's engagement"—was not changed by the Sarbanes-Oxley Act. Instead, the Act expands the circumstances that preclude independence. For example, independence is precluded if any audit partner earns compensation for providing the audit client products or services other than audit, review or attest services. Key practices will include the following:

- **Due Diligence Prior to Engagement.** Prior to engaging an auditor, the audit committee should examine a written report of the firm as to its own internal quality controls, its policies for partner rotation (which must comply with minimum SEC standards as described below), engagements the firm has completed or pending with the company and the fees paid or payable for those engagements.

- **Rotation of Key Auditor Personnel.** Lead and concurring audit partners must now rotate every five years, while other significant audit partners must rotate every seven years. These persons must also observe "time out" periods (five years for lead and concurring partners and two years for other significant audit partners). The audit committee should also consider rotating the audit firm periodically, although rotation is not mandatory.

- **Hiring Policy.** NYSE proposals and new SEC rules require companies to assume responsibility for employment relationships with the auditor that may affect independence. NYSE proposals require the audit committee of a listed U.S. company to establish hiring policies for former employees of the independent auditor. SEC rules applicable to both U.S. and non-U.S. companies generally preclude independence, with respect to an audit of a fiscal period, if a company employee occupying a "financial reporting oversight role" was a member of the audit engagement team during the one-year period preceding the date that audit procedures commenced for that fiscal period. Persons in this role are those who exercise or who are in a position to exercise influence over the company's financial statements and any person who prepares the financial statements. They include, at a minimum, the company's directors, CEO, CFO, chief operating officer, general counsel, controller, director of financial reporting, head of internal audit and treasurer.

- **Annual Due Diligence.** NYSE proposals require the audit committee of a listed U.S. company to obtain annually a report from the independent auditor that describes, among other things, the auditor's internal quality control procedures. We expect that the form of this report will be addressed in standards approved by the PCAOB. These proposals also require the audit committee of such companies to evaluate the independent auditor and the lead partner on an annual basis and encourage the committee to report its findings to the full board.

- **Executive Sessions.** Under NYSE proposals, the audit committee of a listed U.S. company must meet in executive session with the independent auditor. These meetings should be scheduled at least quarterly to address areas of particular sensitivity or risk, such as critical accounting policies and alternative treatments, areas of weakness in internal controls, significant or unusual transactions during the period, matters as to

AUDIT COMMITTEE RESPONSIBILITIES

which the national office was consulted and the other matters as to which the auditor is required to communicate with the audit committee (discussed below). Beyond scheduled meetings, the lead audit partner should be encouraged to speak directly with the chairman of the audit committee about material issues, such as the application of GAAP in a manner that is not preferable or appropriate.

Pre-Approval of Audit and Permitted Non-Audit Services. Beginning May 6, 2003, the audit committee of each issuer must pre-approve all audit services and permitted non-audit services to be provided by the independent auditor, subject to a *de minimis* exception that is not expected to be of practical utility. Key implementing practices include:

- **Elimination of Prohibited Services.** An issuer's independent auditor is prohibited from providing eight types of non-audit services, and the PCAOB is authorized to prohibit others. The prohibitions reflect the principle that independence is impaired if the auditor audits its own work, performs management functions for an audit client or acts as an advocate for the client. Most of these prohibitions were included in prior SEC rules, but some have been expanded. Notably, an issuer may not outsource any part of its internal audit function to its independent auditor, nor may the independent auditor provide "expert services unrelated to the audit" in legal proceedings or investigations involving the company. The rules also expand the scope of prohibited actuarial services and clarify that prohibited legal services include those provided under non-U.S. law.

- **Adoption of Pre-Approval Policy.** The audit committee may approve audit and permissible non-audit services on a case-by-case basis or it may establish detailed pre-approval procedures and policies. We expect most issuers to use a combination of these approaches, with pre-approval procedures used, on a class basis, to address non-controversial, recurring services.

- **Delegation of Pre-Approval Authority.** Pre-approval authority may be delegated to one or more members of the audit committee (but not to management), so long as the delegate reports back to the committee at its next meeting. Procedures for delegation should be included in the issuer's pre-approval policies.

- **Possible Prohibition of Other Services.** To avoid even the appearance of compromised independence, the audit committee may decide to prohibit the independent auditor from providing certain permitted non-audit services. For example, recent controversies involving an auditor's provision of tax services to a client's executive officers have caused some companies to reconsider the appropriateness of those services. Whether the independent auditor should perform a permitted non-audit service will depend on a variety of factors, such as whether its knowledge of the issuer is essential to the efficient provision of the service.

Required Auditor Communications with Audit Committee. Prior to the Sarbanes-Oxley Act, the principal requirements governing the relationship between the audit committee and the independent auditor were set out in Statement of Auditing Standards No. 61, as amended, which specifies the required communications between the independent auditor and the audit committee. Under the new reforms, applicable to both U.S. and non-U.S. companies, these communications should occur at least quarterly and cover:

- the responsibilities of the independent auditor under generally accepted auditing standards;

- management judgments and accounting estimates;

- audit adjustments;

- the views of the independent auditor concerning the quality of the company's accounting principles as applied in its financial statements;

- consultations with other accountants;

- major issues discussed with management prior to retention;

- critical accounting policies and practices used by the company, all possible alternative accounting treatments discussed with management and the treatment preferred by the independent auditor;

- any other material written communications between the independent auditor and management, such as any "management letter" or schedule of unadjusted differences (which should be provided to the audit committee);

- any difficulties encountered during the audit, including whether there were restrictions placed on the independent auditor's activities or access to requested information; and

- the nature and resolution of the independent auditor's disagreements with management.

AUDIT COMMITTEE RESPONSIBILITIES

HEIGHTENED FINANCIAL OVERSIGHT

Monitoring Risk. The audit committee should review the risk profile of the company at least annually and more frequently where the company's business or operating environment is volatile. Typically, this risk assessment should be part of developing the annual internal audit plan. At meetings throughout the year, the committee should also schedule presentations by major divisions or business lines to develop an understanding of the company's business, the financial (*e.g.*, foreign exchange or interest rate exposures), operating and legal risks it faces and the strategies used to manage these risks.

Heightened Oversight of Internal Audit Function. NYSE proposals require a listed U.S. company to have an internal audit function, which may be outsourced (but not, as stated above, to the company's independent auditor). The Sarbanes-Oxley Act does not require the audit committee to oversee the internal audit function, and the SEC has declined to impose this requirement. We believe that many companies will nonetheless increase the involvement of the audit committee in the review of the internal audit function and provide, at a minimum, for "dotted line" reporting to the committee by the head of internal audit. Key practices will include:

- **Oversight of Key Internal Audit Personnel.** The audit committee should oversee the selection or replacement of the head of the company's internal audit function, as well as performance reviews for senior personnel within that function. Because the internal audit function is expected to play a key role in the evaluation of a company's internal control over financial reporting, the audit committee should focus in particular on the independence of internal audit personnel from operating personnel charged with designing and implementing such control. Where the function is outsourced, the audit committee should also review the basis on which the service provider was selected, the service provider's quality control procedures and the terms of the engagement. The performance of outside service providers should be reviewed at least annually.

- **Internal Control Over Financial Reporting.** New SEC rules mandate, subject to a lengthy transition period, that reporting companies maintain effective internal control over financial reporting. Other rules will require that management state its conclusions about the effectiveness of that control in a report that must be attested by the company's independent auditor.[5] These reporting and attestation requirements are expected to require significant preparatory work by companies and their independent auditors, notably in the area of documentation and testing of con-

---

[5] Internal control over financial reporting is discussed in greater detail in Chapter VI.

trols. While the audit committee cannot be expected to review all documentation relating to a company's internal control over financial reporting, the committee should have a sound understanding of the scope of such control (considered alone and as part of the company's overall internal control structure), the organization of the internal audit function and the nature and appropriateness of the evaluative framework that management will use for purposes of its reports.[6] Of course, the audit committee should also review management's reports on internal control over financial reporting and should separately discuss those reports and the related attestations with the independent auditor.

- **Executive Sessions.** Under NYSE proposals, the audit committee of a listed U.S. company must meet in executive session with the internal auditor, without other members of management present. These sessions should be scheduled at least quarterly and should address, among other matters, areas of weakness or risk within the internal control structure and adequacy of staffing and other resources. Even where there is no direct reporting line to the audit committee, the head of internal audit should be encouraged to speak directly with the chairman of the audit committee on a regular basis.

Increased Review of Financial Disclosures. Under NYSE proposals, the audit committee of listed U.S. companies must discuss with management and the independent auditor the company's annual audited financial statements and quarterly or semi-annual financial statements and MD&A disclosures. New SEC rules and guidance restrict the presentation by U.S. and, subject to certain exemptions, non-U.S. companies of "non-GAAP financial measures" (which must be reconciled to GAAP, among other requirements) and impose special disclosure requirements for off-balance sheet arrangements and contractual commitments and

---

[6] The framework must be "a suitable, recognized control framework that is established by a body or group that has followed due-process procedures, including the broad distribution of the framework for public comment." *See, e.g.,* Rules 13a-15(c) and 15d-15(c) under the Exchange Act. The SEC has stated that the so-called "COSO Report" would be a suitable framework. SEC Release No. 33-8238 (June 5, 2003) (citing Committee of Sponsoring Organizations of the Treadway Commission, *Internal Control—Integrated Framework* (1992)), 68 Fed. Reg. 36636, 36642, n. 67 (June 18, 2003). The SEC also identified the *Guidance on Assessing Control,* published by the Canadian Institute of Chartered Accountants, and the *Turnbull Report,* published by the Institute of Chartered Accountants in England & Wales, as suitable frameworks. *Id.*

Audit committee understanding of the company's internal control over financial reporting is particularly important since the SEC's rules define such control, consistent with existing accounting literature, as a process designed by management, but "effected" by the company's board of directors, management and other personnel for specified purposes. Rules 13a-15(f) and 15d-15(f) under the Exchange Act; *see also* Codification of Statements on Auditing Standards (AU) § 319, *Consideration of Internal Control in a Financial Statement Audit.* Thus, the board of directors is directly implicated in the implementation and operation of the company's internal control over financial reporting, a responsibility likely to be delegated to the audit committee given that body's required mandate.

AUDIT COMMITTEE RESPONSIBILITIES

contingencies. The audit committee should inquire about the appropriateness of these disclosures and their compliance with applicable law.

NYSE proposals would also require the audit committee of a listed U.S. company to discuss earnings press releases and financial information and earnings guidance provided to analysts and rating agencies. Discussion of earnings releases and guidance may address the types of information and presentation to be provided or made.

HEIGHTENED COMPLIANCE OVERSIGHT

Monitoring Process, Controls and Procedures. Although the audit committee is not responsible for developing the company's financial or other controls, it should regularly consider their continuing appropriateness. In part, this review will be conducted in conjunction with the committee's regular sessions with the independent and internal auditors and could involve liaising with any "disclosure committee" established as recommended by the SEC. The audit committee should also use the CEO and CFO certifications and, as noted above, management's internal control reports as a basis for inquiry into the effectiveness of the company's disclosure controls and procedures and internal control over financial reporting. These controls and procedures should be adequate to ensure that information about the company's operations and results is accumulated and communicated to management so as to allow timely decisions about public disclosures and to provide reasonable assurance regarding the reliability of the company's financial reporting in accordance with GAAP.[7]

Complaint Procedures. Under SEC rules, the audit committee of each U.S. and non-U.S. listed company must establish procedures for the receipt, retention and treatment of complaints about accounting, auditing and related matters and the confidential, anonymous submission by company employees of concerns about questionable auditing or accounting matters. These procedures must be in place by the earlier of their first annual shareholders' meeting after January 15, 2004 or October 31, 2004. Foreign private issuers must comply by July 31, 2005.

There are no mandatory complaint procedures. We expect that companies will use a combination of telephone "hotline," e-mail and regular mail services,

---

[7] Particularly for companies with complex or geographically dispersed operations, it may be prudent to establish a committee of key senior management that is responsible for oversight of the development and execution of the internal audit plan, as well as issues that may be raised during the course of the internal audit. Persons who could be involved in this committee could include the chief financial officer, the controller, the head of internal audit, the head of risk management, the head of information systems and the general counsel (or other legal and compliance representatives). Given the ongoing nature of the documentation and testing procedures associated with execution of an internal audit plan during a fiscal year, as well as the likely scope and number of controls, monitoring internal control over financial reporting may be too cumbersome for a disclosure committee, which will typically be more focused on the process of preparing specific periodic reports or other disclosures.

each with restricted access by company personnel. As a best practice, we believe that companies will maintain a central log of complaints detailing the complaint and its status. Management is not prohibited from playing a role in these procedures, but the audit committee should not delegate full responsibility to management. The audit committee should, at a minimum, review material complaints and investigations with the chief legal or compliance officer on a quarterly basis and should consider requiring immediate notification of certain matters, such as material fraud or other financial impropriety. While it may also be appropriate for the company's chief legal or compliance officer to make an initial determination as to which complaints require investigation or other action, the audit committee should have the authority to review those determinations and to direct additional action or identify other matters for investigation. Audit committee members should also have unrestricted access to all complaint logs and supporting materials. As the NYSE will require listed U.S. companies to disclose a way to contact outside directors, the complaint procedure should contemplate treatment of concerns received through this means.

Other new SEC rules impose special reporting obligations on lawyers—whether in-house or external—who "appear and practice before the SEC" and who have credible evidence of a material violation of securities laws or similar violations.[8] Generally, the rules require lawyers to report these violations to a company's chief legal officer and, if an appropriate response is not received, "up the ladder" to the company's audit committee. While the rules permit companies to establish a special compliance committee (consisting entirely of independent directors, including at least one member of the audit committee) to address these reports, we expect that many companies will rely on their general counsel or chief compliance officer to develop policies and procedures for administering these rules. Because the audit committee will be charged with oversight of a company's legal compliance under the NYSE proposals, it should be advised of the manner in which the company plans to address these rules. The committee should also receive regular presentations by the chief legal officer (or special compliance committee) regarding material violations reported and the results of investigations or other resolution of the issues raised.

Code of Ethics. Beginning with annual reports for fiscal years ending on or after July 15, 2003, SEC rules will require each reporting company to disclose whether it has a code of ethics for its CEO and senior financial officers or, if not, why not. NYSE proposals will require a code of ethics for the directors, officers and employees of each listed U.S. company. SEC rules and NYSE proposals specify in broad terms the scope of a complying code and require public disclosure of the code. Given its compliance oversight responsibility, the audit committee should take responsibility for periodic review of the company's code of ethics and oversight of compliance with its terms (including the granting of waivers to di-

---

[8] These rules are discussed in greater detail in Chapter X.

AUDIT COMMITTEE RESPONSIBILITIES

rectors and executive officers). After the improprieties at Enron and other companies, related party transactions should be a particular focus.

Officer Certifications. The audit committee is not required to review the required CEO and CFO certifications as a whole, although the officers must certify that they have discussed certain internal control matters with the committee (generally, significant deficiencies and material weaknesses[9] in the design or operation of internal control over financial reporting and fraud by management or other employees with a significant role in such control). The committee should nevertheless discuss with the certifying officers not only the required disclosures, but also their willingness to certify and whether there were any issues that arose during any procedures they have implemented to support the certifications.

HEIGHTENED STANDARDS FOR AUDIT COMMITTEE MEMBERSHIP

The Sarbanes-Oxley Act, SEC rules and NYSE proposals set out new standards of independence for audit committees of listed U.S. and non-U.S. companies. A chart detailing the requirements (including those proposed by the NASD with respect to Nasdaq) is attached.

SEC Independence Requirement. SEC rules will prohibit audit committee members from accepting, directly or indirectly, any consulting, advisory or other compensatory fees from the company (other than in the member's capacity as a member of the board of directors or any board committee). This restriction will bar payments to law firms, accounting or consulting firms, investment banks and financial advisory firms of which an audit committee member is a partner, member or executive officer or holds a similar position. Fixed payments under retirement plans for prior service to the company will, in contrast, be permitted. The SEC has also stated that other business or personal relationships, such as ordinary course commercial relationships (including commercial banking relationships), are not inconsistent with independence, although they may not be permissible under the NYSE proposals.

Audit committee members will also be prohibited from being affiliated persons of the company and its subsidiaries. This element of the test will require a facts-and-circumstances analysis of whether the director controls, is controlled by or is under common control with the company. The SEC has stated that a director

---

[9] These terms are defined by reference to existing accounting literature, particularly AU § 325; *see also* Chapter VI, Note 39.

While the required disclosures are, by the terms of the certification, to be based on the most recent evaluation conducted by the CEO and CFO of internal control over financial reporting, the SEC has stated its expectation that these matters should be disclosed to the audit committee even if they are discovered outside the formal evaluation process or after the completion of such evaluation. SEC Release No. 33-8238 (June 5, 2003), 68 Fed. Reg. 36636, 36647 (June 18, 2003).

will be deemed not to control the company if he or she is not an executive officer or a shareholder owning more than 10% of any class of voting security of the company but that executive officers, employee directors, general partners and managing members of a company affiliate are affiliated persons of the company.

Audit committees of listed U.S. companies must be comprised solely of independent directors by the earlier of their first annual shareholders' meeting after January 15, 2004 or October 31, 2004. Foreign private issuers must comply by July 31, 2005.[10]

NYSE Independence Requirement. NYSE proposals must reflect, at a minimum, the requirements of the SEC rules. As proposed, the NYSE intends to impose a more stringent independence requirement on listed U.S. companies. For example, the proposals would use a broader definition of "immediate family member" for purposes of determining prohibited relationships. In addition, all directors must satisfy a "basic" independence test that requires the full board to determine that no "material relationship" exists between the director and the company, either directly or from the director's role as a partner, shareholder or officer of an entity with a relationship with the company. The NYSE would also impose a "look-back" provision requiring companies to examine specified past relationships between the director and the company.

Audit Committee Financial Expert. New SEC rules require U.S. and non-U.S. companies to disclose in their annual reports for fiscal years ending on or after July 15, 2003 whether any member of their audit committee is an "audit committee financial expert." If so, the company must disclose the person's name and whether he or she is independent under the listing standards of the securities exchange on which the company's securities are listed. Foreign private issuers need not disclose whether an audit committee financial expert is independent until July 31, 2005. If more than one member of the committee satisfies the definition, disclosure of the additional experts is optional. If no member is qualified, the company must disclose why not.

Qualification requires expertise meeting detailed requirements set out in the SEC's rules, which also prescribe the acceptable means to acquire the expertise. Many CEOs, CFOs and persons in the accounting and investment banking professions may qualify, but this experience does not alone guarantee qualification. The SEC has stated that designation as an audit committee financial expert will not impose any duties, obligations or liability on that person that are greater than that person's duties as a member of the audit committee and the board.

---

[10] Special rules apply to companies making an initial public offering. The SEC rules also provide relief in the case of listings of non-equity securities by a direct or indirect consolidated majority-owned subsidiary of a parent company, if the parent company is already subject to the requirements as a result of listing a class of its common equity securities (or similar securities). This relief does not extend to the subsidiary's listing of its equity securities, other than non-convertible, non-participating preferred securities or trust preferred securities.

AUDIT COMMITTEE RESPONSIBILITIES

NYSE rules require all members of the audit committees of U.S. companies (regardless of the type of security listed) to be financially literate on appointment or within a reasonable time thereafter. One member must have "accounting or related financial management experience," and a board of directors may presume that an audit committee member who satisfies the SEC's test for an audit committee financial expert has this experience.

Service on Multiple Audit Committees. The NYSE proposes to require a U.S. company (regardless of the type of security listed) to disclose whether any audit committee member serves on the audit committees of more than two other public companies. If so, the company must disclose its determination that this will not impair the member's ability to serve. Companies may avoid this disclosure by limiting a member's service to the audit committees of two other public companies.

LIABILITY CONSIDERATIONS

Many audit committee members are concerned about the heightened possibility of personal liability following the reforms. Although liability considerations remain important, committee members who act conscientiously and in good faith are not likely to face a materially greater risk of personal liability than in the past.

Civil Liability. The Sarbanes-Oxley Act does not alter a director's general duties of care, loyalty and candor, which are governed by state law. In addition, although the Act provides the SEC with expanded enforcement tools, it does not create new causes of action under which a director might incur civil liability to private plaintiffs or alter any substantive elements of existing causes of action. However, the requirements applicable to qualification of audit committee members, as well as the additional responsibilities conferred on the audit committee, may under state law impose a heightened duty of care on audit committee members than on other board members. In addition, the current enforcement environment may also lead to greater scrutiny of the audit committee and independent directors more generally.[11] As a result, audit committee members should ensure that the company provides adequate director and officer liability insurance and indemnifies them to the fullest extent permitted by law.

Criminal Liability. The Sarbanes-Oxley Act adds new criminal offenses for obstruction of justice in any federal investigation and for knowing execution of a scheme to defraud any person in connection with any security. It also increases penalties for several existing white-collar crimes. These new provisions are discussed more fully in Chapter I.

---

[11] Recent cases have, for example, emphasized the degree of care that independent directors must demonstrate when exercising their business judgment, as well as a heightened sensitivity to conflicts of interest. *See In re Oracle Corp. Derivative Litigation,* 2003 WL 21396449 (Del. Ch., June 17, 2003); *In re The Walt Disney Company Derivative Litigation,* 2003 WL 21267266 (Del. Ch., May 28, 2003); *In re Lernout & Haupsie Securities Litigation,* 286 B.R. 33 (D. Mass 2002).

ANNEX A
Audit Committee Independence Requirements Under Exchange Act Rule 10A-3 and Proposals of the NYSE and NASD (Nasdaq)

Rule 10A-3	NYSE Proposal	NASD Proposal
Implementation Schedule		
All listed issuers (except foreign private issuers and small business issuers) must be in compliance with the new SRO listing rules by the earlier of: • the issuer's first annual shareholders' meeting after January 15, 2004; or • October 31, 2004. Foreign private issuers and small business issuers must be in compliance with the new listing rules by July 31, 2005. New public companies will be required to have one fully independent audit committee member at the time of listing, a majority of independent members within 90 days of listing and a fully independent audit committee within one year.	Companies would have 18 months to comply with the general director independence requirements (with a longer period allowed for companies with a classified board). Newly listed companies would be afforded two years to comply with the general independence requirements. Companies transferring from another market would also have two years to the extent they were not already subject to particular requirements on the previous market. Companies transferring from another market with a substantially similar requirement would be given at least as long a transition period as would have been available to them on the other market.	Companies would be required to comply with the general director independence and non-Rule 10A-3 audit committee member independence requirements by the company's next annual meeting after January 1, 2004. Newly listed companies would be afforded two years to comply with the non-Rule 10A-3 board composition requirements. Companies transferring from other markets with substantially similar requirements would be afforded the balance of any grace period afforded by the other market.

AUDIT COMMITTEE RESPONSIBILITIES

Rule 10A-3	NYSE Proposal	NASD Proposal
Rule 10A-3 only sets out independence requirements for audit committee members.	**General Independence Requirements for Directors**	
	Passive business organizations in the form of trusts, derivatives and special purpose securities would not be subject to any of the corporate governance requirements.	
	The general independence requirements would not apply to foreign private issuers, closed-end management companies or companies listing only preferred or debt securities. (The audit committee member independence requirements, described below, would apply to such companies.)	Under a separate proposal for non-U.S. listed companies,[12] an exemption would be available for foreign private issuers from the applicability of the corporate governance standards as may be necessary or appropriate, except to the extent that such exemption would be contrary to the federal securities laws.
	A majority of independent directors on the board would be required. (Not applicable to controlled companies, foreign private issuers, limited partnerships and companies in bankruptcy proceedings, companies listing only preferred or debt securities and closed-end management companies.)	A majority of independent directors on the board would be required. (Not applicable to controlled companies.)
No requirement that board of directors make	Board of directors would be required to determine	Board of directors would be required to determine

---

[12] Form 19b-4 Proposed Rule Change; File No. SR-NASD-2002-138 (Oct. 8, 2002).

Rule 10A-3	NYSE Proposal	NASD Proposal
a determination with respect to audit committee member independence.	affirmatively that the director has no material relationship with the listed company, either directly or indirectly. Proxy statement disclosure (or if the company does not file an annual proxy statement, Form 10-K) disclosure would be required of the basis for the board's independence determination. Categorical standards would be permitted (disclosure required). Material relationships could include commercial, industrial, banking, consulting, legal, accounting, charitable and familial relationships, among others.	affirmatively that the director has no relationship, which in the opinion of the company's board of directors, would interfere with the exercise of independent judgment.
No look-back period.	Five-year cooling off period (with transition period from time rules become effective).	Three-year cooling off period.
Family members whose relationships with the listed issuer compromise independence limited to spouses, minor children or stepchildren or children or stepchildren sharing a home with the member.	Immediate family members' relationships with the issuer would preclude independence or create a negative presumption. Immediate family members would include a person's spouse, parents, children, siblings, mothers and fathers-in-law, sons and daughters-in-law, brothers and sisters-in-law, and anyone (other than domestic employees) who shares such person's home.	Family members whose relationships with the issuer compromise independence would include any person who is a relative by blood, marriage or adoption or who has the same residence.

AUDIT COMMITTEE RESPONSIBILITIES

Rule 10A-3	NYSE Proposal	NASD Proposal
Executive officers, directors who are also employees, general partners and managing members of an affiliate are deemed to be affiliates of the issuer.	Current employees could not be deemed independent of management.	Officers and current employees of the listed issuer or any subsidiary[13] could not be considered independent. A director who is, or during the past three years was, employed by the company or by any parent or subsidiary of the company could not be considered independent. A director who is a family member of an individual who is, or during the past three years was, employed by the company or by any parent or subsidiary of the company as an executive officer could not be considered independent.
An audit committee member may not accept, directly or indirectly, any consulting, advisory or other compensatory fee from the issuer or any of its subsidiaries. Direct or indirect acceptance includes payments: • to an audit committee member's spouse, minor child or stepchild or child or stepchild sharing a home with the member; and • to an entity in which an audit committee member is a partner, member, officer such as a managing director	Payments of more than $100,000 in direct compensation from the listed company to the director or to a member of the director's immediate family would give rise to a negative presumption. • Director and committee fees and pension or other forms of deferred compensation for prior service (provided such compensation is not contingent in any way on continued service) would not be taken into account. • Compensation received by a director	A director who accepts, or who has a family member who accepts, any payments from the company or any parent or subsidiary of the company in excess of $60,000 during the current fiscal year or any of the past three fiscal years could not be considered independent. Certain compensation and payments are excluded: • compensation for board service; • payments arising solely from investments in the company's securities;

[13] Under the NASD proposal, references to parents or subsidiaries would mean consolidated entities.

Rule 10A-3	NYSE Proposal	NASD Proposal
occupying a comparable position or executive officer or occupies a similar position (except limited partners, non-managing members and those occupying similar positions who, in each case, have no active role in providing services to the entity) and which provides accounting, consulting, legal, investment banking or financial advisory services to the issuer or any subsidiary. Prohibited compensatory fees do not include: • fees for member's service as a member of the board of directors or any board committee; • the receipt of fixed amounts of compensation under a retirement plan, including deferred compensation, for prior service with the listed issuer (provided that such compensation is not contingent in any way on continued service); or • payments to an entity for the provision of non-advisory financial services, such as lending, check clearing, maintaining customer accounts, stock brokerage services or cus-	for former service as an interim Chairman or CEO would not be required to be a factor in board determination of independence under this presumption. • The negative presumption would not end until five years after he or she ceases to receive more than $100,000 per year in such compensation (subject to an initial transition rule). • The presumption would end immediately if the immediate family member who received the direct compensation of more than $100,000 per year dies or becomes incapacitated.	• compensation paid to a family member who is an employee of the company or any parent or subsidiary of the company, but not if such person is an executive officer of the company or any parent or subsidiary of the company; • benefits under a tax-qualified retirement plan; and • non-discretionary compensation.

AUDIT COMMITTEE RESPONSIBILITIES

Rule 10A-3	NYSE Proposal	NASD Proposal
dial and cash management services.		
Ordinary-course commercial relationships are not precluded.	A director who is an executive officer or an employee, or whose immediate family member is an executive officer, of another company (i) that accounts for at least 2% or $1 million, whichever is greater, of the listed company's consolidated gross revenues; or (ii) for which the listed company accounts for at least 2% or $1 million, whichever is greater, of such other company's consolidated gross revenues, in each case would not be independent until five years after falling below such threshold.	A director who is a partner in, or a controlling shareholder or an executive officer of, any organization to which the company made, or from which the company received, payments (other than those arising solely from investments in the company's securities) that exceed 5% of the recipient's consolidated gross revenues for that year, or $200,000, whichever is more, in the current fiscal year or any of the past three fiscal years could not be considered independent.
Independence criteria do not reference relationships with the company's internal or independent auditor.	A director who is affiliated with or employed by, or whose immediate family member is affiliated with or employed in a professional capacity by, a present or former internal or external auditor of the company would not be independent until five years after the end of either the affiliation or the auditing relationship.	A director who is or was a partner or employee of the company's outside auditor, and worked on the company's audit, during the past three years could not be considered independent.
Independence criteria do not reference relationships between the director and another company's compensation committee.	A director who is employed, or whose immediate family member is employed, as an executive officer of another company where any of the listed company's present executives	A director of the listed company who is employed as an executive officer of another entity where any of the executive officers of the listed company serves on the compensation committee

77

Rule 10A-3	NYSE Proposal	NASD Proposal
	serves on that company's compensation committee would not be independent until five years after the end of such service or employment relationship.	of such other entity, or if such relationship existed during the past three years, could not be considered independent.
	Additional Independence Requirements Applicable Only to Audit Committee Members	
Audit committee members must meet the independence requirements of Rule 10A-3, which bar audit committee members from (i) receiving certain fees; and (ii) being affiliates of the issuer or any of its subsidiaries, subject to specific exemptions.	Audit committee members would be required to meet the independence requirements of Rule 10A-3, subject to Rule 10A-3's exemptions.	Audit committee members would be required to meet the independence criteria of § 10A(m)(3) of the Exchange Act.
No upper limit on stock ownership of audit committee members (facts-and-circumstances test).	No upper limit on stock ownership of audit committee members (factor for board to consider in determining independence).	Audit committee members would not be able to own or control 20% or more of the issuer's voting securities. Stock ownership would not preclude a determination of independence for directors not on the audit committee. An employee of an entity that owns or controls such securities would also be an affiliated person.
No exceptional and limited circumstances exception.	No exceptional and limited circumstances exception.	Exceptional and limited circumstances exception for one audit committee member who does meet the special requirements applicable only to audit committee members but not the general independence requirements applicable to independent

AUDIT COMMITTEE RESPONSIBILITIES

Rule 10A-3	NYSE Proposal	NASD Proposal
		directors. A member appointed under this exception would not be able to serve longer than two years or chair the audit committee. An issuer relying on this exception would have to disclose, in its next annual proxy statement, the nature of the relationship and the reasons for its determination that membership on the committee is required by the best interests of the corporation and its shareholders.
Exchanges permitted to provide a limited accommodation for an audit committee member who ceases to be independent for reasons outside of the member's reasonable control.	No such accommodation has been proposed.	No such accommodation has been proposed.
	Additional Requirements Relating to Corporate Governance	
No requirement for how many members an issuer's audit committee must have. Issuers are not required to have audit committees. In the absence of an audit committee, the entire board of directors (or in two-tier board systems, the supervisory board) is an issuer's audit committee. Sets forth responsibilities requirements, complaint procedure requirements, advisor requirements and funding requirements applic-	Listed companies would be required to have a minimum three-person audit committee and a written audit committee charter addressing certain issues. The charter requirement would not be applicable to foreign private issuers or companies listing only preferred or debt securities. Listed companies would be required to follow the non-independence audit committee requirements set forth in Rule 10A-3.	Listed companies would be required to have a minimum three-person audit committee and an audit committee charter addressing certain issues, including those required by § 10A(m) of the Exchange Act.

79

Rule 10A-3	NYSE Proposal	NASD Proposal
able to audit committees, subject to exemptions and clarifying instructions.	Audit committees would be required to have additional responsibilities, and the listed company would be required to have an internal audit function. Not applicable to foreign private issuers or companies listing only preferred or debt securities.	
Compare Section 407 of the Sarbanes-Oxley Act.	Each audit committee member would be required to be financially literate or to become financially literate within a reasonable period of time after his or her appointment to the audit committee. One member would be required to have accounting or related financial management expertise. A person satisfying the SEC's definition of audit committee financial expert would satisfy this requirement. Not applicable to foreign private issuers. If an audit committee member simultaneously serves on the audit committee of more than three public companies, and the listed company does not limit the number of audit committees on which its audit committee members serve, the board would be required to determine that such simultaneous service would not impair the ability of the member to serve effectively on the listed company's audit committee and dis-	Audit committee members would be required to be able to read and understand fundamental financial statements, including a company's balance sheet, income statement and cash flow statement. One member would be required to have past employment experience in finance or accounting, requisite professional certification in accounting or other comparable experience or background which results in the individual's financial sophistication, including being or having been a CEO, CFO or other senior officer with financial oversight responsibilities.

AUDIT COMMITTEE RESPONSIBILITIES

Rule 10A-3	NYSE Proposal	NASD Proposal
	close such determination in the annual proxy statement, or if the company does not file an annual proxy statement, in the company's annual report on Form 10-K filed with the SEC.	
	The non-management directors would be required to meet at regularly scheduled executive sessions without management. Not applicable to closed-end management companies, foreign private issuers or companies listing only preferred or debt securities.	Independent directors would be required to have regularly scheduled executive sessions at which only independent directors are present. Not applicable to controlled companies.
	Listed companies would be required to have a nominating/corporate governance committee, composed entirely of independent directors, which has a written charter addressing certain issues and performs an annual evaluation of the committee. Not applicable to controlled companies, limited partnerships and companies in bankruptcy, closed-end management companies, foreign private issuers and companies listing only preferred or debt securities or in cases where a third party has the legal right to nominate a director.	No requirement to have a nominating committee. Nomination of directors would have to be determined either by a majority of the independent directors or by a nominating committee comprised solely of independent directors (with an exceptional and limited circumstances exception subject to disclosure and another exception for a director who is also an officer if certain conditions are met). Not applicable to controlled companies or in cases where a third party has the legal right to nominate a director.
	Listed companies would be required to have a compensation committee, composed entirely	No requirement to have a compensation committee.

Rule 10A-3	NYSE Proposal	NASD Proposal
	of independent directors, which has a written charter addressing certain issues and performs an annual evaluation of the committee. Not applicable to controlled companies, limited partnerships and companies in bankruptcy, closed-end management companies, foreign private issuers and companies listing only preferred or debt securities.	Compensation of the chief executive officer would have to be determined either by a majority of the independent directors meeting in executive session or by a compensation committee composed solely of independent directors meeting in executive session (with an exceptional and limited circumstances exception subject to disclosure). Not applicable to controlled companies.
		Compensation of all other officers would have to be determined either by a majority of the independent directors or by a compensation committee comprised solely of independent directors (with an exceptional and limited circumstances exception subject to disclosure). The CEO could be present but could not vote. Not applicable to controlled companies.
	The proposals include additional requirements relating to corporate governance guidelines and a code of ethics. Not applicable to closed-end management companies, foreign private issuers and companies listing only preferred or debt securities.	
	Listed foreign private issuers would be required to disclose any signifi-	Under a separate proposal, foreign private issuers who receive ex-

AUDIT COMMITTEE RESPONSIBILITIES

Rule 10A-3	NYSE Proposal	NASD Proposal
	cant ways in which their corporate governance practices differ from those followed by domestic companies under NYSE listing standards.	emptions from corporate governance standards would be required to disclose their reliance on such exemptions and to describe the alternative practice, if any, in lieu of the standards.
Exchanges must require a listed issuer to notify the applicable exchange promptly after an executive officer of the issuer becomes aware of any material noncompliance by the listed issuer with the Rule's requirements.	Each listed company CEO would be required to certify to the NYSE each year that he or she is not aware of any violation by the company of NYSE corporate governance listing standards (and to promptly notify the NYSE of any material noncompliance with NYSE corporate governance requirements). The first requirement would not be applicable to closed-end management companies, foreign private issuers and companies listing only preferred or debt securities. The NYSE would be able to issue a public reprimand letter to any listed company that violates an NYSE listing standard.	

IV LISTED COMPANY AUDIT COMMITTEE STANDARDS

The SEC has adopted new Rule 10A-3 under the Exchange Act,[1] which implements requirements for listing standards relating to audit committees as established by the Sarbanes-Oxley Act and requires additional disclosure regarding audit committees.

Rule 10A-3 implements § 10A(m)(1) of the Exchange Act, which was added by Section 301 of the Sarbanes-Oxley Act. Section 301 sets out requirements relating to audit committees and requires the SEC to direct the national securities exchanges and national securities associations[2] to prohibit the listing of any security of an issuer that is not in compliance with these requirements. The listing standards to be adopted under the Rule will apply to both U.S. and non-U.S. listed issuers, subject to limited exemptions. The SROs will not be able to grant any additional exemptions or waivers in their listing standards or on a case-by-case basis, and to the extent an issuer has obtained exemptions that conflict with Rule 10A-3, such exemptions will no longer be valid. Rule 10A-3:

- clarifies the audit committee requirements, particularly independence requirements;
- provides certain exemptions, in particular for foreign private issuers, from certain of the audit committee requirements;
- updates disclosure requirements regarding audit committees; and
- sets out the timing of implementation of the Rule by the SROs and compliance with the Rule's requirements by issuers.

LISTING STANDARDS

Rule 10A-3 implements the five audit committee listing requirements[3] established by Section 301:

---

[1] SEC Release No. 33-8220 (Apr. 9, 2003) (the "Adopting Release").
[2] These institutions include the NYSE and the American Stock Exchange LLC (the "AMEX"), as well as the NASD, which is the only national securities association and regulates Nasdaq, and are sometimes referred to as self-regulatory organizations or "SROs."
[3] Neither Section 301 nor Rule 10A-3 explicitly requires that an issuer have an audit committee. As previously noted, the Sarbanes-Oxley Act defines the term "audit committee" to encompass the entire board of directors of the issuer, if the issuer does not have a separate audit committee. As a result, the

- each member of the audit committee must be independent according to the criteria specified in the Sarbanes-Oxley Act, which bar committee members from (i) receiving certain fees; and (ii) being affiliates of the issuer or any of its subsidiaries;

- the audit committee must be directly responsible for the appointment, compensation, retention and oversight of the independent auditor (including the resolution of disagreements between management and the auditor regarding financial reporting), and the independent auditor must report directly to the audit committee;

- the audit committee must establish procedures for the receipt, retention and treatment of complaints received by the issuer regarding accounting, internal accounting controls or auditing matters and for the confidential, anonymous submission by employees of concerns regarding questionable accounting or auditing matters;

- the audit committee must have the authority to engage independent counsel and other advisors as the committee determines necessary to carry out its duties; and

- the issuer must provide appropriate funding, as determined by the audit committee, for the payment of compensation to (i) the independent auditor; and (ii) any outside advisors engaged by the audit committee.

Rule 10A-3 applies only to issuers that have securities listed or quoted on a national securities exchange or an automated interdealer quotation system of a national securities association. It does not apply to other companies that have reporting obligations under § 13(a) or 15(d) of the Exchange Act. SROs are required to adopt listing standards in compliance with the Rule's requirements but are not prevented from adopting listing standards that are more stringent or more specific.[4] Rather, the Rule's requirements for audit committees build and rely on the listing standards of the SROs.

---

independence and other requirements imposed by Section 301 and Rule 10A-3 would apply to a listed issuer's entire board of directors, if there is no audit committee.

[4] In 2003, the NYSE and the NASD submitted to the SEC proposed changes to their listing standards, including more stringent standards relating to audit committees. The NYSE proposal amends and restates its original proposal filed with the SEC on August 16, 2002 and replaces the amendments filed on March 12, 2003. *See* Amendment No. 1 to the NYSE's Corporate Governance Rule Proposals; SEC Release No. 34-4762 (Apr. 4, 2003). The NASD proposal amends its previous proposal filed with the SEC on October 9, 2002. *See* Amendment 1: Rules 4200 and 4350 Regarding Board Independence and Independent Committees; SEC Release No. 34-47516 (Mar. 17, 2003).

LISTED COMPANY AUDIT COMMITTEE STANDARDS

INDEPENDENCE OF AUDIT COMMITTEE MEMBERS

Criteria. The definition of independence in Section 301 of the Sarbanes-Oxley Act has two basic criteria:

- an audit committee member may not accept any consulting, advisory or other compensatory fee from the issuer or any of its subsidiaries, other than in the member's capacity as a member of the board of directors or any board committee; and

- an audit committee member may not be an "affiliated person" of the issuer or any subsidiary of the issuer, apart from his or her capacity as a member of the board of directors or any board committee.

Under Rule 10A-3, payments that are disallowed by the first criterion include any payments made "directly or indirectly" to the audit committee member. Indirect payments include any payments to a spouse, a minor child or stepchild or a child or stepchild sharing a home with the member. They also include payments to an entity in which the audit committee member is a partner, member, officer such as a managing director occupying a comparable position or executive officer or occupies a similar position (except limited partners, non-managing members and those occupying similar positions who, in each case, have no active role in providing services to the entity) and which provides accounting, consulting, legal, investment banking or financial advisory services to the issuer or any subsidiary.

Rule 10A-3 does not restrict additional business or personal relationships, such as ordinary-course commercial relationships between the issuer and an entity in which an audit committee member holds a position.[5] In the Adopting Release,

---

[5] The proposals of the NYSE and the NASD include more stringent requirements precluding additional relationships. For example, the NYSE has proposed that no director, including a director who serves on the audit committee, would qualify as "independent" unless the board determines there is no material relationship between the director and the issuer. *See* proposed § 303A(2)(a) of the NYSE proposal. The NASD proposal includes a similar requirement that the board make an affirmative determination. *See* proposed NASD Rule 4200(a)(15). Under the NASD's proposed listing standards, an independent director could not be a partner, controlling shareholder or executive officer of any organization to which the issuer has made, or from which the issuer has received, payments exceeding the greater of 5% of the recipient's annual consolidated gross revenues and $200,000 in the current fiscal year or any of the past three fiscal years. *See* proposed NASD Rule 4200(a)(15)(D). The NYSE proposal also would preclude a determination of independence for a director who is an executive officer or an employee, or whose immediate family member is an executive officer, of another company (A) that accounts for at least 2% or $1 million, whichever is greater, of the listed company's consolidated gross revenues; or (B) for which the listed company accounts for at least 2% or $1 million, whichever is greater, of such other company's consolidated gross revenues. *See* proposed § 303A(2)(b)(iv) of the NYSE proposal. The NASD proposal also includes a broad definition of "family member" as "any person who is a relative by blood, marriage or adoption or who has the same residence." *See* proposed NASD Rule 4200(a)(14).

the SEC states that the prohibitions do not include non-advisory financial services, such as lending, check clearing, maintaining customer accounts, stock brokerage services or custodial and cash management services. Rule 10A-3 also specifies that "compensatory fees" do not include the receipt of fixed amounts of compensation under a retirement plan (including deferred compensation) for prior service with the listed issuer (provided that such compensation is not contingent in any way on continued service).[6] Rule 10A-3 also does not include any look-back period in determining an audit committee member's independence.[7] Rule 10A-3 does not provide an exception for *de minimis* payments.

Rule 10A-3 includes a definition of the term "affiliated person"[8] that is consistent with other definitions of the term "affiliate" in the federal securities laws, such as Exchange Act Rule 12b-2 and Rule 144 under the Securities Act, subject to an additional safe harbor. Under Rule 10A-3, the term "affiliate" of, or person "affiliated" with, a specified person means a person that directly or indirectly controls, or is controlled by or is under common control with, the person specified. The term "control" means "the possession, direct or indirect, of the power to direct or cause the direction of the management and policies of a person, whether through the ownership of voting securities, by contract, or otherwise."[9] Rule 10A-3 also provides that persons with specified kinds of positions at an affiliate will themselves be deemed to be affiliates. The specified positions are executive officer, director (if the director is also an employee), general partner and managing member. The Adopting Release specifies that an outside director or another person with a passive, non-control position, such as a limited partner, will not be deemed to be an affiliate. In a change from the proposal, the final version of Rule 10A-3 does not say that a "designee" of an affiliate is deemed to be an affiliate, but the Adopting Release cautions that an affiliate cannot evade the prohibitions in Rule 10A-3 simply by designating a representative or agent that it directs to act in its place.

The determination of affiliate status requires a factual analysis based on all the relevant facts and circumstances. Because this can be difficult, Rule 10A-3 contains an explicit safe harbor for audit committee members who are not execu-

---

[6] The requirement that the compensation be fixed does not preclude customary, objectively determined adjustment provisions such as cost of living adjustments. *See* the Adopting Release, 68 Fed. Reg. 18788, 18792, n. 57 (Apr. 16, 2003).

[7] The NYSE and the NASD propose look-back periods of five years and three years, respectively.

[8] Section 301 of the Sarbanes-Oxley Act does not define "affiliated person." Without a specific definition, § 3(a)(19) of the Exchange Act would result in the application of the definition of "affiliated person" contained in § 2(a)(3) of the Investment Company Act. This definition will continue to apply for investment companies and business development companies, for which Rule 10A-3 requires that a member of the audit committee not be an "interested person" of the investment company as defined in § 2(a)(19) of the Investment Company Act.

[9] *See* Rule 10A-3(e)(4).

LISTED COMPANY AUDIT COMMITTEE STANDARDS

tive officers[10] or beneficial owners,[11] directly or indirectly, of more than 10% of any class of voting equity securities.[12] These persons are deemed not to control the issuer for the purposes of Rule 10A-3. The Rule specifies that the safe harbor does not create a presumption that those outside the safe harbor are affiliates. A facts-and-circumstances analysis will still need to be undertaken in such cases.[13]

Exemptions. In addition to certain exemptions provided for foreign private issuers discussed below, Rule 10A-3 includes two exemptions (one for new issuers and one for overlapping boards) from the independence requirements.

First, a new issuer need only have one fully independent member at the time of its initial listing, a majority of independent members within 90 days and a fully independent audit committee within one year.[14] Reliance on this exemption is subject to disclosure.

The second exemption allows an audit committee member to sit on the board of directors of both a listed issuer and an affiliate of the listed issuer if the member, except for being a director on each board of directors, otherwise meets the independence requirements for each entity.[15] The proposal limited this exemption to situations where the two companies are parent and subsidiary, but the SEC expanded it in the final version of Rule 10A-3 to cover affiliates, responding to commenters who argued that "sibling" companies or unconsolidated sub-

---

[10] The Rule defines "executive officer" as it is defined in Rule 3b-7 under the Exchange Act. This definition differs from that in the final rule implementing Section 306(a) of the Sarbanes-Oxley Act (relating to restrictions on insider trades during a pension plan blackout period, *see* SEC Release No. 34-47225 (Jan. 22, 2003)), which uses the definition of "officer" provided in Rule 16a-1 under the Exchange Act. These two definitions differ only in that Rule 16a-1(f) explicitly includes an issuer's principal financial officer and principal accounting officer (or, if there is no such accounting officer, the controller).

[11] Beneficial ownership is to be calculated consistent with Rule 13d-3 under the Exchange Act.

[12] Except for the definition of executive officer and the elimination of the requirement that the person not be a director, the safe harbor is similar to the test used for determining "insider" status under § 16 of the Exchange Act and to the safe harbor the SEC proposed in 1997 to include in Rule 144 under the Securities Act. *See* SEC Release No. 33-7391 (Feb. 20, 1997).

[13] The NASD has proposed a 20% ownership limit, beyond which an audit committee member would not be independent. *See* proposed NASD Rule 4350(d)(2)(A)(i)(c). The NYSE had proposed in June 2002 to permit an affiliate of a 20% or greater shareholder to be a non-voting member of the audit committee, but later eliminated this provision in light of Section 301 of the Sarbanes-Oxley Act. *See* note 6 of the NYSE's Corporate Governance Rule Proposals Reflecting Recommendations from the NYSE Corporate Accountability and Listing Standards Committee (Aug. 1, 2002). The NYSE's current proposals explicitly state, "as the concern is independence from management, the [NYSE] does not view ownership of even a significant amount of stock, by itself, as a bar to an independence finding." *See* Commentary to proposed § 303A(2)(a) of the NYSE proposal.

[14] Rule 10A-3(b)(1)(iv)(A) under the Exchange Act.

[15] Rule 10A-3(b)(1)(iv)(B) under the Exchange Act.

sidiaries and joint ventures should be able to share board members without compromising independence for purposes of audit committee eligibility.

In addition, Rule 10A-3 provides an accommodation for foreign private issuers that operate under a dual holding company structure.[16] Given their unique structure, the companies may establish a joint audit committee made up of directors who serve on one or both companies' boards of directors. The Rule provides that where a listed company is one of two dual holding companies, such companies may designate one audit committee for both companies so long as each member of the audit committee is a member of the board of directors of at least one of such dual holding companies.[17] The Rule also provides that dual holding companies will not be deemed affiliates of each other by virtue of their dual holding company arrangements.[18]

Beyond these two specific exemptions, the SEC does not intend to entertain exemptions or waivers for particular relationships on a case-by-case basis, and notes expressly in the Adopting Release that the staff will not entertain no-action letter or exemption requests in this area.[19] The SEC, however, notes that it has the exemptive authority to respond to, and will remain sensitive to, evolving standards of corporate governance, including changes in U.S. and foreign law, to address any new conflicts that cannot be anticipated at this time.[20]

POWERS AND DUTIES OF THE AUDIT COMMITTEE

Responsibilities Relating to Independent Auditors. Under Rule 10A-3, the audit committee is required to be directly responsible for the appointment, compensation, retention and oversight of the work of the independent auditor engaged for the purpose of preparing an audit report or performing other audit, review or attest services for the issuer, and the independent auditor must report directly to the audit committee (the "Responsibility Requirement"). The Rule generally tracks the description of the audit committee's responsibilities in Section 301 of

---

[16] Under Rule 10A-3, "dual holding companies" means two foreign private issuers that are organized in different national jurisdictions, collectively own and supervise the management of one or more businesses which are conducted as a single economic enterprise and do not conduct any business other than collectively owning and supervising such businesses and activities reasonably incidental thereto. *See* Rule 10A-3(e)(5) under the Exchange Act. Examples of these dual holding companies include Reed Elsevier PLC, Royal Dutch Petroleum Company and Unilever PLC.

[17] Rule 10A-3(b)(1)(i) under the Exchange Act.

[18] Rule 10A-3(e)(1)(iv) under the Exchange Act.

[19] *See* the Adopting Release, 68 Fed. Reg. 18788, 18795, n.87 (Apr. 16, 2003).

[20] Rule 10A-3(b)(1)(iv)(F) under the Exchange Act provides that in addition to the enumerated exemptions, the SEC may exempt from the independence requirements a particular relationship with respect to audit committee members, as the SEC determines appropriate in light of the circumstances. This provision implements the exemptive authority granted to the SEC in Section 301 of the Sarbanes-Oxley Act.

LISTED COMPANY AUDIT COMMITTEE STANDARDS

the Sarbanes-Oxley Act, but adds the word "retention" to clarify that the audit committee must be directly responsible for the decision to retain or terminate the outside auditor.[21]

Procedures to Handle Complaints. Rule 10A-3 requires that an audit committee establish procedures for the receipt, retention and treatment of complaints received by the issuer regarding accounting, internal accounting controls or auditing matters and for the confidential, anonymous submission by employees of concerns regarding questionable accounting or auditing matters. The Rule thus strictly reflects the requirements of the Sarbanes-Oxley Act and neither imposes obligations beyond the scope of the Act nor provides any guidance as to the nature of complying procedures. In the absence of additional limitations imposed by the pending SRO initiatives, the implementation of a complaint procedure, apparently including the allocation of responsibilities between management and the audit committee, is left to an issuer's judgment.[22]

Advisors and Funding Requirements. Rule 10A-3 requires that an audit committee have the authority to engage outside advisors, including counsel, as it determines necessary to carry out its duties. The Rule also requires the issuer to provide appropriate funding, as determined by the audit committee, for payment of compensation to the issuer's independent auditor and to any advisors employed by the audit committee. These requirements strictly reflect the requirements of Section 301 of the Sarbanes-Oxley Act. The funding requirement, however, includes an additional obligation that the issuer provide appropriate funding for the ordinary administrative expenses of the audit committee.

Conflicts with Other Applicable Rules. The duties and powers imposed on the audit committee under the Sarbanes-Oxley Act may conflict with applicable law, the issuer's governing documents or other rules such as listing requirements of non-U.S. exchanges. This problem is particularly important for foreign private issuers, and it was the subject of extensive comment. The SEC has sought to address many of the conflicts by means of three instructions to the final version of Rule 10A-3, which have been expanded and clarified from what was contained in the original proposal. The SEC has proceeded by means of instructions rather than exemptions as many commenters requested, but it is clear from the Adopting Release that the SEC intends for the audit committee standards to yield in the event of conflicts of the kinds described in these instructions.

---

[21] In addition, the phrase "or related work," which appears in Section 301 of the Sarbanes-Oxley Act, does not appear in the Rule.

[22] For a discussion of considerations pertinent to the audit committee's establishment of complaint procedures, *see* Chapter III.

The instructions state that the requirements described above (the Responsibility Requirement, the complaint procedures requirement, the advisors requirement and the funding requirement) "do not conflict with" other rules giving the same powers to (i) the shareholders; (ii) the full board of directors without the ability to delegate; or (iii) a governmental entity or tribunal. The instructions do not cover all conflicts between Rule 10A-3 and other applicable law. In particular, the instructions would not seem to address a circumstance in which applicable law, bylaws or listing requirements give the specified responsibilities to management.[23] They also permit powers to be allocated to the shareholders by the issuer's bylaws, while for allocations to the full board or a governmental entity or tribunal the instructions apply only if the allocation is required by law or listing requirements.

If the audit committee cannot have its full responsibilities under Rule 10A-3 due to a conflict of the kinds described, then the instructions do require that it have certain lesser responsibilities. For example, if the shareholders have the power to select the auditors, but the issuer provides a nomination, the audit committee must be responsible for making the nomination. Similarly, if the board of directors is not permitted to delegate a specified responsibility, the audit committee must have "such responsibilities, which can include advisory powers, with respect to such matters to the extent permitted by law, including submitting nominations or recommendations to the full board."

MULTIPLE LISTINGS EXEMPTION

The application of Section 301 of the Sarbanes-Oxley Act does not depend on the type of listed security. As a result, Rule 10A-3 applies to any listed security, including debt securities and derivative securities. Recognizing, however, that many companies issue multiple classes of securities through various ownership structures on various markets, and that issuers often issue non-equity securities through wholly- or majority-owned subsidiaries for various reasons, the Rule provides an exemption relating to multiple listings.[24]

Under Rule 10A-3, additional listings of an issuer's securities are exempt from the audit committee requirements if the issuer is already subject to them as a result of listing any class of securities on any market subject to the Rule. This

---

[23] In contrast, the exemption for foreign private issuers that rely on an alternative mechanism, which is described below, specifies that the alternative body must have the specified powers and duties "to the extent permitted by law."

[24] Rule 10A-3 also provides an exemption from the audit committee requirements for the listing of securities futures products or standardized options, if the listing meets certain requirements relating to the clearing agency, as well as for the securities of asset-backed issuers and certain other passive issuers and certain types of investment companies (the Rule applies to the securities of closed-end investment companies and exchange-traded securities of open-end investment companies, but not to exchange-traded securities of unit investment trusts).

LISTED COMPANY AUDIT COMMITTEE STANDARDS

exemption extends to listings of non-equity securities by a direct or indirect subsidiary that is consolidated or at least 50% beneficially owned by a parent company, if the parent is subject to the requirements as a result of the listing of a class of its equity securities. It does *not* extend to a listing by such subsidiary of its own equity securities (other than non-convertible, non-participating preferred securities or trust preferred securities). The multiple listings exemption is available to U.S. subsidiaries if the parent is a foreign private issuer, even if the foreign parent is relying on one of the special exemptions for foreign private issuers, as discussed below.

As noted below, there is no disclosure requirement relating to the use of the multiple listings exemption.

APPLICATION OF REQUIREMENTS TO FOREIGN PRIVATE ISSUERS

Section 301 of the Sarbanes-Oxley Act does not distinguish between domestic and foreign issuers.[25] The SEC, however, is aware that the requirements of Rule 10A-3 may conflict with legal requirements, corporate governance standards and methods for providing auditor oversight in some foreign jurisdictions. The instructions described above are one attempt to accommodate these conflicts. In addition, the SEC has attempted to address these concerns by providing exemptions in specific areas in which non-U.S. and U.S. corporate governance practices differ. It has not provided any broad-based exemption for non-U.S. companies. The exemptions are exclusive, and the SROs will not be able to grant any additional exemptions or waivers in their listing standards for foreign private issuers or on a case-by-case basis.

Independence Exemptions. Rule 10A-3 includes three exemptions from the independence requirements for audit committees of foreign private issuers:

- **Employee Representation.** Any employee who is not an executive officer of the foreign private issuer may sit on the audit committee if the employee is elected or named to the board of directors or audit committee pursuant to the issuer's governing law or documents, an employee collective bargaining or similar agreement or other home country legal or listing requirements.[26]

---

[25] Rule 10A-3 does provide an exemption for securities listed by foreign governments. *See* Rule 10A-3(c)(6)(iii) under the Exchange Act. This includes any Schedule B issuer. *See* the Adopting Release, 68 Fed. Reg. 18788, 18803, n.159 (Apr. 16, 2003).

[26] In the Adopting Release, the SEC notes that this exemption is provided in recognition that some countries, such as Germany, require a non-management employee representative to serve on the supervisory board or audit committee.

- **Affiliate Representation.** An affiliate or representative of an affiliate (including a controlling shareholder) of the foreign private issuer may sit on the audit committee as an observer if such representative is not a voting member or chair of the audit committee or an executive officer of the issuer and does not receive any compensation prohibited by the independence requirements.

- **Foreign Government Representation.** A representative of a foreign government or foreign governmental entity[27] that is an affiliate of the foreign private issuer may sit on the audit committee if such representative is not an executive officer of the issuer and does not receive any compensation prohibited by the independence requirements.

Each of these exemptions would be available for more than one member of the audit committee.

In addition, Rule 10A-3 clarifies the application of the requirements to issuers with a two-tier board of directors, which is a required or common practice in some countries (*e.g.*, Germany and The Netherlands). In that structure, one tier is the management board, and the other is the supervisory or non-management board. Under the Rule, the term "board of directors" means the supervisory or non-management board.

Exemption for an Alternative Mechanism. Rule 10A-3 also permits a foreign private issuer to be exempt from all of the audit committee requirements if it has an alternative mechanism for overseeing the independent auditor, such as a board of auditors or statutory auditors.[28] The alternative body must be separate from the issuer's board of directors. The exemption is subject to the further conditions that:

- the board of auditors or statutory auditors are established and selected pursuant to home country legal or listing provisions requiring or permitting such board or similar body, and such legal or listing provisions set forth standards of independence for such body;

- management does not elect the board or statutory auditors, and no executive officer of the foreign private issuer is a member of such board or statutory auditors;

---

[27] In the Adopting Release, the SEC indicates that the legal form of the entity that holds the government's shareholdings is not determinative, and that the exemption applies regardless of the manner in which the foreign government owns its interest.

[28] According to the SEC, such alternative mechanisms are permitted under Japanese and Brazilian law and required under Italian law.

LISTED COMPANY AUDIT COMMITTEE STANDARDS

- such board or statutory auditors, in accordance with any applicable home country legal or listing requirements or the issuer's governing documents, is responsible, to the extent permitted by law, for the appointment, retention and oversight of the work of the independent auditor engaged by the issuer (including, to the extent permitted by law, the resolution of disagreements between management and the auditor regarding financial reporting); and

- the remaining requirements of Rule 10A-3, such as those pertaining to complaint procedures, advisors and committee funding, apply to such board or statutory auditors, to the extent permitted by law.

Foreign private issuers relying on any of the above exemptions will need to disclose such reliance.

Foreign private issuers relying on the board of auditors exemption will have to consider a number of interpretive issues relating to the responsibilities of the audit committee under other Sarbanes-Oxley Act rules, auditing rules and home country law.

DISCLOSURE REQUIREMENTS

Disclosure Regarding Exemptions. Rule 10A-3 requires disclosure by any listed issuer that relies on certain of the exemptions described above. Specifically, a listed issuer that relies on the exemptions from the independence requirements or certain of the general exemptions[29] is required to disclose that fact and its assessment of whether such reliance will materially adversely affect the ability of the audit committee to act independently and to satisfy the other requirements of the Rule. This disclosure will need to appear in, or be incorporated by reference into, the issuer's annual reports filed with the SEC,[30] as well as in proxy statements or information statements for shareholders' meetings at which elections for directors are held.

---

[29] Rule 10A-3 will not require issuers relying on the general exemption for unit investment trusts, asset-backed issuers and foreign governments, the multiple listings exemption, the overlapping boards exemption and the securities futures products and standardized options exemptions to make such disclosure.

[30] The disclosure will need to be included in, or be incorporated by reference from the proxy statement into, Part III of annual reports on Form 10-K (through an addition to Item 401 of Regulation S-K). For foreign private issuers that file their annual reports on Form 20-F or Form 40-F, the disclosure requirement will appear in new Item 16D or paragraph (14) to General Instruction B, respectively. For registered investment companies, the disclosure will appear in Item 5(b) of Form N-CSR and Item 22(b)(14) of Schedule 14A.

Identification of the Audit Committee in Annual Reports. Currently, an issuer subject to the proxy rules of § 14 of the Exchange Act is required to disclose the names of each audit committee member in its proxy statement or information statement with respect to the election of directors.[31] Rule 10A-3 will require an issuer subject to the proxy rules also to disclose such information in its annual report, either by including it or by incorporating it by reference from the proxy statement. Foreign private issuers, which are not generally subject to the proxy rules, are already required to identify the members of the audit committee in their annual reports.[32] An issuer that does not have a separately designated audit committee, as permitted by the Sarbanes-Oxley Act,[33] will be required to disclose in its annual report that the entire board is acting as the audit committee.[34]

Updates to Existing Audit Committee Disclosure. Issuers subject to the proxy rules currently must disclose other audit committee information in their proxy statements or information statements with respect to the election of directors, including whether the members of the committee are independent.[35] An issuer with securities listed on the NYSE or the AMEX or quoted on Nasdaq also must disclose whether the audit committee members are independent as defined in the applicable listing standards. Issuers not so listed are now required to disclose whether the audit committee members are independent according to the definition of independence of any of the NYSE, the AMEX or the NASD.

Rule 10A-3 clarifies that for a listed issuer that does not have a separately designated or chosen audit committee, the required disclosure must address all members of the board of directors. The Rule also permits a non-listed issuer to choose any definition for audit committee member independence of a national securities exchange or national securities association that has been approved by the SEC.

Because foreign private issuers generally are not subject to the proxy rules, they are not currently required to disclose this additional audit committee information, including with respect to audit committee member independence. Rule 10A-3 does not require foreign private issuers to provide this additional disclosure.[36]

---

[31] *See* Item 7(d)(1) of Schedule 14A.
[32] *See* Item 6(C)(3) of Form 20-F.
[33] *See* Note 3 *supra*.
[34] Similar disclosure will be required for registered management investment companies.
[35] *See* Item 7(d)(3)(iv) of Schedule 14A. Item 7(d)(3) of Schedule 14A also requires the inclusion of an audit committee report disclosing whether the audit committee has reviewed and discussed the audited financial statements with management and discussed certain matters with the independent auditors (as specified in Item 306 of Regulation S-K). In addition, Item 7(d)(3) requires disclosure about whether the audit committee is governed by a charter, and, if so, inclusion of the charter as an appendix to the proxy statement at least once every three years.
[36] The NYSE proposal would require foreign private issuers to disclose any significant ways in which their corporate governance practices differ from those followed by domestic companies under

LISTED COMPANY AUDIT COMMITTEE STANDARDS

Audit Committee Financial Expert Disclosure for Foreign Private Issuers. The SEC has also adopted amendments to the audit committee financial expert disclosure provisions as they apply to foreign private issuers. Under these amendments, a U.S.-listed foreign private issuer will be required to disclose whether its audit committee financial expert is independent, as that term is defined by the SRO listing standards applicable to that issuer. A non-U.S. listed foreign private issuer will disclose the independence of its audit committee financial expert (if it has one) using any of the SRO definitions that have been approved by the SEC.[37] Foreign private issuers will not be required to comply with these disclosure requirements until July 31, 2005.

CLARIFICATION OF THE SEC'S AUDITOR INDEPENDENCE RULES

Under the SEC's auditor independence rules, an issuer's audit committee must pre-approve audit and non-audit services provided to the issuer and its consolidated subsidiaries by the independent auditor.[38] In the Adopting Release, the SEC clarifies that the audit committee of a parent company that controls another consolidated entity can perform the pre-approval function for the parent company and any consolidated subsidiaries, and that the audit committee (whether that of the parent or the subsidiary) best positioned to review the impact of the service should perform the review. These functions may also be performed by the issuer's board of auditors (or statutory auditors) or the entire board if the issuer does not have a separate audit committee. The Adopting Release further clarifies that the same body responsible for pre-approval of audit and non-audit services also should be the body to which the issuer's auditor communicates certain information required by the SEC's rules.[39]

TIMING AND COMPLIANCE ASPECTS OF THE RULE

Under the Sarbanes-Oxley Act, the final rule must be effective by April 26, 2003. However, Rule 10A-3 incorporates delayed implementation dates. Under

---

NYSE listing standards, including with respect to audit committee member independence. *See* proposed § 303A(11) of the NYSE proposal. An NASD proposal that has not yet been published by the SEC would require a foreign private issuer that receives exemptions from the corporate governance requirements to disclose in its annual report filed with the SEC each requirement from which it is exempted and the alternative practice, if any, of the issuer in lieu of these requirements. *See* Form 19b-4 Proposed Rule Change; File No. SR-NASD-2002-138 (Oct. 8, 2002).

[37] When these rules require a foreign private issuer to refer to the independence standards of an SRO, there is some ambiguity as to whether it should refer to the specific standards applicable to audit committee members pursuant to the Rule, or to the additional, more demanding standards of independence that will almost certainly not otherwise apply to foreign private issuers. Presumably the narrower standards were intended, and in the case of a listed issuer the wording of the rules supports this reading.

[38] *See* SEC Release No. 33-8183 (Jan. 28, 2003).

[39] *See* Rule 2-07 of Regulation S-X.

the Rule, each SRO must provide proposed rules or rule amendments that comply with the Rule no later than July 15, 2003. The Rule also requires that each SRO have final rules or rule amendments that comply with the Rule approved by the SEC no later than December 1, 2003. Listed issuers (other than foreign private issuers and small business issuers) must be in compliance with the new listing standards by the earlier of their first annual shareholders' meeting after January 15, 2004 or October 31, 2004. Listed foreign private issuers and small business issuers must be in compliance by July 31, 2005.

Rule 10A-3 does not establish specific mechanisms for determining compliance with the requirements. Instead, the Adopting Release directs the SROs to require self-reporting from issuers promptly after an executive officer becomes aware of any material non-compliance with the Rule's requirements.

The Rule permits an issuer the opportunity to cure any defects that would result in delisting of its securities. The SEC also permits the SROs to provide an accommodation for an audit committee member who ceases to be independent for reasons outside the member's reasonable control.[40] No new procedures will need to be implemented except to the extent an SRO's current rules do not provide definite procedures and time periods for compliance with the requirements.

---

[40] The SROs may provide that if an audit committee member ceases to be independent for reasons outside the member's reasonable control, that person, with notice by the issuer to the applicable SRO, may remain an audit committee member of the listed issuer until the earlier of the next annual meeting of the listed issuer or one year from the occurrence of the event that caused the member to be no longer independent. However, neither the NYSE nor the NASD proposal seems to include this accommodation.

V NYSE AND NASDAQ GOVERNANCE PROPOSALS

The following chart summarizes the proposed corporate governance rules submitted to the SEC by the NYSE and the NASD (through its subsidiary, Nasdaq) for review and approval by the SEC, and highlights which of these provisions are required by the Sarbanes-Oxley Act.

Proposal	NYSE	Nasdaq
Board Independence	• Independent directors will be required to comprise a majority of the board. A "controlled company" will not be subject to this requirement. A controlled company is one in which more than 50% of the voting power is held by an individual, group or another issuer, rather than the public. A controlled company taking advantage of this exemption must disclose in its proxy its status and the basis for its determination. • Board must affirmatively find independent directors to have no "material" direct or indirect relationship with the issuer. These relationships "can include commercial, industrial, banking, consulting, legal, accounting, charitable and familial relationships (among others)." The basis for the board's determination must be disclosed in the	• Independent directors will be required to comprise a majority of the board. A "controlled company" will not be subject to this requirement. A controlled company is one in which more than 50% of the voting power is held by an individual, group or another company. A controlled company taking advantage of this exemption must disclose in its proxy its status and the basis for its determination. • "Independent director" means a person other than an officer or employee of the issuer or its subsidiaries or any other individual having a relationship that, in the opinion of the issuer's board of directors, will interfere with the exercise of independent judgment in carrying out the responsibilities of a director.

Proposal	NYSE	Nasdaq
	issuer's proxy or, if no proxy is prepared, its Form 10-K. • Ownership of a significant amount of stock will not be a *per se* bar to independence. • Non-management directors will be required to meet regularly in executive sessions. • A director will not be independent if such director is: (i) a person who the board determines has a material relationship with the issuer, directly or indirectly; (ii) an employee of the issuer; (iii) a person who receives more than $100,000 per year in direct compensation from the issuer, other than director and committee fees or deferred compensation for prior services only. This creates a presumption of non-independence which can be negated if the issuer's board determines (and no independent director dissents) that relationship is not material, the relationship is disclosed and the relationship is not covered by a categorical standard; (iv) affiliated with or employed by the internal or external auditor of the issuer;	• Ownership of company stock by itself is not a *per se* bar to independence. • Independent directors will be required to hold regularly scheduled executive sessions. • A director is not independent if such director is: (i) a person who the board determines has a relationship with the issuer that would interfere with the exercise of independent judgment; (ii) an employee of the issuer, its parent or subsidiary; (iii) a person who receives, or whose family member receives, more than $60,000 in *any* payments (other than for board service; payments arising solely from investments in the issuer's securities; compensation paid to a family member who is an employee of the issuer or a subsidiary or parent, unless the family member is an executive officer; or retirement benefits or non-discretionary compensation) from the issuer, its parent or subsidiary (including political contributions); (iv) a partner or employee of the issuer's outside auditor and works on the audit;

NYSE AND NASDAQ PROPOSALS

Proposal	NYSE	Nasdaq
	(v) an executive officer of another company whose compensation committee's membership includes an executive officer of the issuer;	(v) an executive officer of another company whose compensation committee's membership includes an executive officer of the issuer;
	(vi) an executive officer or employee of another company that (a) accounts for at least 2% or $1 million, whichever is greater, of the issuer's consolidated gross revenues; or (b) for which the issuer accounts for at least 2% or $1 million, whichever is greater, of such other company's consolidated gross revenues; and	(vi) a partner, controlling shareholder or executive officer of *any* organization (including charities) to which the issuer makes, or from which the issuer receives (other than those arising solely from investments in the organization's securities), payments in excess of $200,000 or 5% of the issuer's or the organization's gross revenues, whichever is more; and
	(vii) any immediate family members of an individual listed in (iii) through (vi) above.	(vii) a family member of an executive officer of the issuer, its parent or subsidiary.
	• Five-year cooling off period before non-independent directors can be considered independent. This cooling off period will be subject to a transition period so that events or circumstances occurring prior to the adoption of the rules will not disqualify the director.	• Three-year cooling off period before non-independent directors can be considered independent.
	• Issuers will have 18 months (30 months in the case of directors on staggered boards who would not normally stand for election within the 18 month period) to implement this standard once it is approved, except for the requirement to hold exec-	• Issuers will be required to implement this standard by the issuer's first annual meeting occurring after January 1, 2004, except for the requirement to hold executive sessions, which must be implemented within six months from SEC approval of the standard.

Proposal	NYSE	Nasdaq
	utive sessions, which must be implemented within six months from SEC approval of the standard.	
Audit Committee	• *Issuers will be required to have an audit committee comprised solely of independent directors. • NYSE will require the audit committee to be comprised of three or more independent directors. • *Audit committee members must satisfy the independence requirements under the Sarbanes-Oxley Act, subject to exemptions adopted by the SEC, in addition to the NYSE independence standards.[1] • Audit committee members must be financially literate or must become financially literate within a reasonable time after appointment. • One member must have accounting or related management expertise. A person who qualifies as an "audit committee financial expert" under the Sarbanes-Oxley Act could be presumed to	• *Issuers will be required to have an audit committee comprised solely of independent directors. • Nasdaq will require the audit committee to be comprised of three or more independent directors, except for the limited exception described below. • *Audit committee members must satisfy the independence requirements under the Sarbanes-Oxley Act, subject to exemptions adopted by the SEC, in addition to the Nasdaq independence standards. • Audit committee members must be able to read and understand financial statements at the time of appointment. • One member must have accounting or related management expertise. A person that qualifies as an "audit committee financial expert" under

* Denotes a requirement of the Sarbanes-Oxley Act.

[1] The Sarbanes-Oxley Act requires issuers to have an audit committee comprised of independent directors or, if the issuer so chooses, its entire board may serve as the audit committee, in which case its entire board will be subject to the independence requirements. To be independent under the Sarbanes-Oxley Act, an audit committee member may not be an "affiliate" of the issuer or accept (directly or indirectly) any consulting, advisory or other compensatory fees from the issuer. An "affiliate" of the issuer is a person who controls, is controlled by or is under common control with the issuer. The SEC has stated that a person who owns or controls 10% or less of the issuer's shares will not be deemed to be in control of the issuer, and therefore not an affiliate of the issuer.

NYSE AND NASDAQ PROPOSALS

Proposal	NYSE	Nasdaq
	have this expertise. • Board must determine that simultaneous service on audit committees of more than two other companies (where issuer does not have lower limit) will not impair the member's service and must disclose that determination in the proxy or, if no proxy is prepared, the Form 10-K. • Issuers must have an internal audit function, which may be outsourced, except to the independent auditor. Audit committee members must meet periodically with persons responsible for internal audit functions without the presence of management. • The audit committee will be required to have a charter specifying the purpose, duties and evaluation procedures of the committee. • Audit committees will be required to (subject to any exemptions under the Sarbanes-Oxley Act): *(i) directly appoint, retain, compensate, evaluate and terminate the issuer's independent auditors; *(ii) approve, in advance, the provision by the audi-	the Sarbanes-Oxley Act could be presumed to have this expertise. • Heightened standard of independence for audit committee members. In addition to satisfying the independence standard for directors generally, the members of the audit committee may not: (i) receive *any* payment for services other than board or committee service; and (ii) serve if an affiliated person of the issuer or any subsidiary (*i.e.*, owns 20% or more of the issuer's voting securities (or such lower number as may be established by the SEC)).[2] • The audit committee will be required to have a charter specifying the scope of its responsibilities and the means by which it will carry out those responsibilities. • Audit committees will be required to: *(i) have sole authority to appoint, determine funding for and oversee outside auditors; *(ii) approve, in advance, the provision by the au-

* Denotes a requirement of the Sarbanes-Oxley Act.

[2] While the SEC has established a safe harbor with respect to affiliate status, the board may determine that a director who owns more than 10% is not an affiliate and, therefore, still independent for purposes of the Sarbanes-Oxley Act.

Proposal	NYSE	Nasdaq
	tor of all audit services and permissible non-audit services;[3]	ditor of all audit services and permissible non-audit services;
	*(iii) establish procedures for the receipt, retention and treatment of complaints received by the issuer regarding accounting, internal accounting controls or auditing matters and ensure that such complaints are treated confidentially and anonymously;	*(iii) establish procedures for the receipt, retention and treatment of complaints received by the issuer regarding accounting, internal accounting controls or auditing matters and ensure that such complaints are treated confidentially and anonymously;
	*(iv) have authority to consult with, retain and determine funding for legal, accounting and other advisors;	*(iv) have authority to consult with, retain and determine funding for legal, accounting and other advisors; and
	(v) review reports by the auditor describing the auditor's internal quality control procedures, material issues raised by its most recent internal quality control (or peer) review, all relationships between the auditor and the issuer, and any audit problems or difficulties and management's response; (vi) discuss annual and quarterly reports (including MD&A), earnings releases, information and guidance provided to analysts and rating agencies and guidelines and policies governing risk management; and (vii) establish clear hiring	*(v) review *and approve* all related-party transactions. • A single non-independent, non-management director (or family member of such person) may serve for up to two years on the audit committee in "exceptional and limited circumstances," but may not chair the committee. This exception requires determination by the board that an individual's service on the committee is in the best interest of the issuer and its shareholders. If an issuer relies on this exception, its reliance and the nature of the relationship must be disclosed in its proxy. Only directors that satisfy the audit committee inde-

* Denotes a requirement of the Sarbanes-Oxley Act.
[3] Unlike the NASD proposal, the NYSE proposal does not specifically set forth this requirement, which is contained in the Sarbanes-Oxley Act. We have included the requirement here for completeness.

NYSE AND NASDAQ PROPOSALS

Proposal	NYSE	Nasdaq
	policies for employees or former employees of the independent auditors. • The new independence standards for audit committee members will be subject to the same 18- and 30-month transition periods applicable to the election of a majority of the board. The requirements to increase the responsibility of the audit committee, adopt the committee charter and establish an internal audit function will require implementation within six months of SEC approval of the proposal. In respect of NYSE proposals that reflect the requirements of the Sarbanes-Oxley Act, issuers (other than foreign private issuers) must be in compliance by the earlier of their first annual shareholders meeting after January 15, 2004, or October 31, 2004.	pendence requirements of the Sarbanes-Oxley Act will be eligible to serve pursuant to the "exceptional and limited circumstances" exception. • Issuers will be required to implement the new independence standards for audit committee members by the issuer's first annual meeting occurring after January 1, 2004. Other requirements, such as adoption of a charter, must be implemented within six months from SEC approval of the standard. In respect of Nasdaq proposals that reflect the requirements of the Sarbanes-Oxley Act, issuers (other than foreign private issuers) must be in compliance by the earlier of their first annual shareholders meeting after January 15, 2004, or October 31, 2004.
Audit Committee Compensation	• *An audit committee member may not accept any consulting, advisory or other compensatory fee from the issuer other than as a member of the audit committee or the board of directors.	• *An audit committee member may not accept any consulting, advisory or other compensatory fee from the issuer other than as a member of the audit committee or the board of directors.
Compensation Committee	• Executive officer compensation must be approved by a compensation committee (or equivalent) comprised solely of independent di-	• Executive officer compensation must be approved by either a compensation committee comprised solely of independent directors, or

* Denotes a requirement of the Sarbanes-Oxley Act.

Proposal	NYSE	Nasdaq
	rectors. Controlled companies are exempt. • The compensation committee will be required to have a charter specifying the purpose, duties and evaluation procedures of the committee. • Issuers will be required to establish the compensation (or equivalent) committee with the requisite charter within six months of SEC approval of the proposal; however, the "full independence" requirement is subject to the same 18- and 30-month transition periods applicable to the election of a majority of the board.	by a majority of the independent directors. Controlled companies are exempt. • "Exceptional and limited circumstances" exception for one non-independent, non-management director. Reliance on this exception will require that the committee be comprised of at least three members and will be subject to disclosure in the proxy. • Issuers will be required to implement these standards by their first annual meeting occurring after January 1, 2004.
Nominating Committee	• Issuers will be required to have a nominating committee (or equivalent) responsible for nominating directors comprised solely of independent directors. This requirement does not apply to controlled companies or companies that are legally required by contract (*e.g.*, by shareholder agreement) to permit a third party to appoint directors. • The committee will be required to have a charter specifying the purpose,	• Director nominations must be approved by a nominating committee comprised solely of independent directors or by a majority of the independent directors. This requirement does not apply to controlled companies or companies that are legally required by contract (*e.g.*, by shareholder agreement) to permit a third party to appoint directors. • A single non-independent

NYSE AND NASDAQ PROPOSALS

Proposal	NYSE	Nasdaq
	duties and evaluation procedures of the committee. • Issuers will be required to establish the nominating (or equivalent) committee with the requisite charter within six months of SEC approval of the proposal; however, the "full independence" requirement is subject to the same 18- and 30-month transition periods applicable to the election of a majority of the board.	director will be allowed to serve for up to two years if (i) the individual is an officer who owns or controls more than 20% of the issuer's voting securities; or (ii) in "exceptional and limited" circumstances. Reliance on these exemptions will require that the committee be comprised of at least three independent members and will be subject to disclosure in the proxy. • Issuers will be required to implement these standards by their first annual meeting occurring after January 1, 2004.
Corporate Governance/ Code of Ethics	• Issuers will have to adopt governance guidelines, a code of business conduct and ethics standards. Issuers will be required to publish these items on their websites and to state in their annual reports that these documents are available on their website and in hard copy on request. • *The Sarbanes-Oxley Act requires an issuer to disclose whether it has adopted a code of ethics for its principal executive officer, principal financial officer, principal accounting officer or controller, or persons performing similar functions, and if	• Issuers will be required to have a code of conduct, for all directors and employees. The code of conduct must be publicly available. • *The Sarbanes-Oxley Act requires an issuer to disclose whether it has adopted a code of ethics for its principal executive officer, principal financial officer, principal accounting officer or controller, or persons performing similar func-

* Denotes a requirement of the Sarbanes-Oxley Act.

Proposal	NYSE	Nasdaq
	not, the reasons why it has not done so. • Codes of conduct and ethics should address, at a minimum, conflicts of interest; corporate opportunities; confidentiality; fair dealing; protection and use of issuer assets; legal compliance; and reporting of illegal and unethical behavior. • The issuer's board of directors may grant waivers to executive officers and directors. Any waivers must be disclosed. • Corporate governance guidelines must address, at a minimum, directors' qualifications, responsibilities and compensation; access to management and independent advisers; management succession; director orientation; and annual performance evaluation of the board. • Issuers will be required to adopt corporate governance guidelines and codes within six months of SEC approval of the standard.	tions, and if not, the reasons why it has not done so. • The code of conduct must address, at a minimum, conflicts of interest and compliance with applicable laws, rules and regulations. • The code must also contain an appropriate compliance mechanism. • The issuer's board of directors may grant waivers to executive officers and directors. Any waivers must be disclosed. • Issuers will be required to adopt a code of conduct within six months of SEC approval of the standard.
Foreign Private Issuers	• *Foreign private issuers will be required to comply with the requirements of the Sarbanes-Oxley Act regarding audit committees and financial experts.	• *Foreign private issuers will be required to comply with the requirements of the Sarbanes-Oxley Act regarding audit committees and financial experts.

* Denotes a requirement of the Sarbanes-Oxley Act.

NYSE AND NASDAQ PROPOSALS

Proposal	NYSE	Nasdaq
	• Foreign private issuers are generally exempt from the other corporate governance rules but will be required to disclose (in English) any significant ways in which their corporate governance practices differ from NYSE listing standards. Such disclosure may be made in a brief, general summary on the issuer's website and/or in its annual report. If disclosure is made only on the website, the annual report must so state and provide the website address. • CEOs must promptly notify NYSE after any executive officer of the issuer becomes aware of any material non-compliance with the applicable NYSE rules. • Foreign private issuers will have until July 31, 2005 to comply with the audit committee requirements (with disclosure about the independence of financial experts required in any annual report for a fiscal year ending on or after July 15, 2005) and six months after the SEC approves the new corporate governance rules to satisfy the other requirements listed above.	• Foreign private issuers may obtain exemptions from Nasdaq's other corporate governance rules and will be required to disclose any exemptions from those rules, at the time of their first U.S. listing and annually (as well as any alternative measures taken in lieu of the waived requirements). Such disclosure must be made in a registration statement or annual report filed with the SEC. • Foreign private issuers will have until July 31, 2005 to comply with the audit committee requirements (with disclosure about the independence of financial experts required in any annual report for a fiscal year ending on or after July 15, 2005). The additional disclosure requirement described above will take effect for new listings and filings made on or after January 1, 2004.
Equity Compensation Plans	• Shareholders must be given an opportunity to vote on approval or material modification of all stock option plans, excluding employment-in-	• Shareholders must approve the adoption of all stock option plans and any material modification of such plans (including material modifi-

Proposal	NYSE	Nasdaq
	duced awards, option plans acquired through mergers and acquisitions, "excess benefit plans" and tax-qualified plans. With respect to the approval of a stock option plan, a broker will be able to vote a customer's shares only pursuant to that customer's instructions.[4]	cations to existing plans), excluding employment-induced awards, option plans acquired through mergers and acquisitions, "excess benefit plans," tax-qualified plans and plans that merely provide a convenient way to purchase shares on the open market or from the issuer at fair market value.
CEO Certifications	• Annually, the CEO will be required to certify that he or she is unaware of any violation by the issuer of NYSE corporate governance standards. • The CEO must notify NYSE after any executive officer becomes aware of any material non-compliance with the corporate governance standards. • Issuers will have six months to implement this standard once the proposal is approved by the SEC.	
Sanctions	• In addition to possible suspension and delisting, NYSE may issue a public reprimand letter for violation of a listing standard.	• Material misrepresentations or omissions by companies to Nasdaq may result in delisting. • Nasdaq will have the authority to deny re-listing to an issuer based upon a corporate governance violation that occurred while that issuer's appeal of the delisting was pending.

[4] The NYSE notified its listed companies on June 20, 2003 that its final rule regarding this listing standard is expected to become effective on June 30, 2003. The final text of the rule has not been published, although it is expected to be substantially similar to the NYSE's original proposal and subject to more specific transition rules than those originally proposed. The NASD also filed with the SEC a further amendment of its proposal. *See* Amendment No. 3: Shareholder Approval Requirement under Rule 4350(i), SR-NASD-2002-14 (June 23, 2003).

NYSE AND NASDAQ PROPOSALS

Proposal	NYSE	Nasdaq
Additional Proposals	NYSE may develop a corporate governance institute in conjunction with leading authorities.	• Nasdaq-mandated disclosure of material information may be disclosed through methods expressly approved in Regulation FD (this proposal has been approved by the SEC and is currently effective). • Going-concern qualifications in audit reports will require disclosure by press release, with prior notification to Nasdaq. • Nasdaq will presume a change of control (for purposes of the shareholder approval rules) once an investor acquires 20% of an issuer's outstanding voting power, unless a larger ownership and/or voting position is held on a post-transaction basis by (i) a shareholder or identified group of shareholders unaffiliated with the investor; or (ii) the issuer's directors and officers that are unaffiliated with the investor. • Nasdaq is considering whether to require continuing education for all directors.

VI   OFFICER CERTIFICATIONS AND INTERNAL CONTROL REPORTS

Among the more controversial aspects of the Sarbanes-Oxley Act has been the interplay between Sections 302 and 906 of the Act, which require a company's CEO and CFO to make specified certifications about the company's required public disclosures.[1] While apparently directed at a common principle—that senior officers of U.S. and non-U.S. public companies should take personal responsibility for those disclosures—the two provisions require substantively different certifications.[2]

Section 302 and related regulations of the SEC require the CEO and CFO to certify, among other matters, that the applicable report contains no material misstatements or omissions of material facts and that the financial statements and other financial information in the report fairly present in all material respects the issuer's financial condition, results of operations and cash flows. Although Section 906 requires these officers to make a similar "fair presentation" certification, it also requires a certification to the effect that the report "fully complies" with the requirements of the Exchange Act. The confusion arising from these substantive differences has been compounded insofar as the SEC is charged with implement-

---

[1] The forms of the certifications are reproduced in Appendix D. In addition to these certifications, proposed rules of NYSE would require the CEO of each NYSE-listed company to certify to the NYSE each year that he or she is not aware of any violation by the company of NYSE corporate governance listing standards. *See* Amendment No. 1 to the NYSE's Corporate Governance Rule Proposals; SEC Release 34-47672 (Apr. 4, 2003). The NASD has also proposed amendments to its rules requiring that the CEO and chief compliance officers of its members certify as to the adequacy of their compliance and supervisory policies and procedures. *See* NASD Notice to Members 03-29 (June 2003).

[2] *See* Opening Statement of Rep. Michael Oxley, Chairman of the House Financial Services Committee, in the Conference Committee Transcript accompanying the Sarbanes-Oxley Act: "Jail time for corporate executives who commit crimes is clearly in order." Conference Committee Transcript (July 24, 2002). The Senate Conference Report indicates that some degree of confusion about the interplay of Sections 302 and 906 existed at the time of the adoption of the Sarbanes-Oxley Act. For example, Sen. Michael Enzi remarked that "I also realize inconsistencies appear in sections 302 and 906. The SEC is required to complete rulemaking within 30 days after the date of enactment with regard to CEO certification under section 302. However, section 906 suggests that certification would be required upon enactment, thus the penalties would go into effect before the certification requirement is completed through the rulemaking process. I believe it was the intent of the Conferees that the penalties under section 906 should not become effective until the rulemaking process is finalized." 148 CONG. REC. S7356 (July 25, 2002). *But see* Statement of Sen. Joseph R. Biden, Jr., "Legislative History of Title IX of the Sarbanes-Oxley Act of 2002," 149 CONG. REC. S5325 (daily ed. Apr. 11, 2003), discussed at Note 55 *infra*.

ing Section 302, whereas Section 906 amended the U.S. criminal code and is thus within the jurisdiction of the Department of Justice.[3]

Other differences between the two provisions have also provided cause for debate as to their application. For example, Section 302 applies to "companies" that file periodic reports under § 13(a) or 15(d) of the Exchange Act; Section 906 applies to "issuers."[4] Indeed, the language of Sections 302 and 906 suggests that the certification requirements may be applied to different reports. Section 302 refers to annual and quarterly reports, whereas Section 906 refers to "periodic report[s] containing financial statements." The statutory language also suggests that the certifications could be provided to the SEC using different means. Consistent with the statutory requirement that the Section 302 certification appear "in" a report, the SEC's original rules required that it appear below the signature block of the applicable report. By contrast, since the Section 906 certification must only "accompany" the report, companies have submitted it in a number of ways. Some have filed it as an exhibit to the report or, in the case of U.S. issuers, on a separate Form 8-K. Others have submitted it as non-public paper or electronic correspondence.

The officer certification requirements present special questions for foreign private issuers, since the language of the required certifications reflects U.S.-style governance practices. Some foreign private issuers must determine which persons serve as the CEO and CFO, as well as which body functions as the audit committee of the board of directors, since the Section 302 certification requires the CEO and CFO to make various disclosures to the committee.[5]

The SEC recently adopted amendments to its rules and reporting forms to facilitate access to the Section 302 and 906 certifications by both the public and the SEC and to standardize the method by which the Section 906 certification is provided.[6] Although members of the SEC staff had previously suggested in infor-

---

[3] 18 U.S.C. § 1350.

[4] "Issuer" is defined in the Act as a company that has securities registered under § 12 of the Exchange Act, or that is required to file reports under § 15(d) of the Exchange Act, or that has filed a registration statement under the Securities Act that has not yet become effective and that it has not withdrawn.

[5] In its release adopting rules under Section 301 of the Sarbanes-Oxley Act relating to listed company audit committees, the SEC stated that "[s]ome foreign private issuers have a two-tier board, with one tier designated as the management board and the other tier designated as the supervisory or non-management board. In this circumstance, we believe that the supervisory or non-management board is the body within the company best equipped to comply with the requirements [relating to audit committees]. Our final rule clarifies that in the case of foreign private issuers with two-tier board systems, the term 'board of directors' means the supervisory or non-management board for purposes of Rule 10A-3 under the Exchange Act. As such, the supervisory or non-management board can either form a separate audit committee or, if the entire supervisory or non-management board is independent within the provisions and exceptions of the rule, the entire board can be designated as the audit committee." SEC Release No. 33-8220 (Apr. 9, 2003), 68 Fed. Reg. 18788, 18802 (Apr. 16, 2003).

[6] SEC Release No. 33-8238 (June 5, 2003).

CERTIFICATIONS AND INTERNAL CONTROL REPORTS

mal statements the possibility that the two certifications would be combined, the amendments do not address this approach.

While the disparities in certification will persist, the SEC's amendments do attempt to clarify some substantive uncertainties in the Section 302 certification, notably with respect to an issuer's internal control over financial reporting. These amendments were driven in large measure by the requirement of Section 404 of the Act that each issuer disclose annually an internal control report stating management's responsibility for the issuer's internal control structure and procedures for financial reporting and its conclusions regarding the effectiveness thereof.[7]

The certification requirements are discussed below. We have also addressed the requirement that management report on internal control over financial reporting in light of its impact on the Section 302 certification.

SECTION 302 CERTIFICATION

Generally. The SEC adopted rules implementing Section 302 of the Sarbanes-Oxley Act in August 2002.[8] As noted above, the Section 302 rules apply to annual and (in the case of U.S. companies) quarterly reports filed after that date by all reporting companies, including foreign private issuers, investment companies and issuers of asset-backed securities.[9] The SEC amended the Section 302 certification in 2003 to implement changes that will become effective in two stages.[10] The changes in the first stage, effective August 14, 2003, primarily reorganize the certification and clarify the nature of the disclosures that must be made in an issuer's Exchange Act reports and by the CEO and CFO to the issuer's independent auditor and audit committee. Changes effective in the second stage reflect new obligations of issuers to maintain and evaluate their internal control over financial reporting and are subject to a lengthy transition period as described below.

Upon effectiveness of all of the recent amendments, an issuer's CEO and CFO (or persons performing similar functions) must certify that:

- he or she has reviewed the report;

---

[7] Section 404(a) of the Sarbanes-Oxley Act. The SEC's rules under Section 404 are also discussed in our memorandum entitled "SEC Adopts New Rules on CEO/CFO Certification and Internal Controls."

[8] SEC Release No. 33-8124 (Aug. 29, 2002) (the "Original Release").

[9] The SEC has clarified that issuers that voluntarily file reports under the Exchange Act (*e.g.*, pursuant to an indenture provision) are subject to the Section 302 certification requirement. Division of Corporation Finance: Sarbanes-Oxley Act of 2002—Frequently Asked Questions, Question 9 (last revised Nov. 14, 2002).

[10] SEC Release No. 33-8238 (June 5, 2003). The SEC staff has indicated that the revised Section 302 certification should be used by U.S. issuers that report on a calendar year basis in connection with their quarterly reports on Form 10-Q for the second quarter of 2003, even if they are filed before August 14, 2003.

- based on his or her knowledge, the report contains no material misstatements or omissions;

- based on his or her knowledge, the financial statements, and other financial information included in the report, fairly present in all material respects the financial condition, results of operations and cash flows of the issuer as of, and for, the periods presented in the report;

- he or she and the other certifying officers:

    — are responsible for establishing and maintaining the issuer's disclosure controls and procedures and internal control over financial reporting and have properly designed them (or supervised their design);[11]

    — have evaluated the issuer's disclosure controls and procedures and presented their conclusions in the report; and

    — have disclosed any change in the issuer's internal control over financial reporting that occurred during the most recent fiscal quarter (or fiscal year, in the case of foreign private issuers) that has materially affected, or is reasonably likely to materially affect, the issuer's internal control over financial reporting; and

- he or she and the other certifying officers have disclosed, based on their most recent evaluation of internal control over financial reporting, to the issuer's independent auditor and audit committee all significant deficiencies and material weaknesses in the design or operation of internal control over financial reporting that are reasonably likely to affect the issuer's ability to record, process, summarize and report financial information and any fraud (regardless of materiality) involving management or other employees having a significant role in the issuer's internal control over financial reporting.

Covered Reports under Section 302. The Section 302 certification requirements apply to annual reports on Forms 10-K, 20-F and 40-F, quarterly reports on Forms 10-Q, transition reports on any of these forms, and amendments to any of these reports.[12] They do not apply to reports on Form 6-K furnished by foreign pri-

---

[11] The apparent requirement of the original Section 302 certification that the CEO and CFO themselves "design" the company's disclosure controls and procedures generated significant criticism, prompting the SEC to clarify in subsequent amendments that the officers need only "cause" them to be properly designed under their supervision. This change will be effective for reports filed on or after August 14, 2003. SEC Release No. 33-8238 (June 5, 2003).

[12] The Section 302 certification does not apply to foreign private issuers that furnish materials to the SEC pursuant to Rule 12g3-2(b) under the Exchange Act. The Section 302 rules also exempt filings relating to employee benefit plans made on Form 11-K from the certification requirement. Original Release, 67 Fed. Reg. 57276, 57278, n. 47 (Sept. 9, 2002).

CERTIFICATIONS AND INTERNAL CONTROL REPORTS

vate issuers or current reports on Form 8-K, regardless of their content or timing. Certifications are also not required in connection with filings of proxy statements and information statements. The Original Release notes, however, that issuers may in certain circumstances satisfy their disclosure obligations under Part III of Form 10-K—information regarding directors and officers, executive compensation, security ownership and related party transactions—by incorporating the information by reference from a definitive proxy or information statement, and that in these instances the certification in the Form 10-K would be considered to cover any such information as of the filing date of the proxy or information statement.[13]

Fair Presentation of Financial Information. The Section 302 rules require a certification that the financial statements and other financial information in a covered report "fairly present in all material respects" the financial condition, results of operations and cash flows of the issuer. The Original Release explains that this certification covers financial statements (including footnotes), selected financial data, MD&A and other financial information in a report. The "fairly presents" standard addresses the financial information in a report viewed in its entirety, and is broader than a requirement to present financial information in conformity with GAAP. According to the Original Release, it encompasses the selection of appropriate accounting policies, proper application of those policies, disclosure of financial information that is informative and reasonably reflects the underlying transactions and events and the inclusion of any additional disclosure necessary to provide investors with a materially accurate and complete picture of the issuer's financial condition, results of operations and cash flows.

In support of this disclosure standard, the Original Release cites Rule 12b-20 under the Exchange Act,[14] as well as certain key court decisions and SEC enforcement proceedings that stand for the proposition that presentation of financial information in conformity with GAAP may not necessarily satisfy the disclosure obligations under the anti-fraud provisions of the federal securities laws.[15] The Original Release does not suggest, however, that issuers can override or not comply with GAAP in order to fairly present financial information, or adopt *pro forma* presentations for that purpose.[16]

---

[13] The SEC requested comment as to whether the certification requirement should be extended to other Exchange Act reports, such as registration statements on Form 10 and definitive proxy and information statements. SEC Release No. 33-8124 (Aug. 29, 2002). No action has yet been proposed or taken to extend the scope of the Section 302 certification requirement.

[14] Rule 12b-20 under the Exchange Act provides that "[i]n addition to the information expressly required to be included in a statement or report, there shall be added such further material information, if any, as may be necessary to make the required statements, in the light of the circumstances under which they were made not misleading."

[15] *See United States v. Simon*, 425 F.2d 796 (2d Cir. 1969); *In re Caterpillar, Inc.*, SEC Release No. 34-30532 (Mar. 31, 1992); *Edison Schools, Inc.*, SEC Release No. 34-45925 (May 14, 2002).

[16] Indeed, in separate rules adopted pursuant to Section 401(b) of the Sarbanes-Oxley Act, *pro forma* financial information—so called "non-GAAP financial measures"—included in any report filed

THE SARBANES-OXLEY ACT: ANALYSIS AND PRACTICE

Disclosure Controls and Procedures. Consistent with the Section 302 certification requirement, Rules 13a-15 and 15d-15 under the Exchange Act require that all reporting companies (other than asset-backed issuers) maintain disclosure controls and procedures. The term "disclosure controls and procedures" is defined as controls and other procedures of an issuer that are designed to ensure that information—whether financial or non-financial—required to be disclosed in reports filed or submitted under the Exchange Act is recorded, processed, summarized and reported within the required time periods.[17] They thus encompass both controls and procedures to assure the accuracy and completeness of narrative disclosures and internal financial controls of the type covered by the Foreign Corrupt Practices Act and § 13(b)(2) of the Exchange Act.[18]

Disclosure controls and procedures include measures designed to ensure that information required to be disclosed in Exchange Act reports is accumulated or communicated to the issuer's management, including its CEO and CFO, as appropriate to allow timely decisions regarding required disclosure. All Exchange Act reporting obligations are intended to be covered, including requirements to file current reports on Form 8-K (in the case of domestic issuers) or to furnish reports on Form 6-K (in the case of foreign private issuers), as well as definitive proxy materials, definitive information statements and beneficial ownership reports filed under § 13(d) of the Exchange Act.[19] According to the Original Release, disclosure controls and procedures are designed to capture the following:

- information potentially subject to disclosure under Regulation S-K, Regulation S-X and Forms 20-F and 40-F;

---

with the SEC, or in any other public disclosure, must be presented in a manner that does not contain any material misstatements or omissions and that reconciles the pro forma information with a GAAP presentation. SEC Release No. 33-8176 (Jan. 22, 2003).

[17] A company that fails to maintain adequate disclosure controls and procedures, to review them as required and otherwise to comply with the rules could be subject to SEC action for violating § 13(a) or § 15(d) of the Exchange Act even where the failure did not lead to flawed disclosure. Considerations relevant to the design of disclosure controls and procedures are discussed in Chapter VIII.

[18] § 13(b)(2) of the Exchange Act requires companies to maintain adequate books and records and adequate internal accounting controls. *See also* Exchange Act Rules 13b2-1 (prohibiting falsification of accounting records) and 13b2-2 (prohibiting false statements in connection with an audit or preparation or filing of any document or report required to be filed with the SEC).

[19] This requirement presents special issues for foreign private issuers insofar as they generally furnish to the SEC a significantly greater number of Form 6-K reports relative to the number of Form 8-K reports filed by U.S. issuers. This is often because many foreign private issuers simply furnish all press releases on Form 6-K rather than make case-by-case determinations as to their materiality. In light of the new rules, foreign private issuers should consider reviewing their current Form 6-K practices with a view to furnishing Form 6-K reports only with respect to information that is material. The disclosure controls and procedures maintained by foreign private issuers should be designed to ensure timely submission of Form 6-K reports and to take into account that information submitted in Form 6-K reports is subject to Rule 12b-20 under the Exchange Act.

CERTIFICATIONS AND INTERNAL CONTROL REPORTS

- information relevant to an assessment of the need to disclose developments and risks that pertain to the issuer's businesses (including, in some cases, an assessment and evaluation of operational and regulatory risks); and

- information that must be evaluated for disclosure under Exchange Act Rule 12b-20, as noted above.

Internal Control Over Financial Reporting. Because the original form of Section 302 certification was thought to be unclear in its application to internal financial controls, particularly their evaluation, the SEC amended the certification to introduce a new term, "internal control over financial reporting."[20] Subject to a lengthy transition period,[21] the SEC will require that issuers maintain and periodically evaluate their internal control over financial reporting. The changes to the certification derive from the separate SEC rulemaking noted above that implements Section 404 of the Act. That initiative will require, subject to the same transition period, each reporting company to include in its annual filings with the SEC a report of management containing, among other things, a statement of management's responsibility for establishing and maintaining adequate internal control over financial reporting and its conclusions about the effectiveness of the control. The company's independent auditor must attest to, and report separately on, management's report.

Relying substantially on the framework set out in the 1992 Report of the Committee of Sponsoring Organizations of the Treadway Commission (the "COSO Report"), as codified in existing auditing standards,[22] the SEC stated that internal control over financial reporting is but one element of a company's internal control structure.[23] Specifically, internal control over financial reporting is defined in the SEC's new rules as:

---

[20] SEC Release No. 33-8238 (June 5, 2003).

[21] The SEC's rules under Section 404 will become effective for "accelerated filers" (generally U.S. issuers with an equity capitalization of more than $75 million that have filed an annual report with the SEC) beginning with the annual report for their first fiscal year ending on or after June 15, 2004 (April 15, 2005 for all other issuers, including foreign private issuers).

[22] Committee of Sponsoring Organizations, *Internal Control—Integrated Framework* (1992); Codification of Statements on Auditing Standards (AU) § 319, *Consideration of Internal Control in a Financial Statement Audit.* The COSO Report has been supplemented twice, in 1994 and 1996. *See* Addendum to *Reporting to External Parties* (1994); *Internal Control Issues in Derivatives Usage—An Information Tool* (1996).

[23] SEC Release No. 33-8238 (June 5, 2003). According to the COSO Report and AU § 319, a company's internal control structure must also address the effectiveness and efficiency of a company's operations and its compliance with laws and regulations (not restricted to the U.S. federal securities laws). The SEC clarified, however, that compliance with laws and regulations directly related to the preparation of financial statements are included as part of internal control over financial reporting. *Id.* (citing AU § 317, *Illegal Acts by Clients*), 68 Fed. Reg. 36636, 36640 (June 18, 2003). For a foreign

a process designed by, or under the supervision of, the registrant's principal executive and principal financial officers, or persons performing similar functions, and effected by the registrant's board of directors, management and other personnel, to provide reasonable assurance regarding the reliability of financial reporting and the preparation of financial statements for external purposes in accordance with generally accepted accounting principles and includes those policies and procedures that

- pertain to the maintenance of records that in reasonable detail accurately and fairly reflect the transactions and dispositions of the assets of the registrant;

- provide reasonable assurance that transactions are recorded as necessary to permit preparation of financial statements in accordance with generally accepted accounting principles, and receipts and expenditures of the registrant are being made only in accordance with authorizations of management and directors of the registrant; and

- provide reasonable assurance regarding prevention or timely detection of unauthorized acquisition, use or disposition of the registrant's assets that could have a material effect on the financial statements.[24]

The relationship between disclosure controls and procedures and internal control over financial reporting remains somewhat unclear. The SEC has stated that there is "substantial overlap" between the two concepts, but has declined to provide any more specific guidance.[25] Instead, it has stated that:

. . . in designing their disclosure controls and procedures, companies can be expected to make judgments regarding the processes on which they will rely to meet applicable requirements. In doing so, some companies might design their disclosure controls and

---

private issuer, an important consequence of the SEC's statement is that internal control over financial reporting must also address the numerical reconciliation, required in Securities Act registration statements and Exchange Act reports, of the differences in the issuer's financial results and principal balance sheet items reported under home country GAAP and those that would have been obtained under U.S. GAAP and SEC regulations.

[24] *Id.*; *see also* Rules 13a-15(f) and 15d-15(f) under the Exchange Act. The SEC explicitly declined to incorporate existing auditing standards in its definition, referring to the view of commenters that accounting literature is oriented toward the planning and performance of financial statement audits, and not toward a determination of whether internal control is effective.

[25] SEC Release No. 33-8238 (June 5, 2003), 68 Fed. Reg. 36636, 36645 (June 18, 2003).

procedures so that certain components of internal control over financial reporting pertaining to the accurate recording of transactions and disposition of assets or to the safeguarding of assets are not included. For example, a company might have developed internal control over financial reporting that includes as a component of safeguarding assets dual signature requirements or limitations on signature authority on checks. That company could nonetheless determine that this component is not part of disclosure controls and procedures.[26]

Notwithstanding this commentary, the inclusion of the recordkeeping requirements of § 13(b)(2) within disclosure controls and procedures—and the consistency of those requirements, in the SEC's view, with internal control over financial reporting[27]—suggests that areas of disjunction are limited. The distinction seems most pertinent to the required evaluations, with internal control over financial reporting requiring a more detailed focus at all levels of the financial reporting structure.

Evaluation of Controls and Procedures. An issuer's management is required, with the participation of the CEO and CFO, to evaluate the effectiveness of the issuer's disclosure controls and procedures.[28] Subject to the transition period for management's internal control reports, management must also, with the participation of the CEO and CFO, evaluate the effectiveness of the issuer's internal control over financial reporting and changes in such control that occurred during the period that have materially affected, or are reasonably likely to materially affect, such control.[29]

In the Original Release, the SEC did not mandate any particular evaluation methodology with the expectation that each issuer will develop a process that is consistent with its business and internal management and supervisory practices. The SEC has stated, however, that evaluations (particularly interim evaluations) should generally focus on developments since the most recent evaluation.[30] These may include changes in the business of the company, significant corporate trans-

---

[26] *Id.*

[27] *Id.*, 68 Fed. Reg. 36636, 36640 (June 18, 2003).

[28] Rules 13a-15(b) and 15d-15(b) under the Exchange Act. This evaluation must be completed quarterly by U.S. issuers and annually by foreign private issuers. Commencing August 14, 2003, the evaluation must be conducted "as of" the end of the period covered by the relevant report. SEC Release No. 33-8238 (June 5, 2003). Questions that may be appropriate to address in connection with an evaluation are set out in Chapter VII.

[29] Rules 13a-15(c) and (d) and 15d-15(c) and (d) under the Exchange Act. The evaluation of the effectiveness of internal control over financial reporting must be made as of the issuer's fiscal year-end. The evaluation of material changes in such control must be made quarterly by U.S. issuers and annually by foreign private issuers.

[30] SEC Release No. 33-8238 (June 5, 2003), 68 Fed. Reg., 36636, 36645 (June 18, 2003).

actions (*e.g.*, mergers or divestitures), expansion into new geographic regions, significant changes in management or the organizational structure of the company and, of course, any significant deficiencies or material weaknesses in the controls and procedures or fraud or other improprieties that have been identified. Particular attention should be given to any development that suggests the potential for a systemic deficiency in the preparation of the company's disclosures.

The SEC also recommended that each company establish a "disclosure committee." The disclosure committee would be responsible for considering the materiality of information and determining disclosure obligations on a timely basis. The disclosure committee could also play an important role in evaluating an issuer's controls and procedures. The SEC suggested that the members of the committee could include:

- the principal accounting officer or the controller;

- the general counsel or other senior legal officer with responsibility for disclosure matters who reports to the general counsel;

- the principal risk management officer;

- the chief investor relations officer (or an officer with equivalent responsibilities); and

- such other officers or employees, including individuals associated with the company's business units, as the company deems appropriate.

The requirement to evaluate internal control over financial reporting, particularly for purposes of management's internal control reports, will require substantial action beyond the typical mandate of any disclosure committee. We expect that evaluations in this area will be largely conducted by a company's controllers and its internal audit personnel, although other personnel (*e.g.*, risk management and compliance) will play an important role. Because the principal accounting officer or controller can be expected to be a member of the disclosure committee, the key personnel involved in preparing disclosure will nonetheless be informed of potential concerns. Some companies may elect to have a separate committee charged with development and oversight of the internal audit plan and its ongoing execution. In this regard, the SEC recognized that the operation of controls can vary and stated that "management should perform evaluations of the design and operation of the company's entire system of internal control over financial reporting over a period of time that is adequate for it to determine whether, as of the end of the company's fiscal year, the design and operation of [such control] are effec-

CERTIFICATIONS AND INTERNAL CONTROL REPORTS

tive."[31] The SEC also stated that "quarterly evaluations of those components of internal control over financial reporting . . . subsumed within disclosure controls and procedures should be informed by the purposes of disclosure controls and procedures."[32]

While methodologies may vary among companies, management's evaluation of internal control over financial reporting must be based on a "suitable, recognized control framework that is established by a body or group that has followed due-process procedures, including the broad distribution of the framework for public comment."[33] For most U.S. companies, this framework will be that advanced in the COSO Report, while foreign private issuers may look to home country GAAP for guidance as to an appropriate framework.[34] Procedures undertaken to evaluate internal control over financial reporting must also be sufficient to evaluate its design and test its effectiveness.[35] Mere inquiry by management will generally not be sufficient.[36]

Of equal significance is the requirement, implemented as part of the rules under Section 404 of the Act, that evaluations be supported by sufficient "evidential matter," which must provide "reasonable support for management's assessment of the effectiveness of the registrant's internal control over financial reporting," including with respect to the design of internal control over financial reporting, and not only its operational effectiveness.[37] Specifically, the evidential matter should provide reasonable support "for the evaluation of whether the control is designed to prevent or detect material misstatements or omissions; for the

---

[31] SEC Release No. 33-8238 (June 5, 2003), 68 Fed. Reg. 36636, 36645 (June 18, 2003).

[32] *Id.*

[33] Rules 13a-15(c) and 15d-15(c) under the Exchange Act. A suitable framework must "be free from bias; permit reasonably consistent qualitative and quantitative measurements of a company's internal control; be sufficiently complete so that those relevant factors that would alter a conclusion about the effectiveness of a company's internal controls are not omitted; and be relevant to an evaluation of internal control over financial reporting." SEC Release No. 33-8238 (June 5, 2003) (citing Codification of Statements on Standards for Attestation Engagements (AT) § 101, *Attestation Engagements*, paragraph 24), 68 Fed. Reg. 36636, 36642 (June 18, 2003).

[34] The SEC identified *Guidance on Assessing Control*, published by the Canadian Institute of Chartered Accountants, and the *Turnbull Report*, published by the Institute of Chartered Accountants in England & Wales, as examples of appropriate frameworks. SEC Release No. 33-8238 (June 5, 2003), 68 Fed. Reg. 36636, 36642, n. 67 (June 18, 2003).

[35] The SEC has stated that controls subject to this assessment include "controls over initiating, recording, processing and reconciling account balances, classes of transactions and disclosure and related assertions included in the financial statements; controls related to the initiation and processing of non-routine and non-systematic transactions; controls related to the selection and application of appropriate accounting policies; and controls related to the prevention, identification and detection of fraud." SEC Release No. 33-8238 (June 5, 2003), 68 Fed. Reg. 36636, 36643 (June 18, 2003).

[36] *Id.*

[37] *See e.g.*, Instruction 1 to Item 308 of Regulation S-K and to Item 15 of Form 20-F.

THE SARBANES-OXLEY ACT: ANALYSIS AND PRACTICE

conclusion that the tests were appropriately planned and performed; and that the results of the tests were appropriately considered."[38]

Required Disclosures. A number of disclosure obligations accompany the Section 302 certification and the rules implementing Section 404 of the Act, which we discuss below.

The CEO and CFO must disclose to the independent auditor and the audit committee of the issuer all significant deficiencies and material weaknesses in the design or operation of internal control over financial reporting that are reasonably likely to adversely affect the company's ability to record, process, summarize and report financial information.[39] The certifying officers must also disclose to the independent auditor and the audit committee any fraud (regardless of materiality) involving management or other employees having a significant role in the issuer's internal control over financial reporting. Finally, the issuer must disclose in its periodic reports the conclusions of the CEO and the CFO as to the effectiveness of its disclosure controls and procedures and any material changes in internal control over financial reporting identified as part of the required evaluation.[40]

---

[38] SEC Release No. 33-8238 (June 5, 2003), 68 Fed. Reg. 36636, 36643 (June 18, 2003); *see also* AU § 326, *Evidential Matter.*

[39] This requirement is effective on August 14, 2003. The prior form of certification required that significant deficiencies be so disclosed, but that material weaknesses be identified only to the independent auditor.

Under existing auditing standards, an independent auditor must familiarize itself with internal controls in connection with the design and performance of the audit and report to the audit committee significant deficiencies or material weaknesses in internal controls. *See* AU § 325, *Communication of Internal Control Related Matters Noted in an Audit.*

Under AU § 325, a "material weakness" is defined as "a reportable condition in which the design or operation of one or more of the internal control components does not reduce to a relatively low degree the risk that misstatements caused by errors or fraud in amounts that would be material to the financial statements being audited may occur and not be detected within a timely period." The term will have the same meaning for purposes of the SEC's rules, and the term "significant deficiency" will have the same meaning as "reportable condition." A "reportable condition" is defined as "a significant deficiency in the design or operation of internal control, which could adversely affect the company's ability to record, process, summarize and report financial data consistent with the assertions of management in the financial statements." Noting the relationship between the two concepts, the SEC stated that an aggregation of significant deficiencies could constitute a material weakness, a conclusion that is consistent with existing accounting guidance. SEC Release No. 33-8238 (June 5, 2003); *see also* AT § 501, *Reporting on an Entity's Internal Control over Financial Reporting*, paragraph 39.

[40] *See, e.g.,* Items 307 and 308(c) of Regulation S-K. Many issuers have sought to elaborate the concept of "effectiveness" in their disclosures. Some have, for example, indicated that their disclosure controls and procedures are designed only to provide "reasonable assurance" that they will meet their objectives. The SEC staff has generally not objected to this disclosure, although the staff has required issuers to state, if true, that their disclosure controls and procedures are effective to provide that level of assurance, and the staff has not permitted companies to state that there can be "no assurance" as to the effective operation of the controls and procedures under all circumstances. The SEC has also noted that the definition of internal control over financial reporting includes the concept of reasonable assurance. SEC Release No. 33-8238 (June 5, 2003), 68 Fed. Reg. 36636, 36647 (June 18, 2003).

CERTIFICATIONS AND INTERNAL CONTROL REPORTS

As previously noted,[41] the requirement to evaluate internal control over financial reporting and material changes in such control is subject to an extended transition period. Nevertheless, the requirement *to disclose* material changes in internal control over financial reporting becomes effective on August 14, 2003. The requirement to make certain disclosures to the issuer's independent auditor and audit committee is also effective on that date, notwithstanding that it is to be "based on the most recent evaluation of internal control over financial reporting."

This approach reflects the staff's view that these new disclosure requirements are not a departure from existing requirements. During the transition period, companies should continue to follow the guidance that the SEC staff provided in its answers to "frequently asked questions" about the Sarbanes-Oxley Act.[42] Question 20 of that "FAQ" stated that, pending final rules under Section 404, the staff would interpret "internal controls and procedures for financial reporting" and "internal controls" by reference to existing accounting literature, *viz.* AU § 319. In Question 22, the staff also reiterated that some elements of internal control are included within disclosure controls and procedures, notably those maintained under § 13(b)(2) of the Exchange Act.

Subject to the extended transition period previously noted, management's report on internal control over financial reporting must be disclosed in the issuer's annual report. The report must:

- state management's responsibility for establishing and maintaining adequate internal control over financial reporting for the issuer;

- identify the framework used by management to evaluate the effectiveness of such control;

- state management's assessment of the effectiveness of the issuer's internal control over financial reporting as of the issuer's fiscal year-end, including a statement as to whether or not such control is effective and a disclosure of any material weakness identified by management;[43] and

- state that the issuer's independent auditor has issued an attestation report on management's assessment of the issuer's internal control over financial reporting.

The attestation report of the independent auditor with respect to management's report must also be included in the annual report. The PCAOB is respon-

---

[41] *See* Note 21 *supra.*

[42] Division of Corporation Finance: Sarbanes-Oxley Act of 2002—Frequently Asked Questions (last revised Nov. 14, 2002).

[43] Management may not conclude that internal control over financial reporting is effective if one or more material weaknesses have been identified.

sible for adopting the relevant attestation standard. In doing so, the PCAOB has stated that it will consider both the existing standard (AT § 501), as well as an exposure draft issued by the AICPA in March 2003.[44]

Issuers of Asset-Backed Securities. Because the information required to be reported under the Exchange Act by asset-backed issuers differs significantly from that required of operating companies, the rules apply separate certification requirements to issuers of asset-backed securities. The SEC also elected not to extend to asset-backed issuers the new requirements concerning internal control over financial reporting and management's related reporting obligation.[45] Rules 13a-14 and 15d-14 under the Exchange Act require asset-backed issuers[46] to provide a certification addressing:

- review by the certifying officer of the annual report and other reports containing distribution information for the period covered by the annual report;

- the absence in the report, to the best of the certifying officer's knowledge, of any material misstatements or omissions;

- the inclusion in the report, to the best of the certifying officer's knowledge, of the financial information required to be provided to the trustee under the governing documents of the issuer; and

- compliance by the servicer with the servicing obligations and minimum servicing standards.

The certification must be executed by the trustee of the trust (if the trustee signs the annual periodic report) or the senior officer in charge of securitization of the depositor (if the depositor signs the annual periodic report). Alternatively, the rules provide that the senior officer in charge of the servicing function of the master servicer (or entity performing equivalent functions) may execute the certification. While the SEC did not prescribe a form of certification, the staff of the SEC's

---

[44] *See* AICPA Auditing Standards Board, Proposed Statements on Auditing Standards, *Auditing an Entity's Internal Control Over Financial Reporting in Conjunction with the Financial Statement Audit*, and Proposed Statement on Standards for Attestation Engagements, *Reporting on an Entity's Internal Control Over Financial Reporting* (Mar. 18, 2003).

[45] SEC Release No. 33-8238 (June 5, 2003).

[46] The term "asset-backed issuer" is defined as any issuer whose reporting obligation results from the registration of securities it issued that are primarily serviced by the cash flows of a discrete pool of receivables or other financial assets, either fixed or revolving, that by their terms convert into cash within a finite time period plus any rights or other assets designed to assure the servicing or timely distribution of proceeds to security holders.

CERTIFICATIONS AND INTERNAL CONTROL REPORTS

Division of Corporation Finance issued a separate statement including a form that it believes satisfies the rules.[47]

Registered Investment Companies. Rules 30a-2 and 30a-3 under the Investment Company Act implement the certification and related requirements of Section 302 for registered investment companies.[48] Registered management investment companies, including mutual funds, regardless of whether they are subject to § 13(a) or § 15(d) of the Exchange Act, must file certified semi-annual shareholder reports with the SEC on a new Form N-CSR. They must also maintain and regularly evaluate disclosure controls and procedures designed to ensure that the information required in the investment company's Exchange Act reports is collected, processed and disclosed on a timely basis. While Section 404 of the Sarbanes-Oxley Act is not applicable to registered investment companies, the SEC has nevertheless imposed on them the requirement to maintain internal control over financial reporting.[49] As a result, the original form of certification for investment companies has been amended in several respects.

Execution of Section 302 Certification. Each officer must provide a separate certification, and the certifications must be filed as exhibits to the related periodic report.[50] In addition, the certification must be in a prescribed form and "may not be changed in any respect (even if the change would appear to be inconsequential in nature)."[51] The certification must be signed directly by each officer, and may not be signed on his or her behalf pursuant to a power of attorney.

Liability for False Section 302 Certifications. Although a certifying officer who is a signatory to a report has Exchange Act liability in that capacity, an

---

[47] Revised Statement: Compliance by Asset-Backed Issuers with Exchange Act Rules 13a-14 and 15d-14 (Feb. 21, 2003). The original SEC interpretation is set out in Statement by the Staff of the Division of Corporation Finance of the Securities and Exchange Commission Regarding Compliance by Asset-Backed Issuers with Exchange Act Rules 13a-14 and 15d-14 (Aug. 27, 2002).

[48] SEC Release No. 34-47262 (Jan. 27, 2003). Rule 30a-2 was also amended to require that the certifications be provided as exhibits to Form N-CSR. SEC Release No. 33-8238 (June 5, 2003).

[49] SEC Release No. 33-8238 (June 5, 2003); *see also* Rule 30a-3 under the Investment Company Act.

[50] The SEC originally required that the Section 302 certifications be included on the signature page of the related periodic report. In its release proposing the amended filing approach, the SEC stated that the placement of Section 302 certifications below the signature block does not allow investors to access them easily using the EDGAR filing system. SEC Release No. 33-8212 (Mar. 21, 2003) (the "March Release"). The original approach also required the SEC staff to review the text of a periodic report to determine compliance with Section 302. The SEC reasoned that, as exhibits, the Section 302 certifications would continue to form part of the related reports, as required by the Sarbanes-Oxley Act.

[51] Because the SEC's most recent amendments of the Section 302 certification requirement will become effective in two stages, the SEC has stated that issuers may temporarily modify the form of certification to eliminate language that will become effective only in the second stage.

THE SARBANES-OXLEY ACT: ANALYSIS AND PRACTICE

officer providing a false certification could be subject, on a separate basis in his or her personal capacity, to SEC action for violating § 13(a) or 15(d) of the Exchange Act and to SEC and private actions for violating Exchange Act § 10(b) and Rule 10b-5 thereunder. The Director of the SEC's Division of Corporation Finance stated in connection with the adoption of the original certification rules that this liability could include criminal penalties separate and apart from those provided by Section 906 of the Sarbanes-Oxley Act.[52]

Transition Period. All covered reports filed after August 29, 2002 (including amendments to reports previously filed before that date) must include the certifications regarding review of the report, the absence of material misstatements and omissions and fair presentation of financial information.[53] As noted above, the recent amendments to the Section 302 certification will generally become effective on August 14, 2003. The principal exception to this effective date is the certification stating the CEO's and CFO's responsibility for the company's internal control over financial reporting. That requirement will be effective for U.S. issuers that are "accelerated filers" beginning with the annual report for their first fiscal year ending on or after June 15, 2004 (April 15, 2005 for all other issuers, including foreign private issuers).

SECTION 906 CERTIFICATION

Section 906 of the Sarbanes-Oxley Act requires a separate officer certification to "accompany" each "periodic report containing financial statements filed by an issuer with the [SEC]." The certification is to the effect that "the periodic report containing the financial statements fully complies with the requirements of section 13(a) or 15(d) of the [Exchange Act] and that information contained in the periodic report fairly presents, in all material respects, the financial condition and results of operations of the issuer." As Section 906 amends the U.S. criminal code, it is subject to enforcement by the Department of Justice and requires no rulemaking by the SEC.

---

[52] In an administrative proceeding brought against HealthSouth Corporation and its former chief executive officer alleging a $1.4 billion accounting fraud, the SEC alleged that the chief executive officer "knew or was reckless in not knowing that [HealthSouth's] financial statements materially overstated its operating results [but nevertheless] certified under oath that [HealthSouth's] 2001 Form 10-K contained no 'untrue statement of material fact.'" SEC Litigation Release No. 18044 (Mar. 20, 2003). While the certification involved was made pursuant to a special SEC order (*see* Order 4-460, Order Requiring the Filing of Sworn Statements Pursuant to § 21(a)(1) of the Securities Exchange Act of 1934 (June 27, 2002)), and not pursuant to the Section 302 certification rules, the SEC's allegations demonstrate its intention to use the officer certification requirement as a basis for asserting the personal liability of senior officials of public companies.

[53] However, only covered reports filed for periods ending after August 29, 2002 must include the certifications regarding disclosure controls and procedures and internal controls. In addition, the requirement to evaluate disclosure controls and procedures also applies only to covered reports filed for periods ending after August 29, 2002.

CERTIFICATIONS AND INTERNAL CONTROL REPORTS

There is some inconsistency in the SEC's rules and other pronouncements in the use of the terms "periodic" and "filed" and whether those terms apply to reports on Forms 8-K and 6-K. The better view is that Section 906 was not intended to apply to reports on these forms that contain financial statements filed with (in the case of Form 8-K) or submitted to (in the case of Form 6-K) the SEC. The Original Release supports this interpretation of Section 906, as it refers to reports on Forms 8-K and 6-K as "current reports . . . rather than periodic (quarterly and annual) reports," and also states that the SEC "[does] not believe that a Form 6-K constitutes a 'periodic' report analogous to a quarterly report." The March Release confirms this conclusion by stating that the Section 906 certification only applies to quarterly, semi-annual and annual reports that contain financial statements,[54] making it comparable to the Section 302 requirement.[55]

As stated above, the Section 906 certification need only "accompany" the relevant report, and companies have provided the certification in a variety of ways. Effective August 14, 2003, companies must file the Section 906 certification as an exhibit to the relevant report.[56] Periodic reports failing to include the Section 906 certifications will therefore be incomplete and not in compliance with

---

[54] The March Release does not, however, expressly exempt from the Section 906 certification requirement an employee stock purchase plan's annual report on Form 11-K as is the case with the Section 302 certification requirement. While members of the SEC staff have informally indicated their view that Section 906 applies to Form 11-K, the SEC has stated only that it will continue to discuss the applicability of Section 906 in that context in light of recent statements by Sen. Joseph R. Biden, Jr. See Note 55 infra. SEC Release No. 33-8238 (June 5, 2003), 68 Fed. Reg. 36636, 36652 (June 18, 2003). The SEC has confirmed that amendments to periodic reports that do not contain financial statements are not subject to Section 906. SEC Release No. 33-8238 (June 5, 2003), 68 Fed. Reg. 36636, 36653 (June 18, 2003).

[55] In a statement read into the Congressional Record on April 11, 2003, Sen. Joseph R. Biden, Jr. stated that the scope of the certification under Section 302 of the Sarbanes-Oxley Act was intentionally narrower than that of the certification required under Section 906. See Statement of Sen. Joseph R. Biden, Jr., "Legislative History of Title IX of the Sarbanes-Oxley Act of 2002," 149 CONG. REC. S5325 (daily ed. Apr. 11, 2003). The Senator also stated that Section 906 was intended to apply to "so-called 'current' reports like Forms 8-K and 6-K . . . ." *Id.* Nonetheless—and notwithstanding its title—whether Senator Biden's statement should be accorded weight as legislative history of the Act is dubious. *See, e.g., Chicasaw Nation v. United States*, 534 U.S. 84 (2001) (citing *Heinz v. Jenkins*, U.S. 291 (1995)); *Clarke v. Securities Industry Association*, 479 U.S. 388 (1987). In light of these Supreme Court decisions, Senator Biden's commentary would likely be viewed solely as the views of one "informed person," rather than as a statement upon which legislators relied in adopting Section 906. In acknowledging Senator Biden's statement, the SEC expressed concern that the extension of Section 906 to reports on Forms 8-K and 6-K "could potentially chill the disclosure of information by companies." SEC Release No. 33-8238 (June 5, 2003), 68 Fed. Reg. 36636, 36652 (June 18, 2003). Nevertheless, in light of the Senator's statement, the SEC is continuing to consider the scope of Section 906 with the Department of Justice. *Id.*

[56] SEC Release No. 33-8238 (June 5, 2003). The Section 906 certifications would as a result become subject to the signature requirements of Rule 302 of Regulation S-T. These requirements relate primarily to submission of documents with signatures in typed form via the EDGAR system and to retention of the related manually-signed signature pages.

§ 13(a) of the Exchange Act. Because Section 906 certifications need only "accompany" the related periodic report, these certifications will be deemed only to be "furnished," rather than "filed." Accordingly, Section 906 certifications will not be subject to the civil anti-fraud provisions of Exchange Act § 18, nor will they be automatically incorporated by reference into an issuer's Securities Act registration statements.

Pending effectiveness of the above requirement, the SEC has encouraged issuers to submit Section 906 certifications as "additional exhibits" to the applicable report under Item 99 of Item 601(b) of Regulation S-K or, in the case of foreign private issuers, in accordance with the requirements of the applicable form. Consistent with the effect of the new rules, the March Release states that Section 906 certifications so submitted will be treated as "accompanying" the related report, rather than "filed" as part of the report.

As is the case for the Section 302 certification, the certifying officers may not sign by power of attorney. However, only a single certification is required, which in that event must be signed by both the CEO and CFO.

Section 906 imposes criminal liability for inaccurate certifications knowingly or willfully furnished by a CEO or CFO. Companies could also be subject to civil liability under common law theories of fraud and other causes of action.[57]

---

[57] While Section 906 penalizes willfully or knowingly false certifications, it fails explicitly to penalize the failure to file any certification whatsoever. In an exchange of letters between Sen. Joseph R. Biden, Jr. and the Department of Justice, however, the latter clarified that it would "utilize [the criminal provisions of the Exchange Act, codified at 15 U.S.C. 78ff] to prosecute executives who violate the Sarbanes-Oxley Act by willfully failing to file Section 906's required certification." *See* Letter of Assistant Attorney General Daniel J. Bryant to the Honorable Joseph R. Biden, Jr. (Dec. 26, 2002). In any event, the SEC may refer violations of the Exchange Act to the Department of Justice for criminal prosecution under § 32 of the Exchange Act, and the Department of Justice can independently bring criminal proceedings for willful violations of any provision of the Exchange Act or the rules and regulations thereunder. As noted above, the failure to file a Section 906 certification as an exhibit to a periodic report would result in a violation of the Exchange Act and related rules and thus exposure of the relevant officers to criminal prosecution if the failure were willful.

VII QUESTIONS TO ASK BEFORE CERTIFYING PERIODIC REPORTS

In August 2002, the SEC issued rules implementing the certification requirements of Section 302 of the Sarbanes-Oxley Act. These rules, together with Section 906 of the Sarbanes-Oxley Act, require CEOs and CFOs of all SEC-reporting companies to certify the accuracy of their annual and (in the case of U.S. companies) quarterly reports.[1] The forms of certification required under Sections 302 and 906 are reproduced in Appendix D.

Under the new rules, CEOs and CFOs are also responsible for the design, maintenance and evaluation of their companies' disclosure controls and procedures and, subject to a lengthy transition period, their internal control over financial reporting.[2] (We sometimes refer below to a company's "controls and procedures" to address both concepts.) Although current reports on Form 8-K by U.S. issuers and on Form 6-K by foreign private issuers are not subject to certification, controls and procedures are required to be designed, maintained and evaluated to ensure full and timely disclosure in those reports, as well as in definitive proxy and information statements. We recommend that every CEO and CFO review existing procedures for preparing SEC filings with a view to formalizing them and determining a method for evaluating them.[3]

While the CEO and CFO must certify as to their conduct of evaluation of the company's controls and procedures, this does not preclude reliance on subordinates to assist in that evaluation.[4] Some of the areas of inquiry we suggest should be addressed by senior management personnel who have played a significant role in the implementation of the company's controls and procedures. These personnel are well positioned to offer views about the efficacy of the company's controls and procedures both as a general matter and as they apply to the report in question. Those companies that have established "disclosure committees" as suggested by

---

[1] These certification requirements and related SEC rules are discussed more fully in Chapter VI.

[2] Some elements of the certification pertaining to internal control over financial reporting are effective commencing August 14, 2003, notwithstanding that the requirements to maintain and evaluate such control are not yet effective. *See* Note 5 *infra* and accompanying text.

[3] Issues that should be considered in designing controls and procedures are addressed in Chapter VIII.

[4] Indeed, Rules 13a-15 and 15d-15 under the Exchange Act require that "management, . . . with the participation of" the CEO and CFO, must conduct the evaluation of the company's controls and procedures.

the SEC generally also require that the committee members assist in the evaluation of the company's controls and procedures.

Before providing the required certifications, CEOs and CFOs should consider the following questions:

WERE YOU PERSONALLY INVOLVED?

This is a *personal* certification. While you of course must rely on your subordinates for help in formalizing and evaluating the company's controls and procedures and preparing the report you are certifying, you must participate directly in the review of that report and in the design (or supervision of the design), maintenance and evaluation of your company's controls and procedures as they apply to all of the company's public disclosures, including current reports on Forms 8-K and 6-K as stated above.

DID YOU MAKE THE REPORTING PROCESS A PRIORITY?

Setting the right "tone at the top" has never been more important. Emphasize to management and employees at every opportunity the importance you place on accurate and timely disclosure, and make it clear that people should treat disclosure preparation seriously.

DID YOU READ THE REPORT CAREFULLY?

To state the obvious, you must read carefully the report that will be covered by the certifications. Does the report provide an accurate and complete picture of the company's financial condition, performance and cash flows as you know it? Does the report reflect material trends in your industry, general economic conditions or other factors that could affect the company's financial condition or results? Consider your disclosure in light of best practices. Ask questions about anything you do not understand.

DID YOU EVALUATE THE PROCEDURES USED TO PREPARE THE REPORT?

How much confidence do the company's controls and procedures give you that the company is able to record, process, summarize and report to the SEC required information on a timely basis? Are the controls and procedures adequate to ensure that there are no material errors or omissions in the company's reports generally, as well as in the report you are certifying?

- Review staffing. Are the right people involved in the preparation of the company's public disclosures, including the report you are certifying?

BEFORE CERTIFYING PERIODIC REPORTS

- —Do the people responsible for preparing initial drafts of the company's public disclosures have the appropriate level of skill and experience?

- —Do the preparers have access to the people with the information required to be disclosed? Are the people with that information responsive to inquiries and requests from the preparers, including in the case of the report you are certifying?

- —In the case of the report you are certifying, was additional staffing required? Would it have improved the quality of that report?

- —Did there continue to be sufficient staffing in light of employee turnover during this period? Should more staff be involved in future periods?

• Evaluate whether there was enough time. Do the procedures afford enough time to prepare quality disclosure, including in the case of the report you are certifying?

- —Was there enough time to prepare a high quality initial draft of the report you are certifying?

- —Was there enough time for a thorough review and exchange of comments on that draft and any subsequent drafts?

• Test the accuracy of the controls and procedures. Assign company personnel the specific responsibility of confirming how well the company's controls and procedures worked with respect to selected important transactions or contracts. Review the results of their inquiries with those personnel.

- —Were the files and underlying documentation provided to the preparers of the company's reports in the most recent period adequate?

- —Was the disclosure prepared in a timely manner? Was it included in the initial draft? If not, at what point in the process was the transaction or contract flagged for disclosure?

- —Was the disclosure of the transaction or contract accurate?

- —Make sure that there is an employee with specific responsibility for confirming that the disclosure complies with SEC form and rule requirements. Did the "form check" reveal any instances in which the information provided was not responsive to SEC requirements? If so, were they corrected?

- Focus on key areas of risk. What steps is the company taking to identify and address these areas both as a general matter and in the case of the period covered by the report you are certifying?

- Review the disclosure in the report you are certifying that addresses the effectiveness of your company's disclosure controls and procedures and material changes in the company's internal control over financial reporting. Does this disclosure accurately reflect the conclusions reached in your evaluation?

- Where a problem occurred, determine why and modify the company's controls and procedures to address the problem. How serious was the problem? Did it involve low-level employees or senior management? Did it involve active misconduct? It will be important not only to make appropriate changes, but also to follow up to ensure implementation and effectiveness of the changes.

DID YOU REVIEW THE COMPANY'S INTERNAL CONTROL OVER FINANCIAL REPORTING?

Consider whether the company's internal control structure and current systems give you enough comfort that financial disclosures are accurate.

While you must certify only as to changes in internal control over financial reporting during the most recent quarterly period (or annual period in the case of foreign private issuers) that have materially affected or are reasonably likely to materially affect such control, doing so requires an understanding of the company's internal control structure.[5] Some questions that can aid in a preliminary understanding of internal control are set out below.

In future periods, this element of the certification will also depend largely on the work preparatory to management's separate report on the company's inter-

---

[5] This element of the certification is effective beginning August 14, 2003. As previously noted, the maintenance and evaluation of internal control over financial reporting will not then be required. This element must therefore be interpreted based on prior interim guidance of the staff of the SEC provided with respect to "internal controls" shortly after enactment of the Sarbanes-Oxley Act. Under that guidance, the basis for this certification would be a review of those internal controls that are part of an issuer's disclosure controls and procedures (*e.g.*, books and records maintained pursuant to § 13(b)(2) of the Exchange Act). *See* Division of Corporation Finance: Sarbanes-Oxley Act of 2002—Frequently Asked Questions (last revised Nov. 14, 2002); *see also* Chapter VI, text accompanying Note 41.

BEFORE CERTIFYING PERIODIC REPORTS

nal control over financial reporting. The requirement for this report will become effective in the case of U.S. "accelerated filers" beginning with the annual report for their first fiscal year ending on or after June 15, 2004 (April 15, 2005 for all other issuers, including foreign private issuers). In this connection, the SEC has stated that "an assessment of the effectiveness of internal control over financial reporting must be supported by evidential matter, including documentation, regarding both the design of internal controls and the testing processes."[6] The SEC has also emphasized the importance of adequate testing for these purposes by stating that "inquiry alone generally will not provide an adequate basis for management's assessment."[7]

- Does management have an appropriate framework for evaluating the adequacy of internal control over financial reporting (*e.g.*, the 1992 Report of the Committee of Sponsoring Organizations of the Treadway Commission, sometimes known as the "COSO Report")? Does management engage in sufficient and appropriate testing and evaluation of its internal control over financial reporting? Is there appropriate evidence of testing procedures and the results?[8]

- What is the structure of the company's internal control over financial reporting (*i.e.*, senior management and departmental responsibilities, internal reporting lines and the reporting line to the company's audit committee)? Is it appropriate in light of the scope and complexity of the company's operations?

- Is the internal audit plan appropriately prioritized to reflect the current risk profile of the company? Is the internal audit for the current fiscal year subject to an appropriate planning and documentation process? Is the internal audit on target for completion as planned? Do adjustments need to be made?

---

[6] SEC Release No. 33-8238 (June 5, 2003), 68 Fed. Reg. 36636, 36643 (June 18, 2003); *see also* AU § 326, *Evidential Matter*.

[7] *Id*. The SEC expects that management will perform evaluations of the company's entire system of internal control over financial reporting over a period of time that will be "adequate for it to determine whether, as of the end of the company's fiscal year, the design and operation of [such] control are effective." *Id*., 68 Fed. Reg. 36636, 36644 (June 18, 2003).

[8] § 13(b)(2) of the Exchange Act requires that reporting companies "make and keep books, records, and accounts, which in reasonable detail, accurately and fairly reflect the transactions and dispositions of the assets of the issuer." The SEC has stated that these books and records should include "not only general ledgers and accounting entries, but also memoranda and internal corporate reports." SEC Release No. 33-8238 (June 5, 2003), 68 Fed. Reg. 36636, 36643, n. 76 (June 18, 2003) (citing *In re Microsoft*, Admin. Proc. File No. 3-10789 (June 3, 2002)); *see also* SEC Release No. 34-17500 (Jan. 29, 1981).

- Are the financial and reporting systems (including the company's use of the Internet and other electronic systems) adequate and secure so as to produce consistently accurate results?

- What controls exist to prevent and detect fraud and other financial or accounting improprieties? Are they adequate?

  — Does the company have a system by which employees or others can report financial or accounting impropriety on a confidential and anonymous basis and without fear of punishment? Does the company have a system by which internal and external lawyers can report evidence of a material violation of the securities laws or similar violations? Were any reports made?

  — Were there any instances of fraud, whether or not material, uncovered during the most recent period that involve management or other employees who have a significant role in the company's internal control over financial reporting?

- Are significant controls appropriately documented? For these purposes, significant controls would include any controls the failure of which could result in a material misstatement in the company's financial statements, such as controls over significant accounts (*i.e.*, initiating, recording, processing and reconciling account balances, transactions, disclosure and assertions in the financial statements), areas of disclosure that involve a high degree of subjectivity or judgment, manual journal entries and consolidating entries.

- Are there adequate controls over special or non-routine or non-systematic transactions (*e.g.*, related party transactions, transactions involving special purpose entities or other off-balance sheet transactions)?

- Where are the weak points in the system? Have the internal auditors or the independent auditor raised any issues about the adequacy of internal controls? In particular, were there any significant deficiencies or material weaknesses that were discovered in the most recent period or that are pending from prior periods?[9] If so, are they appropriately disclosed and what steps are being taken to address them?[10]

---

[9] *See* Chapter VI, Note 39, for guidance as to the meanings of these terms.
[10] It is noteworthy that in connection with management's report on internal control over financial reporting, management will be expressly prohibited from concluding that such control is effective if there are one or more material weaknesses in the company's internal control over financial reporting. Item 308(a)(3) of Regulation S-K.

BEFORE CERTIFYING PERIODIC REPORTS

DID YOU TALK TO THE KEY PEOPLE RESPONSIBLE FOR PREPARING THE REPORT?

Convene a "cabinet" session or a meeting of the company's disclosure committee (*i.e.*, a meeting of the key senior personnel responsible for implementing the company's controls and procedures and for the disclosures included in the report you are certifying) to ask questions including:

- Is there any area of our company's disclosure that makes you uncomfortable?

- Is there any area of our financial reporting that is questionable?

- Are you aware of any attempt by company personnel to improperly influence or hinder the independent auditor in the performance of its engagement?

- If it were you, and you faced criminal penalties if you were wrong, would you sign this certification?

- If the company's controls and procedures call for internal chains of certifications or other special verification procedures, were the internal certifications with respect to the report you are certifying completed without qualification? Were the verification procedures completed and effective?

DID YOU IDENTIFY THE DISCLOSURE AREAS THAT ARE MOST PRONE TO ERROR AND MERIT A SECOND LOOK?

Questions that may help identify these areas include:

- If there were errors in the report, where would they be most likely to appear?

- What areas of the company's disclosure have raised questions in the past?

- Where have others in the industry recently experienced problems?

- What are the hot button issues for the SEC that are relevant to the company? (*e.g.*, critical accounting estimates, revenue recognition, reserves, asset impairment, off-balance sheet arrangements, window dressing transactions, related party transactions and use of non-GAAP financial measures)

DID YOU FOLLOW UP ON SPECIAL ISSUES?

Questions that may help identify these issues include:

- Have there been any disagreements with the independent auditor?

- Did the company consult with any other auditor for any reason during the period? What were the circumstances? What was the resolution?

- What comments has the SEC made on the company's filings in the past?

- Have there been any significant audit or other post-closing adjustments?

- Have analysts or other third party observers publicly questioned any of the company's accounting or disclosure practices?

- Are there areas of disclosure where the company's key competitors (or others in the industry) provide significantly greater detail than the company? Would the additional detail also be appropriate for the company's disclosure?

- Does the company have an internal code of conduct? Have there been any violations or waivers of its provisions?

- What other "diligence" inquiries were conducted to support the disclosures included in the report you are certifying? Did they raise any issues?

DID YOU TALK TO YOUR INDEPENDENT AUDITOR?

Discuss the certifications with your independent auditor. Discuss any significant deficiencies or material weaknesses in your company's internal control over financial reporting, or any fraud involving management or other employees with a significant role in internal control over financial reporting. Questions you may wish to ask the independent auditor include:

- If the independent auditor were solely responsible for preparing the financial statements, is there anything it would have done differently?

- Did the independent auditor raise any key issues in the course of the audit of the annual financial statements or any required review of the company's interim financial statements? Did the independent auditor consult with its national office about any matter pertaining to the company's financial statements or accounting for any particular transaction? If so, what was the resolution?

BEFORE CERTIFYING PERIODIC REPORTS

- Did the independent auditor have any concerns about the company's controls and procedures and, particulary, the company's internal control over financial reporting? Is the interface between internal and independent auditors working well so that the independent auditor is getting the information and cooperation it needs? Did any company personnel attempt to hinder or improperly influence the independent auditor?

- In what ways is the company's accounting aggressive? Where are there alternative treatments possible under GAAP? Why were the alternatives rejected?

- What adjustments suggested by the independent auditor in the period have not been made?

- If the company were doing a registered offering with the SEC right now, what areas of its accounting might the SEC question?

DID YOU MEET WITH YOUR AUDIT COMMITTEE?

Discuss with the audit committee (or persons performing the equivalent function) the certifications, the verification procedures you have undertaken and any significant issues that have been raised. Based on your most recent annual evaluation of the company's internal control over financial reporting,[11] discuss any significant deficiencies or material weaknesses in such control or any fraud involving management or other employees with a significant role in internal controls.

- Ask the audit committee about its involvement in the preparation or review of the report. Did it fulfill the obligations set out in its mandate or charter? Did it receive all the cooperation it needed? Did it or the internal or independent auditor identify any significant issues?

- Confirm that your audit committee is comfortable with the content of the certification and the procedures supporting it.

- Is the audit committee satisfied with the company's controls and procedures?

---

[11] This element of the certification is effective beginning August 14, 2003, notwithstanding that it is explicitly based on an evaluation of internal control over financial reporting. See Note 5 *supra*.

DID YOU KEEP A RECORD?

You should keep a record of the steps you take in reviewing the report you are certifying and in evaluating the company's controls and procedures. If you require that other company personnel or external advisors provide certifications, a record of those documents should also be kept.

DID YOU CONSULT WITH OUTSIDE COUNSEL?

If you have elected to involve outside counsel as part of your evaluation, did counsel have adequate time to make a meaningful contribution? Even where counsel has not been involved, if the above steps give rise to any significant issues, you should consider the need to consult outside counsel to formulate a response.

VIII DESIGNING DISCLOSURE CONTROLS AND PROCEDURES

The SEC's final rules under Section 302 of the Sarbanes-Oxley Act, effective on August 29, 2002, require the CEO and CFO of each SEC-reporting company (whether U.S. or non-U.S.) to take responsibility for the company's disclosure controls and procedures and the company's internal control over financial reporting. (We sometimes refer below to a company's "controls and procedures" to address both concepts.) As part of the new regime, the CEO and CFO must certify, in connection with each periodic report filed with the SEC, the quality of the company's public disclosure and the effectiveness of these controls and procedures.

Separately, Section 906 of the Sarbanes-Oxley Act imposes a second officer certification requirement that also addresses the quality of a reporting company's disclosures. This requirement became effective on July 30, 2002.[1]

The following are considerations that should be taken into account to satisfy the new rules with respect to a company's controls and procedures and to ensure that the CEO and CFO can provide the required certifications.

DEFINITION OF CONTROLS AND PROCEDURES

As defined by the SEC, "disclosure controls and procedures" are controls and other procedures of an issuer that are designed to ensure that information required to be disclosed by the issuer in the reports that it files or submits under the Exchange Act is recorded, processed, summarized and reported within the time periods specified in the SEC's rules and forms.[2] A company's disclosure controls and procedures must include measures designed to ensure that information required to be disclosed is accumulated and communicated to the issuer's management, including its CEO and CFO, or persons performing similar functions, to allow timely decisions regarding required disclosures. The disclosure controls and

---

[1] The forms of certification required under Sections 302 and 906 are reproduced in Appendix D. The certification requirement and the requirement to maintain controls and procedures are discussed more fully in Chapter VI.

[2] *See* Rules 13a-14 and 15d-14 under the Exchange Act. Effective August 14, 2003, the definition will be moved to new Rules 13a-15(e) and 15d-15(e) under the Exchange Act. SEC Release No. 33-8238 (June 5, 2003).

procedures should be broad enough to capture information that is potentially material and subject to disclosure.

In its original release on this subject, the SEC distinguished between "internal controls" and "disclosure controls and procedures," and stated that disclosure controls and procedures should cover both narrative and financial disclosures. In recently adopted rules implementing Section 404 of the Sarbanes-Oxley Act, the SEC clarified this point by introducing the term "internal control over financial reporting."[3] Under relevant accounting literature, this control is a subset of internal controls and would effectively represent those controls that are maintained by reporting companies under § 13(b)(2) of the Exchange Act, which pertains to financial reporting.[4]

Specifically, the term "internal control over financial reporting" is defined as:

a process designed by, or under the supervision of, the issuer's principal executive and principal financial officers, or persons performing similar functions, and effected by the issuer's board of directors, management and other personnel, to provide reasonable assurance regarding the reliability of financial reporting and the preparation of financial statements for external purposes in accordance with GAAP and includes those policies and procedures that

- pertain to the maintenance of records that in reasonable detail accurately and fairly reflect the transactions and dispositions of the assets of the issuer;

- provide reasonable assurance that transactions are recorded as necessary to permit preparation of financial statements in accordance with GAAP, and that receipts and expenditures of the issuer are being made only in accordance with authorizations of management and directors of the issuer; and

- provide reasonable assurance regarding prevention or timely detection of unauthorized acquisition, use or disposition of the issuer's assets that could have a material effect on the financial statements.[5]

The SEC's certification requirements cover periodic reports, such as Forms 10-K and 10-Q for U.S. issuers and Form 20-F for foreign private issuers and

---

[3] SEC Release No. 33-8238 (June 5, 2003).

[4] *See, e.g.*, Codification of Statements on Auditing Standards (AU) § 319, *Consideration of Internal Control in a Financial Statement Audit*, under which a company's internal control structure also includes the effectiveness and efficiency of its operations and compliance with laws and regulations.

[5] SEC Release No. 33-8238 (June 5, 2003).

DISCLOSURE CONTROLS AND PROCEDURES

Form 40-F for eligible Canadian issuers. The rules relating to controls and procedures, however, also cover current reports of U.S. companies on Form 8-K, as well as Form 6-K reports of foreign private issuers.

NO "ONE SIZE FITS ALL" APPROACH

A company's controls and procedures should be in writing and tailored to reflect the operations of the company and its particular risk profile. The need for adequate documentation is particularly acute in the case of internal control over financial reporting. The SEC has stated that "a company must maintain evidential matter, including documentation, to provide reasonable support for management's assessment of the effectiveness of the company's internal control over financial reporting."[6]

The starting point for creating a system of controls and procedures that complies should be an inventory and review of the company's existing practices and controls. While reporting companies will already have a system of internal financial controls as a result of their obligations under § 13(b)(2) of the Exchange Act (and therefore a starting point for the requirement to maintain internal control over financial reporting), most companies will need to systematize their practices for compiling and analyzing information and the process of preparing public disclosures. In this regard, consideration should be given not only to the requirements of the particular reports filed with or submitted to the SEC by the company, but also to the manner in which information is disclosed in those reports. For example, if the company reports according to business segments, controls and procedures should be developed to reflect that reporting pattern. Care should be taken, however, to establish controls and procedures for which meaningful compliance is possible. Perfunctory or inconsistent compliance can give rise to adverse inferences in the event the company's disclosures are challenged as defective.

STATEMENT OF PURPOSE

The CEO and CFO of each reporting company must certify as to the design and effectiveness of the company's controls and procedures, among other matters, and companies have an independent obligation to maintain controls and procedures. Any compilation of controls and procedures should indicate that it has been adopted for these purposes and that the controls and procedures should be considered in conjunction with the company's other compliance policies, controls and procedures.

---

[6] SEC Release No. 33-8238 (June 5, 2003), 68 Fed. Reg. 36636, 36643 (June 18, 2003); *see also* Instruction 1 to Item 308 of Regulation S-K and to Item 15 of Form 20-F (setting out requirements for management's report on internal control over financial reporting pursuant to Section 404 of the Sarbanes-Oxley Act).

CONSULTATION WITH OUTSIDE ADVISORS

The company should develop its controls and procedures in consultation with its outside counsel and, to the extent permitted by new SEC rules pertaining to auditor independence, its independent auditor.[7] This consideration is particularly relevant in light of management's internal control report referred to above, which must be subject to attestation by the independent auditor.[8]

While the SEC's rules under Section 404 will not become effective for most U.S. issuers until the annual report for their first fiscal year ending on or after June 15, 2004 (April 15, 2005 for foreign private issuers), it is expected to require substantial time for issuers to establish and document their internal controls over financial reporting in order to permit a "clean" attestation. Management should take steps now to ensure that its controls and evaluation framework will constitute an appropriate basis both for its report and the attestation by the company's independent auditor. It is expected, for example, that the independent auditor will require that the company's significant controls be adequately documented and that there be appropriate testing of the controls by company personnel, with sufficient evidence thereof. For these purposes, significant controls include those controls the failure of which could result in a material misstatement in the company's financial statements, including controls over significant account balances, significant or non-routine transactions, manual journal entries, consolidating entries and areas of disclosure involving significant subjectivity or judgment. It is also expected that the independent auditor will be required to perform additional testing procedures to determine the effectiveness of a company's controls and management's process for evaluating the controls.

Depending on their existing level of preparedness, some companies will likely find it necessary to engage a separate accounting firm to assist them in assessing the quality of their controls and in formulating an action plan for documenting new or existing controls, particularly as the PCAOB finalizes the relevant attestation standard.[9]

INTERNAL APPROVAL OF CONTROLS AND PROCEDURES

Although the SEC does not require it, we recommend that a company's disclosure controls and procedures be presented (together with the results of the periodic evaluation of the controls and procedures by the CEO and CFO) for review

---

[7] The SEC has stated that "auditors may assist management in documenting internal controls. When the auditor is engaged to assist management in documenting internal controls, management must be actively involved in the process." SEC Release No. 33-8238 (June 5, 2003), 68 Fed. Reg. 36636, 36642 (June 18, 2003); *see also* SEC Release No. 33-8183 (Jan. 28, 2003).

[8] *See* Item 308(b) of Regulation S-K.

[9] *See* Chapter I, Note 97.

DISCLOSURE CONTROLS AND PROCEDURES

and approval by the company's board of directors and/or the audit committee and, if created, the company's "disclosure committee." While the audit committee cannot be expected to review the entirety of a company's internal control over financial reporting, it would nevertheless be appropriate for the head of the company's internal audit function to make a detailed presentation to the committee as to the overall scope of the company's controls, the structure of the internal audit function and the framework that management will use for purposes of evaluating the company's internal control over financial reporting, as required by SEC rules.

DISCLOSURE COMMITTEE

Personnel responsible for implementing a company's controls and procedures will vary depending on its organization and reporting lines. It is important that these personnel have appropriate skills, experience and positions within the company to assure that implementation will be effective. We recommend that, at a minimum, the following company officers be involved in developing and overseeing implementation of a company's controls and procedures:

- General counsel and senior legal official responsible for disclosure who reports to the general counsel (also recommended by the SEC);

- Chief investor relations officer (also recommended by the SEC);

- Principal accounting officer (or controller) (also recommended by the SEC);

- Principal risk manager officer (also recommended by the SEC);

- Heads of major business units (also recommended by the SEC);

- Head of pension & benefits/human resources department; and

- If applicable, head of external reporting.

If they are not directly involved in the development of the company's controls and procedures, the CEO and CFO should approve them in consultation with the general counsel, the controller and the head of the company's internal audit function.

The SEC has recommended that companies establish a disclosure committee for purposes of implementing controls and procedures on an ongoing basis. The committee should include at least the personnel recommended by the SEC as noted above and should report to senior management, including the CEO and CFO.

The existence and effective operation of such a committee would be helpful in establishing the basis for the CEO and CFO certifications as to controls and procedures. The practical utility of such a committee and the scope of its responsibilities will, however, depend on the nature of the company, the complexity of its operations and other considerations. If created, the committee's responsibilities should be clearly established, and it should meet periodically to assure execution of its responsibilities, which could include the following:

- Assisting the CEO and CFO (or equivalent certifying officers) in the design, implementation and evaluation of controls and procedures and, in consultation with the internal and independent auditors, the company's internal control over financial reporting;[10]

- Resolving questions about the materiality of a development or other information;

- Reviewing and advising on the scope and content of disclosure; and

- Recommending to the CEO, CFO (and any other certifying officers) and the company's board of directors (or audit committee or comparable body) the filing of each annual or quarterly report.

MATTERS COVERED BY CONTROLS AND PROCEDURES

Under the new rules, a company must have effective disclosure controls and procedures to meet its obligations under both periodic and current reports (including matters reportable on Form 6-K), and this requirement also extends to internal control over financial reporting. Proposed NYSE governance standards require the audit committee of a U.S. company to review other significant communications, including earnings guidance, which we believe should be a best practice for all reporting companies.[11] We recommend that a company's controls and procedures thus cover a broader range of public disclosures than is strictly required by the new SEC rules. We believe the controls and procedures should be developed to cover the following reports and other matters:

---

[10] Given the more technical considerations associated with the implementation and evaluation of internal control over financial reporting, companies with complex or dispersed operations may find it prudent to establish a separate committee with responsibility for oversight of the internal audit plan and issues that may be raised during the course of its execution throughout the year.

[11] Amendment No. 1 to the NYSE's Corporate Governance Proposals; SEC Release No. 34-47672 (Apr. 11, 2003).

DISCLOSURE CONTROLS AND PROCEDURES

U.S. Reporting Companies

- Annual reports on Form 10-K;

- Proxy and information statements;

- Quarterly reports on Form 10-Q;

- Current reports on Form 8-K, including earnings press releases for completed periods as required by new SEC rules, with particular emphasis on any non-GAAP financial measures included and the reconciliations thereof to GAAP;

- Forms 3, 4 and 5, if the company prepares these filings for officers and directors; and

- Special financial reports required by regulated entities under applicable law.

Foreign Private Issuers

- Annual reports on Form 20-F (or 40-F in the case of eligible Canadian issuers); and

- Financial and other material information reported on Form 6-K.

All Reporting Companies

- Other financial press releases and "scripts" for earnings calls;

- Earnings guidance;

- Rating agency reports;

- Other miscellaneous reports (*e.g.*, Schedules 13D and 13G);

- Website disclosure practices and other communication policies, particularly with respect to financial information;

- Whistleblowing procedures with respect to complaints about the company's disclosure, whether internal or external;[12]

---

[12] SEC rules adopted under Section 301 of the Sarbanes-Oxley Act will require that the audit committees of all listed companies in the United States establish these procedures. SEC Release No. 33-8220 (Apr. 9, 2003). This requirement is discussed in greater detail in Chapter III.

THE SARBANES-OXLEY ACT: ANALYSIS AND PRACTICE

- Reports by internal and external lawyers with respect to material violations of securities laws, breaches of fiduciary duty or similar violations;[13] and

- Review and consideration of matters raised by other components of the disclosure process, including the independent auditor's "management letter" and the new attestation by the independent auditor of management's conclusions about the effectiveness of the company's internal control over financial reporting.

PLAN FOR NEW FORM 8-K REQUIREMENTS

A pending SEC proposal would require Form 8-K reports to be filed by U.S. reporting companies within two business days, and would also require reporting by U.S. companies of several new events, some of which may be difficult to track.[14] Companies should plan now for procedures that would capture relevant information and reflect the possibility that the SEC will in fact impose the two business day filing deadline. The new disclosures would cover:

- Material agreements outside the ordinary course (which as proposed would include non-binding letters of intent);

- Termination of a material agreement not made in the ordinary course;

- Termination of or reduction in a customer relationship representing specified amount of the company's revenues;

- Material direct or contingent financial obligations;

- Events triggering material direct or contingent financial obligations;

- "Exit activities," including any material write-off or restructuring;

- Material impairments;

- Change in rating or outlook or issuance of a credit watch;

- Listing change, delisting and notice of non-compliance with listing standards;

---

[13] SEC rules adopted under Section 307 of the Sarbanes-Oxley Act will generally require that all lawyers who practice before the SEC report "up the ladder" to a company's chief legal officer any credible evidence they may have of such violations. These rules are discussed in greater detail in Chapter X.

[14] SEC Release No. 34-46084 (June 17, 2002).

DISCLOSURE CONTROLS AND PROCEDURES

- Notice of withdrawal of previous audit report or that the company may not rely on a previous audit report;

- Material limitations, restrictions or prohibitions regarding the company's employee benefit, retirement and stock ownership plans;

- Unregistered sales of equity securities; and

- Material modifications to securityholders' rights.

Existing current reporting items would also be changed to include disclosure about a director's departure for reasons other than a disagreement or removal for cause, the appointment or departure of a principal officer and the election of directors, and amendments to the company's constitutive documents.

REVIEW FORM 6-K SUBMISSION POLICY

Many foreign private issuers file a Form 6-K each time they disseminate any information in their home markets or make any required filing with their local stock exchange. Depending on the scope and frequency of the home country reporting requirements, the result is often that a foreign private issuer furnishes to the SEC a significantly greater number of reports on Form 6-K relative to the number of Form 8-K reports filed by a comparable U.S. issuer. In light of the new rules, foreign private issuers should review with outside counsel their current Form 6-K practices with a view to furnishing Form 6-K reports only with respect to information that is material. In making materiality determinations, foreign private issuers should consider SEC requirements (including the SEC's proposal about new Form 8-K current disclosures, even though it is applicable only to U.S. reporting companies) and U.S. judicial pronouncements, as well as any home country judicial, administrative or regulatory guidance as to materiality determinations.

The controls and procedures maintained by foreign private issuers should be designed to ensure timely submission of Form 6-K reports via EDGAR (required as of November 4, 2002) and to take into account that information submitted in Form 6-K reports is subject to Rule 12b-20 under the Exchange Act (*i.e.*, a requirement that the report include all necessary information to make it complete and accurate in all material respects).

STEPS TO CONSIDER FOR EACH REPORT OR COMMUNICATION

The procedures for the various SEC reports and other disclosures are likely to vary. We would expect, for example, that the procedures for preparing a non-financial press release would be different in scope from procedures used to prepare earnings releases or required quarterly reports. In determining the appropriate scope of procedures for each type of report, document or other communication covered by disclosure procedures, the following should be considered:

- Determination of responsibility for preparation of each part of the relevant report, document or communication;

- Ultimate approval responsibility for each part and the entirety of the report, document or communication;

- General "closing" procedures for information subject to a reporting obligation;

- Time required to complete preparation and review of drafts;

- Need for and timing of "due diligence" meetings, whether wholly internal or with outside advisors, including those necessary to satisfy CEO and CFO certification requirements;

- Responsibility for preparation and revision of drafts;

- Responsibility for confirming compliance with SEC or stock exchange rules and form requirements (sometimes called the "form check");

- Responsibility for review and sign-off on drafts and the final version of SEC and other disclosures;

- Special documentation and other procedures (*e.g.*, sub-certifications to support CEO and CFO certifications and "cabinet" sessions of management, or meetings of the disclosure committee if created) to assist the CEO and the CFO in complying with their certification obligations;[15]

---

[15] It appears that most companies are implementing some form of sub-certification requirement by subordinate officers, although practice varies widely as to the number of officials required to certify and their level of seniority.

The scope of sub-certifications also appears to vary widely, depending primarily on the nature of the certifying official's responsibility. For example, officials responsible for financial reporting and internal control for the consolidated entity may be expected to provide certifications substantially identical to those provided by the CEO and CFO. By contrast, company officials with operating responsibility may be required to certify solely as to trends and commitments within their business units. Certifications by legal personnel may be even more limited, with some companies requiring certification only as to litigations or other proceedings required to be reported.

Where a company requires sub-certifications, the company's controls and procedures should require that a record be maintained of those that have been provided from period to period. Of course, any exceptions to a sub-certification (or the failure to provide a required sub-certification) should be pursued and addressed prior to the filing of the relevant report.

DISCLOSURE CONTROLS AND PROCEDURES

- Need for review by the company's board of directors and/or the audit committee (or comparable body);

- Need for external validation or consultation (*e.g.*, audit report, SAS 100 review report on interim results of U.S. companies, discussions with the audit committee, outside counsel or independent auditor) and impact on the timeline for preparation of the report; and

- Filing or other external dissemination procedures (*e.g.*, some of the NYSE governance proposals and new SEC rules require publication by both SEC filing and website posting).

CREATING A TIMELINE

It may be useful to create a timeline for the steps involved in preparing a company's principal reports. This can help assure that information is timely reported internally so as to facilitate thoughtful, rather than hurried, preparation of disclosure. Preparation of a timeline will also focus the attention of those persons critical to the disclosure process on the time they need to execute their responsibility to gather, verify and report the required information to those responsible for preparing the disclosures.[16] The company should also consider whether there are technological solutions, such as extranets, that can facilitate sharing of drafts and other necessary information more expeditiously. Whether the company achieves its timeline for its major reports can also be a key metric in determining the effectiveness of a company's controls and procedures.

RESPONSIBILITIES OF AUDIT COMMITTEE OR COMPARABLE BODY

A clear practical implication of the recent initiatives by Congress, the SEC and others is that the role of the audit committee (or the body performing an equivalent function) has been expanded.[17] All reporting companies should review the responsibilities that they now accord to their audit committee (or comparable body) and whether they are appropriate in light of the new and anticipated requirements. The audit committee (or comparable body) should plan to review periodic reports, as well as material current reports (*e.g.*, those containing financial information, such as earnings releases or guidance). It may also be appropriate to

---

[16] The use of a timeline has particular importance for "accelerated filers" (generally U.S. issuers with an equity capitalization of more than $75 million that have filed an annual report with the SEC), which will become subject to shortened reporting deadlines commencing with their first fiscal year ending on or after December 15, 2003. *See* SEC Release No. 33-8128 (Sept. 5, 2002); SEC Release No. 33-8128A (Apr. 8, 2003) (technical amendments).

[17] Audit committee responsibilities under the Sarbanes-Oxley Act and related listing standards are addressed more fully in Chapters III and IV.

increase the number or length of audit committee meetings to assure sufficient time for meaningful execution of the committee's responsibilities.

DOCUMENT RETENTION POLICIES

Consider which supporting documents should be retained, by whom, where and for how long. Some documentation must be retained by gatekeepers (*e.g.*, independent auditors are now required to retain their work papers for seven years) or the company (*e.g.*, the "evidential matter" supporting management's reports on internal control over financial reporting). Other documentation, however, may not be necessary or appropriate to retain. It is important that document retention be subject to a careful policy that is implemented consistently, rather than on the basis of *ad hoc* judgments.

DISSEMINATION OF CONTROLS AND PROCEDURES

The company should make sure that personnel responsible for implementing the company's controls and procedures understand and have adequate access to them. Consideration should be given to written acknowledgements by key personnel as to their receipt and understanding of same.

TRAINING SESSIONS

The disclosure requirements under the federal securities laws can be complex, both in terms of the factual information called for, as well as in the application of the law to that information. Special training and orientation sessions for persons with significant involvement in the disclosure process or a significant role in internal control may be worthwhile. Training topics could include, at a minimum, a description of relevant requirements and standards, including both legal and accounting, and the types of due diligence that may be appropriate from period to period. These sessions should involve members of the legal staff or outside counsel. Of course, training programs with respect to internal control over financial reporting will involve significantly greater focus on matters of GAAP application, recordkeeping and internal reporting systems, and there should be participation in these programs by the independent auditor (subject to the SEC's rules on auditor independence) or other accounting experts.

PERIODIC EVALUATION OF CONTROLS AND PROCEDURES

CEOs and CFOs are required to conduct a review of the effectiveness of their companies' controls and procedures within the 90-day period preceding the filing date of the report containing the certification. Commencing with covered reports filed on or after August 14, 2003, the evaluation must be made as of the end of the period covered by the report. As a result, controls and procedures should be

DISCLOSURE CONTROLS AND PROCEDURES

reviewed no less frequently than quarterly, in the case of U.S. issuers, or annually, in the case of foreign private issuers. More frequent interim evaluations may be appropriate where there are significant changes in SEC or stock exchange reporting requirements or in the circumstances or prospects of the company. An individual or group should be allocated responsibility for ensuring this review takes place in a responsible manner.

It will be crucial to develop appropriate metrics for evaluating controls and procedures, particularly those not within the scope of internal control over financial reporting, which will be subject to well-developed evaluative frameworks under relevant accounting guidance. Companies should consult with their internal and independent auditors as to ways in which the internal control and audit process might be extended to address such controls and procedures. For example, a company that had engaged in material transactions during a reporting period could selectively "audit" the process for one or more of the transactions. The company could solicit input from the persons involved as to whether the right information was provided on a timely basis and to the right persons for evaluation in light of disclosure requirements and whether processes for sharing draft disclosure or views about the materiality of the event worked well.

Any evaluation should also take into account the following general considerations:[18]

- Whether other participants should be included in the disclosure process;

- Staffing inadequacies (either as to number or quality of personnel);

- The impact of incompatible information systems on the reliability of internal information flows;

- Whether there are other impediments to consistently accurate information and, if so, what steps are appropriate to correct them;

- The desirability of training efforts for those persons who have significant involvement in the process;

- Whether adequate time is allowed to air issues and whether there is sufficient dialogue among gatekeepers (*i.e.*, are comments on disclosure conveyed and included, but not discussed more broadly); and

---

[18] Specific questions that may be useful in connection with an evaluation of a company's controls and procedures are addressed in Chapter VII.

- The nature and scope of the review of all or relevant portions of the disclosure by committees of the company's board of directors, particularly the audit committee, by any "cabinet" session of management representatives or by the company's disclosure committee, and where such review is contemplated, whether there is adequate time for such review and comment.

The following specific areas involving the company's operations should also be taken into account insofar as the company's circumstances may have changed:

- Operational and reputational risks;

- Information technology risks;

- Strategic risks;

- Financial and market risks (*e.g.*, credit, market and liquidity);

- Other "hot button" areas, such as related party transactions, off-balance sheet transactions and derivatives activities;

- Regulatory developments;

- Risks associated with cross-border activities; and

- Litigation and other contingencies.

REQUIRED COMMUNICATIONS

The CEO and CFO must discuss with the independent auditor and the company's audit committee (or body performing an equivalent function), at a minimum, significant deficiencies and material weaknesses in the design or operation of the company's internal control over financial reporting that are reasonably likely to adversely affect the company's ability to record, process, summarize or report financial data and any fraud, whether or not material, by the company's management who have a significant role in the company's internal control over financial reporting. Despite the limited nature of this reporting requirement, it would be prudent for the CEO and CFO to discuss with the audit committee the entirety of the matters covered by the Section 302 and Section 906 officer certifications.

DISCLOSURE CONTROLS AND PROCEDURES

The SEC's periodic reporting forms also require a company to disclose the conclusions of the CEO and CFO about the effectiveness of the company's disclosure controls and procedures and material changes to the company's internal control over financial reporting.[19] The SEC has provided no guidance as to the scope or content of this requirement, and practice has varied widely. The SEC has, however, indicated that it would be inappropriate for a company to include as part of this disclosure significant disclaimers as to the ultimate effectiveness of its controls and procedures and, in certain circumstances, has required companies to amend their disclosures to delete these disclaimers.[20]

---

[19] *See, e.g.*, Item 14 of Form 10-K and Item 4 of Form 10-Q, each referring to Item 307 of Regulation S-K, and Item 15 of Form 20-F.

[20] SEC Release No. 33-8238 (June 5, 2003). The SEC stated that its staff has generally not objected to disclosure that disclosure controls and procedures are designed to provide only "reasonable assurance" that they will meet their objectives, although the staff has requested that companies state, if true, that such controls and procedures are effective to provide such level of assurance. *Id.*, 68 Fed. Reg. 36636, 36647 (June 18, 2003).

IX PRACTICAL CONSIDERATIONS FOR EARNINGS RELEASES

In January 2003, the SEC adopted Regulation G and Item 10(e) of Regulation S-K, which address the use of "non-GAAP financial measures" by public companies in their SEC filings and other public disclosures.[1] The SEC also adopted Item 12 of Form 8-K, which requires that U.S. companies furnish to the SEC on Form 8-K "earnings releases" and other material financial information that is made publicly available with respect to any completed annual or quarterly fiscal period. The rules raise a number of practical questions for companies that issue earnings press releases and discuss their results in earnings webcasts or conference calls.

The application of the new rules depends in significant part on whether the company is a U.S. domestic issuer or a foreign private issuer. In particular, Regulation G exempts foreign private issuers from its limitations in certain circumstances. Foreign private issuers that do not qualify for this exemption should be guided by the rules and practices discussed below that are applicable to U.S. companies.

U.S. DOMESTIC ISSUERS

Earnings Press Release. If the earnings press release contains any non-GAAP financial measure, Regulation G requires that the earnings press release also present the most directly comparable financial measure calculated and presented in accordance with GAAP and a quantitative reconciliation of the two measures.

In addition, new Item 12 of Form 8-K requires U.S. domestic issuers to *furnish* their quarterly earnings releases to the SEC and to comply with the requirements of new Item 10(e)(1)(i) of Regulation S-K in connection with any non-GAAP financial measures contained in the releases. Item 10(e)(1)(i) imposes two further requirements in addition to those imposed by Regulation G. First, the comparable GAAP measure must be presented with equal or greater prominence. Second, there must be a statement regarding management's belief as to why the non-

---

[1] SEC Release No. 33-8176 (Jan. 22, 2003); *see also* Division of Corporation Finance: Frequently Asked Questions Regarding the Use of Non-GAAP Financial Measures (June 13, 2003). The new rules are discussed in greater detail in our memorandum entitled "SEC Adopts Rules to Implement Section 401(b) of the Sarbanes-Oxley Act and to Require Furnishing of Earnings Releases on Form 8-K."

GAAP financial measure is useful to investors (and, if material, regarding the additional reasons for which management uses the non-GAAP financial measure). This last requirement can be satisfied either in the earnings press release or in the related Form 8-K.[2]

Earnings Webcast or Conference Call. An earnings press release typically is followed shortly by a webcast or conference call with securities analysts, which for purposes of compliance with Regulation FD is made accessible to the public and announced to the public by means designed to ensure broad, non-exclusionary access. The announcement generally is made a week to ten days prior to the earnings webcast or conference call and repeated in the earnings press release.

Oral Presentation of Non-GAAP Financial Measures

The requirements of Regulation G are satisfied with respect to non-GAAP financial measures made public orally, telephonically or by webcast, broadcast or similar means if:

- the information required by Regulation G (*i.e.*, comparable GAAP measure and quantitative reconciliation) is provided on the issuer's website at the time the non-GAAP financial measure is made public; and

- the location of the website is made public in the same presentation in which the non-GAAP financial measure is used.

To ensure compliance in this manner, the earnings press release should be posted on the issuer's website prior to the start of the earnings webcast or conference call. The following oral disclaimer also should be made at the beginning of the presentation[3] if non-GAAP financial measures will be presented orally during the earnings webcast or conference call or may be presented in response to questions:

> Our earnings press release, including a reconciliation of certain *pro forma* financial information to the most directly comparable measures under generally accepted accounting principles, is posted on our website at www.[company].com/[insert name of relevant page].

Use of Slides and Written Materials

While the matter was not expressly addressed by the SEC in adopting Regulation G, we believe that disclosure made during an earnings webcast or confer-

---

[2] The explanation of the utility of the non-GAAP financial measure also need not be included if this information was already included in the issuer's most recent annual report on Form 10-K (or a more recent Form 10-Q) or 20-F, except to the extent necessary to update it.

[3] This disclaimer may accompany the disclaimer regarding "forward-looking statements" that most companies make as part of their public announcements or conferences as permitted by the safe harbor contained in § 21E of the Exchange Act. *See* Chapter I, Note 89.

EARNINGS RELEASES

ence call by means of slides that are not distributed or made available electronically or in hard copy should be viewed as disclosure "orally . . . or by similar means" within the meaning of the "oral disclosures" requirements of Regulation G. Under this view, the required comparable GAAP measure and quantitative reconciliation need not be set forth in the slides themselves, provided that each requirement applicable to "oral disclosures" has been satisfied.

By contrast, if slides or other written materials are distributed or made available electronically or in hard copy to participants in the earnings webcast or conference call and contain non-GAAP financial measures, we believe that the most directly comparable GAAP measures and the required reconciliations must be presented in the slides or other written or electronic materials and should be presented in close proximity to the non-GAAP financial measures.

Material Information Not Contained in Earnings Press Release

An exemption from the obligation to furnish a report on Form 8-K to the SEC under new Item 12 of Form 8-K is available for information disclosed orally, telephonically or by webcast, broadcast or similar means if:

- the information is provided as part of a presentation that is complementary to, and initially occurs within 48 hours after, a related written announcement or release that has been furnished to the SEC under Item 12 of Form 8-K prior to the presentation;[4]

- the presentation is broadly accessible to the public by dial-in conference call, by webcast, broadcast or similar means;

- any financial and other statistical information contained in the presentation is provided on the issuer's website;[5] and

---

[4] The SEC staff has stated that no additional filing on Form 8-K is necessary where an issuer releases its earnings after the close of the market and files the earnings press release as an exhibit to a quarterly report on Form 10-Q the next day prior to its earnings webcast or conference call, assuming the other conditions of the exception from filing are met. Division of Corporation Finance: Frequently Asked Questions Regarding the Use of Non-GAAP Financial Measures, Question 25 (June 13, 2003).

[5] The SEC staff has stated that an audio file of the initial webcast would satisfy this condition only if (i) it contains all material financial and other statistical information included in the presentation that was not previously disclosed; and (ii) investors can access it and replay it through the company's website. Alternatively, the staff stated, slides posted on the website at the time of the presentation containing the required, previously undisclosed, material information would also satisfy the condition. In each case, the information must include any material information provided in connection with any questions and answers during the presentation. *Id.*, Question 22.

- the presentation was announced by a widely disseminated press release that included instructions as to the location on the registrant's website where the information would be available.

The simplest means of ensuring availability of the exemption is to:

- include in the press release announcing the earnings webcast or conference call a statement identifying the page on the issuer's website where the webcast or call will be archived;

- ensure that the announcement is "widely disseminated" (which would be the case if the issuer has chosen to satisfy its obligations under Regulation FD by distributing the announcement through a widely circulated news or wire service); and

- ensure that the earnings press release has been furnished to the SEC under Item 12 of Form 8-K before the earnings webcast or conference call begins.[6]

If any material information not contained in, but complementary to the information contained in, the earnings press release is made public orally during the earnings webcast or conference call, the complementary information must be posted on the issuer's website.[7] Although this requirement should not prove difficult to comply with for any material, complementary information planned to be disclosed in the webcast or call, it raises a practical problem if the information is disclosed in response to a question during the presentation. While not expressly addressed by the SEC, this requirement should be satisfied in such circumstances if the complementary information is posted on the issuer's website by the open of business on the business day following the webcast or call.[8] Archiving the webcast or a transcript of the conference call on the issuer's website within that time

---

[6] Although the SEC will shortly begin a pilot program to open the EDGAR filing system beginning at 6 a.m. (Eastern standard time), it is currently open to accept filings only between the hours of 8 a.m. and 10 p.m. (Eastern standard time). Based on these hours of operation, it would be advisable to (i) furnish the earnings press release to the SEC prior to 10 p.m. on the business day before the earnings webcast or conference call; or (ii) start the webcast or call no earlier than 8:15 a.m. to allow sufficient time for the release to be furnished to the SEC at 8 a.m. on the day of the webcast or call and to appear in the SEC's EDGAR filing system prior to the start of the company's remarks. The SEC staff has confirmed that, where the earnings release is issued after the close of the market and the conference call or webcast includes material previously undisclosed information (thus precluding reliance on this exception), an issuer must file a transcript of the relevant portion of the conference call or slides including the information on Form 8-K. *Id.*, Question 23.

[7] Alternatively, the complementary information could be furnished to the SEC under Item 12 of Form 8-K within five business days after having been made public.

[8] The SEC staff has confirmed that the posting must occur "promptly" (but without specifying a deadline) and that a webcast of the oral presentation would be sufficient to meet this requirement. *Id.*, Question 24.

EARNINGS RELEASES

period will satisfy this requirement. Issuers should note, however, that the SEC "encourages" issuers to provide "ongoing website access" to information not furnished under Item 12 of Form 8-K in reliance on this exemption and "suggests" that website access be provided for at least a 12-month period.[9]

Material information made public during the earnings webcast or conference call must be furnished to the SEC under Item 12 of Form 8-K within five business days after it is made public if that information was not contained in, and is not complementary to the information contained in, the earnings press release. The SEC's adopting release relating to Item 12 of Form 8-K suggests that information may be viewed as complementary to the information contained in the earnings press release to the extent that the issuer merely continues its practices (as in effect prior to adoption of Item 12 of Form 8-K) regarding allocation of information between the earnings press release and the earnings webcast or conference call.[10]

We also believe that material information made public during the webcast or conference call should be furnished to the SEC under Item 12 of Form 8-K within five business days after it is made public if that information was not contained in the earnings release and was disclosed in slides or other written materials that were distributed or made available electronically or in hard copy to participants.[11]

---

[9] SEC Release No. 33-8176 (Jan. 22, 2003).

[10] The SEC stated, however, that "[we] do not intend this exception to foster changes in practice whereby disclosure is shifted from the written release or announcement to the complementary presentation." SEC Release No. 33-8176 (Jan. 22, 2003), 68 Fed. Reg. 4820, 4826, n. 58 (Jan. 30, 2003).

[11] Many companies conduct "one on one" meetings with investors or attend analyst conferences throughout the year that may not fall within the "complementary disclosures" exception given the limited timeframe during which the exception is available. If these presentations include only a repetition of information previously furnished to the SEC, no new obligation to furnish the information on Form 8-K should arise, even where the information is provided in a different format (*e.g.*, graphic, rather than numerical presentation). By contrast, a public update of information previously furnished to the SEC under Item 12 of Form 8-K must itself also be furnished on that Form. *See* Item 12(a) of Form 8-K.

An issue is also raised as to whether a "one on one" meeting constitutes a "public announcement" for purposes of Item 12 of Form 8-K. Form 8-K provides no guidance on this point, although in adopting Regulation G, the SEC stated that "whether disclosure is 'public' will . . . depend on all the facts and circumstances." SEC Release No. 33-8176 (Jan. 22, 2003), 68 Fed. Reg. 4820, 4823, n. 31 (Jan. 30, 2003).

One area that may provide guidance is the statutory and regulatory regime surrounding offers of securities under the Securities Act. In that context, the number of offerees would not affect whether a "public" distribution has occurred, but the sophistication of the investors involved would. Building on those principles, if persons attending the "one on one" meeting were "accredited investors" within the meaning of Rule 501 of Regulation D under the Securities Act or "qualified institutional buyers" within the meaning of Rule 144A under the Securities Act, an argument could be made that a disclosure is not "public" for purposes of reporting on Form 8-K.

As these meetings are typically held with securities analysts and institutional investors, the company would in any event be obligated to make a wider public disclosure under Regulation FD, if it dis-

FOREIGN PRIVATE ISSUERS

Earnings Press Release. A foreign private issuer benefits from an exemption from the requirements of Regulation G if:

- the securities of the issuer are listed on a securities exchange or quoted in an inter-dealer quotation system outside the United States;

- the non-GAAP financial measure is not derived from or based on a measure calculated and presented in accordance with U.S. GAAP; and

- the disclosure is made in a written communication that is released outside the United States prior to or contemporaneously with its release in the United States and is not otherwise targeted at persons located in the United States.[12]

As a result, the earnings press releases of most foreign private issuers, whose primary financial statements are prepared under non-U.S. GAAP, need not comply with Regulation G.

In addition, foreign private issuers are exempt from the requirements of Form 8-K, including Item 12 of Form 8-K. Thus, while foreign private issuers generally furnish their earnings press releases to the SEC on Form 6-K, they are not required to comply with the requirements of Item 10(e)(1)(i) of Regulation S-K in their earnings press releases or in the reports on Form 6-K used to furnish those earnings press releases to the SEC.

Because the contents of any earnings press release may affect investment decisions by U.S. investors and therefore result in liability under U.S. federal and state securities laws, however, foreign private issuers should consult with U.S. counsel about the contents of their earnings press releases, notwithstanding that those releases will in many cases not be subject to the requirements of Regulation G.[13] In addition, foreign private issuers that have outstanding shelf registration statements under the Securities Act should bear in mind that Form 6-Ks used to furnish earnings releases to the SEC must comply with the full requirements of Item 10(e) of

---

closed material information not previously disclosed to the public. Despite this practical result, in adopting Regulation G, the SEC specifically rejected Regulation FD as a precedent for determining when a disclosure is "public." SEC Release No. 33-8176 (Jan. 22, 2003).

[12] We believe that a press release should not be viewed as "targeted at persons located in the United States" solely because it is in the English language.

[13] Disclosures furnished on Form 6-K are also be subject to Rule 12b-20 under the Exchange Act (*i.e.*, a requirement that the report include all necessary information to make it complete and accurate in all material respects).

EARNINGS RELEASES

Regulation S-K if they are incorporated by reference into those (or similar) registration statements.[14]

Earnings Webcast or Conference Call. In the case of a foreign private issuer that is exempt from the requirements of Regulation G with respect to earnings webcasts or conference calls, no new steps need be taken. Foreign private issuers should, however, continue to take into account best practices and the views of the SEC to avoid selective disclosure of material information and to monitor the content of these oral presentations in light of the anti-fraud provisions of the U.S. federal and state securities laws.

---

[14] In addition to the comparable GAAP measure, quantitative reconciliation and management statement required by Item 10(e)(1)(i), Item 10(e) prohibits the presentation of certain types of non-GAAP financial measures, including:
- non-GAAP liquidity measures (other than earnings before interest, taxes, depreciation and amortization, or "EBITDA") excluding charges or liabilities that, generally speaking, required or will require cash settlement; and
- non-GAAP performance measures adjusted to exclude items identified as non-recurring, infrequent or unusual, when the nature of any excluded item is such that it is reasonably likely to recur within two years or there was a similar gain or charge within the prior two years.

A report on Form 6-K is incorporated by reference into a Securities Act registration statement only if the foreign private issuer so indicates. The SEC staff has stated that a foreign private issuer that wishes to incorporate only a portion of an earnings press release (*e.g.*, the portion that does not contain a non-GAAP measure) has two options. Either it can furnish a single report on From 6-K, specifying which portion of the release is incorporated and which is not, or it can file two reports, only one of which is incorporated by reference. The SEC staff has stated its preference for the latter approach, although it also noted that the company should consider whether its disclosure is rendered misleading by virtue of having incorporated only a portion of its earnings press release. Division of Corporation Finance: Frequently Asked Questions Regarding the Use of Non-GAAP Financial Measures, Question 29 (June 13, 2003).

X ATTORNEY PROFESSIONAL CONDUCT STANDARDS

The SEC has published final rules setting forth the professional responsibilities of attorneys "appearing and practicing" before the SEC in the representation of issuers (the "Final Rules").[1] Adopted under Section 307 of the Sarbanes-Oxley Act's mandate to issue rules defining "minimum standards of professional conduct for attorneys appearing and practicing before the [SEC],"[2] the Final Rules prescribe new reporting requirements for attorneys who become aware of evidence of misconduct by issuer clients. Concurrently with adopting the Final Rules, the SEC deferred action on the controversial "noisy withdrawal" provisions of its proposed rules (the "Proposed Rules") to implement Section 307, extending the comment period for these provisions until April 7, 2003. The SEC also proposed an alternative "reporting out" proposal for comment by April 7, 2003.[3]

The effective date for the Final Rules is August 5, 2003. We describe the new requirements below and suggest practical recommendations for complying with them.

OVERVIEW

In November 2002, the SEC issued the Proposed Rules to implement Section 307 of the Sarbanes-Oxley Act.[4] The Proposed Rules responded to Section 307's mandate to adopt "up the ladder" reporting requirements, but also went beyond that mandate in two important respects. First, the SEC included a provision that would require "noisy withdrawal" by outside counsel from representation of the issuer in the event the issuer fails to respond appropriately to evidence of a material violation that the attorney reasonably believes is ongoing or about to occur and likely to result in substantial financial harm to the issuer or investors. Second, the SEC proposed new exceptions to an attorney's obligation to maintain client confidences.

The Final Rules retain the core "up the ladder" reporting requirements set forth in the Proposed Rules. Thus, an attorney representing an issuer before the SEC who becomes aware of evidence of a material violation of securities laws,

---

[1] SEC Release No. 33-8185 (Jan. 29, 2003) (the "Adopting Release").
[2] Sarbanes-Oxley Act of 2002, Pub. L. No. 107-204, 116 Stat. 745 (2002).
[3] SEC Release No. 33-8186 (Jan. 29, 2003) (the "Companion Release").
[4] SEC Release No. 33-8150 (Nov. 21, 2002) (the "Proposing Release").

breach of fiduciary duty or similar violation within the client issuer must report that evidence to the chief legal officer ("CLO") or to both the CLO and the CEO of the issuer. If the CLO does not "appropriately respond" to the report within a reasonable time, the attorney must report the evidence further "up the ladder" to the audit committee, another committee made up solely of independent board members, or the issuer's board of directors itself. As an alternative, the Final Rules offer a second reporting procedure under which issuers may establish a qualified legal compliance committee ("QLCC") to handle these reports. In addition, in keeping with the original proposal, the Final Rules establish new exceptions described below to an attorney's obligation to maintain client confidences.

Despite the similarities, the Final Rules differ from the Proposed Rules in several important respects.

- First, the Final Rules limit the reporting obligations' scope to attorneys having an attorney-client relationship with the issuer. This excludes persons employed by issuers who are attorneys by training but who do not provide legal advice to the issuer.

- Second, the Final Rules create a safe harbor from the reporting obligations for attorneys admitted to practice outside the United States that qualify as "non-appearing foreign attorneys" under the definitions below.

- Third, the Final Rules adopt an evidentiary threshold that requires reporting whenever it would be unreasonable for a reasonable and prudent attorney to fail to conclude that the evidence makes it "reasonably likely" that a material violation has occurred, is ongoing or is about to occur. While it will be challenging for the SEC to show that it was unreasonable for an attorney to fail to reach a particular conclusion, the "reasonably likely" standard—which is lower than "more likely than not"—could create a flood of reports by cautious attorneys unsure of the scope of the Final Rules.

- Fourth, the Final Rules withdraw the documentation requirements initially offered for comment. Under the Proposed Rules, an attorney would have been required to document his report to the CLO and any response made to it and to retain that documentation for a reasonable amount of time. Similarly, the CLO would have been required to document any inquiry undertaken in response to a report. These requirements were withdrawn in the Final Rules.

- Finally, in response to widespread comments calling for the SEC to defer action on the controversial "noisy withdrawal" provisions of the Pro-

ATTORNEY CONDUCT STANDARDS

posed Rules, the SEC extended the comment period for these provisions until April 7, 2003. The SEC also proposed for comment an alternative "reporting out" proposal. Under this alternative, an attorney retained by the issuer would still be required to resign, but the issuer, rather than the attorney, would be required to make the resignation public. The attorney would have no obligation to disaffirm any tainted filing or submission. Comments on the alternative proposal were also due on April 7, 2003.

REPORTING REQUIREMENTS

The Final Rules, which create Part 205 of the Code of Federal Regulations, are surprisingly complex. Annexes A and B to this Chapter include flow charts that depict the various requirements.

The heart of the Final Rules is § 205.3. It sets forth the up-the-ladder reporting requirements. The principal features of the reporting procedure are:

- **Governing Principle.** Section 205.3(a) sets forth the governing principle of the Final Rules, which is that an attorney appearing and practicing before the SEC in the representation of an issuer owes his or her professional and ethical duties to the issuer as organization, and not to the issuer's officers, directors or employees.[5]

- **Duty to Report Evidence of a Material Violation.** Under § 205.3(b)(1) of the Final Rules, whenever an attorney appearing and practicing before the SEC in the representation of an issuer becomes aware of "evidence of a material violation" by the issuer or by any officer, director, employee or agent of the issuer, the attorney must report the evidence to the issuer's CLO or to both the CLO and the CEO.

- **Appropriate Response by CLO.** Upon receiving these reports, the CLO must cause such inquiry into the reported matter as he or she reasonably believes is "appropriate" to determine if a material violation has occurred, is ongoing or is about to occur. If the CLO reasonably finds no material violation, or concludes after being advised by outside counsel (retained with the consent of the issuer's board of directors, an appropriate board committee or a QLCC) that the issuer has a colorable de-

---

[5] The final version of § 205.3(a) does not include the language included in the Proposed Rules to the effect that an attorney must "act in the best interest of the issuer and its shareholders." 67 Fed. Reg. 71670, 71680 (Dec. 2, 2002). The SEC deleted this language in response to comments noting that such a duty would be inconsistent with existing state ethics rules and might have the unintended effect of creating a private right of action for breach of a new fiduciary duty to shareholders.

fense to the reported violation, then he or she must notify the reporting attorney of that conclusion and its basis. If instead the CLO concludes that a material violation has occurred, is ongoing or is about to occur, he or she must take reasonable steps to ensure the issuer adopts remedial measures, including sanctions if appropriate.

- **Duty to Report Higher Up the Ladder.** A reporting attorney who receives what he or she reasonably believes to be an appropriate and timely response from the CLO has no further obligation under the Final Rules. If the reporting attorney does not receive an appropriate and timely response from the CLO, or if the attorney believes that it would be futile to report to the CLO or CEO because either or both may be implicated in the misconduct, the attorney must report the evidence to either the audit committee of the issuer's board of directors or to another board committee consisting solely of independent directors. If the issuer has neither an audit committee nor such an independent committee, the attorney must, in the absence of an appropriate response from the issuer's CLO, report the evidence to the full board of directors. The CLO must inform the reporting attorney of any course of action taken in response to the report.

- **Appropriate Responses End the Reporting Obligation.** A reporting attorney who receives what he or she reasonably believes to be an appropriate response from the audit committee, independent committee of the board of directors or the board itself has no further reporting obligation. If, on the other hand, the reporting attorney does not reasonably believe the issuer has made an appropriate response within a reasonable time, § 205.3(b)(9) of the Final Rules requires the attorney to inform the CLO, the CEO and directors to whom the attorney reported of that belief and the reasons behind it.[6]

- **Qualified Legal Compliance Committee.** Section 205.3(c) of the Final Rules establishes an alternative reporting procedure under which an attorney may report evidence of a material violation to an issuer's QLCC, rather than to the issuer's CLO. A CLO may also refer reports to the QLCC. Attorneys who report to the QLCC satisfy their obligations under the Final Rules and are not required to assess the appropriateness of the issuer's response to the reported evidence.

---

[6] As further described below, the SEC has proposed for comment two alternative provisions that, upon such failure to receive an adequate response within a reasonable time, and assuming certain other conditions are met, would require resignation (by outside counsel) or similar steps (by inside counsel) and would cause notice of such resignation or steps to be given.

ATTORNEY CONDUCT STANDARDS

- **Obligations of Investigating Attorneys.** An attorney retained to investigate reported evidence of a material violation must inform the CLO of the results of the investigation. Unless each of the investigating attorney and the CLO reasonably believes that no material violation has occurred, is ongoing or is about to occur, the CLO must notify the issuer's board of directors, an independent board committee or the QLCC of the results of the investigation. If the CLO does not do so, the investigating attorney must report up the ladder. The attorney has no duty to make this report if the attorney was retained or is directed by the CLO to assert, consistent with his or her professional obligations, a colorable defense on behalf of the issuer in any investigation or proceeding arising from the alleged misconduct. In that case, the CLO must nevertheless keep the board informed as to the progress and outcome of the investigation or proceeding.[7]

COVERED ATTORNEYS; "NON-APPEARING FOREIGN ATTORNEYS"

The scope of the Final Rules comes, in large part, from how they define various key terms. The principal terms are discussed in the sections that follow.

"Attorney"

The Final Rules define an "attorney" as "any person who is admitted, licensed, or otherwise qualified to practice law in any jurisdiction, domestic or foreign, or who holds himself or herself out as admitted, licensed, or otherwise qualified to practice law."

"Appearing and Practicing" Before the SEC

Categories of Conduct. Section 205.2(a) of the Final Rules identifies four categories of conduct that cause an attorney to be "appearing and practicing" before the SEC. They are:

- transacting any business with the SEC, including communications in any form;

- representing an issuer in an SEC administrative proceeding or in connection with any SEC investigation, inquiry, information request or subpoena;

---

[7] If the investigating attorney is retained or directed by the QLCC to investigate the evidence or to assert a colorable defense, the investigating attorney need not report evidence of a material violation further within the client issuer. 17 C.F.R. § 205.3(b)(7).

- providing advice in respect of the U.S. securities laws or SEC rules or regulations regarding any document that the attorney has notice will be filed with or submitted to, or incorporated into any document that will be filed with or submitted to, the SEC. This includes providing such advice in the context of preparing, or participating in the preparation of, any such document; or

- advising an issuer as to whether information or a statement, opinion or other writing is required to be filed with or submitted to, or incorporated into any document that will be filed with or submitted to, the SEC.

This broad definition is designed to capture the full range of individuals who contribute, edit or prepare information contained in materials filed with the SEC, even if these individuals are not directly responsible for the actual filing.

Participation in the preparation of a document filed with the SEC will not be deemed "appearing and practicing" unless the attorney has notice that the document will be submitted to or filed with the SEC and provides securities law advice regarding the document. Thus, for example, an attorney that does nothing more than negotiate and draft a contract will not thereby be deemed to appear and practice before the SEC, even if the attorney knows the contract will be filed with the SEC as an exhibit. However, if the attorney provides securities law advice concerning the contract—for example, advises as to whether information concerning that contract must be filed with the SEC—the attorney will be deemed to appear and practice before the SEC.

This definition is quite broad, though more narrow than that originally proposed. It encompasses attorneys with only peripheral roles in the issuer's representation before the SEC. The attorney need not specialize in securities law, and the attorney may be covered even if he or she is not significantly involved in preparation of the filing. The Final Rules also apply to attorneys who advise the issuer that no action is necessary (*e.g.,* that no document need be filed, or disclosure made, under the circumstances).

Exemption for Non-Practicing Attorneys. An attorney will not be deemed to appear and practice before the SEC to the extent that he or she does not provide legal services to an issuer with whom that attorney has an attorney-client relationship. Whether an attorney-client relationship exists turns on the expectations and understandings between the two parties and is a question of federal law. This provision should exempt, for example, attorneys by training who work in investment banks but do not provide legal services.

ATTORNEY CONDUCT STANDARDS

"In the Representation of an Issuer"

Representation of an Issuer. The Final Rules define "in the representation of an issuer" as "providing legal services as an attorney for an issuer, regardless of whether the attorney is employed or retained by the issuer."[8] Under this definition, an attorney need not be employed by an issuer to act "in the representation of" that issuer. For example, an attorney employed by an investment adviser who helps prepare materials for a registered investment company that he or she knows will be submitted to the SEC, appears and practices before the SEC in the representation of the issuer even though he or she is not employed by that investment company.

Issuer. Section 205.2(h) of the Final Rules defines an "issuer" to mean an issuer that has securities registered under § 12 of the Exchange Act or that is required to file reports under § 15(d) of the Exchange Act. The definition also includes companies that have filed a registration statement under the Securities Act that has not yet become effective but that has not been withdrawn. The definition excludes foreign government issuers.[9]

Non-Public Subsidiaries of a Public Parent Company. The SEC also considers an attorney for entities controlled by an issuer to be acting "in the representation of an issuer" if the attorney provides legal services to the controlled entity on behalf of, at the behest, or for the benefit of the issuer.[10] Similarly, if that attorney completes work that will ultimately be submitted to the SEC by the parent (*e.g.*, as part of a disclosure document), he or she appears and practices before the SEC "in the representation of an issuer."

Safe Harbor for "Non-Appearing Foreign Attorneys"

In response to widespread concerns raised by non-U.S. attorneys, the Final Rules create a safe harbor from the reporting requirements for "non-appearing foreign attorneys." To qualify as a "non-appearing foreign attorney," an attorney:

- must be admitted to practice in a foreign jurisdiction;

---

[8] Underwriters' counsel would not be covered by the reporting requirements because such counsel would not provide legal services to the issuer. *See* the Adopting Release, 68 Fed. Reg. 6296, 6302, n. 52 (Feb. 6, 2003).

[9] Foreign government issuers are those eligible to register securities on Schedule B of the Securities Act.

[10] 17 C.F.R. § 205.2(h). In the Adopting Release, the SEC indicated that this definition is also intended to reflect the duty of an attorney retained by the issuer to report to the issuer evidence of misconduct by an agent (such as an underwriter) of the issuer.

- cannot hold himself or herself out as practicing, or give legal advice regarding, U.S. federal or state securities or other laws;[11] and

- must conduct activities that would constitute appearing and practicing before the SEC only (i) incidentally to, and in the ordinary course of, his or her foreign law practice; or (ii) in consultation with U.S. counsel.

Attorneys who satisfy the above conditions are exempt from the reporting requirements set forth in the Final Rules. Although the Final Rules do not exempt all foreign attorneys, the scope of the work customarily performed by most foreign attorneys should allow them to qualify for the exemption. Together with the provision described below excusing non-compliance with any provision of the Final Rules to the extent that it conflicts with home country law, the non-appearing foreign attorney provision should significantly lessen the burden of the Final Rules on foreign attorneys.

Evidence that Triggers a Reporting Obligation

The Final Rules require reporting when a covered attorney becomes aware of "evidence" of "a material violation." The Final Rules clarify the type of evidence that triggers the reporting requirement, and also identify what constitutes a "material violation."

"Evidence"

The Final Rules define "evidence of a material violation" as credible evidence,[12] based upon which it would be unreasonable, under the circumstances, for a prudent and competent attorney not to conclude that it is "reasonably likely" that a material violation has occurred, is ongoing or is about to occur.[13]

- The evidentiary standard, while objective, takes into account the fact that there may be a range of views an attorney could hold without being unreasonable. In the Adopting Release, the SEC also indicates that an attorney's particular circumstances, including his or her professional skills, background and experience, familiarity with the issuer and other factors, must be considered when assessing the reasonableness of an attorney's views.

---

[11] One example of conduct that might constitute holding oneself out as practicing U.S. federal or state securities laws might be distributing business cards highlighting one's admission to a U.S. state bar. Foreign attorneys who hold themselves out as practicing or advising on U.S. legal matters would not qualify for the safe harbor.

[12] This excludes "gossip, hearsay or innuendo." SEC Release No. 33-8185 (Jan. 29, 2003); 68 Fed. Reg. 6296, 6302 (Feb. 6, 2003) (citing comments of the Association of the Bar, dated Apr. 7, 2003).

[13] 17 C.F.R. § 205.2(e).

ATTORNEY CONDUCT STANDARDS

- The triggering standard is, however, relatively low. An attorney must report evidence raising a "reasonable likelihood" that a material violation has occurred, is ongoing or is about to occur. While surpassing mere suspicion, this standard encompasses evidence that would not be implicated by an actual knowledge standard or even by a standard based on probability (*e.g.*, a "more likely than not" standard).[14] Thus, even in situations where the evidence suggests that a violation probably has not occurred, reporting may still be required.

"Material Violation"

An attorney must report evidence of a "material violation" by an issuer or related parties. In response to concerns about the ability of an attorney to assess matters of foreign law, the final definition of "material violation" is limited to "a material violation of an applicable U.S. federal or state securities law, a material breach of fiduciary duty arising under U.S. federal or state law, or a similar material violation of any U.S. federal or state law."[15] For purposes of this definition, "material" retains its customary definition under the federal securities laws—*i.e.*, violations are material if a reasonable investor would consider them important when making decisions to buy, sell or hold securities, or when determining how to vote based on proxy materials.[16]

Material Violations of Federal or State Securities Laws. The definition of "material violation of securities laws" encompasses both federal and state securities laws. Attorneys working on a multi-state transaction are expected to report evidence of material violations stemming from *all* the securities laws applicable to the deal.

Material Breach of Fiduciary Duties. The Final Rules identify the typical common law breaches of fiduciary duties that give rise to an obligation to report. Section 205.2(d) of the Final Rules defines "breach of fiduciary duty" as "any breach of fiduciary or similar duty to the issuer recognized under an applicable federal or state statute or at common law, including but not limited to misfeasance, nonfeasance, abdication of duty, abuse of trust, and approval of unlawful transactions."

---

[14] In the Adopting Release, the SEC indicated that it intends the term "reasonably likely" to be consistent with the discussion of the term included in the adopting release for the final rule regarding disclosure of off-balance sheet arrangements. *See* SEC Release No. 34-47264 (Jan. 27, 2003) (reaffirming the SEC's view that "reasonably likely" is a lower disclosure threshold than "more likely than not" but one higher than "more than remote").

[15] 17 C.F.R. § 205.2(i). Although the Final Rules on their face do not require reporting of material violations of foreign law, in practice, a non-disclosed material violation of foreign law could give rise to a violation of Rule 10b-5 under the Exchange Act, thereby triggering a reporting obligation.

[16] *See generally Basic, Inc. v. Levinson*, 485 U.S. 224, 231-36 (1988).

Similar Material Violation. Section 307 of the Sarbanes-Oxley Act provides no guidance as to what types of violations Congress intended to include in the definition of "similar violation." Perhaps because the SEC itself does not know what the term means, the SEC similarly does not give direction, stating in the Proposing Release only that "it appears...the term [similar violation] is intended to extend beyond a breach of fiduciary duty or a violation of the securities laws"[17] and failing to discuss the term at all in the Adopting Release. Other possible "similar violations" may include breaches of fiduciary duties under ERISA.[18]

APPROPRIATE RESPONSE TO REPORTS

Generally

If an attorney does not receive an "appropriate response" within a "reasonable time"[19] to his report of evidence of a material violation from the CLO, the reporting attorney must report that evidence "up the ladder" as described above. The Final Rules define an "appropriate response" to be a response to reported evidence as a result of which the attorney "reasonably believes" that:

- no material violation has occurred, is ongoing or is about to occur;

- the issuer has adopted appropriate remedial measures (*i.e.,* steps or sanctions to stop any material violations that are ongoing, steps to prevent any material violation that has yet to occur and steps to remedy or "otherwise appropriately address" past material violations and to minimize the likelihood of their recurrence); or

- the issuer, with the consent of the issuer's board of directors, independent board committee or QLCC, has retained or directed an attorney to investigate the reported evidence and has either:

  —substantially implemented any remedial recommendation made by such attorney after a reasonable investigation; or

---

[17] Proposing Release, 67 Fed. Reg. 71672, 71679 (Dec. 2, 2002).
[18] *See* the Adopting Release, 68 Fed. Reg. 6296, 6301, n.40 (Feb. 6, 2003).
[19] The Final Rules do not define a "reasonable time." In the Adopting Release, the SEC notes that many remedial measures, such as disclosures and the cessation of ongoing material violations, will occur in "short order" after the decision to pursue them has been made, but that some remedial measures may take longer to implement. In the latter case, the Adopting Release suggests that a reasonable time means a reasonable period of time for the issuer to complete its remediation.

—been advised that such attorney may, consistent with his or her professional obligations, assert a colorable defense on behalf of the issuer in any investigation or proceeding relating to the reported evidence.

Attorneys may struggle somewhat with the notion of "appropriate remedial measures," for these are not established legal concepts. We would be surprised if any enforcement action turns on the adequacy of these measures.

"Reasonable Belief"

The attorney must "reasonably believe" that the issuer's response is appropriate before the reporting obligation is terminated. In the Adopting Release, the SEC indicates that in assessing the reasonableness of the attorney's belief, it will take into account "all attendant circumstances." These might include the "amount and weight of the evidence of a material violation, the severity of the apparent material violation and the scope of the investigation into the report." The SEC further indicates that while a CLO's assurance that no material violation exists would be relevant to the reasonableness of the belief, it cannot be dispositive. The attorney may, however, rely on reasonable and appropriate factual representations and legal determinations of persons on whom a reasonable attorney would rely.

Colorable Defense

Section 205.2(b)(3) of the Final Rules clarifies that the assertion of a colorable defense in an investigation or judicial or administrative proceeding is an appropriate response to reported evidence of a material violation. For these purposes, a "colorable defense" is any defense that an attorney could appropriately take consistent with his or her professional obligation to avoid asserting frivolous defenses.[20] Colorable defenses may include asserting a colorable basis for contending that the SEC staff should not prevail or requiring the SEC's staff or other litigant to bear the burden of its case. At the same time, the Final Rules require that the assertion of such a defense be made with the consent of the issuer's board of directors, an appropriate board committee or a QLCC. This provision is designed to prevent a CLO from avoiding the obligation to keep the board informed simply by retaining a new attorney to investigate so as to assert a colorable, but perhaps weak, defense.

---

[20] *See generally, e.g.*, FED. R. CIV. PROC. Rule 11 (prohibiting an attorney from raising frivolous claims or defenses).

QUALIFIED LEGAL COMPLIANCE COMMITTEE

The Final Rules allow, but do not require, an issuer's board of directors to create a qualified legal compliance committee as an alternative recipient of attorney reports.[21] An attorney who reports evidence of a material violation to the QLCC satisfies his or her obligations under the Final Rules and need not assess the appropriateness of the issuer's response. A CLO who receives an attorney's report may pass the report on to the QLCC and likewise fulfill his or her duties.

Composition

The QLCC, which may also be an audit or other committee [22] of the issuer's board of directors, must have at least one member of the issuer's audit committee[23] and two or more additional independent board members,[24] and must have adopted written procedures for the confidential receipt, retention and consideration of any report of evidence of a material violation under the Final Rules. All QLCC members must meet the independence standards set forth in § 205.2(k)(1), which prohibits direct or indirect employees of the issuer (or "interested persons," in the case of a registered investment companies) from serving as QLCC members. In the Adopting Release, the SEC indicates that it anticipates that these provisions will be amended to conform to the definition of "independent director" adopted in the final rules under Section 301 of the Sarbanes-Oxley Act.[25]

Authority and Responsibilities

When the QLCC receives an attorney's report, it is required to notify the issuer's CEO and CLO. The QLCC must then determine if the evidence warrants an investigation and, if so, direct the CLO or outside counsel to oversee the investigation. The QLCC must also notify the audit committee or the full board of directors that it has initiated an investigation and, at the conclusion of any such investigation, inform the CLO, the CEO and the board of directors of the results of the investigation. Finally, the QLCC has the authority and responsibility to recom-

---

[21] An issuer cannot simply establish a QLCC to respond to a specific incident. Under § 205.3(c), evidence of a material violation can be referred only to a QLCC that has been previously formed.

[22] This change was introduced in the Final Rules in response to comments that issuers should not be required to create a new committee to serve as a QLCC, so long as an existing committee contains the required number of independent directors.

[23] If the issuer does not have an audit committee, such member must be from an equivalent committee of independent directors.

[24] Although the Final Rules do not explicitly state that all members of the QLCC must be members of the board, this appears to be the intention.

[25] *See generally* SEC Release No. 33-8220 (Apr. 9, 2003) (adopting standards related to listed company audit committees) (the "Audit Committee Release"). These standards are discussed more fully in Chapters III and IV.

ATTORNEY CONDUCT STANDARDS

mend, by majority vote, remedial measures to the issuer in the event of wrongdoing.

If an issuer fails in any material respect to implement an appropriate response recommended by the QLCC, the QLCC must have the authority and responsibility, acting by majority vote, to "take all other appropriate action, including the authority to notify the [SEC]."[26] Thus, the QLCC must be authorized from the outset to notify the SEC of a failure by the issuer to implement the QLCC's recommendations, but it is neither required to do so nor may it be limited in its authority to do so by the degree of financial harm involved in the issuer's violation.

EXCEPTIONS TO DUTY TO MAINTAIN CONFIDENCES

New Exceptions

Section 205.3(d) of the Final Rules sets forth new exceptions to the attorney's obligation to maintain client confidences.[27] The exceptions permit, but do not require, an attorney to disclose, under specified circumstances, confidential client information. Section 205.3(d) supersedes any state ethics rules or laws that prohibit such disclosure. The exceptions are:

- **Self-Defense.** Section 205.3(d)(1) of the Final Rules permits disclosure by an attorney in order to defend against charges of failure to abide by the obligations set forth in the Final Rules. Permitted disclosure includes the report made of evidence of a material violation, the issuer's response to that report and any contemporaneous documentation relating to the report or subsequent response to it.

- **Prevent Financial Injury and Fraud.** Section 205.3(d)(2) of the Final Rules further permits attorneys to reveal, without the issuer's consent, confidential client information relating to a representation before the SEC, to the extent the attorney reasonably believes such disclosure is necessary:

    — to prevent a material violation that is likely to cause substantial injury to the financial interest or property of the issuer or investors;

---

[26] 17 C.F.R. § 205.2(k)(4).

[27] The Final Rules withdraw the provision included in the Proposing Rules that would have expressly provided that information an issuer shares with the SEC pursuant to a confidentiality agreement does not constitute a waiver of any other applicable privilege. The SEC withdrew this provision out of concern that some courts might not accept the SEC's analysis of the issue. The SEC will nonetheless continue its policy of entering into such confidentiality agreements and will vigorously argue in defense of such agreements where waiver of privilege is asserted.

— to prevent the issuer from committing or suborning perjury, or committing an act that is likely to perpetrate a fraud upon the SEC; or

— to rectify the consequences of material violation by the issuer that caused, or may cause, substantial injury to the financial interest or property of the issuer or investors in furtherance of which the attorney's services were used.

Comparison to Existing Confidentiality Rules

ABA Rules on Confidentiality. The SEC's exceptions follow established legal ethics concepts. Model Rule 1.6 of the American Bar Association (the "ABA") prohibits attorneys from disclosing information relating to a representation unless the disclosure is necessary to prevent "imminent death or substantial bodily harm."[28] The Ethics 2000 project within the ABA sought to include an exception to the obligation of confidentiality to prevent clients from committing a crime or fraud "that is reasonably certain to result in substantial injury to the financial interests or property of another." The ABA committee also suggested an exception "to prevent or mitigate substantial injury to the financial interests or property of another." Both of these exceptions would come into play only when the client is using the lawyer's services in furtherance of the wrongdoing.[29] The ABA rejected the proposal in 2000, but in July 2002 its Task Force on Corporate Responsibility included in its preliminary report (the "Cheek Report") another recommendation that the ABA adopt the Ethics 2000 exceptions to the attorney-client privilege.[30]

New York State Rules on Confidentiality. The New York Lawyer's Code of Professional Responsibility also prohibits lawyers from revealing confidential client information. The Code does, however, allow a lawyer to disclose "the intention of a client to commit a crime and the information necessary to prevent the crime."[31] The Code does not limit the types of crimes giving rise to this exception to the attorney-client privilege, thus allowing a lawyer to reveal information about a client's intention to commit fraud or other financial crimes.

The Final Rules are consistent with the Cheek Report and the New York Code's permissive, not mandatory, disclosure to prevent financial harm. There are differences among the codes, though, regarding the extent to which the attorney

---

[28] ABA/BNA LAWYERS' MANUAL ON PROFESSIONAL CONDUCT, American Bar Association and The Bureau of National Affairs, Inc. (2002), Rule 1.16 at 1:115.
[29] "Rule 1.6: Confidentiality of Information." ABA website, Ethics 2000 Report at http://www.abanet.org/cpr/e2k-rule16h.html.
[30] *Preliminary Report of the ABA Task Force on Corporate Responsibility*, July 16, 2002, at http://www.abanet.org/buslaw/corporateresponsibility.
[31] THE LAWYER'S CODE OF PROFESSIONAL RESPONSIBILITY, New York State Bar Association (2002), DR 4-101: Preservation of Confidences and Secrets of a Client, at 38.

ATTORNEY CONDUCT STANDARDS

involvement in the illegal action is a condition to allowing disclosure. The Cheek Report proposes permissive disclosure where the attorney's services are used to commit or facilitate a crime. The New York Code allows disclosure where the client intends to commit a crime, regardless of the attorney's actions or how the attorney knows of the impending crime. The Final Rules chart a third path by allowing the attorney to disclose confidential client information "related to the representation," thus limiting the information the attorney would be allowed to disclose to that uncovered in the course of representation.

CONFLICT WITH STATE AND FOREIGN LAW

The Final Rules supersede all state ethical regulations that would impose lower standards of reporting on attorneys facing material misconduct by a client issuer. Therefore, while the Final Rules override any state bar rules limiting reporting obligations or prohibiting disclosure of client confidences under circumstances in which reporting would be required, and disclosure allowed, by the Final Rules, they would not limit application of state rules that would require disclosure where the SEC would not.

Under the Final Rules, the SEC may sanction an attorney regardless of the discipline imposed upon him by a state bar association for the same actions. An attorney who complies in good faith with the SEC's requirements will not, however, be liable for violating any conflicting state ethics rules.

Section 205.6(d) of the Final Rules provides that attorneys practicing outside the United States will not be required to comply with the requirements set forth in the Final Rules to the extent that such compliance is prohibited by applicable foreign law.

SUPERVISORY ATTORNEYS

The Final Rules distinguish between the respective reporting responsibilities of supervisory and subordinate attorneys. "Supervisory" attorneys are those who direct or supervise another attorney who is appearing and practicing before the SEC in the representation of an issuer.[32] "Subordinate" attorneys are attorneys who appear and practice before the SEC in the representation of an issuer "under the supervision or direction of another attorney" other than the issuer's CLO.[33] A CLO is considered a supervisory attorney under the Final Rules.[34]

---

[32] 17 C.F.R. § 205.4(a).
[33] 17 C.F.R. § 205.5(a).
[34] 17 C.F.R. § 205.4(a).

Supervisory Attorney

Section 205.4(b) of the Final Rules requires a supervisory attorney to make "reasonable efforts" to ensure that a subordinate attorney under his or her supervision or direction is aware of and complies with the Final Rules. Whenever a subordinate attorney "appears and practices" before the SEC, so too does the supervisory attorney overseeing that subordinate attorney's work. The Final Rules do not specify exactly how supervisory attorneys would be required to fulfill their obligations, but examples could include providing appropriate training, creating procedures for subordinate attorneys to report evidence of material violations they encounter and adopting measures to monitor and enforce compliance with the procedures.

Subordinate Attorney

Section 205.5 provides that a subordinate attorney's reporting obligations are satisfied if the subordinate attorney reports to his or her supervising attorney evidence of a material violation of which the subordinate attorney has become aware in appearing and practicing before the SEC. Once a supervisory attorney receives a report from a subordinate attorney, the supervisory attorney, in effect, stands in the shoes of the reporting attorney and takes on the obligations that the subordinate attorney otherwise would have had under the Final Rules. Subordinate attorneys are permitted, but not required, to report up the ladder within a client issuer if they believe the supervisory attorney has failed to comply with the reporting obligations.

Law Firms

It is not clear whether a law firm could be found liable for a breach of the Final Rules. The definition of attorney speaks in terms of a "person," not just a "natural person," but many of the rules are written as if they would apply only to a natural person. It would not, however, be unprecedented for the SEC to apply its rules of professional conduct to law firms,[35] and the SEC also could issue a cease-and-desist order to a firm found to be a "cause" of an individual's violation.[36]

PENALTIES FOR VIOLATIONS OF THE FINAL RULES

A violation of the Final Rules would be treated the same as any other violation of the federal securities laws, with possible injunctive action and civil penalties. The SEC also may commence cease-and-desist and Rule 102(e) proceedings

---

[35] *See, e.g., In the Matter of Keating, Muething & Klekamp*, SEC Release No. 34-15982 (July 2, 1979).

[36] *See KPMG, LLP v. SEC*, 289 F.3d 109 (D.C. Cir. 2002).

ATTORNEY CONDUCT STANDARDS

against violating attorneys.[37] The Final Rules do not provide for criminal penalties, and § 205.7 makes clear that no private rights of action are available under the Final Rules.

NOISY WITHDRAWAL AND REPORTING OUT

Noisy Withdrawal

Generally. The SEC left open for comment until April 7, 2003 the controversial "noisy withdrawal" provisions set forth in the Proposing Release. Those provisions would go beyond Section 307's reporting requirements to oblige, under certain circumstances, reporting attorneys who do not receive an appropriate response to make a noisy withdrawal from the representation of the issuer. Only outside attorneys would be required to make a noisy withdrawal and only if:

- they have reported up the ladder within an issuer a material violation that they reasonably believe is ongoing or is about to occur;

- they reasonably believe the material violation is likely to result in substantial injury to the financial interest or property of the issuer or of investors; and

- they have not received within a reasonable time an appropriate response from the issuer's CLO or board of directors.

Because an attorney who reports evidence of a material violation to a QLCC has no further duty to assess the appropriateness of the response to that evidence, noisy withdrawal would not be required for an attorney using the QLCC reporting procedure.

For outside counsel, noisy withdrawal would include resigning from the representation, notifying the SEC that the withdrawal is based on "professional considerations" and disaffirming any submission to the SEC that the attorney helped prepare and believes is or may be materially false or misleading. In-house counsel also would be required to disaffirm any tainted submission, but would not be required to resign. CLOs would be required to inform attorneys subsequently retained after a reporting attorney's withdrawal that the previous attorney withdrew for "professional considerations." Attorneys may, but would not be required to, make a noisy withdrawal if the violation has already occurred but has no lasting effect. If the violation is not likely to injure substantially the financial interest

---

[37] Rule 102(e) provides that the SEC may discipline attorneys for "improper professional conduct." 60 Fed. Reg. 32738 (June 23, 1995).

or property of the issuer, there would be no ongoing duty for the attorney to disaffirm any SEC filing or submission.

Standard and Timing for Withdrawal. Unlike the "reasonably likely" evidentiary standard for reporting, the withdrawing attorney must "reasonably believe" a violation is ongoing or about to occur. An outside attorney would then be obliged to withdraw "forthwith" if the issuer fails to respond appropriately to his report and would be required to inform the SEC of the withdrawal within one day thereafter. Outside counsel would be directed to "promptly" disaffirm submissions to the SEC that they believe are tainted by the violation. In-house counsel disaffirming submissions to the SEC would be required to notify the SEC of this decision within one day of concluding that the issuer's response to a report is either inappropriate or unreasonably delayed, and disaffirm the documents "promptly" thereafter.

Alternative Reporting Out Proposal

The SEC has proposed an alternative "reporting out" procedure when attorneys receive an inappropriate response to the evidence reported.

Attorney Obligations. Under the proposed alternative, an attorney who has reported evidence of a material violation within an issuer but has not received within a reasonable time an appropriate response, and who:

- "reasonably concludes" that there is "substantial evidence" of a material violation;[38]

- that is ongoing or about to occur; and

- is likely to cause substantial injury to the financial interest or property of the issuer or of investors;

would be required either to:

- in the case of outside counsel, withdraw from representation and notify the issuer in writing of this withdrawal for "professional considerations"; or

- in the case of in-house counsel, cease participating in any matter related to the violation and notify the issuer in writing that he or she has not re-

---

[38] The Companion Release indicates that the words "reasonably concludes there is substantial evidence" are intended to provide a "different and higher evidentiary standard" for withdrawal than the "reasonably believes" standard used in the "noisy withdrawal" rules. The SEC requested comment on whether this higher standard is appropriate. If this standard is adopted, it should narrow considerably the circumstances requiring withdrawal. 68 Fed. Reg. 6324, 6328 (Feb. 6, 2003).

ceived an appropriate response in a reasonable time to his or her report of evidence of misconduct.[39]

Similarly, attorneys who reported evidence of a material violation and who reasonably believe they were discharged as a result of that report would be required to notify the issuer's CLO. CLOs would be required to advise any attorneys subsequently retained that the previous attorney resigned for "professional considerations." In addition, if the issuer fails to comply with its obligation to make an appropriate filing as described below, the proposed alternative would permit, but not require, an attorney to inform the SEC that he or she has provided the issuer with a notice as described above, indicating that such action was based on "professional considerations."

Because an attorney who reports to the QLCC has no duty to assess the appropriateness of the issuer's response, the reporting out procedure would not apply to an attorney who reports to a QLCC.

Issuer Obligations. After notifying the issuer in writing and withdrawing or ceasing activities, as appropriate, the attorney would have no further obligations under the proposed alternative. Within two days of receiving the notice, however, the issuer would be required to report the attorney's action to the SEC in an appropriate public filing on a Form 8-K, 20-F, or 40-F, as applicable.[40] The filing would report the attorney's action and describe the surrounding circumstances. The SEC seeks comment on whether an issuer should be permitted not to disclose the withdrawal after receiving independent legal advice that the reporting attorney acted unreasonably, or if the issuer implements an appropriate response to the evidence after receiving the attorney's withdrawal notice. It is unclear in the latter situation who may determine the appropriateness of the response if the reporting attorney has withdrawn.

---

[39] An attorney who, after having sought leave to withdraw from representation or to cease participation or assistance in a matter, would be prohibited from taking these actions by order or rule of any court, administrative body or other authority with jurisdiction over the attorney, need not take such actions. However, in that event the attorney must give notice to the issuer that, but for such prohibition, he or she would have taken such actions, and that notice will be deemed the equivalent of such action. *See* § 205.3(d)(2) of the "reporting out" proposal.

[40] Under the proposed amendments to Forms 20-F and 40-F, an issuer would be permitted for this purpose to file only the facing page of the form, the information required under this item and a signature page. Issuers would not be required to file a complete Form 20-F or 40-F each time they made a disclosure of an attorney's written notice. Nor would certifications of such filings by the CEO and CFO be required under Rule 13a-14 or 15d-14 under the Exchange Act. In the Companion Release, the SEC requested comment on whether Forms 20-F and 40-F are the appropriate forms for this disclosure, or whether the SEC should instead create a new form or require reporting on Form 6-K.

THE SARBANES-OXLEY ACT: ANALYSIS AND PRACTICE

RECOMMENDATIONS FOR COMPLYING WITH THE NEW RULES

To comply with the Final Rules, issuers should consider taking the following steps.

- **Develop a Written Policy for Reporting.** The policy should identify the person or entity to whom attorneys should report in the first instance. An alternative contact should also be identified in the event the initial contact is implicated in the misconduct. The policy should include procedures for how reports will be addressed. Matters that may be relevant to these procedures could include creation of a report log, a timeline for instigating an inquiry, a method for disposing of frivolous reports and documentation requirements to record results of investigations and reporting back to the attorney.

- **Circulate the Written Policy to All Attorneys.** Circulating the policy will effectively give attorneys notice of their new responsibilities and the issuer's processes for fulfilling them. The reporting policy should be re-circulated on an annual basis to in-house and regular outside counsel to remind them of their reporting duties and the procedures for meeting them.

- **Provide for Certification by Recipients.** Require in-house attorneys to sign certifications acknowledging that they have received the written policy and understand it. In-house attorneys should also affirmatively state their agreement to be bound by the written policy.

- **Insert Language in Engagement Letters.** Include in all new engagement letters language instructing outside lawyers to comply with the new rules and requiring their commitment to abide by the issuer's policy for reporting. The letter should include as an attachment the issuer's written policy, modified as necessary to address outside attorneys' obligations under the rules.

- **Provide Training for All Lawyers.** Develop training programs for lawyers as soon as possible, and include training on the Final Rules as part of a new lawyer's orientation. By providing this training and documenting attendance, issuers can demonstrate their good faith effort to educate attorneys about the Final Rules.

- **Consider Creating a QLCC.** QLCCs have the benefit of relieving reporting attorneys of their obligation to judge the "appropriateness" of the issuer's response. In addition, attorneys who report to a QLCC would not be required to make a "noisy withdrawal" or to follow the "reporting out" procedures under the SEC's proposals. On the other hand, despite the fact that the Final Rules are clear that they do not create a private right of action against QLCC members for failure to comply with their duties, independent directors may be hesitant to take on the obligations mandated by this new role. Given this concern, and considering that the audit committee is already required to consider complaints regarding accounting, internal controls and auditing matters,[41] issuers may find it preferable to use the audit committee as the QLCC, rather than creating a new stand-alone committee.

- **Foreign Lawyers Should Consult with U.S. Counsel on SEC-Related Matters.** Foreign lawyers wishing to qualify for the non-appearing foreign lawyer exemption should avoid holding themselves out as practicing or advising on U.S. law, and should advise on SEC matters only in consultation with U.S. counsel.

- **Provide for Mechanism to Monitor Compliance.** It is far worse to have procedures that are not followed than to have no procedures at all. Attorneys and firms should adopt mechanisms to monitor compliance and to follow up on indications of non-compliance.

- **Create Internal Consultative Mechanism.** Attorneys may be uncertain whether information indicates a potential violation or a permissible and common course of action for an issuer. Issuers should institutionalize a consultative mechanism by appointing a specific legal department ethics or compliance person to whom attorneys can address specific questions about suspicious information.

- **Provide for Regular Executive Sessions Among the Key Players.** The general counsel of an issuer should meet regularly with the QLCC or head of the audit committee to discuss any reports that have been made and the resulting actions by the issuer, as well as the adequacy of the reporting procedure for implementing the Final Rules.[42]

---

[41] *See* the Audit Committee Release. Similarly, the NYSE has proposed rules that would require audit committees to assist the board in its oversight of the issuer's compliance with legal and regulatory requirements. *See* Amendment No. 1 to the NYSE's Corporate Governance Rule Proposals; SEC Release No. 34-47672 (Apr. 11, 2003).

[42] This process should be coordinated with the audit committee's consideration of complaints concerning accounting, internal accounting controls or auditing matters. *See* the Audit Committee Release. Audit committee responsibilities under the Sarbanes-Oxley Act are addressed more fully in Chapter III.

THE SARBANES-OXLEY ACT: ANALYSIS AND PRACTICE

ANNEX A
Procedures Absent a Qualified Legal Compliance Committee

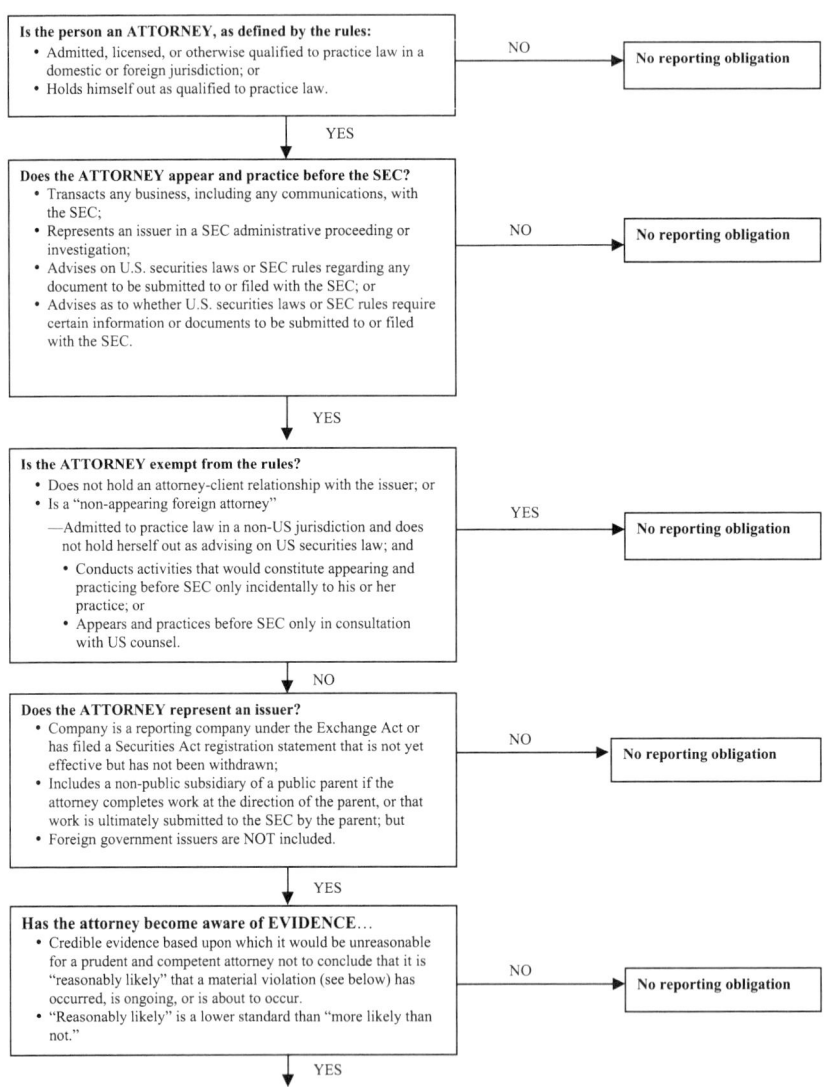

ATTORNEY CONDUCT STANDARDS

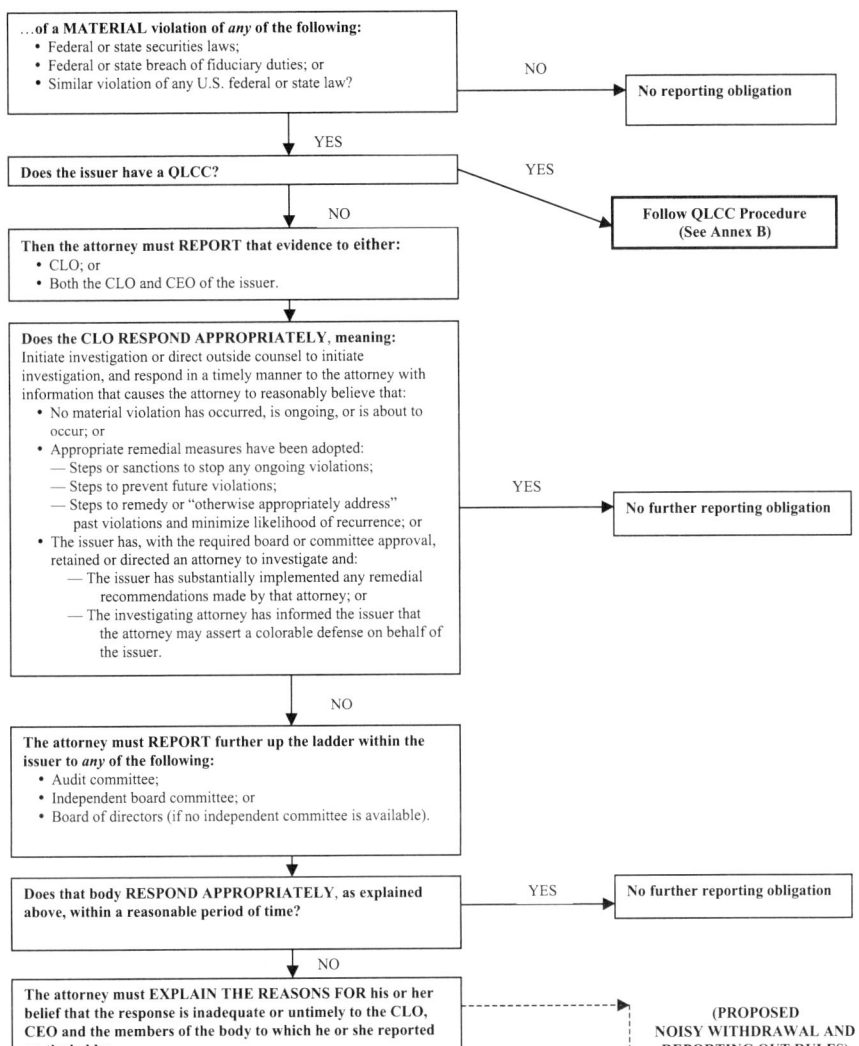

THE SARBANES-OXLEY ACT: ANALYSIS AND PRACTICE

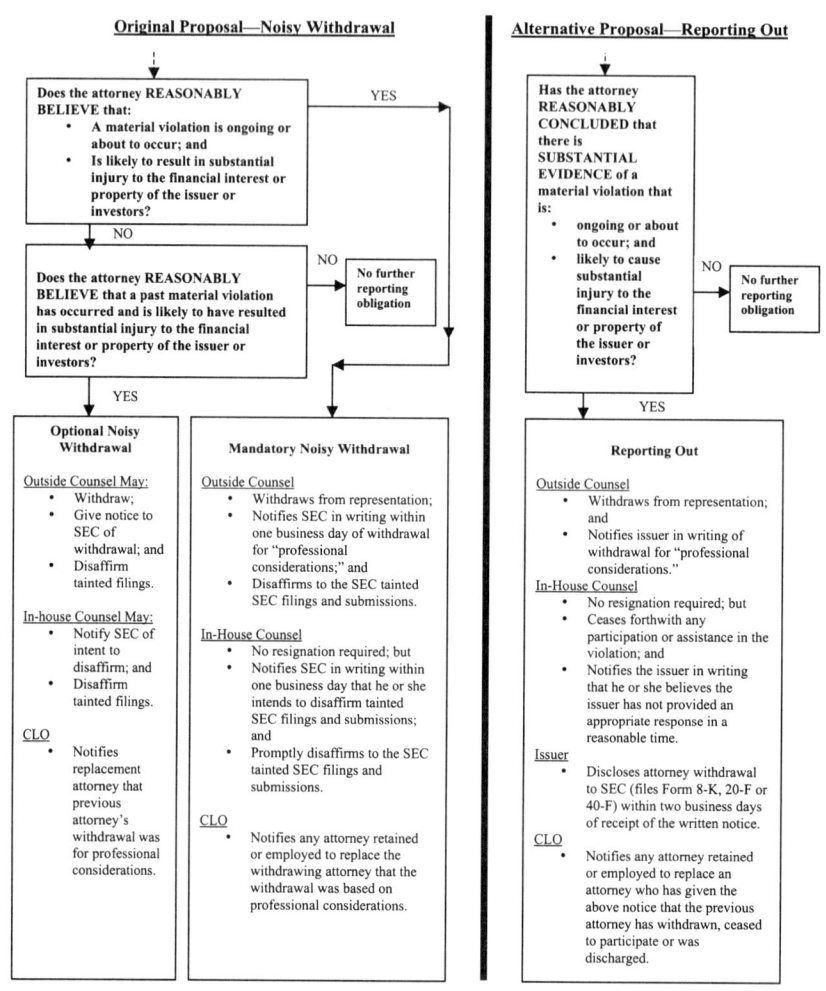

ATTORNEY CONDUCT STANDARDS

ANNEX B
Qualified Legal Compliance Committee Procedure

Does the issuer have a properly formed QLCC?
- Consists of at least one member of the issuer's audit committee and two or more independent board members;
- With adopted written procedures for the confidential receipt, retention, and consideration of a report;
- Established by board of directors before the attorney reports evidence of misconduct; and
- With the authority and responsibility, acting by majority vote, to take all other appropriate actions, including the authority to notify the SEC if the issuer fails to implement an appropriate response.

NO → **Attorney must REPORT using CLO procedures described in previous chart**

↓ YES

Then the attorney may REPORT evidence of a material violation to the QLCC...
- No further obligation on part of reporting attorney.
- CLO may refer reports to QLCC.

↓

After receiving a report, the QLCC must RESPOND APPROPRIATELY, meaning:
- Inform the CLO or CEO of the report;
- Determine whether an investigation is necessary;
- If an investigation is warranted:
  —Notify the audit committee or full board of directors;
  —Initiate an investigation, conducted either by the CLO or outside attorneys; and
  —Retain such additional expert personnel as necessary; and
- At the conclusion of the investigation:
  —Recommend, by majority vote, an appropriate response by the issuer;
  —Inform the CLO, CEO, and board of directors of the results of the investigations and the appropriate remedial measures to be adopted:
    - Steps or sanctions to stop any ongoing violations;
    - Steps to prevent future violations; and
    - Steps to remedy or "otherwise appropriately address" past violations and minimize likelihood of recurrence.

Appendix A
Sarbanes-Oxley Act of 2002

One Hundred Seventh Congress
of the
United States of America

AT THE SECOND SESSION

Begun and held at the City of Washington on Wednesday, the twenty-third day of January, two thousand and two

An Act

To protect investors by improving the accuracy and reliability of corporate disclosures made pursuant to the securities laws, and for other purposes.

Be it enacted by the Senate and House of Representatives of the United States of America in Congress assembled,

SECTION 1. SHORT TITLE; TABLE OF CONTENTS.

(a) SHORT TITLE.—This Act may be cited as the "Sarbanes-Oxley Act of 2002".

(b) TABLE OF CONTENTS.—The table of contents for this Act is as follows:

Sec. 1. Short title; table of contents.
Sec. 2. Definitions.
Sec. 3. Commission rules and enforcement.

TITLE I—PUBLIC COMPANY ACCOUNTING OVERSIGHT BOARD

Sec. 101. Establishment; administrative provisions.
Sec. 102. Registration with the Board.
Sec. 103. Auditing, quality control, and independence standards and rules.
Sec. 104. Inspections of registered public accounting firms.
Sec. 105. Investigations and disciplinary proceedings.
Sec. 106. Foreign public accounting firms.
Sec. 107. Commission oversight of the Board.
Sec. 108. Accounting standards.
Sec. 109. Funding.

TITLE II—AUDITOR INDEPENDENCE

Sec. 201. Services outside the scope of practice of auditors.
Sec. 202. Preapproval requirements.
Sec. 203. Audit partner rotation.
Sec. 204. Auditor reports to audit committees.
Sec. 205. Conforming amendments.
Sec. 206. Conflicts of interest.
Sec. 207. Study of mandatory rotation of registered public accounting firms.
Sec. 208. Commission authority.
Sec. 209. Considerations by appropriate State regulatory authorities.

TITLE III—CORPORATE RESPONSIBILITY

Sec. 301. Public company audit committees.
Sec. 302. Corporate responsibility for financial reports.
Sec. 303. Improper influence on conduct of audits.
Sec. 304. Forfeiture of certain bonuses and profits.
Sec. 305. Officer and director bars and penalties.
Sec. 306. Insider trades during pension fund blackout periods.
Sec. 307. Rules of professional responsibility for attorneys.
Sec. 308. Fair funds for investors.

TITLE IV—ENHANCED FINANCIAL DISCLOSURES

Sec. 401. Disclosures in periodic reports.
Sec. 402. Enhanced conflict of interest provisions.
Sec. 403. Disclosures of transactions involving management and principal stockholders.

Sec. 404. Management assessment of internal controls.
Sec. 405. Exemption.
Sec. 406. Code of ethics for senior financial officers.
Sec. 407. Disclosure of audit committee financial expert.
Sec. 408. Enhanced review of periodic disclosures by issuers.
Sec. 409. Real time issuer disclosures.

TITLE V—ANALYST CONFLICTS OF INTEREST

Sec. 501. Treatment of securities analysts by registered securities associations and national securities exchanges.

TITLE VI—COMMISSION RESOURCES AND AUTHORITY

Sec. 601. Authorization of appropriations.
Sec. 602. Appearance and practice before the Commission.
Sec. 603. Federal court authority to impose penny stock bars.
Sec. 604. Qualifications of associated persons of brokers and dealers.

TITLE VII—STUDIES AND REPORTS

Sec. 701. GAO study and report regarding consolidation of public accounting firms.
Sec. 702. Commission study and report regarding credit rating agencies.
Sec. 703. Study and report on violators and violations.
Sec. 704. Study of enforcement actions.
Sec. 705. Study of investment banks.

TITLE VIII—CORPORATE AND CRIMINAL FRAUD ACCOUNTABILITY

Sec. 801. Short title.
Sec. 802. Criminal penalties for altering documents.
Sec. 803. Debts nondischargeable if incurred in violation of securities fraud laws.
Sec. 804. Statute of limitations for securities fraud.
Sec. 805. Review of Federal Sentencing Guidelines for obstruction of justice and extensive criminal fraud.
Sec. 806. Protection for employees of publicly traded companies who provide evidence of fraud.
Sec. 807. Criminal penalties for defrauding shareholders of publicly traded companies.

TITLE IX—WHITE-COLLAR CRIME PENALTY ENHANCEMENTS

Sec. 901. Short title.
Sec. 902. Attempts and conspiracies to commit criminal fraud offenses.
Sec. 903. Criminal penalties for mail and wire fraud.
Sec. 904. Criminal penalties for violations of the Employee Retirement Income Security Act of 1974.
Sec. 905. Amendment to sentencing guidelines relating to certain white-collar offenses.
Sec. 906. Corporate responsibility for financial reports.

TITLE X—CORPORATE TAX RETURNS

Sec. 1001. Sense of the Senate regarding the signing of corporate tax returns by chief executive officers.

TITLE XI—CORPORATE FRAUD AND ACCOUNTABILITY

Sec. 1101. Short title.
Sec. 1102. Tampering with a record or otherwise impeding an official proceeding.
Sec. 1103. Temporary freeze authority for the Securities and Exchange Commission.
Sec. 1104. Amendment to the Federal Sentencing Guidelines.
Sec. 1105. Authority of the Commission to prohibit persons from serving as officers or directors.
Sec. 1106. Increased criminal penalties under Securities Exchange Act of 1934.
Sec. 1107. Retaliation against informants.

SEC. 2. DEFINITIONS.

(a) IN GENERAL.—In this Act, the following definitions shall apply:

(1) APPROPRIATE STATE REGULATORY AUTHORITY.—The term "appropriate State regulatory authority" means the State agency or other authority responsible for the licensure or other regulation of the practice of accounting in the State or States

having jurisdiction over a registered public accounting firm or associated person thereof, with respect to the matter in question.

(2) AUDIT.—The term "audit" means an examination of the financial statements of any issuer by an independent public accounting firm in accordance with the rules of the Board or the Commission (or, for the period preceding the adoption of applicable rules of the Board under section 103, in accordance with then-applicable generally accepted auditing and related standards for such purposes), for the purpose of expressing an opinion on such statements.

(3) AUDIT COMMITTEE.—The term "audit committee" means—

(A) a committee (or equivalent body) established by and amongst the board of directors of an issuer for the purpose of overseeing the accounting and financial reporting processes of the issuer and audits of the financial statements of the issuer; and

(B) if no such committee exists with respect to an issuer, the entire board of directors of the issuer.

(4) AUDIT REPORT.—The term "audit report" means a document or other record—

(A) prepared following an audit performed for purposes of compliance by an issuer with the requirements of the securities laws; and

(B) in which a public accounting firm either—

(i) sets forth the opinion of that firm regarding a financial statement, report, or other document; or

(ii) asserts that no such opinion can be expressed.

(5) BOARD.—The term "Board" means the Public Company Accounting Oversight Board established under section 101.

(6) COMMISSION.—The term "Commission" means the Securities and Exchange Commission.

(7) ISSUER.—The term "issuer" means an issuer (as defined in section 3 of the Securities Exchange Act of 1934 (15 U.S.C. 78c)), the securities of which are registered under section 12 of that Act (15 U.S.C. 78l), or that is required to file reports under section 15(d) (15 U.S.C. 78o(d)), or that files or has filed a registration statement that has not yet become effective under the Securities Act of 1933 (15 U.S.C. 77a *et seq.*), and that it has not withdrawn.

(8) NON-AUDIT SERVICES.—The term "non-audit services" means any professional services provided to an issuer by a registered public accounting firm, other than those provided to an issuer in connection with an audit or a review of the financial statements of an issuer.

(9) PERSON ASSOCIATED WITH A PUBLIC ACCOUNTING FIRM.—

(A) IN GENERAL.—The terms "person associated with a public accounting firm" (or with a "registered public accounting firm") and "associated person of a public accounting firm" (or of a "registered public accounting firm") mean any individual proprietor, partner, shareholder, principal, accountant, or other professional employee of a public accounting firm, or any other independent contractor or entity that, in connection with the preparation or issuance of any audit report—

(i) shares in the profits of, or receives compensation in any other form from, that firm; or
(ii) participates as agent or otherwise on behalf of such accounting firm in any activity of that firm.
(B) EXEMPTION AUTHORITY.—The Board may, by rule, exempt persons engaged only in ministerial tasks from the definition in subparagraph (A), to the extent that the Board determines that any such exemption is consistent with the purposes of this Act, the public interest, or the protection of investors.
(10) PROFESSIONAL STANDARDS.—The term "professional standards" means—
(A) accounting principles that are—
(i) established by the standard setting body described in section 19(b) of the Securities Act of 1933, as amended by this Act, or prescribed by the Commission under section 19(a) of that Act (15 U.S.C. 17a(s)) or section 13(b) of the Securities Exchange Act of 1934 (15 U.S.C. 78a(m)); and
(ii) relevant to audit reports for particular issuers, or dealt with in the quality control system of a particular registered public accounting firm; and
(B) auditing standards, standards for attestation engagements, quality control policies and procedures, ethical and competency standards, and independence standards (including rules implementing title II) that the Board or the Commission determines—
(i) relate to the preparation or issuance of audit reports for issuers; and
(ii) are established or adopted by the Board under section 103(a), or are promulgated as rules of the Commission.
(11) PUBLIC ACCOUNTING FIRM.—The term "public accounting firm" means—
(A) a proprietorship, partnership, incorporated association, corporation, limited liability company, limited liability partnership, or other legal entity that is engaged in the practice of public accounting or preparing or issuing audit reports; and
(B) to the extent so designated by the rules of the Board, any associated person of any entity described in subparagraph (A).
(12) REGISTERED PUBLIC ACCOUNTING FIRM.—The term "registered public accounting firm" means a public accounting firm registered with the Board in accordance with this Act.
(13) RULES OF THE BOARD.—The term "rules of the Board" means the bylaws and rules of the Board (as submitted to, and approved, modified, or amended by the Commission, in accordance with section 107), and those stated policies, practices, and interpretations of the Board that the Commission, by rule, may deem to be rules of the Board, as necessary or appropriate in the public interest or for the protection of investors.
(14) SECURITY.—The term "security" has the same meaning as in section 3(a) of the Securities Exchange Act of 1934 (15 U.S.C. 78c(a)).

APPENDIX A: SARBANES-OXLEY ACT OF 2002

(15) SECURITIES LAWS.—The term "securities laws" means the provisions of law referred to in section 3(a)(47) of the Securities Exchange Act of 1934 (15 U.S.C. 78c(a)(47)), as amended by this Act, and includes the rules, regulations, and orders issued by the Commission thereunder.

(16) STATE.—The term "State" means any State of the United States, the District of Columbia, Puerto Rico, the Virgin Islands, or any other territory or possession of the United States.

(b) CONFORMING AMENDMENT.—Section 3(a)(47) of the Securities Exchange Act of 1934 (15 U.S.C. 78c(a)(47)) is amended by inserting "the Sarbanes-Oxley Act of 2002," before "the Public".

SEC. 3. COMMISSION RULES AND ENFORCEMENT.

(a) REGULATORY ACTION.—The Commission shall promulgate such rules and regulations, as may be necessary or appropriate in the public interest or for the protection of investors, and in furtherance of this Act.—

(b) ENFORCEMENT.—

(1) IN GENERAL.—A violation by any person of this Act, any rule or regulation of the Commission issued under this Act, or any rule of the Board shall be treated for all purposes in the same manner as a violation of the Securities Exchange Act of 1934 (15 U.S.C. 78a et seq.) or the rules and regulations issued thereunder, consistent with the provisions of this Act, and any such person shall be subject to the same penalties, and to the same extent, as for a violation of that Act or such rules or regulations.

(2) INVESTIGATIONS, INJUNCTIONS, AND PROSECUTION OF OFFENSES.—Section 21 of the Securities Exchange Act of 1934 (15 U.S.C. 78u) is amended—

(A) in subsection (a)(1), by inserting "the rules of the Public Company Accounting Oversight Board, of which such person is a registered public accounting firm or a person associated with such a firm," after "is a participant,";

(B) in subsection (d)(1), by inserting "the rules of the Public Company Accounting Oversight Board, of which such person is a registered public accounting firm or a person associated with such a firm," after "is a participant,";

(C) in subsection (e), by inserting "the rules of the Public Company Accounting Oversight Board, of which such person is a registered public accounting firm or a person associated with such a firm," after "is a participant,"; and

(D) in subsection (f), by inserting "or the Public Company Accounting Oversight Board" after "self-regulatory organization" each place that term appears.

(3) CEASE-AND-DESIST PROCEEDINGS.—Section 21C(c)(2) of the Securities Exchange Act of 1934 (15 U.S.C. 78u–3(c)(2)) is amended by inserting "registered public accounting firm (as defined in section 2 of the Sarbanes-Oxley Act of 2002)," after "government securities dealer,".

(4) ENFORCEMENT BY FEDERAL BANKING AGENCIES.—Section 12(i) of the Securities Exchange Act of 1934 (15 U.S.C. 78l(i)) is amended by—

(A) striking "sections 12," each place it appears and inserting "sections 10A(m), 12,"; and

(B) striking "and 16," each place it appears and inserting "and 16 of this Act, and sections 302, 303, 304, 306, 401(b), 404, 406, and 407 of the Sarbanes-Oxley Act of 2002,".

(c) EFFECT ON COMMISSION AUTHORITY.—Nothing in this Act or the rules of the Board shall be construed to impair or limit—

(1) the authority of the Commission to regulate the accounting profession, accounting firms, or persons associated with such firms for purposes of enforcement of the securities laws;

(2) the authority of the Commission to set standards for accounting or auditing practices or auditor independence, derived from other provisions of the securities laws or the rules or regulations thereunder, for purposes of the preparation and issuance of any audit report, or otherwise under applicable law; or

(3) the ability of the Commission to take, on the initiative of the Commission, legal, administrative, or disciplinary action against any registered public accounting firm or any associated person thereof.

TITLE I—PUBLIC COMPANY ACCOUNTING OVERSIGHT BOARD

SEC. 101. ESTABLISHMENT; ADMINISTRATIVE PROVISIONS.

(a) ESTABLISHMENT OF BOARD.—There is established the Public Company Accounting Oversight Board, to oversee the audit of public companies that are subject to the securities laws, and related matters, in order to protect the interests of investors and further the public interest in the preparation of informative, accurate, and independent audit reports for companies the securities of which are sold to, and held by and for, public investors. The Board shall be a body corporate, operate as a nonprofit corporation, and have succession until dissolved by an Act of Congress.

(b) STATUS.—The Board shall not be an agency or establishment of the United States Government, and, except as otherwise provided in this Act, shall be subject to, and have all the powers conferred upon a nonprofit corporation by, the District of Columbia Nonprofit Corporation Act. No member or person employed by, or agent for, the Board shall be deemed to be an officer or employee of or agent for the Federal Government by reason of such service.

(c) DUTIES OF THE BOARD.—The Board shall, subject to action by the Commission under section 107, and once a determination is made by the Commission under subsection (d) of this section—

(1) register public accounting firms that prepare audit reports for issuers, in accordance with section 102;

(2) establish or adopt, or both, by rule, auditing, quality control, ethics, independence, and other standards relating to the preparation of audit reports for issuers, in accordance with section 103;

(3) conduct inspections of registered public accounting firms, in accordance with section 104 and the rules of the Board;

(4) conduct investigations and disciplinary proceedings concerning, and impose appropriate sanctions where justified upon,

registered public accounting firms and associated persons of such firms, in accordance with section 105;

(5) perform such other duties or functions as the Board (or the Commission, by rule or order) determines are necessary or appropriate to promote high professional standards among, and improve the quality of audit services offered by, registered public accounting firms and associated persons thereof, or otherwise to carry out this Act, in order to protect investors, or to further the public interest;

(6) enforce compliance with this Act, the rules of the Board, professional standards, and the securities laws relating to the preparation and issuance of audit reports and the obligations and liabilities of accountants with respect thereto, by registered public accounting firms and associated persons thereof; and

(7) set the budget and manage the operations of the Board and the staff of the Board.

(d) COMMISSION DETERMINATION.—The members of the Board shall take such action (including hiring of staff, proposal of rules, and adoption of initial and transitional auditing and other professional standards) as may be necessary or appropriate to enable the Commission to determine, not later than 270 days after the date of enactment of this Act, that the Board is so organized and has the capacity to carry out the requirements of this title, and to enforce compliance with this title by registered public accounting firms and associated persons thereof. The Commission shall be responsible, prior to the appointment of the Board, for the planning for the establishment and administrative transition to the Board's operation.

(e) BOARD MEMBERSHIP.—

(1) COMPOSITION.—The Board shall have 5 members, appointed from among prominent individuals of integrity and reputation who have a demonstrated commitment to the interests of investors and the public, and an understanding of the responsibilities for and nature of the financial disclosures required of issuers under the securities laws and the obligations of accountants with respect to the preparation and issuance of audit reports with respect to such disclosures.

(2) LIMITATION.—Two members, and only 2 members, of the Board shall be or have been certified public accountants pursuant to the laws of 1 or more States, provided that, if 1 of those 2 members is the chairperson, he or she may not have been a practicing certified public accountant for at least 5 years prior to his or her appointment to the Board.

(3) FULL-TIME INDEPENDENT SERVICE.—Each member of the Board shall serve on a full-time basis, and may not, concurrent with service on the Board, be employed by any other person or engage in any other professional or business activity. No member of the Board may share in any of the profits of, or receive payments from, a public accounting firm (or any other person, as determined by rule of the Commission), other than fixed continuing payments, subject to such conditions as the Commission may impose, under standard arrangements for the retirement of members of public accounting firms.

(4) APPOINTMENT OF BOARD MEMBERS.—

(A) INITIAL BOARD.—Not later than 90 days after the date of enactment of this Act, the Commission, after consultation with the Chairman of the Board of Governors of the Federal Reserve System and the Secretary of the Treasury, shall appoint the chairperson and other initial members of the Board, and shall designate a term of service for each.

(B) VACANCIES.—A vacancy on the Board shall not affect the powers of the Board, but shall be filled in the same manner as provided for appointments under this section.

(5) TERM OF SERVICE.—

(A) IN GENERAL.—The term of service of each Board member shall be 5 years, and until a successor is appointed, except that—

(i) the terms of office of the initial Board members (other than the chairperson) shall expire in annual increments, 1 on each of the first 4 anniversaries of the initial date of appointment; and

(ii) any Board member appointed to fill a vacancy occurring before the expiration of the term for which the predecessor was appointed shall be appointed only for the remainder of that term.

(B) TERM LIMITATION.—No person may serve as a member of the Board, or as chairperson of the Board, for more than 2 terms, whether or not such terms of service are consecutive.

(6) REMOVAL FROM OFFICE.—A member of the Board may be removed by the Commission from office, in accordance with section 107(d)(3), for good cause shown before the expiration of the term of that member.

(f) POWERS OF THE BOARD.—In addition to any authority granted to the Board otherwise in this Act, the Board shall have the power, subject to section 107—

(1) to sue and be sued, complain and defend, in its corporate name and through its own counsel, with the approval of the Commission, in any Federal, State, or other court;

(2) to conduct its operations and maintain offices, and to exercise all other rights and powers authorized by this Act, in any State, without regard to any qualification, licensing, or other provision of law in effect in such State (or a political subdivision thereof);

(3) to lease, purchase, accept gifts or donations of or otherwise acquire, improve, use, sell, exchange, or convey, all of or an interest in any property, wherever situated;

(4) to appoint such employees, accountants, attorneys, and other agents as may be necessary or appropriate, and to determine their qualifications, define their duties, and fix their salaries or other compensation (at a level that is comparable to private sector self-regulatory, accounting, technical, supervisory, or other staff or management positions);

(5) to allocate, assess, and collect accounting support fees established pursuant to section 109, for the Board, and other fees and charges imposed under this title; and

(6) to enter into contracts, execute instruments, incur liabilities, and do any and all other acts and things necessary, appropriate, or incidental to the conduct of its operations and the exercise of its obligations, rights, and powers imposed or granted by this title.

(g) RULES OF THE BOARD.—The rules of the Board shall, subject to the approval of the Commission—

(1) provide for the operation and administration of the Board, the exercise of its authority, and the performance of its responsibilities under this Act;

(2) permit, as the Board determines necessary or appropriate, delegation by the Board of any of its functions to an individual member or employee of the Board, or to a division of the Board, including functions with respect to hearing, determining, ordering, certifying, reporting, or otherwise acting as to any matter, except that—

(A) the Board shall retain a discretionary right to review any action pursuant to any such delegated function, upon its own motion;

(B) a person shall be entitled to a review by the Board with respect to any matter so delegated, and the decision of the Board upon such review shall be deemed to be the action of the Board for all purposes (including appeal or review thereof); and

(C) if the right to exercise a review described in subparagraph (A) is declined, or if no such review is sought within the time stated in the rules of the Board, then the action taken by the holder of such delegation shall for all purposes, including appeal or review thereof, be deemed to be the action of the Board;

(3) establish ethics rules and standards of conduct for Board members and staff, including a bar on practice before the Board (and the Commission, with respect to Board-related matters) of 1 year for former members of the Board, and appropriate periods (not to exceed 1 year) for former staff of the Board; and

(4) provide as otherwise required by this Act.

(h) ANNUAL REPORT TO THE COMMISSION.—The Board shall submit an annual report (including its audited financial statements) to the Commission, and the Commission shall transmit a copy of that report to the Committee on Banking, Housing, and Urban Affairs of the Senate, and the Committee on Financial Services of the House of Representatives, not later than 30 days after the date of receipt of that report by the Commission.

SEC. 102. REGISTRATION WITH THE BOARD.

(a) MANDATORY REGISTRATION.—Beginning 180 days after the date of the determination of the Commission under section 101(d), it shall be unlawful for any person that is not a registered public accounting firm to prepare or issue, or to participate in the preparation or issuance of, any audit report with respect to any issuer.

(b) APPLICATIONS FOR REGISTRATION.—

(1) FORM OF APPLICATION.—A public accounting firm shall use such form as the Board may prescribe, by rule, to apply for registration under this section.

(2) CONTENTS OF APPLICATIONS.—Each public accounting firm shall submit, as part of its application for registration, in such detail as the Board shall specify—

(A) the names of all issuers for which the firm prepared or issued audit reports during the immediately preceding calendar year, and for which the firm expects to prepare or issue audit reports during the current calendar year;

(B) the annual fees received by the firm from each such issuer for audit services, other accounting services, and non-audit services, respectively;

(C) such other current financial information for the most recently completed fiscal year of the firm as the Board may reasonably request;

(D) a statement of the quality control policies of the firm for its accounting and auditing practices;

(E) a list of all accountants associated with the firm who participate in or contribute to the preparation of audit reports, stating the license or certification number of each such person, as well as the State license numbers of the firm itself;

(F) information relating to criminal, civil, or administrative actions or disciplinary proceedings pending against the firm or any associated person of the firm in connection with any audit report;

(G) copies of any periodic or annual disclosure filed by an issuer with the Commission during the immediately preceding calendar year which discloses accounting disagreements between such issuer and the firm in connection with an audit report furnished or prepared by the firm for such issuer; and

(H) such other information as the rules of the Board or the Commission shall specify as necessary or appropriate in the public interest or for the protection of investors.

(3) CONSENTS.—Each application for registration under this subsection shall include—

(A) a consent executed by the public accounting firm to cooperation in and compliance with any request for testimony or the production of documents made by the Board in the furtherance of its authority and responsibilities under this title (and an agreement to secure and enforce similar consents from each of the associated persons of the public accounting firm as a condition of their continued employment by or other association with such firm); and

(B) a statement that such firm understands and agrees that cooperation and compliance, as described in the consent required by subparagraph (A), and the securing and enforcement of such consents from its associated persons, in accordance with the rules of the Board, shall be a condition to the continuing effectiveness of the registration of the firm with the Board.

(c) ACTION ON APPLICATIONS.—

(1) TIMING.—The Board shall approve a completed application for registration not later than 45 days after the date of receipt of the application, in accordance with the rules of the Board, unless the Board, prior to such date, issues a written notice of disapproval to, or requests more information from, the prospective registrant.

(2) TREATMENT.—A written notice of disapproval of a completed application under paragraph (1) for registration shall be treated as a disciplinary sanction for purposes of sections 105(d) and 107(c).

(d) PERIODIC REPORTS.—Each registered public accounting firm shall submit an annual report to the Board, and may be required to report more frequently, as necessary to update the information contained in its application for registration under this section, and to provide to the Board such additional information as the Board or the Commission may specify, in accordance with subsection (b)(2).

(e) PUBLIC AVAILABILITY.—Registration applications and annual reports required by this subsection, or such portions of such applications or reports as may be designated under rules of the Board, shall be made available for public inspection, subject to rules of the Board or the Commission, and to applicable laws relating to the confidentiality of proprietary, personal, or other information contained in such applications or reports, provided that, in all events, the Board shall protect from public disclosure information reasonably identified by the subject accounting firm as proprietary information.

(f) REGISTRATION AND ANNUAL FEES.—The Board shall assess and collect a registration fee and an annual fee from each registered public accounting firm, in amounts that are sufficient to recover the costs of processing and reviewing applications and annual reports.

SEC. 103. AUDITING, QUALITY CONTROL, AND INDEPENDENCE STANDARDS AND RULES.

(a) AUDITING, QUALITY CONTROL, AND ETHICS STANDARDS.—

(1) IN GENERAL.—The Board shall, by rule, establish, including, to the extent it determines appropriate, through adoption of standards proposed by 1 or more professional groups of accountants designated pursuant to paragraph (3)(A) or advisory groups convened pursuant to paragraph (4), and amend or otherwise modify or alter, such auditing and related attestation standards, such quality control standards, and such ethics standards to be used by registered public accounting firms in the preparation and issuance of audit reports, as required by this Act or the rules of the Commission, or as may be necessary or appropriate in the public interest or for the protection of investors.

(2) RULE REQUIREMENTS.—In carrying out paragraph (1), the Board—

(A) shall include in the auditing standards that it adopts, requirements that each registered public accounting firm shall—

(i) prepare, and maintain for a period of not less than 7 years, audit work papers, and other information related to any audit report, in sufficient detail to support the conclusions reached in such report;

(ii) provide a concurring or second partner review and approval of such audit report (and other related information), and concurring approval in its issuance, by a qualified person (as prescribed by the Board) associated with the public accounting firm, other than the person in charge of the audit, or by an independent reviewer (as prescribed by the Board); and

(iii) describe in each audit report the scope of the auditor's testing of the internal control structure and procedures of the issuer, required by section 404(b), and present (in such report or in a separate report)—

(I) the findings of the auditor from such testing;
(II) an evaluation of whether such internal control structure and procedures—
(aa) include maintenance of records that in reasonable detail accurately and fairly reflect the transactions and dispositions of the assets of the issuer;
(bb) provide reasonable assurance that transactions are recorded as necessary to permit preparation of financial statements in accordance with generally accepted accounting principles, and that receipts and expenditures of the issuer are being made only in accordance with authorizations of management and directors of the issuer; and
(III) a description, at a minimum, of material weaknesses in such internal controls, and of any material noncompliance found on the basis of such testing.

(B) shall include, in the quality control standards that it adopts with respect to the issuance of audit reports, requirements for every registered public accounting firm relating to—
(i) monitoring of professional ethics and independence from issuers on behalf of which the firm issues audit reports;
(ii) consultation within such firm on accounting and auditing questions;
(iii) supervision of audit work;
(iv) hiring, professional development, and advancement of personnel;
(v) the acceptance and continuation of engagements;
(vi) internal inspection; and
(vii) such other requirements as the Board may prescribe, subject to subsection (a)(1).

(3) AUTHORITY TO ADOPT OTHER STANDARDS.—
(A) IN GENERAL.—In carrying out this subsection, the Board—
(i) may adopt as its rules, subject to the terms of section 107, any portion of any statement of auditing standards or other professional standards that the Board determines satisfy the requirements of paragraph (1), and that were proposed by 1 or more professional groups of accountants that shall be designated or recognized by the Board, by rule, for such purpose, pursuant to this paragraph or 1 or more advisory groups convened pursuant to paragraph (4); and
(ii) notwithstanding clause (i), shall retain full authority to modify, supplement, revise, or subsequently amend, modify, or repeal, in whole or in part, any portion of any statement described in clause (i).

(B) INITIAL AND TRANSITIONAL STANDARDS.—The Board shall adopt standards described in subparagraph (A)(i) as initial or transitional standards, to the extent the Board determines necessary, prior to a determination of the

APPENDIX A: SARBANES-OXLEY ACT OF 2002

Commission under section 101(d), and such standards shall be separately approved by the Commission at the time of that determination, without regard to the procedures required by section 107 that otherwise would apply to the approval of rules of the Board.

(4) ADVISORY GROUPS.—The Board shall convene, or authorize its staff to convene, such expert advisory groups as may be appropriate, which may include practicing accountants and other experts, as well as representatives of other interested groups, subject to such rules as the Board may prescribe to prevent conflicts of interest, to make recommendations concerning the content (including proposed drafts) of auditing, quality control, ethics, independence, or other standards required to be established under this section.

(b) INDEPENDENCE STANDARDS AND RULES.—The Board shall establish such rules as may be necessary or appropriate in the public interest or for the protection of investors, to implement, or as authorized under, title II of this Act.

(c) COOPERATION WITH DESIGNATED PROFESSIONAL GROUPS OF ACCOUNTANTS AND ADVISORY GROUPS.—

(1) IN GENERAL.—The Board shall cooperate on an ongoing basis with professional groups of accountants designated under subsection (a)(3)(A) and advisory groups convened under subsection (a)(4) in the examination of the need for changes in any standards subject to its authority under subsection (a), recommend issues for inclusion on the agendas of such designated professional groups of accountants or advisory groups, and take such other steps as it deems appropriate to increase the effectiveness of the standard setting process.

(2) BOARD RESPONSES.—The Board shall respond in a timely fashion to requests from designated professional groups of accountants and advisory groups referred to in paragraph (1) for any changes in standards over which the Board has authority.

(d) EVALUATION OF STANDARD SETTING PROCESS.—The Board shall include in the annual report required by section 101(h) the results of its standard setting responsibilities during the period to which the report relates, including a discussion of the work of the Board with any designated professional groups of accountants and advisory groups described in paragraphs (3)(A) and (4) of subsection (a), and its pending issues agenda for future standard setting projects.

SEC. 104. INSPECTIONS OF REGISTERED PUBLIC ACCOUNTING FIRMS.

(a) IN GENERAL.—The Board shall conduct a continuing program of inspections to assess the degree of compliance of each registered public accounting firm and associated persons of that firm with this Act, the rules of the Board, the rules of the Commission, or professional standards, in connection with its performance of audits, issuance of audit reports, and related matters involving issuers.

(b) INSPECTION FREQUENCY.—

(1) IN GENERAL.—Subject to paragraph (2), inspections required by this section shall be conducted—

(A) annually with respect to each registered public accounting firm that regularly provides audit reports for more than 100 issuers; and

(B) not less frequently than once every 3 years with respect to each registered public accounting firm that regularly provides audit reports for 100 or fewer issuers.

(2) ADJUSTMENTS TO SCHEDULES.—The Board may, by rule, adjust the inspection schedules set under paragraph (1) if the Board finds that different inspection schedules are consistent with the purposes of this Act, the public interest, and the protection of investors. The Board may conduct special inspections at the request of the Commission or upon its own motion.

(c) PROCEDURES.—The Board shall, in each inspection under this section, and in accordance with its rules for such inspections—

(1) identify any act or practice or omission to act by the registered public accounting firm, or by any associated person thereof, revealed by such inspection that may be in violation of this Act, the rules of the Board, the rules of the Commission, the firm's own quality control policies, or professional standards;

(2) report any such act, practice, or omission, if appropriate, to the Commission and each appropriate State regulatory authority; and

(3) begin a formal investigation or take disciplinary action, if appropriate, with respect to any such violation, in accordance with this Act and the rules of the Board.

(d) CONDUCT OF INSPECTIONS.—In conducting an inspection of a registered public accounting firm under this section, the Board shall—

(1) inspect and review selected audit and review engagements of the firm (which may include audit engagements that are the subject of ongoing litigation or other controversy between the firm and 1 or more third parties), performed at various offices and by various associated persons of the firm, as selected by the Board;

(2) evaluate the sufficiency of the quality control system of the firm, and the manner of the documentation and communication of that system by the firm; and

(3) perform such other testing of the audit, supervisory, and quality control procedures of the firm as are necessary or appropriate in light of the purpose of the inspection and the responsibilities of the Board.

(e) RECORD RETENTION.—The rules of the Board may require the retention by registered public accounting firms for inspection purposes of records whose retention is not otherwise required by section 103 or the rules issued thereunder.

(f) PROCEDURES FOR REVIEW.—The rules of the Board shall provide a procedure for the review of and response to a draft inspection report by the registered public accounting firm under inspection. The Board shall take such action with respect to such response as it considers appropriate (including revising the draft report or continuing or supplementing its inspection activities before issuing a final report), but the text of any such response, appropriately redacted to protect information reasonably identified by the accounting firm as confidential, shall be attached to and made part of the inspection report.

(g) REPORT.—A written report of the findings of the Board for each inspection under this section, subject to subsection (h), shall be—

APPENDIX A: SARBANES-OXLEY ACT OF 2002

(1) transmitted, in appropriate detail, to the Commission and each appropriate State regulatory authority, accompanied by any letter or comments by the Board or the inspector, and any letter of response from the registered public accounting firm; and

(2) made available in appropriate detail to the public (subject to section 105(b)(5)(A), and to the protection of such confidential and proprietary information as the Board may determine to be appropriate, or as may be required by law), except that no portions of the inspection report that deal with criticisms of or potential defects in the quality control systems of the firm under inspection shall be made public if those criticisms or defects are addressed by the firm, to the satisfaction of the Board, not later than 12 months after the date of the inspection report.

(h) INTERIM COMMISSION REVIEW.—

(1) REVIEWABLE MATTERS.—A registered public accounting firm may seek review by the Commission, pursuant to such rules as the Commission shall promulgate, if the firm—

(A) has provided the Board with a response, pursuant to rules issued by the Board under subsection (f), to the substance of particular items in a draft inspection report, and disagrees with the assessments contained in any final report prepared by the Board following such response; or

(B) disagrees with the determination of the Board that criticisms or defects identified in an inspection report have not been addressed to the satisfaction of the Board within 12 months of the date of the inspection report, for purposes of subsection (g)(2).

(2) TREATMENT OF REVIEW.—Any decision of the Commission with respect to a review under paragraph (1) shall not be reviewable under section 25 of the Securities Exchange Act of 1934 (15 U.S.C. 78y), or deemed to be "final agency action" for purposes of section 704 of title 5, United States Code.

(3) TIMING.—Review under paragraph (1) may be sought during the 30-day period following the date of the event giving rise to the review under subparagraph (A) or (B) of paragraph (1).

SEC. 105. INVESTIGATIONS AND DISCIPLINARY PROCEEDINGS.

(a) IN GENERAL.—The Board shall establish, by rule, subject to the requirements of this section, fair procedures for the investigation and disciplining of registered public accounting firms and associated persons of such firms.

(b) INVESTIGATIONS.—

(1) AUTHORITY.—In accordance with the rules of the Board, the Board may conduct an investigation of any act or practice, or omission to act, by a registered public accounting firm, any associated person of such firm, or both, that may violate any provision of this Act, the rules of the Board, the provisions of the securities laws relating to the preparation and issuance of audit reports and the obligations and liabilities of accountants with respect thereto, including the rules of the Commission issued under this Act, or professional standards, regardless of how the act, practice, or omission is brought to the attention of the Board.

(2) TESTIMONY AND DOCUMENT PRODUCTION.—In addition to such other actions as the Board determines to be necessary or appropriate, the rules of the Board may—

(A) require the testimony of the firm or of any person associated with a registered public accounting firm, with respect to any matter that the Board considers relevant or material to an investigation;

(B) require the production of audit work papers and any other document or information in the possession of a registered public accounting firm or any associated person thereof, wherever domiciled, that the Board considers relevant or material to the investigation, and may inspect the books and records of such firm or associated person to verify the accuracy of any documents or information supplied;

(C) request the testimony of, and production of any document in the possession of, any other person, including any client of a registered public accounting firm that the Board considers relevant or material to an investigation under this section, with appropriate notice, subject to the needs of the investigation, as permitted under the rules of the Board; and

(D) provide for procedures to seek issuance by the Commission, in a manner established by the Commission, of a subpoena to require the testimony of, and production of any document in the possession of, any person, including any client of a registered public accounting firm, that the Board considers relevant or material to an investigation under this section.

(3) NONCOOPERATION WITH INVESTIGATIONS.—

(A) IN GENERAL.—If a registered public accounting firm or any associated person thereof refuses to testify, produce documents, or otherwise cooperate with the Board in connection with an investigation under this section, the Board may—

(i) suspend or bar such person from being associated with a registered public accounting firm, or require the registered public accounting firm to end such association;

(ii) suspend or revoke the registration of the public accounting firm; and

(iii) invoke such other lesser sanctions as the Board considers appropriate, and as specified by rule of the Board.

(B) PROCEDURE.—Any action taken by the Board under this paragraph shall be subject to the terms of section 107(c).

(4) COORDINATION AND REFERRAL OF INVESTIGATIONS.—

(A) COORDINATION.—The Board shall notify the Commission of any pending Board investigation involving a potential violation of the securities laws, and thereafter coordinate its work with the work of the Commission's Division of Enforcement, as necessary to protect an ongoing Commission investigation.

(B) REFERRAL.—The Board may refer an investigation under this section—

(i) to the Commission;

APPENDIX A: SARBANES-OXLEY ACT OF 2002

(ii) to any other Federal functional regulator (as defined in section 509 of the Gramm-Leach-Bliley Act (15 U.S.C. 6809)), in the case of an investigation that concerns an audit report for an institution that is subject to the jurisdiction of such regulator; and

(iii) at the direction of the Commission, to—

(I) the Attorney General of the United States;

(II) the attorney general of 1 or more States; and

(III) the appropriate State regulatory authority.

(5) USE OF DOCUMENTS.—

(A) CONFIDENTIALITY.—Except as provided in subparagraph (B), all documents and information prepared or received by or specifically for the Board, and deliberations of the Board and its employees and agents, in connection with an inspection under section 104 or with an investigation under this section, shall be confidential and privileged as an evidentiary matter (and shall not be subject to civil discovery or other legal process) in any proceeding in any Federal or State court or administrative agency, and shall be exempt from disclosure, in the hands of an agency or establishment of the Federal Government, under the Freedom of Information Act (5 U.S.C. 552a), or otherwise, unless and until presented in connection with a public proceeding or released in accordance with subsection (c).

(B) AVAILABILITY TO GOVERNMENT AGENCIES.—Without the loss of its status as confidential and privileged in the hands of the Board, all information referred to in subparagraph (A) may—

(i) be made available to the Commission; and

(ii) in the discretion of the Board, when determined by the Board to be necessary to accomplish the purposes of this Act or to protect investors, be made available to—

(I) the Attorney General of the United States;

(II) the appropriate Federal functional regulator (as defined in section 509 of the Gramm-Leach-Bliley Act (15 U.S.C. 6809)), other than the Commission, with respect to an audit report for an institution subject to the jurisdiction of such regulator;

(III) State attorneys general in connection with any criminal investigation; and

(IV) any appropriate State regulatory authority,

each of which shall maintain such information as confidential and privileged.

(6) IMMUNITY.—Any employee of the Board engaged in carrying out an investigation under this Act shall be immune from any civil liability arising out of such investigation in the same manner and to the same extent as an employee of the Federal Government in similar circumstances.

(c) DISCIPLINARY PROCEDURES.—

(1) NOTIFICATION; RECORDKEEPING.—The rules of the Board shall provide that in any proceeding by the Board to determine

whether a registered public accounting firm, or an associated person thereof, should be disciplined, the Board shall—

(A) bring specific charges with respect to the firm or associated person;

(B) notify such firm or associated person of, and provide to the firm or associated person an opportunity to defend against, such charges; and

(C) keep a record of the proceedings.

(2) PUBLIC HEARINGS.—Hearings under this section shall not be public, unless otherwise ordered by the Board for good cause shown, with the consent of the parties to such hearing.

(3) SUPPORTING STATEMENT.—A determination by the Board to impose a sanction under this subsection shall be supported by a statement setting forth—

(A) each act or practice in which the registered public accounting firm, or associated person, has engaged (or omitted to engage), or that forms a basis for all or a part of such sanction;

(B) the specific provision of this Act, the securities laws, the rules of the Board, or professional standards which the Board determines has been violated; and

(C) the sanction imposed, including a justification for that sanction.

(4) SANCTIONS.—If the Board finds, based on all of the facts and circumstances, that a registered public accounting firm or associated person thereof has engaged in any act or practice, or omitted to act, in violation of this Act, the rules of the Board, the provisions of the securities laws relating to the preparation and issuance of audit reports and the obligations and liabilities of accountants with respect thereto, including the rules of the Commission issued under this Act, or professional standards, the Board may impose such disciplinary or remedial sanctions as it determines appropriate, subject to applicable limitations under paragraph (5), including—

(A) temporary suspension or permanent revocation of registration under this title;

(B) temporary or permanent suspension or bar of a person from further association with any registered public accounting firm;

(C) temporary or permanent limitation on the activities, functions, or operations of such firm or person (other than in connection with required additional professional education or training);

(D) a civil money penalty for each such violation, in an amount equal to—

(i) not more than $100,000 for a natural person or $2,000,000 for any other person; and

(ii) in any case to which paragraph (5) applies, not more than $750,000 for a natural person or $15,000,000 for any other person;

(E) censure;

(F) required additional professional education or training; or

(G) any other appropriate sanction provided for in the rules of the Board.

APPENDIX A: SARBANES-OXLEY ACT OF 2002

(5) INTENTIONAL OR OTHER KNOWING CONDUCT.—The sanctions and penalties described in subparagraphs (A) through (C) and (D)(ii) of paragraph (4) shall only apply to—

(A) intentional or knowing conduct, including reckless conduct, that results in violation of the applicable statutory, regulatory, or professional standard; or

(B) repeated instances of negligent conduct, each resulting in a violation of the applicable statutory, regulatory, or professional standard.

(6) FAILURE TO SUPERVISE.—

(A) IN GENERAL.—The Board may impose sanctions under this section on a registered accounting firm or upon the supervisory personnel of such firm, if the Board finds that—

(i) the firm has failed reasonably to supervise an associated person, either as required by the rules of the Board relating to auditing or quality control standards, or otherwise, with a view to preventing violations of this Act, the rules of the Board, the provisions of the securities laws relating to the preparation and issuance of audit reports and the obligations and liabilities of accountants with respect thereto, including the rules of the Commission under this Act, or professional standards; and

(ii) such associated person commits a violation of this Act, or any of such rules, laws, or standards.

(B) RULE OF CONSTRUCTION.—No associated person of a registered public accounting firm shall be deemed to have failed reasonably to supervise any other person for purposes of subparagraph (A), if—

(i) there have been established in and for that firm procedures, and a system for applying such procedures, that comply with applicable rules of the Board and that would reasonably be expected to prevent and detect any such violation by such associated person; and

(ii) such person has reasonably discharged the duties and obligations incumbent upon that person by reason of such procedures and system, and had no reasonable cause to believe that such procedures and system were not being complied with.

(7) EFFECT OF SUSPENSION.—

(A) ASSOCIATION WITH A PUBLIC ACCOUNTING FIRM.—It shall be unlawful for any person that is suspended or barred from being associated with a registered public accounting firm under this subsection willfully to become or remain associated with any registered public accounting firm, or for any registered public accounting firm that knew, or, in the exercise of reasonable care should have known, of the suspension or bar, to permit such an association, without the consent of the Board or the Commission.

(B) ASSOCIATION WITH AN ISSUER.—It shall be unlawful for any person that is suspended or barred from being associated with an issuer under this subsection willfully to become or remain associated with any issuer in an accountancy or a financial management capacity, and for any issuer that knew, or in the exercise of reasonable care should have known, of such suspension or bar, to permit such an association, without the consent of the Board or the Commission.

(d) REPORTING OF SANCTIONS.—

(1) RECIPIENTS.—If the Board imposes a disciplinary sanction, in accordance with this section, the Board shall report the sanction to—

(A) the Commission;

(B) any appropriate State regulatory authority or any foreign accountancy licensing board with which such firm or person is licensed or certified; and

(C) the public (once any stay on the imposition of such sanction has been lifted).

(2) CONTENTS.—The information reported under paragraph (1) shall include—

(A) the name of the sanctioned person;

(B) a description of the sanction and the basis for its imposition; and

(C) such other information as the Board deems appropriate.

(e) STAY OF SANCTIONS.—

(1) IN GENERAL.—Application to the Commission for review, or the institution by the Commission of review, of any disciplinary action of the Board shall operate as a stay of any such disciplinary action, unless and until the Commission orders (summarily or after notice and opportunity for hearing on the question of a stay, which hearing may consist solely of the submission of affidavits or presentation of oral arguments) that no such stay shall continue to operate.

(2) EXPEDITED PROCEDURES.—The Commission shall establish for appropriate cases an expedited procedure for consideration and determination of the question of the duration of a stay pending review of any disciplinary action of the Board under this subsection.

SEC. 106. FOREIGN PUBLIC ACCOUNTING FIRMS.

(a) APPLICABILITY TO CERTAIN FOREIGN FIRMS.—

(1) IN GENERAL.—Any foreign public accounting firm that prepares or furnishes an audit report with respect to any issuer, shall be subject to this Act and the rules of the Board and the Commission issued under this Act, in the same manner and to the same extent as a public accounting firm that is organized and operates under the laws of the United States or any State, except that registration pursuant to section 102 shall not by itself provide a basis for subjecting such a foreign public accounting firm to the jurisdiction of the Federal or State courts, other than with respect to controversies between such firms and the Board.

(2) BOARD AUTHORITY.—The Board may, by rule, determine that a foreign public accounting firm (or a class of such firms) that does not issue audit reports nonetheless plays such a substantial role in the preparation and furnishing of such reports for particular issuers, that it is necessary or appropriate, in light of the purposes of this Act and in the public interest or for the protection of investors, that such firm (or class of firms) should be treated as a public accounting firm

APPENDIX A: SARBANES-OXLEY ACT OF 2002

(or firms) for purposes of registration under, and oversight by the Board in accordance with, this title.

(b) PRODUCTION OF AUDIT WORKPAPERS.—

(1) CONSENT BY FOREIGN FIRMS.—If a foreign public accounting firm issues an opinion or otherwise performs material services upon which a registered public accounting firm relies in issuing all or part of any audit report or any opinion contained in an audit report, that foreign public accounting firm shall be deemed to have consented—

(A) to produce its audit workpapers for the Board or the Commission in connection with any investigation by either body with respect to that audit report; and

(B) to be subject to the jurisdiction of the courts of the United States for purposes of enforcement of any request for production of such workpapers.

(2) CONSENT BY DOMESTIC FIRMS.—A registered public accounting firm that relies upon the opinion of a foreign public accounting firm, as described in paragraph (1), shall be deemed—

(A) to have consented to supplying the audit workpapers of that foreign public accounting firm in response to a request for production by the Board or the Commission; and

(B) to have secured the agreement of that foreign public accounting firm to such production, as a condition of its reliance on the opinion of that foreign public accounting firm.

(c) EXEMPTION AUTHORITY.—The Commission, and the Board, subject to the approval of the Commission, may, by rule, regulation, or order, and as the Commission (or Board) determines necessary or appropriate in the public interest or for the protection of investors, either unconditionally or upon specified terms and conditions exempt any foreign public accounting firm, or any class of such firms, from any provision of this Act or the rules of the Board or the Commission issued under this Act.

(d) DEFINITION.—In this section, the term "foreign public accounting firm" means a public accounting firm that is organized and operates under the laws of a foreign government or political subdivision thereof.

SEC. 107. COMMISSION OVERSIGHT OF THE BOARD.

(a) GENERAL OVERSIGHT RESPONSIBILITY.—The Commission shall have oversight and enforcement authority over the Board, as provided in this Act. The provisions of section 17(a)(1) of the Securities Exchange Act of 1934 (15 U.S.C. 78q(a)(1)), and of section 17(b)(1) of the Securities Exchange Act of 1934 (15 U.S.C. 78q(b)(1)) shall apply to the Board as fully as if the Board were a "registered securities association" for purposes of those sections 17(a)(1) and 17(b)(1).

(b) RULES OF THE BOARD.—

(1) DEFINITION.—In this section, the term "proposed rule" means any proposed rule of the Board, and any modification of any such rule.

(2) PRIOR APPROVAL REQUIRED.—No rule of the Board shall become effective without prior approval of the Commission in accordance with this section, other than as provided in section 103(a)(3)(B) with respect to initial or transitional standards.

(3) APPROVAL CRITERIA.—The Commission shall approve a proposed rule, if it finds that the rule is consistent with the requirements of this Act and the securities laws, or is necessary or appropriate in the public interest or for the protection of investors.

(4) PROPOSED RULE PROCEDURES.—The provisions of paragraphs (1) through (3) of section 19(b) of the Securities Exchange Act of 1934 (15 U.S.C. 78s(b)) shall govern the proposed rules of the Board, as fully as if the Board were a "registered securities association" for purposes of that section 19(b), except that, for purposes of this paragraph—

(A) the phrase "consistent with the requirements of this title and the rules and regulations thereunder applicable to such organization" in section 19(b)(2) of that Act shall be deemed to read "consistent with the requirements of title I of the Sarbanes-Oxley Act of 2002, and the rules and regulations issued thereunder applicable to such organization, or as necessary or appropriate in the public interest or for the protection of investors"; and

(B) the phrase "otherwise in furtherance of the purposes of this title" in section 19(b)(3)(C) of that Act shall be deemed to read "otherwise in furtherance of the purposes of title I of the Sarbanes-Oxley Act of 2002".

(5) COMMISSION AUTHORITY TO AMEND RULES OF THE BOARD.—The provisions of section 19(c) of the Securities Exchange Act of 1934 (15 U.S.C. 78s(c)) shall govern the abrogation, deletion, or addition to portions of the rules of the Board by the Commission as fully as if the Board were a "registered securities association" for purposes of that section 19(c), except that the phrase "to conform its rules to the requirements of this title and the rules and regulations thereunder applicable to such organization, or otherwise in furtherance of the purposes of this title" in section 19(c) of that Act shall, for purposes of this paragraph, be deemed to read "to assure the fair administration of the Public Company Accounting Oversight Board, conform the rules promulgated by that Board to the requirements of title I of the Sarbanes-Oxley Act of 2002, or otherwise further the purposes of that Act, the securities laws, and the rules and regulations thereunder applicable to that Board".

(c) COMMISSION REVIEW OF DISCIPLINARY ACTION TAKEN BY THE BOARD.—

(1) NOTICE OF SANCTION.—The Board shall promptly file notice with the Commission of any final sanction on any registered public accounting firm or on any associated person thereof, in such form and containing such information as the Commission, by rule, may prescribe.

(2) REVIEW OF SANCTIONS.—The provisions of sections 19(d)(2) and 19(e)(1) of the Securities Exchange Act of 1934 (15 U.S.C. 78s (d)(2) and (e)(1)) shall govern the review by the Commission of final disciplinary sanctions imposed by the Board (including sanctions imposed under section 105(b)(3) of this Act for noncooperation in an investigation of the Board), as fully as if the Board were a self-regulatory organization and the Commission were the appropriate regulatory agency for such organization for purposes of those sections 19(d)(2) and 19(e)(1), except that, for purposes of this paragraph—

(A) section 105(e) of this Act (rather than that section 19(d)(2)) shall govern the extent to which application for, or institution by the Commission on its own motion of, review of any disciplinary action of the Board operates as a stay of such action;

(B) references in that section 19(e)(1) to "members" of such an organization shall be deemed to be references to registered public accounting firms;

(C) the phrase "consistent with the purposes of this title" in that section 19(e)(1) shall be deemed to read "consistent with the purposes of this title and title I of the Sarbanes-Oxley Act of 2002";

(D) references to rules of the Municipal Securities Rulemaking Board in that section 19(e)(1) shall not apply; and

(E) the reference to section 19(e)(2) of the Securities Exchange Act of 1934 shall refer instead to section 107(c)(3) of this Act.

(3) COMMISSION MODIFICATION AUTHORITY.—The Commission may enhance, modify, cancel, reduce, or require the remission of a sanction imposed by the Board upon a registered public accounting firm or associated person thereof, if the Commission, having due regard for the public interest and the protection of investors, finds, after a proceeding in accordance with this subsection, that the sanction—

(A) is not necessary or appropriate in furtherance of this Act or the securities laws; or

(B) is excessive, oppressive, inadequate, or otherwise not appropriate to the finding or the basis on which the sanction was imposed.

(d) CENSURE OF THE BOARD; OTHER SANCTIONS.—

(1) RESCISSION OF BOARD AUTHORITY.—The Commission, by rule, consistent with the public interest, the protection of investors, and the other purposes of this Act and the securities laws, may relieve the Board of any responsibility to enforce compliance with any provision of this Act, the securities laws, the rules of the Board, or professional standards.

(2) CENSURE OF THE BOARD; LIMITATIONS.—The Commission may, by order, as it determines necessary or appropriate in the public interest, for the protection of investors, or otherwise in furtherance of the purposes of this Act or the securities laws, censure or impose limitations upon the activities, functions, and operations of the Board, if the Commission finds, on the record, after notice and opportunity for a hearing, that the Board—

(A) has violated or is unable to comply with any provision of this Act, the rules of the Board, or the securities laws; or

(B) without reasonable justification or excuse, has failed to enforce compliance with any such provision or rule, or any professional standard by a registered public accounting firm or an associated person thereof.

(3) CENSURE OF BOARD MEMBERS; REMOVAL FROM OFFICE.— The Commission may, as necessary or appropriate in the public interest, for the protection of investors, or otherwise in furtherance of the purposes of this Act or the securities laws, remove

from office or censure any member of the Board, if the Commission finds, on the record, after notice and opportunity for a hearing, that such member—

(A) has willfully violated any provision of this Act, the rules of the Board, or the securities laws;

(B) has willfully abused the authority of that member; or

(C) without reasonable justification or excuse, has failed to enforce compliance with any such provision or rule, or any professional standard by any registered public accounting firm or any associated person thereof.

SEC. 108. ACCOUNTING STANDARDS.

(a) AMENDMENT TO SECURITIES ACT OF 1933.—Section 19 of the Securities Act of 1933 (15 U.S.C. 77s) is amended—

(1) by redesignating subsections (b) and (c) as subsections (c) and (d), respectively; and

(2) by inserting after subsection (a) the following:

"(b) RECOGNITION OF ACCOUNTING STANDARDS.—

"(1) IN GENERAL.—In carrying out its authority under subsection (a) and under section 13(b) of the Securities Exchange Act of 1934, the Commission may recognize, as 'generally accepted' for purposes of the securities laws, any accounting principles established by a standard setting body—

"(A) that—

"(i) is organized as a private entity;

"(ii) has, for administrative and operational purposes, a board of trustees (or equivalent body) serving in the public interest, the majority of whom are not, concurrent with their service on such board, and have not been during the 2-year period preceding such service, associated persons of any registered public accounting firm;

"(iii) is funded as provided in section 109 of the Sarbanes-Oxley Act of 2002;

"(iv) has adopted procedures to ensure prompt consideration, by majority vote of its members, of changes to accounting principles necessary to reflect emerging accounting issues and changing business practices; and

"(v) considers, in adopting accounting principles, the need to keep standards current in order to reflect changes in the business environment, the extent to which international convergence on high quality accounting standards is necessary or appropriate in the public interest and for the protection of investors; and

"(B) that the Commission determines has the capacity to assist the Commission in fulfilling the requirements of subsection (a) and section 13(b) of the Securities Exchange Act of 1934, because, at a minimum, the standard setting body is capable of improving the accuracy and effectiveness of financial reporting and the protection of investors under the securities laws.

APPENDIX A: SARBANES-OXLEY ACT OF 2002

"(2) ANNUAL REPORT.—A standard setting body described in paragraph (1) shall submit an annual report to the Commission and the public, containing audited financial statements of that standard setting body.".

(b) COMMISSION AUTHORITY.—The Commission shall promulgate such rules and regulations to carry out section 19(b) of the Securities Act of 1933, as added by this section, as it deems necessary or appropriate in the public interest or for the protection of investors.

(c) NO EFFECT ON COMMISSION POWERS.—Nothing in this Act, including this section and the amendment made by this section, shall be construed to impair or limit the authority of the Commission to establish accounting principles or standards for purposes of enforcement of the securities laws.

(d) STUDY AND REPORT ON ADOPTING PRINCIPLES-BASED ACCOUNTING.—

(1) STUDY.—

(A) IN GENERAL.—The Commission shall conduct a study on the adoption by the United States financial reporting system of a principles-based accounting system.

(B) STUDY TOPICS.—The study required by subparagraph (A) shall include an examination of—

(i) the extent to which principles-based accounting and financial reporting exists in the United States;

(ii) the length of time required for change from a rules-based to a principles-based financial reporting system;

(iii) the feasibility of and proposed methods by which a principles-based system may be implemented; and

(iv) a thorough economic analysis of the implementation of a principles-based system.

(2) REPORT.—Not later than 1 year after the date of enactment of this Act, the Commission shall submit a report on the results of the study required by paragraph (1) to the Committee on Banking, Housing, and Urban Affairs of the Senate and the Committee on Financial Services of the House of Representatives.

SEC. 109. FUNDING.

(a) IN GENERAL.—The Board, and the standard setting body designated pursuant to section 19(b) of the Securities Act of 1933, as amended by section 108, shall be funded as provided in this section.

(b) ANNUAL BUDGETS.—The Board and the standard setting body referred to in subsection (a) shall each establish a budget for each fiscal year, which shall be reviewed and approved according to their respective internal procedures not less than 1 month prior to the commencement of the fiscal year to which the budget pertains (or at the beginning of the Board's first fiscal year, which may be a short fiscal year). The budget of the Board shall be subject to approval by the Commission. The budget for the first fiscal year of the Board shall be prepared and approved promptly following the appointment of the initial five Board members, to permit action by the Board of the organizational tasks contemplated by section 101(d).

(c) SOURCES AND USES OF FUNDS.—

(1) RECOVERABLE BUDGET EXPENSES.—The budget of the Board (reduced by any registration or annual fees received under section 102(e) for the year preceding the year for which the budget is being computed), and all of the budget of the standard setting body referred to in subsection (a), for each fiscal year of each of those 2 entities, shall be payable from annual accounting support fees, in accordance with subsections (d) and (e). Accounting support fees and other receipts of the Board and of such standard-setting body shall not be considered public monies of the United States.

(2) FUNDS GENERATED FROM THE COLLECTION OF MONETARY PENALTIES.—Subject to the availability in advance in an appropriations Act, and notwithstanding subsection (i), all funds collected by the Board as a result of the assessment of monetary penalties shall be used to fund a merit scholarship program for undergraduate and graduate students enrolled in accredited accounting degree programs, which program is to be administered by the Board or by an entity or agent identified by the Board.

(d) ANNUAL ACCOUNTING SUPPORT FEE FOR THE BOARD.—

(1) ESTABLISHMENT OF FEE.—The Board shall establish, with the approval of the Commission, a reasonable annual accounting support fee (or a formula for the computation thereof), as may be necessary or appropriate to establish and maintain the Board. Such fee may also cover costs incurred in the Board's first fiscal year (which may be a short fiscal year), or may be levied separately with respect to such short fiscal year.

(2) ASSESSMENTS.—The rules of the Board under paragraph (1) shall provide for the equitable allocation, assessment, and collection by the Board (or an agent appointed by the Board) of the fee established under paragraph (1), among issuers, in accordance with subsection (g), allowing for differentiation among classes of issuers, as appropriate.

(e) ANNUAL ACCOUNTING SUPPORT FEE FOR STANDARD SETTING BODY.—The annual accounting support fee for the standard setting body referred to in subsection (a)—

(1) shall be allocated in accordance with subsection (g), and assessed and collected against each issuer, on behalf of the standard setting body, by 1 or more appropriate designated collection agents, as may be necessary or appropriate to pay for the budget and provide for the expenses of that standard setting body, and to provide for an independent, stable source of funding for such body, subject to review by the Commission; and

(2) may differentiate among different classes of issuers.

(f) LIMITATION ON FEE.—The amount of fees collected under this section for a fiscal year on behalf of the Board or the standards setting body, as the case may be, shall not exceed the recoverable budget expenses of the Board or body, respectively (which may include operating, capital, and accrued items), referred to in subsection (c)(1).

(g) ALLOCATION OF ACCOUNTING SUPPORT FEES AMONG ISSUERS.—Any amount due from issuers (or a particular class of issuers) under this section to fund the budget of the Board or the standard setting body referred to in subsection (a) shall be allocated among and payable by each issuer (or each issuer in a particular class, as applicable) in an amount equal to the total of such amount, multiplied by a fraction—

(1) the numerator of which is the average monthly equity market capitalization of the issuer for the 12-month period immediately preceding the beginning of the fiscal year to which such budget relates; and

(2) the denominator of which is the average monthly equity market capitalization of all such issuers for such 12-month period.

(h) CONFORMING AMENDMENTS.—Section 13(b)(2) of the Securities Exchange Act of 1934 (15 U.S.C. 78m(b)(2)) is amended—

(1) in subparagraph (A), by striking "and" at the end; and

(2) in subparagraph (B), by striking the period at the end and inserting the following: "; and

"(C) notwithstanding any other provision of law, pay the allocable share of such issuer of a reasonable annual accounting support fee or fees, determined in accordance with section 109 of the Sarbanes-Oxley Act of 2002.".

(i) RULE OF CONSTRUCTION.—Nothing in this section shall be construed to render either the Board, the standard setting body referred to in subsection (a), or both, subject to procedures in Congress to authorize or appropriate public funds, or to prevent such organization from utilizing additional sources of revenue for its activities, such as earnings from publication sales, provided that each additional source of revenue shall not jeopardize, in the judgment of the Commission, the actual and perceived independence of such organization.

(j) START-UP EXPENSES OF THE BOARD.—From the unexpended balances of the appropriations to the Commission for fiscal year 2003, the Secretary of the Treasury is authorized to advance to the Board not to exceed the amount necessary to cover the expenses of the Board during its first fiscal year (which may be a short fiscal year).

TITLE II—AUDITOR INDEPENDENCE

SEC. 201. SERVICES OUTSIDE THE SCOPE OF PRACTICE OF AUDITORS.

(a) PROHIBITED ACTIVITIES.—Section 10A of the Securities Exchange Act of 1934 (15 U.S.C. 78j–1) is amended by adding at the end the following:

"(g) PROHIBITED ACTIVITIES.—Except as provided in subsection (h), it shall be unlawful for a registered public accounting firm (and any associated person of that firm, to the extent determined appropriate by the Commission) that performs for any issuer any audit required by this title or the rules of the Commission under this title or, beginning 180 days after the date of commencement of the operations of the Public Company Accounting Oversight Board established under section 101 of the Sarbanes-Oxley Act of 2002 (in this section referred to as the 'Board'), the rules of the Board, to provide to that issuer, contemporaneously with the audit, any non-audit service, including—

"(1) bookkeeping or other services related to the accounting records or financial statements of the audit client;

"(2) financial information systems design and implementation;

"(3) appraisal or valuation services, fairness opinions, or contribution-in-kind reports;
"(4) actuarial services;
"(5) internal audit outsourcing services;
"(6) management functions or human resources;
"(7) broker or dealer, investment adviser, or investment banking services;
"(8) legal services and expert services unrelated to the audit; and
"(9) any other service that the Board determines, by regulation, is impermissible.

"(h) PREAPPROVAL REQUIRED FOR NON-AUDIT SERVICES.—A registered public accounting firm may engage in any non-audit service, including tax services, that is not described in any of paragraphs (1) through (9) of subsection (g) for an audit client, only if the activity is approved in advance by the audit committee of the issuer, in accordance with subsection (i).".

(b) EXEMPTION AUTHORITY.—The Board may, on a case by case basis, exempt any person, issuer, public accounting firm, or transaction from the prohibition on the provision of services under section 10A(g) of the Securities Exchange Act of 1934 (as added by this section), to the extent that such exemption is necessary or appropriate in the public interest and is consistent with the protection of investors, and subject to review by the Commission in the same manner as for rules of the Board under section 107.

SEC. 202. PREAPPROVAL REQUIREMENTS.

Section 10A of the Securities Exchange Act of 1934 (15 U.S.C. 78j–1), as amended by this Act, is amended by adding at the end the following:
"(i) PREAPPROVAL REQUIREMENTS.—
"(1) IN GENERAL.—
"(A) AUDIT COMMITTEE ACTION.—All auditing services (which may entail providing comfort letters in connection with securities underwritings or statutory audits required for insurance companies for purposes of State law) and non-audit services, other than as provided in subparagraph (B), provided to an issuer by the auditor of the issuer shall be preapproved by the audit committee of the issuer.
"(B) DE MINIMUS EXCEPTION.—The preapproval requirement under subparagraph (A) is waived with respect to the provision of non-audit services for an issuer, if—
"(i) the aggregate amount of all such non-audit services provided to the issuer constitutes not more than 5 percent of the total amount of revenues paid by the issuer to its auditor during the fiscal year in which the nonaudit services are provided;
"(ii) such services were not recognized by the issuer at the time of the engagement to be non-audit services; and
"(iii) such services are promptly brought to the attention of the audit committee of the issuer and approved prior to the completion of the audit by the audit committee or by 1 or more members of the audit committee who are members of the board of directors to whom authority to grant such approvals has been delegated by the audit committee.

APPENDIX A: SARBANES-OXLEY ACT OF 2002

"(2) DISCLOSURE TO INVESTORS.—Approval by an audit committee of an issuer under this subsection of a non-audit service to be performed by the auditor of the issuer shall be disclosed to investors in periodic reports required by section 13(a).

"(3) DELEGATION AUTHORITY.—The audit committee of an issuer may delegate to 1 or more designated members of the audit committee who are independent directors of the board of directors, the authority to grant preapprovals required by this subsection. The decisions of any member to whom authority is delegated under this paragraph to preapprove an activity under this subsection shall be presented to the full audit committee at each of its scheduled meetings.

"(4) APPROVAL OF AUDIT SERVICES FOR OTHER PURPOSES.—In carrying out its duties under subsection (m)(2), if the audit committee of an issuer approves an audit service within the scope of the engagement of the auditor, such audit service shall be deemed to have been preapproved for purposes of this subsection.".

SEC. 203. AUDIT PARTNER ROTATION.

Section 10A of the Securities Exchange Act of 1934 (15 U.S.C. 78j–1), as amended by this Act, is amended by adding at the end the following:

"(j) AUDIT PARTNER ROTATION.—It shall be unlawful for a registered public accounting firm to provide audit services to an issuer if the lead (or coordinating) audit partner (having primary responsibility for the audit), or the audit partner responsible for reviewing the audit, has performed audit services for that issuer in each of the 5 previous fiscal years of that issuer.".

SEC. 204. AUDITOR REPORTS TO AUDIT COMMITTEES.

Section 10A of the Securities Exchange Act of 1934 (15 U.S.C. 78j–1), as amended by this Act, is amended by adding at the end the following:

"(k) REPORTS TO AUDIT COMMITTEES.—Each registered public accounting firm that performs for any issuer any audit required by this title shall timely report to the audit committee of the issuer—

"(1) all critical accounting policies and practices to be used;

"(2) all alternative treatments of financial information within generally accepted accounting principles that have been discussed with management officials of the issuer, ramifications of the use of such alternative disclosures and treatments, and the treatment preferred by the registered public accounting firm; and

"(3) other material written communications between the registered public accounting firm and the management of the issuer, such as any management letter or schedule of unadjusted differences.".

SEC. 205. CONFORMING AMENDMENTS.

(a) DEFINITIONS.—Section 3(a) of the Securities Exchange Act of 1934 (15 U.S.C. 78c(a)) is amended by adding at the end the following:

"(58) AUDIT COMMITTEE.—The term 'audit committee' means—

"(A) a committee (or equivalent body) established by and amongst the board of directors of an issuer for the purpose of overseeing the accounting and financial reporting processes of the issuer and audits of the financial statements of the issuer; and

"(B) if no such committee exists with respect to an issuer, the entire board of directors of the issuer.

"(59) REGISTERED PUBLIC ACCOUNTING FIRM.—The term 'registered public accounting firm' has the same meaning as in section 2 of the Sarbanes-Oxley Act of 2002.".

(b) AUDITOR REQUIREMENTS.—Section 10A of the Securities Exchange Act of 1934 (15 U.S.C. 78j–1) is amended—

(1) by striking "an independent public accountant" each place that term appears and inserting "a registered public accounting firm";

(2) by striking "the independent public accountant" each place that term appears and inserting "the registered public accounting firm";

(3) in subsection (c), by striking "No independent public accountant" and inserting "No registered public accounting firm"; and

(4) in subsection (b)—

(A) by striking "the accountant" each place that term appears and inserting "the firm";

(B) by striking "such accountant" each place that term appears and inserting "such firm"; and

(C) in paragraph (4), by striking "the accountant's report" and inserting "the report of the firm".

(c) OTHER REFERENCES.—The Securities Exchange Act of 1934 (15 U.S.C. 78a et seq.) is amended—

(1) in section 12(b)(1) (15 U.S.C. 78l(b)(1)), by striking "independent public accountants" each place that term appears and inserting "a registered public accounting firm"; and

(2) in subsections (e) and (i) of section 17 (15 U.S.C. 78q), by striking "an independent public accountant" each place that term appears and inserting "a registered public accounting firm".

(d) CONFORMING AMENDMENT.—Section 10A(f) of the Securities Exchange Act of 1934 (15 U.S.C. 78k(f)) is amended—

(1) by striking "DEFINITION" and inserting "DEFINITIONS"; and

(2) by adding at the end the following: "As used in this section, the term 'issuer' means an issuer (as defined in section 3), the securities of which are registered under section 12, or that is required to file reports pursuant to section 15(d), or that files or has filed a registration statement that has not yet become effective under the Securities Act of 1933 (15 U.S.C. 77a et seq.), and that it has not withdrawn.".

SEC. 206. CONFLICTS OF INTEREST.

Section 10A of the Securities Exchange Act of 1934 (15 U.S.C. 78j–1), as amended by this Act, is amended by adding at the end the following:

"(l) CONFLICTS OF INTEREST.—It shall be unlawful for a registered public accounting firm to perform for an issuer any audit service required by this title, if a chief executive officer, controller, chief financial officer, chief accounting officer, or any person serving in an equivalent position for the issuer, was employed by that registered independent public accounting firm and participated in

APPENDIX A: SARBANES-OXLEY ACT OF 2002

any capacity in the audit of that issuer during the 1-year period preceding the date of the initiation of the audit.".

SEC. 207. STUDY OF MANDATORY ROTATION OF REGISTERED PUBLIC ACCOUNTING FIRMS.

(a) STUDY AND REVIEW REQUIRED.—The Comptroller General of the United States shall conduct a study and review of the potential effects of requiring the mandatory rotation of registered public accounting firms.

(b) REPORT REQUIRED.—Not later than 1 year after the date of enactment of this Act, the Comptroller General shall submit a report to the Committee on Banking, Housing, and Urban Affairs of the Senate and the Committee on Financial Services of the House of Representatives on the results of the study and review required by this section.

(c) DEFINITION.—For purposes of this section, the term "mandatory rotation" refers to the imposition of a limit on the period of years in which a particular registered public accounting firm may be the auditor of record for a particular issuer.

SEC. 208. COMMISSION AUTHORITY.

(a) COMMISSION REGULATIONS.—Not later than 180 days after the date of enactment of this Act, the Commission shall issue final regulations to carry out each of subsections (g) through (l) of section 10A of the Securities Exchange Act of 1934, as added by this title.

(b) AUDITOR INDEPENDENCE.—It shall be unlawful for any registered public accounting firm (or an associated person thereof, as applicable) to prepare or issue any audit report with respect to any issuer, if the firm or associated person engages in any activity with respect to that issuer prohibited by any of subsections (g) through (l) of section 10A of the Securities Exchange Act of 1934, as added by this title, or any rule or regulation of the Commission or of the Board issued thereunder.

SEC. 209. CONSIDERATIONS BY APPROPRIATE STATE REGULATORY AUTHORITIES.

In supervising nonregistered public accounting firms and their associated persons, appropriate State regulatory authorities should make an independent determination of the proper standards applicable, particularly taking into consideration the size and nature of the business of the accounting firms they supervise and the size and nature of the business of the clients of those firms. The standards applied by the Board under this Act should not be presumed to be applicable for purposes of this section for small and medium sized nonregistered public accounting firms.

TITLE III—CORPORATE RESPONSIBILITY

SEC. 301. PUBLIC COMPANY AUDIT COMMITTEES.

Section 10A of the Securities Exchange Act of 1934 (15 U.S.C. 78f) is amended by adding at the end the following:

"(m) STANDARDS RELATING TO AUDIT COMMITTEES.—
   "(1) COMMISSION RULES.—

"(A) IN GENERAL.—Effective not later than 270 days after the date of enactment of this subsection, the Commission shall, by rule, direct the national securities exchanges and national securities associations to prohibit the listing of any security of an issuer that is not in compliance with the requirements of any portion of paragraphs (2) through (6).

"(B) OPPORTUNITY TO CURE DEFECTS.—The rules of the Commission under subparagraph (A) shall provide for appropriate procedures for an issuer to have an opportunity to cure any defects that would be the basis for a prohibition under subparagraph (A), before the imposition of such prohibition.

"(2) RESPONSIBILITIES RELATING TO REGISTERED PUBLIC ACCOUNTING FIRMS.—The audit committee of each issuer, in its capacity as a committee of the board of directors, shall be directly responsible for the appointment, compensation, and oversight of the work of any registered public accounting firm employed by that issuer (including resolution of disagreements between management and the auditor regarding financial reporting) for the purpose of preparing or issuing an audit report or related work, and each such registered public accounting firm shall report directly to the audit committee.

"(3) INDEPENDENCE.—

"(A) IN GENERAL.—Each member of the audit committee of the issuer shall be a member of the board of directors of the issuer, and shall otherwise be independent.

"(B) CRITERIA.—In order to be considered to be independent for purposes of this paragraph, a member of an audit committee of an issuer may not, other than in his or her capacity as a member of the audit committee, the board of directors, or any other board committee—

"(i) accept any consulting, advisory, or other compensatory fee from the issuer; or

"(ii) be an affiliated person of the issuer or any subsidiary thereof.

"(C) EXEMPTION AUTHORITY.—The Commission may exempt from the requirements of subparagraph (B) a particular relationship with respect to audit committee members, as the Commission determines appropriate in light of the circumstances.

"(4) COMPLAINTS.—Each audit committee shall establish procedures for—

"(A) the receipt, retention, and treatment of complaints received by the issuer regarding accounting, internal accounting controls, or auditing matters; and

"(B) the confidential, anonymous submission by employees of the issuer of concerns regarding questionable accounting or auditing matters.

"(5) AUTHORITY TO ENGAGE ADVISERS.—Each audit committee shall have the authority to engage independent counsel and other advisers, as it determines necessary to carry out its duties.

"(6) FUNDING.—Each issuer shall provide for appropriate funding, as determined by the audit committee, in its capacity as a committee of the board of directors, for payment of compensation—

"(A) to the registered public accounting firm employed by the issuer for the purpose of rendering or issuing an audit report; and
"(B) to any advisers employed by the audit committee under paragraph (5).".

SEC. 302. CORPORATE RESPONSIBILITY FOR FINANCIAL REPORTS.

(a) REGULATIONS REQUIRED.—The Commission shall, by rule, require, for each company filing periodic reports under section 13(a) or 15(d) of the Securities Exchange Act of 1934 (15 U.S.C. 78m, 78o(d)), that the principal executive officer or officers and the principal financial officer or officers, or persons performing similar functions, certify in each annual or quarterly report filed or submitted under either such section of such Act that—

(1) the signing officer has reviewed the report;

(2) based on the officer's knowledge, the report does not contain any untrue statement of a material fact or omit to state a material fact necessary in order to make the statements made, in light of the circumstances under which such statements were made, not misleading;

(3) based on such officer's knowledge, the financial statements, and other financial information included in the report, fairly present in all material respects the financial condition and results of operations of the issuer as of, and for, the periods presented in the report;

(4) the signing officers—
 (A) are responsible for establishing and maintaining internal controls;
 (B) have designed such internal controls to ensure that material information relating to the issuer and its consolidated subsidiaries is made known to such officers by others within those entities, particularly during the period in which the periodic reports are being prepared;
 (C) have evaluated the effectiveness of the issuer's internal controls as of a date within 90 days prior to the report; and
 (D) have presented in the report their conclusions about the effectiveness of their internal controls based on their evaluation as of that date;

(5) the signing officers have disclosed to the issuer's auditors and the audit committee of the board of directors (or persons fulfilling the equivalent function)—
 (A) all significant deficiencies in the design or operation of internal controls which could adversely affect the issuer's ability to record, process, summarize, and report financial data and have identified for the issuer's auditors any material weaknesses in internal controls; and
 (B) any fraud, whether or not material, that involves management or other employees who have a significant role in the issuer's internal controls; and

(6) the signing officers have indicated in the report whether or not there were significant changes in internal controls or in other factors that could significantly affect internal controls subsequent to the date of their evaluation, including any corrective actions with regard to significant deficiencies and material weaknesses.

(b) Foreign Reincorporations Have No Effect.—Nothing in this section 302 shall be interpreted or applied in any way to allow any issuer to lessen the legal force of the statement required under this section 302, by an issuer having reincorporated or having engaged in any other transaction that resulted in the transfer of the corporate domicile or offices of the issuer from inside the United States to outside of the United States.

(c) Deadline.—The rules required by subsection (a) shall be effective not later than 30 days after the date of enactment of this Act.

SEC. 303. IMPROPER INFLUENCE ON CONDUCT OF AUDITS.

(a) Rules To Prohibit.—It shall be unlawful, in contravention of such rules or regulations as the Commission shall prescribe as necessary and appropriate in the public interest or for the protection of investors, for any officer or director of an issuer, or any other person acting under the direction thereof, to take any action to fraudulently influence, coerce, manipulate, or mislead any independent public or certified accountant engaged in the performance of an audit of the financial statements of that issuer for the purpose of rendering such financial statements materially misleading.

(b) Enforcement.—In any civil proceeding, the Commission shall have exclusive authority to enforce this section and any rule or regulation issued under this section.

(c) No Preemption of Other Law.—The provisions of subsection (a) shall be in addition to, and shall not supersede or preempt, any other provision of law or any rule or regulation issued thereunder.

(d) Deadline for Rulemaking.—The Commission shall—

(1) propose the rules or regulations required by this section, not later than 90 days after the date of enactment of this Act; and

(2) issue final rules or regulations required by this section, not later than 270 days after that date of enactment.

SEC. 304. FORFEITURE OF CERTAIN BONUSES AND PROFITS.

(a) Additional Compensation Prior to Noncompliance With Commission Financial Reporting Requirements.—If an issuer is required to prepare an accounting restatement due to the material noncompliance of the issuer, as a result of misconduct, with any financial reporting requirement under the securities laws, the chief executive officer and chief financial officer of the issuer shall reimburse the issuer for—

(1) any bonus or other incentive-based or equity-based compensation received by that person from the issuer during the 12-month period following the first public issuance or filing with the Commission (whichever first occurs) of the financial document embodying such financial reporting requirement; and

(2) any profits realized from the sale of securities of the issuer during that 12-month period.

(b) Commission Exemption Authority.—The Commission may exempt any person from the application of subsection (a), as it deems necessary and appropriate.

SEC. 305. OFFICER AND DIRECTOR BARS AND PENALTIES.

(a) Unfitness Standard.—

APPENDIX A: SARBANES-OXLEY ACT OF 2002

(1) SECURITIES EXCHANGE ACT OF 1934.—Section 21(d)(2) of the Securities Exchange Act of 1934 (15 U.S.C. 78u(d)(2)) is amended by striking "substantial unfitness" and inserting "unfitness".

(2) SECURITIES ACT OF 1933.—Section 20(e) of the Securities Act of 1933 (15 U.S.C. 77t(e)) is amended by striking "substantial unfitness" and inserting "unfitness".

(b) EQUITABLE RELIEF.—Section 21(d) of the Securities Exchange Act of 1934 (15 U.S.C. 78u(d)) is amended by adding at the end the following:

"(5) EQUITABLE RELIEF.—In any action or proceeding brought or instituted by the Commission under any provision of the securities laws, the Commission may seek, and any Federal court may grant, any equitable relief that may be appropriate or necessary for the benefit of investors.".

SEC. 306. INSIDER TRADES DURING PENSION FUND BLACKOUT PERIODS.

(a) PROHIBITION OF INSIDER TRADING DURING PENSION FUND BLACKOUT PERIODS.—

(1) IN GENERAL.—Except to the extent otherwise provided by rule of the Commission pursuant to paragraph (3), it shall be unlawful for any director or executive officer of an issuer of any equity security (other than an exempted security), directly or indirectly, to purchase, sell, or otherwise acquire or transfer any equity security of the issuer (other than an exempted security) during any blackout period with respect to such equity security if such director or officer acquires such equity security in connection with his or her service or employment as a director or executive officer.

(2) REMEDY.—

(A) IN GENERAL.—Any profit realized by a director or executive officer referred to in paragraph (1) from any purchase, sale, or other acquisition or transfer in violation of this subsection shall inure to and be recoverable by the issuer, irrespective of any intention on the part of such director or executive officer in entering into the transaction.

(B) ACTIONS TO RECOVER PROFITS.—An action to recover profits in accordance with this subsection may be instituted at law or in equity in any court of competent jurisdiction by the issuer, or by the owner of any security of the issuer in the name and in behalf of the issuer if the issuer fails or refuses to bring such action within 60 days after the date of request, or fails diligently to prosecute the action thereafter, except that no such suit shall be brought more than 2 years after the date on which such profit was realized.

(3) RULEMAKING AUTHORIZED.—The Commission shall, in consultation with the Secretary of Labor, issue rules to clarify the application of this subsection and to prevent evasion thereof. Such rules shall provide for the application of the requirements of paragraph (1) with respect to entities treated as a single employer with respect to an issuer under section 414(b), (c), (m), or (o) of the Internal Revenue Code of 1986 to the extent necessary to clarify the application of such requirements and to prevent evasion thereof. Such rules may also provide for

appropriate exceptions from the requirements of this subsection, including exceptions for purchases pursuant to an automatic dividend reinvestment program or purchases or sales made pursuant to an advance election.

(4) BLACKOUT PERIOD.—For purposes of this subsection, the term "blackout period", with respect to the equity securities of any issuer—

(A) means any period of more than 3 consecutive business days during which the ability of not fewer than 50 percent of the participants or beneficiaries under all individual account plans maintained by the issuer to purchase, sell, or otherwise acquire or transfer an interest in any equity of such issuer held in such an individual account plan is temporarily suspended by the issuer or by a fiduciary of the plan; and

(B) does not include, under regulations which shall be prescribed by the Commission—

(i) a regularly scheduled period in which the participants and beneficiaries may not purchase, sell, or otherwise acquire or transfer an interest in any equity of such issuer, if such period is—

(I) incorporated into the individual account plan; and

(II) timely disclosed to employees before becoming participants under the individual account plan or as a subsequent amendment to the plan; or

(ii) any suspension described in subparagraph (A) that is imposed solely in connection with persons becoming participants or beneficiaries, or ceasing to be participants or beneficiaries, in an individual account plan by reason of a corporate merger, acquisition, divestiture, or similar transaction involving the plan or plan sponsor.

(5) INDIVIDUAL ACCOUNT PLAN.—For purposes of this subsection, the term "individual account plan" has the meaning provided in section 3(34) of the Employee Retirement Income Security Act of 1974 (29 U.S.C. 1002(34), except that such term shall not include a one-participant retirement plan (within the meaning of section 101(i)(8)(B) of such Act (29 U.S.C. 1021(i)(8)(B))).

(6) NOTICE TO DIRECTORS, EXECUTIVE OFFICERS, AND THE COMMISSION.—In any case in which a director or executive officer is subject to the requirements of this subsection in connection with a blackout period (as defined in paragraph (4)) with respect to any equity securities, the issuer of such equity securities shall timely notify such director or officer and the Securities and Exchange Commission of such blackout period.

(b) NOTICE REQUIREMENTS TO PARTICIPANTS AND BENEFICIARIES UNDER ERISA.—

(1) IN GENERAL.—Section 101 of the Employee Retirement Income Security Act of 1974 (29 U.S.C. 1021) is amended by redesignating the second subsection (h) as subsection (j), and by inserting after the first subsection (h) the following new subsection:

"(i) NOTICE OF BLACKOUT PERIODS TO PARTICIPANT OR BENEFICIARY UNDER INDIVIDUAL ACCOUNT PLAN.—
"(1) DUTIES OF PLAN ADMINISTRATOR.—In advance of the commencement of any blackout period with respect to an individual account plan, the plan administrator shall notify the plan participants and beneficiaries who are affected by such action in accordance with this subsection.
"(2) NOTICE REQUIREMENTS.—
"(A) IN GENERAL.—The notices described in paragraph (1) shall be written in a manner calculated to be understood by the average plan participant and shall include—
"(i) the reasons for the blackout period,
"(ii) an identification of the investments and other rights affected,
"(iii) the expected beginning date and length of the blackout period,
"(iv) in the case of investments affected, a statement that the participant or beneficiary should evaluate the appropriateness of their current investment decisions in light of their inability to direct or diversify assets credited to their accounts during the blackout period, and
"(v) such other matters as the Secretary may require by regulation.
"(B) NOTICE TO PARTICIPANTS AND BENEFICIARIES.—Except as otherwise provided in this subsection, notices described in paragraph (1) shall be furnished to all participants and beneficiaries under the plan to whom the blackout period applies at least 30 days in advance of the blackout period.
"(C) EXCEPTION TO 30-DAY NOTICE REQUIREMENT.—In any case in which—
"(i) a deferral of the blackout period would violate the requirements of subparagraph (A) or (B) of section 404(a)(1), and a fiduciary of the plan reasonably so determines in writing, or
"(ii) the inability to provide the 30-day advance notice is due to events that were unforeseeable or circumstances beyond the reasonable control of the plan administrator, and a fiduciary of the plan reasonably so determines in writing,
subparagraph (B) shall not apply, and the notice shall be furnished to all participants and beneficiaries under the plan to whom the blackout period applies as soon as reasonably possible under the circumstances unless such a notice in advance of the termination of the blackout period is impracticable.
"(D) WRITTEN NOTICE.—The notice required to be provided under this subsection shall be in writing, except that such notice may be in electronic or other form to the extent that such form is reasonably accessible to the recipient.
"(E) NOTICE TO ISSUERS OF EMPLOYER SECURITIES SUBJECT TO BLACKOUT PERIOD.—In the case of any blackout period in connection with an individual account plan, the plan administrator shall provide timely notice of such

blackout period to the issuer of any employer securities subject to such blackout period.

"(3) EXCEPTION FOR BLACKOUT PERIODS WITH LIMITED APPLICABILITY.—In any case in which the blackout period applies only to 1 or more participants or beneficiaries in connection with a merger, acquisition, divestiture, or similar transaction involving the plan or plan sponsor and occurs solely in connection with becoming or ceasing to be a participant or beneficiary under the plan by reason of such merger, acquisition, divestiture, or transaction, the requirement of this subsection that the notice be provided to all participants and beneficiaries shall be treated as met if the notice required under paragraph (1) is provided to such participants or beneficiaries to whom the blackout period applies as soon as reasonably practicable.

"(4) CHANGES IN LENGTH OF BLACKOUT PERIOD.—If, following the furnishing of the notice pursuant to this subsection, there is a change in the beginning date or length of the blackout period (specified in such notice pursuant to paragraph (2)(A)(iii)), the administrator shall provide affected participants and beneficiaries notice of the change as soon as reasonably practicable. In relation to the extended blackout period, such notice shall meet the requirements of paragraph (2)(D) and shall specify any material change in the matters referred to in clauses (i) through (v) of paragraph (2)(A).

"(5) REGULATORY EXCEPTIONS.—The Secretary may provide by regulation for additional exceptions to the requirements of this subsection which the Secretary determines are in the interests of participants and beneficiaries.

"(6) GUIDANCE AND MODEL NOTICES.—The Secretary shall issue guidance and model notices which meet the requirements of this subsection.

"(7) BLACKOUT PERIOD.—For purposes of this subsection—

"(A) IN GENERAL.—The term 'blackout period' means, in connection with an individual account plan, any period for which any ability of participants or beneficiaries under the plan, which is otherwise available under the terms of such plan, to direct or diversify assets credited to their accounts, to obtain loans from the plan, or to obtain distributions from the plan is temporarily suspended, limited, or restricted, if such suspension, limitation, or restriction is for any period of more than 3 consecutive business days.

"(B) EXCLUSIONS.—The term 'blackout period' does not include a suspension, limitation, or restriction—

"(i) which occurs by reason of the application of the securities laws (as defined in section 3(a)(47) of the Securities Exchange Act of 1934),

"(ii) which is a change to the plan which provides for a regularly scheduled suspension, limitation, or restriction which is disclosed to participants or beneficiaries through any summary of material modifications, any materials describing specific investment alternatives under the plan, or any changes thereto, or

"(iii) which applies only to 1 or more individuals, each of whom is the participant, an alternate payee (as defined in section 206(d)(3)(K)), or any other beneficiary pursuant to a qualified domestic relations order (as defined in section 206(d)(3)(B)(i)).

"(8) INDIVIDUAL ACCOUNT PLAN.—

"(A) IN GENERAL.—For purposes of this subsection, the term 'individual account plan' shall have the meaning provided such term in section 3(34), except that such term shall not include a one-participant retirement plan.

"(B) ONE-PARTICIPANT RETIREMENT PLAN.—For purposes of subparagraph (A), the term 'one-participant retirement plan' means a retirement plan that—

"(i) on the first day of the plan year—

"(I) covered only the employer (and the employer's spouse) and the employer owned the entire business (whether or not incorporated), or

"(II) covered only one or more partners (and their spouses) in a business partnership (including partners in an S or C corporation (as defined in section 1361(a) of the Internal Revenue Code of 1986)),

"(ii) meets the minimum coverage requirements of section 410(b) of the Internal Revenue Code of 1986 (as in effect on the date of the enactment of this paragraph) without being combined with any other plan of the business that covers the employees of the business,

"(iii) does not provide benefits to anyone except the employer (and the employer's spouse) or the partners (and their spouses),

"(iv) does not cover a business that is a member of an affiliated service group, a controlled group of corporations, or a group of businesses under common control, and

"(v) does not cover a business that leases employees.".

(2) ISSUANCE OF INITIAL GUIDANCE AND MODEL NOTICE.—The Secretary of Labor shall issue initial guidance and a model notice pursuant to section 101(i)(6) of the Employee Retirement Income Security Act of 1974 (as added by this subsection) not later than January 1, 2003. Not later than 75 days after the date of the enactment of this Act, the Secretary shall promulgate interim final rules necessary to carry out the amendments made by this subsection.

(3) CIVIL PENALTIES FOR FAILURE TO PROVIDE NOTICE.—Section 502 of such Act (29 U.S.C. 1132) is amended—

(A) in subsection (a)(6), by striking "(5), or (6)" and inserting "(5), (6), or (7)";

(B) by redesignating paragraph (7) of subsection (c) as paragraph (8); and

(C) by inserting after paragraph (6) of subsection (c) the following new paragraph:

"(7) The Secretary may assess a civil penalty against a plan administrator of up to $100 a day from the date of the plan administrator's failure or refusal to provide notice to participants and beneficiaries in accordance with section 101(i). For purposes of this paragraph, each violation with respect to any single participant or beneficiary shall be treated as a separate violation.".

(3) PLAN AMENDMENTS.—If any amendment made by this subsection requires an amendment to any plan, such plan amendment shall not be required to be made before the first plan year beginning on or after the effective date of this section, if—

    (A) during the period after such amendment made by this subsection takes effect and before such first plan year, the plan is operated in good faith compliance with the requirements of such amendment made by this subsection, and

    (B) such plan amendment applies retroactively to the period after such amendment made by this subsection takes effect and before such first plan year.

(c) EFFECTIVE DATE.—The provisions of this section (including the amendments made thereby) shall take effect 180 days after the date of the enactment of this Act. Good faith compliance with the requirements of such provisions in advance of the issuance of applicable regulations thereunder shall be treated as compliance with such provisions.

SEC. 307. RULES OF PROFESSIONAL RESPONSIBILITY FOR ATTORNEYS.

Not later than 180 days after the date of enactment of this Act, the Commission shall issue rules, in the public interest and for the protection of investors, setting forth minimum standards of professional conduct for attorneys appearing and practicing before the Commission in any way in the representation of issuers, including a rule—

    (1) requiring an attorney to report evidence of a material violation of securities law or breach of fiduciary duty or similar violation by the company or any agent thereof, to the chief legal counsel or the chief executive officer of the company (or the equivalent thereof); and

    (2) if the counsel or officer does not appropriately respond to the evidence (adopting, as necessary, appropriate remedial measures or sanctions with respect to the violation), requiring the attorney to report the evidence to the audit committee of the board of directors of the issuer or to another committee of the board of directors comprised solely of directors not employed directly or indirectly by the issuer, or to the board of directors.

SEC. 308. FAIR FUNDS FOR INVESTORS.

(a) CIVIL PENALTIES ADDED TO DISGORGEMENT FUNDS FOR THE RELIEF OF VICTIMS.—If in any judicial or administrative action brought by the Commission under the securities laws (as such term is defined in section 3(a)(47) of the Securities Exchange Act of 1934 (15 U.S.C. 78c(a)(47)) the Commission obtains an order requiring disgorgement against any person for a violation of such laws or the rules or regulations thereunder, or such person agrees in settlement of any such action to such disgorgement, and the Commission also obtains pursuant to such laws a civil penalty against such person, the amount of such civil penalty shall, on the motion or at the direction of the Commission, be added to and become part of the disgorgement fund for the benefit of the victims of such violation.

(b) ACCEPTANCE OF ADDITIONAL DONATIONS.—The Commission is authorized to accept, hold, administer, and utilize gifts, bequests and devises of property, both real and personal, to the United

States for a disgorgement fund described in subsection (a). Such gifts, bequests, and devises of money and proceeds from sales of other property received as gifts, bequests, or devises shall be deposited in the disgorgement fund and shall be available for allocation in accordance with subsection (a).

(c) STUDY REQUIRED.—

(1) SUBJECT OF STUDY.—The Commission shall review and analyze—

(A) enforcement actions by the Commission over the five years preceding the date of the enactment of this Act that have included proceedings to obtain civil penalties or disgorgements to identify areas where such proceedings may be utilized to efficiently, effectively, and fairly provide restitution for injured investors; and

(B) other methods to more efficiently, effectively, and fairly provide restitution to injured investors, including methods to improve the collection rates for civil penalties and disgorgements.

(2) REPORT REQUIRED.—The Commission shall report its findings to the Committee on Financial Services of the House of Representatives and the Committee on Banking, Housing, and Urban Affairs of the Senate within 180 days after of the date of the enactment of this Act, and shall use such findings to revise its rules and regulations as necessary. The report shall include a discussion of regulatory or legislative actions that are recommended or that may be necessary to address concerns identified in the study.

(d) CONFORMING AMENDMENTS.—Each of the following provisions is amended by inserting ", except as otherwise provided in section 308 of the Sarbanes-Oxley Act of 2002" after "Treasury of the United States":

(1) Section 21(d)(3)(C)(i) of the Securities Exchange Act of 1934 (15 U.S.C. 78u(d)(3)(C)(i)).

(2) Section 21A(d)(1) of such Act (15 U.S.C. 78u-1(d)(1)).

(3) Section 20(d)(3)(A) of the Securities Act of 1933 (15 U.S.C. 77t(d)(3)(A)).

(4) Section 42(e)(3)(A) of the Investment Company Act of 1940 (15 U.S.C. 80a–41(e)(3)(A)).

(5) Section 209(e)(3)(A) of the Investment Advisers Act of 1940 (15 U.S.C. 80b–9(e)(3)(A)).

(e) DEFINITION.—As used in this section, the term "disgorgement fund" means a fund established in any administrative or judicial proceeding described in subsection (a).

TITLE IV—ENHANCED FINANCIAL DISCLOSURES

SEC. 401. DISCLOSURES IN PERIODIC REPORTS.

(a) DISCLOSURES REQUIRED.—Section 13 of the Securities Exchange Act of 1934 (15 U.S.C. 78m) is amended by adding at the end the following:

"(i) ACCURACY OF FINANCIAL REPORTS.—Each financial report that contains financial statements, and that is required to be prepared in accordance with (or reconciled to) generally accepted accounting principles under this title and filed with the Commission shall reflect all material correcting adjustments that have been identified by a registered public accounting firm in accordance with generally accepted accounting principles and the rules and regulations of the Commission.

"(j) OFF-BALANCE SHEET TRANSACTIONS.—Not later than 180 days after the date of enactment of the Sarbanes-Oxley Act of 2002, the Commission shall issue final rules providing that each annual and quarterly financial report required to be filed with the Commission shall disclose all material off-balance sheet transactions, arrangements, obligations (including contingent obligations), and other relationships of the issuer with unconsolidated entities or other persons, that may have a material current or future effect on financial condition, changes in financial condition, results of operations, liquidity, capital expenditures, capital resources, or significant components of revenues or expenses.".

(b) COMMISSION RULES ON *PRO FORMA* FIGURES.—Not later than 180 days after the date of enactment of the Sarbanes-Oxley Act of 2002, the Commission shall issue final rules providing that *pro forma* financial information included in any periodic or other report filed with the Commission pursuant to the securities laws, or in any public disclosure or press or other release, shall be presented in a manner that—

(1) does not contain an untrue statement of a material fact or omit to state a material fact necessary in order to make the pro forma financial information, in light of the circumstances under which it is presented, not misleading; and

(2) reconciles it with the financial condition and results of operations of the issuer under generally accepted accounting principles.

(c) STUDY AND REPORT ON SPECIAL PURPOSE ENTITIES.—

(1) STUDY REQUIRED.—The Commission shall, not later than 1 year after the effective date of adoption of off-balance sheet disclosure rules required by section 13(j) of the Securities Exchange Act of 1934, as added by this section, complete a study of filings by issuers and their disclosures to determine—

(A) the extent of off-balance sheet transactions, including assets, liabilities, leases, losses, and the use of special purpose entities; and

(B) whether generally accepted accounting rules result in financial statements of issuers reflecting the economics of such off-balance sheet transactions to investors in a transparent fashion.

(2) REPORT AND RECOMMENDATIONS.—Not later than 6 months after the date of completion of the study required by paragraph (1), the Commission shall submit a report to the President, the Committee on Banking, Housing, and Urban Affairs of the Senate, and the Committee on Financial Services of the House of Representatives, setting forth—

(A) the amount or an estimate of the amount of off-balance sheet transactions, including assets, liabilities, leases, and losses of, and the use of special purpose entities by, issuers filing periodic reports pursuant to section 13 or 15 of the Securities Exchange Act of 1934;

(B) the extent to which special purpose entities are used to facilitate off-balance sheet transactions;

APPENDIX A: SARBANES-OXLEY ACT OF 2002

(C) whether generally accepted accounting principles or the rules of the Commission result in financial statements of issuers reflecting the economics of such transactions to investors in a transparent fashion;

(D) whether generally accepted accounting principles specifically result in the consolidation of special purpose entities sponsored by an issuer in cases in which the issuer has the majority of the risks and rewards of the special purpose entity; and

(E) any recommendations of the Commission for improving the transparency and quality of reporting off-balance sheet transactions in the financial statements and disclosures required to be filed by an issuer with the Commission.

SEC. 402. ENHANCED CONFLICT OF INTEREST PROVISIONS.

(a) PROHIBITION ON PERSONAL LOANS TO EXECUTIVES.—Section 13 of the Securities Exchange Act of 1934 (15 U.S.C. 78m), as amended by this Act, is amended by adding at the end the following:

"(k) PROHIBITION ON PERSONAL LOANS TO EXECUTIVES.—

"(1) IN GENERAL.—It shall be unlawful for any issuer (as defined in section 2 of the Sarbanes-Oxley Act of 2002), directly or indirectly, including through any subsidiary, to extend or maintain credit, to arrange for the extension of credit, or to renew an extension of credit, in the form of a personal loan to or for any director or executive officer (or equivalent thereof) of that issuer. An extension of credit maintained by the issuer on the date of enactment of this subsection shall not be subject to the provisions of this subsection, provided that there is no material modification to any term of any such extension of credit or any renewal of any such extension of credit on or after that date of enactment.

"(2) LIMITATION.—Paragraph (1) does not preclude any home improvement and manufactured home loans (as that term is defined in section 5 of the Home Owners' Loan Act (12 U.S.C. 1464)), consumer credit (as defined in section 103 of the Truth in Lending Act (15 U.S.C. 1602)), or any extension of credit under an open end credit plan (as defined in section 103 of the Truth in Lending Act (15 U.S.C. 1602)), or a charge card (as defined in section 127(c)(4)(e) of the Truth in Lending Act (15 U.S.C. 1637(c)(4)(e)), or any extension of credit by a broker or dealer registered under section 15 of this title to an employee of that broker or dealer to buy, trade, or carry securities, that is permitted under rules or regulations of the Board of Governors of the Federal Reserve System pursuant to section 7 of this title (other than an extension of credit that would be used to purchase the stock of that issuer), that is—

"(A) made or provided in the ordinary course of the consumer credit business of such issuer;

"(B) of a type that is generally made available by such issuer to the public; and

"(C) made by such issuer on market terms, or terms that are no more favorable than those offered by the issuer to the general public for such extensions of credit.

"(3) RULE OF CONSTRUCTION FOR CERTAIN LOANS.—Paragraph (1) does not apply to any loan made or maintained by an insured depository institution (as defined in section 3 of the Federal Deposit Insurance Act (12 U.S.C. 1813)), if the loan is subject to the insider lending restrictions of section 22(h) of the Federal Reserve Act (12 U.S.C. 375b).".

SEC. 403. DISCLOSURES OF TRANSACTIONS INVOLVING MANAGEMENT AND PRINCIPAL STOCKHOLDERS.

(a) AMENDMENT.—Section 16 of the Securities Exchange Act of 1934 (15 U.S.C. 78p) is amended by striking the heading of such section and subsection (a) and inserting the following:

"**SEC. 16. DIRECTORS, OFFICERS, AND PRINCIPAL STOCKHOLDERS.**

"(a) DISCLOSURES REQUIRED.—

"(1) DIRECTORS, OFFICERS, AND PRINCIPAL STOCKHOLDERS REQUIRED TO FILE.—Every person who is directly or indirectly the beneficial owner of more than 10 percent of any class of any equity security (other than an exempted security) which is registered pursuant to section 12, or who is a director or an officer of the issuer of such security, shall file the statements required by this subsection with the Commission (and, if such security is registered on a national securities exchange, also with the exchange).

"(2) TIME OF FILING.—The statements required by this subsection shall be filed—

"(A) at the time of the registration of such security on a national securities exchange or by the effective date of a registration statement filed pursuant to section 12(g);

"(B) within 10 days after he or she becomes such beneficial owner, director, or officer;

"(C) if there has been a change in such ownership, or if such person shall have purchased or sold a security-based swap agreement (as defined in section 206(b) of the Gramm-Leach-Bliley Act (15 U.S.C. 78c note)) involving such equity security, before the end of the second business day following the day on which the subject transaction has been executed, or at such other time as the Commission shall establish, by rule, in any case in which the Commission determines that such 2-day period is not feasible.

"(3) CONTENTS OF STATEMENTS.—A statement filed—

"(A) under subparagraph (A) or (B) of paragraph (2) shall contain a statement of the amount of all equity securities of such issuer of which the filing person is the beneficial owner; and

"(B) under subparagraph (C) of such paragraph shall indicate ownership by the filing person at the date of filing, any such changes in such ownership, and such purchases and sales of the security-based swap agreements as have occurred since the most recent such filing under such subparagraph.

"(4) ELECTRONIC FILING AND AVAILABILITY.—Beginning not later than 1 year after the date of enactment of the Sarbanes-Oxley Act of 2002—

"(A) a statement filed under subparagraph (C) of paragraph (2) shall be filed electronically;

"(B) the Commission shall provide each such statement on a publicly accessible Internet site not later than the end of the business day following that filing; and

APPENDIX A: SARBANES-OXLEY ACT OF 2002

"(C) the issuer (if the issuer maintains a corporate website) shall provide that statement on that corporate website, not later than the end of the business day following that filing.".

(b) EFFECTIVE DATE.—The amendment made by this section shall be effective 30 days after the date of the enactment of this Act.

SEC. 404. MANAGEMENT ASSESSMENT OF INTERNAL CONTROLS.

(a) RULES REQUIRED.—The Commission shall prescribe rules requiring each annual report required by section 13(a) or 15(d) of the Securities Exchange Act of 1934 (15 U.S.C. 78m or 78o(d)) to contain an internal control report, which shall—

(1) state the responsibility of management for establishing and maintaining an adequate internal control structure and procedures for financial reporting; and

(2) contain an assessment, as of the end of the most recent fiscal year of the issuer, of the effectiveness of the internal control structure and procedures of the issuer for financial reporting.

(b) INTERNAL CONTROL EVALUATION AND REPORTING.—With respect to the internal control assessment required by subsection (a), each registered public accounting firm that prepares or issues the audit report for the issuer shall attest to, and report on, the assessment made by the management of the issuer. An attestation made under this subsection shall be made in accordance with standards for attestation engagements issued or adopted by the Board. Any such attestation shall not be the subject of a separate engagement.

SEC. 405. EXEMPTION.

Nothing in section 401, 402, or 404, the amendments made by those sections, or the rules of the Commission under those sections shall apply to any investment company registered under section 8 of the Investment Company Act of 1940 (15 U.S.C. 80a–8).

SEC. 406. CODE OF ETHICS FOR SENIOR FINANCIAL OFFICERS.

(a) CODE OF ETHICS DISCLOSURE.—The Commission shall issue rules to require each issuer, together with periodic reports required pursuant to section 13(a) or 15(d) of the Securities Exchange Act of 1934, to disclose whether or not, and if not, the reason therefor, such issuer has adopted a code of ethics for senior financial officers, applicable to its principal financial officer and comptroller or principal accounting officer, or persons performing similar functions.

(b) CHANGES IN CODES OF ETHICS.—The Commission shall revise its regulations concerning matters requiring prompt disclosure on Form 8–K (or any successor thereto) to require the immediate disclosure, by means of the filing of such form, dissemination by the Internet or by other electronic means, by any issuer of any change in or waiver of the code of ethics for senior financial officers.

(c) DEFINITION.—In this section, the term "code of ethics" means such standards as are reasonably necessary to promote—

(1) honest and ethical conduct, including the ethical handling of actual or apparent conflicts of interest between personal and professional relationships;

(2) full, fair, accurate, timely, and understandable disclosure in the periodic reports required to be filed by the issuer; and

(3) compliance with applicable governmental rules and regulations.

(d) DEADLINE FOR RULEMAKING.—The Commission shall—

(1) propose rules to implement this section, not later than 90 days after the date of enactment of this Act; and

(2) issue final rules to implement this section, not later than 180 days after that date of enactment.

SEC. 407. DISCLOSURE OF AUDIT COMMITTEE FINANCIAL EXPERT.

(a) RULES DEFINING "FINANCIAL EXPERT".—The Commission shall issue rules, as necessary or appropriate in the public interest and consistent with the protection of investors, to require each issuer, together with periodic reports required pursuant to sections 13(a) and 15(d) of the Securities Exchange Act of 1934, to disclose whether or not, and if not, the reasons therefor, the audit committee of that issuer is comprised of at least 1 member who is a financial expert, as such term is defined by the Commission.

(b) CONSIDERATIONS.—In defining the term "financial expert" for purposes of subsection (a), the Commission shall consider whether a person has, through education and experience as a public accountant or auditor or a principal financial officer, comptroller, or principal accounting officer of an issuer, or from a position involving the performance of similar functions—

(1) an understanding of generally accepted accounting principles and financial statements;

(2) experience in—

(A) the preparation or auditing of financial statements of generally comparable issuers; and

(B) the application of such principles in connection with the accounting for estimates, accruals, and reserves;

(3) experience with internal accounting controls; and

(4) an understanding of audit committee functions.

(c) DEADLINE FOR RULEMAKING.—The Commission shall—

(1) propose rules to implement this section, not later than 90 days after the date of enactment of this Act; and

(2) issue final rules to implement this section, not later than 180 days after that date of enactment.

SEC. 408. ENHANCED REVIEW OF PERIODIC DISCLOSURES BY ISSUERS.

(a) REGULAR AND SYSTEMATIC REVIEW.—The Commission shall review disclosures made by issuers reporting under section 13(a) of the Securities Exchange Act of 1934 (including reports filed on Form 10–K), and which have a class of securities listed on a national securities exchange or traded on an automated quotation facility of a national securities association, on a regular and systematic basis for the protection of investors. Such review shall include a review of an issuer's financial statement.

(b) REVIEW CRITERIA.—For purposes of scheduling the reviews required by subsection (a), the Commission shall consider, among other factors—

(1) issuers that have issued material restatements of financial results;

(2) issuers that experience significant volatility in their stock price as compared to other issuers;

(3) issuers with the largest market capitalization;

(4) emerging companies with disparities in price to earning ratios;

(5) issuers whose operations significantly affect any material sector of the economy; and

(6) any other factors that the Commission may consider relevant.

(c) MINIMUM REVIEW PERIOD.—In no event shall an issuer required to file reports under section 13(a) or 15(d) of the Securities Exchange Act of 1934 be reviewed under this section less frequently than once every 3 years.

SEC. 409. REAL TIME ISSUER DISCLOSURES.

Section 13 of the Securities Exchange Act of 1934 (15 U.S.C. 78m), as amended by this Act, is amended by adding at the end the following:

"(l) REAL TIME ISSUER DISCLOSURES.—Each issuer reporting under section 13(a) or 15(d) shall disclose to the public on a rapid and current basis such additional information concerning material changes in the financial condition or operations of the issuer, in plain English, which may include trend and qualitative information and graphic presentations, as the Commission determines, by rule, is necessary or useful for the protection of investors and in the public interest.".

TITLE V—ANALYST CONFLICTS OF INTEREST

SEC. 501. TREATMENT OF SECURITIES ANALYSTS BY REGISTERED SECURITIES ASSOCIATIONS AND NATIONAL SECURITIES EXCHANGES.

(a) RULES REGARDING SECURITIES ANALYSTS.—The Securities Exchange Act of 1934 (15 U.S.C. 78a et seq.) is amended by inserting after section 15C the following new section:

"SEC. 15D. SECURITIES ANALYSTS AND RESEARCH REPORTS.

"(a) ANALYST PROTECTIONS.—The Commission, or upon the authorization and direction of the Commission, a registered securities association or national securities exchange, shall have adopted, not later than 1 year after the date of enactment of this section, rules reasonably designed to address conflicts of interest that can arise when securities analysts recommend equity securities in research reports and public appearances, in order to improve the objectivity of research and provide investors with more useful and reliable information, including rules designed—

"(1) to foster greater public confidence in securities research, and to protect the objectivity and independence of securities analysts, by—

"(A) restricting the prepublication clearance or approval of research reports by persons employed by the broker or dealer who are engaged in investment banking activities, or persons not directly responsible for investment research, other than legal or compliance staff;

"(B) limiting the supervision and compensatory evaluation of securities analysts to officials employed by the broker or dealer who are not engaged in investment banking activities; and

"(C) requiring that a broker or dealer and persons employed by a broker or dealer who are involved with investment banking activities may not, directly or indirectly, retaliate against or threaten to retaliate against any securities analyst employed by that broker or dealer or its affiliates as a result of an adverse, negative, or otherwise unfavorable research report that may adversely affect the present or prospective investment banking relationship of the broker or dealer with the issuer that is the subject of the research report, except that such rules may not limit the authority of a broker or dealer to discipline a securities analyst for causes other than such research report in accordance with the policies and procedures of the firm;

"(2) to define periods during which brokers or dealers who have participated, or are to participate, in a public offering of securities as underwriters or dealers should not publish or otherwise distribute research reports relating to such securities or to the issuer of such securities;

"(3) to establish structural and institutional safeguards within registered brokers or dealers to assure that securities analysts are separated by appropriate informational partitions within the firm from the review, pressure, or oversight of those whose involvement in investment banking activities might potentially bias their judgment or supervision; and

"(4) to address such other issues as the Commission, or such association or exchange, determines appropriate.

"(b) DISCLOSURE.—The Commission, or upon the authorization and direction of the Commission, a registered securities association or national securities exchange, shall have adopted, not later than 1 year after the date of enactment of this section, rules reasonably designed to require each securities analyst to disclose in public appearances, and each registered broker or dealer to disclose in each research report, as applicable, conflicts of interest that are known or should have been known by the securities analyst or the broker or dealer, to exist at the time of the appearance or the date of distribution of the report, including—

"(1) the extent to which the securities analyst has debt or equity investments in the issuer that is the subject of the appearance or research report;

"(2) whether any compensation has been received by the registered broker or dealer, or any affiliate thereof, including the securities analyst, from the issuer that is the subject of the appearance or research report, subject to such exemptions as the Commission may determine appropriate and necessary to prevent disclosure by virtue of this paragraph of material non-public information regarding specific potential future investment banking transactions of such issuer, as is appropriate in the public interest and consistent with the protection of investors;

"(3) whether an issuer, the securities of which are recommended in the appearance or research report, currently is, or during the 1-year period preceding the date of the appearance or date of distribution of the report has been, a client of the registered broker or dealer, and if so, stating the types of services provided to the issuer;

"(4) whether the securities analyst received compensation with respect to a research report, based upon (among any other factors) the investment banking revenues (either generally or specifically earned from the issuer being analyzed) of the registered broker or dealer; and

"(5) such other disclosures of conflicts of interest that are material to investors, research analysts, or the broker or dealer as the Commission, or such association or exchange, determines appropriate.

"(c) DEFINITIONS.—In this section—

"(1) the term 'securities analyst' means any associated person of a registered broker or dealer that is principally responsible for, and any associated person who reports directly or indirectly to a securities analyst in connection with, the preparation of the substance of a research report, whether or not any such person has the job title of 'securities analyst'; and

"(2) the term 'research report' means a written or electronic communication that includes an analysis of equity securities of individual companies or industries, and that provides information reasonably sufficient upon which to base an investment decision.".

(b) ENFORCEMENT.—Section 21B(a) of the Securities Exchange Act of 1934 (15 U.S.C. 78u–2(a)) is amended by inserting "15D," before "15B".

(c) COMMISSION AUTHORITY.—The Commission may promulgate and amend its regulations, or direct a registered securities association or national securities exchange to promulgate and amend its rules, to carry out section 15D of the Securities Exchange Act of 1934, as added by this section, as is necessary for the protection of investors and in the public interest.

TITLE VI—COMMISSION RESOURCES AND AUTHORITY

SEC. 601. AUTHORIZATION OF APPROPRIATIONS.

Section 35 of the Securities Exchange Act of 1934 (15 U.S.C. 78kk) is amended to read as follows:

"SEC. 35. AUTHORIZATION OF APPROPRIATIONS.

"In addition to any other funds authorized to be appropriated to the Commission, there are authorized to be appropriated to carry out the functions, powers, and duties of the Commission, $776,000,000 for fiscal year 2003, of which—

"(1) $102,700,000 shall be available to fund additional compensation, including salaries and benefits, as authorized in the Investor and Capital Markets Fee Relief Act (Public Law 107–123; 115 Stat. 2390 *et seq.*);

"(2) $108,400,000 shall be available for information technology, security enhancements, and recovery and mitigation activities in light of the terrorist attacks of September 11, 2001; and

"(3) $98,000,000 shall be available to add not fewer than an additional 200 qualified professionals to provide enhanced oversight of auditors and audit services required by the Federal securities laws, and to improve Commission investigative and disciplinary efforts with respect to such auditors and services, as well as for additional professional support staff necessary to strengthen the programs of the Commission involving Full Disclosure and Prevention and Suppression of Fraud, risk management, industry technology review, compliance, inspections, examinations, market regulation, and investment management.".

SEC. 602. APPEARANCE AND PRACTICE BEFORE THE COMMISSION.

The Securities Exchange Act of 1934 (15 U.S.C. 78a *et seq.*) is amended by inserting after section 4B the following:

"SEC. 4C. APPEARANCE AND PRACTICE BEFORE THE COMMISSION.

"(a) AUTHORITY TO CENSURE.—The Commission may censure any person, or deny, temporarily or permanently, to any person the privilege of appearing or practicing before the Commission in any way, if that person is found by the Commission, after notice and opportunity for hearing in the matter—

"(1) not to possess the requisite qualifications to represent others;

"(2) to be lacking in character or integrity, or to have engaged in unethical or improper professional conduct; or

"(3) to have willfully violated, or willfully aided and abetted the violation of, any provision of the securities laws or the rules and regulations issued thereunder.

"(b) DEFINITION.—With respect to any registered public accounting firm or associated person, for purposes of this section, the term 'improper professional conduct' means—

"(1) intentional or knowing conduct, including reckless conduct, that results in a violation of applicable professional standards; and

"(2) negligent conduct in the form of—

"(A) a single instance of highly unreasonable conduct that results in a violation of applicable professional standards in circumstances in which the registered public accounting firm or associated person knows, or should know, that heightened scrutiny is warranted; or

"(B) repeated instances of unreasonable conduct, each resulting in a violation of applicable professional standards, that indicate a lack of competence to practice before the Commission.".

SEC. 603. FEDERAL COURT AUTHORITY TO IMPOSE PENNY STOCK BARS.

(a) SECURITIES EXCHANGE ACT OF 1934.—Section 21(d) of the Securities Exchange Act of 1934 (15 U.S.C. 78u(d)), as amended by this Act, is amended by adding at the end the following:

"(6) AUTHORITY OF A COURT TO PROHIBIT PERSONS FROM PARTICIPATING IN AN OFFERING OF PENNY STOCK.—

"(A) IN GENERAL.—In any proceeding under paragraph (1) against any person participating in, or, at the time of the alleged misconduct who was participating in, an offering of penny stock, the court may prohibit that person from participating in an offering of penny stock, conditionally or unconditionally, and permanently or for such period of time as the court shall determine.

"(B) DEFINITION.—For purposes of this paragraph, the term 'person participating in an offering of penny stock' includes

APPENDIX A: SARBANES-OXLEY ACT OF 2002

any person engaging in activities with a broker, dealer, or issuer for purposes of issuing, trading, or inducing or attempting to induce the purchase or sale of, any penny stock. The Commission may, by rule or regulation, define such term to include other activities, and may, by rule, regulation, or order, exempt any person or class of persons, in whole or in part, conditionally or unconditionally, from inclusion in such term.".

(b) SECURITIES ACT OF 1933.—Section 20 of the Securities Act of 1933 (15 U.S.C. 77t) is amended by adding at the end the following:

"(g) AUTHORITY OF A COURT TO PROHIBIT PERSONS FROM PARTICIPATING IN AN OFFERING OF PENNY STOCK.—

"(1) IN GENERAL.—In any proceeding under subsection (a) against any person participating in, or, at the time of the alleged misconduct, who was participating in, an offering of penny stock, the court may prohibit that person from participating in an offering of penny stock, conditionally or unconditionally, and permanently or for such period of time as the court shall determine.

"(2) DEFINITION.—For purposes of this subsection, the term 'person participating in an offering of penny stock' includes any person engaging in activities with a broker, dealer, or issuer for purposes of issuing, trading, or inducing or attempting to induce the purchase or sale of, any penny stock. The Commission may, by rule or regulation, define such term to include other activities, and may, by rule, regulation, or order, exempt any person or class of persons, in whole or in part, conditionally or unconditionally, from inclusion in such term.".

SEC. 604. QUALIFICATIONS OF ASSOCIATED PERSONS OF BROKERS AND DEALERS.

(a) BROKERS AND DEALERS.—Section 15(b)(4) of the Securities Exchange Act of 1934 (15 U.S.C. 78o) is amended—

(1) by striking subparagraph (F) and inserting the following:

"(F) is subject to any order of the Commission barring or suspending the right of the person to be associated with a broker or dealer;"; and

(2) in subparagraph (G), by striking the period at the end and inserting the following: "; or

"(H) is subject to any final order of a State securities commission (or any agency or officer performing like functions), State authority that supervises or examines banks, savings associations, or credit unions, State insurance commission (or any agency or office performing like functions), an appropriate Federal banking agency (as defined in section 3 of the Federal Deposit Insurance Act (12 U.S.C. 1813(q))), or the National Credit Union Administration, that—

"(i) bars such person from association with an entity regulated by such commission, authority, agency, or officer, or from engaging in the business of securities, insurance, banking, savings association activities, or credit union activities; or "(ii) constitutes a final order based on violations of any laws or regulations that prohibit fraudulent, manipulative, or deceptive conduct.".

(b) INVESTMENT ADVISERS.—Section 203(e) of the Investment Advisers Act of 1940 (15 U.S.C. 80b–3(e)) is amended—

(1) by striking paragraph (7) and inserting the following:

"(7) is subject to any order of the Commission barring or suspending the right of the person to be associated with an investment adviser;";

(2) in paragraph (8), by striking the period at the end and inserting "; or"; and

(3) by adding at the end the following:

"(9) is subject to any final order of a State securities commission (or any agency or officer performing like functions), State authority that supervises or examines banks, savings associations, or credit unions, State insurance commission (or any agency or office performing like functions), an appropriate Federal banking agency (as defined in section 3 of the Federal Deposit Insurance Act (12 U.S.C. 1813(q))), or the National Credit Union Administration, that—

"(A) bars such person from association with an entity regulated by such commission, authority, agency, or officer, or from engaging in the business of securities, insurance, banking, savings association activities, or credit union activities; or

"(B) constitutes a final order based on violations of any laws or regulations that prohibit fraudulent, manipulative, or deceptive conduct.".

(c) CONFORMING AMENDMENTS.—

(1) SECURITIES EXCHANGE ACT OF 1934.—The Securities Exchange Act of 1934 (15 U.S.C. 78a et seq.) is amended—

(A) in section 3(a)(39)(F) (15 U.S.C. 78c(a)(39)(F))—

(i) by striking "or (G)" and inserting "(H), or (G)"; and

(ii) by inserting ", or is subject to an order or finding," before "enumerated";

(B) in each of section 15(b)(6)(A)(i) (15 U.S.C. 78o(b)(6)(A)(i)), paragraphs (2) and (4) of section 15B(c) (15 U.S.C. 78o–4(c)), and subparagraphs (A) and (C) of section 15C(c)(1) (15 U.S.C. 78o–5(c)(1))—

(i) by striking "or (G)" each place that term appears and inserting "(H), or (G)"; and

(ii) by striking "or omission" each place that term appears, and inserting ", or is subject to an order or finding,"; and

(C) in each of paragraphs (3)(A) and (4)(C) of section 17A(c) (15 U.S.C. 78q–1(c))—

(i) by striking "or (G)" each place that term appears and inserting "(H), or (G)"; and

(ii) by inserting ", or is subject to an order or finding," before "enumerated" each place that term appears.

(2) INVESTMENT ADVISERS ACT OF 1940.—Section 203(f) of the Investment Advisers Act of 1940 (15 U.S.C. 80b–3(f)) is amended—

(A) by striking "or (8)" and inserting "(8), or (9)"; and

(B) by inserting "or (3)" after "paragraph (2)".

APPENDIX A: SARBANES-OXLEY ACT OF 2002

TITLE VII—STUDIES AND REPORTS

SEC. 701. GAO STUDY AND REPORT REGARDING CONSOLIDATION OF PUBLIC ACCOUNTING FIRMS.

(a) STUDY REQUIRED.—The Comptroller General of the United States shall conduct a study—
    (1) to identify—
        (A) the factors that have led to the consolidation of public accounting firms since 1989 and the consequent reduction in the number of firms capable of providing audit services to large national and multi-national business organizations that are subject to the securities laws;
        (B) the present and future impact of the condition described in subparagraph (A) on capital formation and securities markets, both domestic and international; and
        (C) solutions to any problems identified under subparagraph (B), including ways to increase competition and the number of firms capable of providing audit services to large national and multinational business organizations that are subject to the securities laws;
    (2) of the problems, if any, faced by business organizations that have resulted from limited competition among public accounting firms, including—
        (A) higher costs;
        (B) lower quality of services;
        (C) impairment of auditor independence; or
        (D) lack of choice; and
    (3) whether and to what extent Federal or State regulations impede competition among public accounting firms.

(b) CONSULTATION.—In planning and conducting the study under this section, the Comptroller General shall consult with—
    (1) the Commission;
    (2) the regulatory agencies that perform functions similar to the Commission within the other member countries of the Group of Seven Industrialized Nations;
    (3) the Department of Justice; and
    (4) any other public or private sector organization that the Comptroller General considers appropriate.

(c) REPORT REQUIRED.—Not later than 1 year after the date of enactment of this Act, the Comptroller General shall submit a report on the results of the study required by this section to the Committee on Banking, Housing, and Urban Affairs of the Senate and the Committee on Financial Services of the House of Representatives.

SEC. 702. COMMISSION STUDY AND REPORT REGARDING CREDIT RATING AGENCIES.

(a) STUDY REQUIRED.—
    (1) IN GENERAL.—The Commission shall conduct a study of the role and function of credit rating agencies in the operation of the securities market.
    (2) AREAS OF CONSIDERATION.—The study required by this subsection shall examine—
        (A) the role of credit rating agencies in the evaluation of issuers of securities;

(B) the importance of that role to investors and the functioning of the securities markets;

(C) any impediments to the accurate appraisal by credit rating agencies of the financial resources and risks of issuers of securities;

(D) any barriers to entry into the business of acting as a credit rating agency, and any measures needed to remove such barriers;

(E) any measures which may be required to improve the dissemination of information concerning such resources and risks when credit rating agencies announce credit ratings; and

(F) any conflicts of interest in the operation of credit rating agencies and measures to prevent such conflicts or ameliorate the consequences of such conflicts.

(b) REPORT REQUIRED.—The Commission shall submit a report on the study required by subsection (a) to the President, the Committee on Financial Services of the House of Representatives, and the Committee on Banking, Housing, and Urban Affairs of the Senate not later than 180 days after the date of enactment of this Act.

SEC. 703. STUDY AND REPORT ON VIOLATORS AND VIOLATIONS.

(a) STUDY.—The Commission shall conduct a study to determine, based upon information for the period from January 1, 1998, to December 31, 2001—

(1) the number of securities professionals, defined as public accountants, public accounting firms, investment bankers, investment advisers, brokers, dealers, attorneys, and other securities professionals practicing before the Commission—

(A) who have been found to have aided and abetted a violation of the Federal securities laws, including rules or regulations promulgated thereunder (collectively referred to in this section as "Federal securities laws"), but who have not been sanctioned, disciplined, or otherwise penalized as a primary violator in any administrative action or civil proceeding, including in any settlement of such an action or proceeding (referred to in this section as "aiders and abettors"); and

(B) who have been found to have been primary violators of the Federal securities laws;

(2) a description of the Federal securities laws violations committed by aiders and abettors and by primary violators, including—

(A) the specific provision of the Federal securities laws violated;

(B) the specific sanctions and penalties imposed upon such aiders and abettors and primary violators, including the amount of any monetary penalties assessed upon and collected from such persons;

(C) the occurrence of multiple violations by the same person or persons, either as an aider or abettor or as a primary violator; and

(D) whether, as to each such violator, disciplinary sanctions have been imposed, including any censure, suspension, temporary bar, or permanent bar to practice before the Commission; and

APPENDIX A: SARBANES-OXLEY ACT OF 2002

(3) the amount of disgorgement, restitution, or any other fines or payments that the Commission has assessed upon and collected from, aiders and abettors and from primary violators.

(b) REPORT.—A report based upon the study conducted pursuant to subsection (a) shall be submitted to the Committee on Banking, Housing, and Urban Affairs of the Senate, and the Committee on Financial Services of the House of Representatives not later than 6 months after the date of enactment of this Act.

SEC. 704. STUDY OF ENFORCEMENT ACTIONS.

(a) STUDY REQUIRED.—The Commission shall review and analyze all enforcement actions by the Commission involving violations of reporting requirements imposed under the securities laws, and restatements of financial statements, over the 5-year period preceding the date of enactment of this Act, to identify areas of reporting that are most susceptible to fraud, inappropriate manipulation, or inappropriate earnings management, such as revenue recognition and the accounting treatment of off-balance sheet special purpose entities.

(b) REPORT REQUIRED.—The Commission shall report its findings to the Committee on Financial Services of the House of Representatives and the Committee on Banking, Housing, and Urban Affairs of the Senate, not later than 180 days after the date of enactment of this Act, and shall use such findings to revise its rules and regulations, as necessary. The report shall include a discussion of regulatory or legislative steps that are recommended or that may be necessary to address concerns identified in the study.

SEC. 705. STUDY OF INVESTMENT BANKS.

(a) GAO STUDY.—The Comptroller General of the United States shall conduct a study on whether investment banks and financial advisers assisted public companies in manipulating their earnings and obfuscating their true financial condition. The study should address the rule of investment banks and financial advisers—

(1) in the collapse of the Enron Corporation, including with respect to the design and implementation of derivatives transactions, transactions involving special purpose vehicles, and other financial arrangements that may have had the effect of altering the company's reported financial statements in ways that obscured the true financial picture of the company;

(2) in the failure of Global Crossing, including with respect to transactions involving swaps of fiberoptic cable capacity, in the designing transactions that may have had the effect of altering the company's reported financial statements in ways that obscured the true financial picture of the company; and

(3) generally, in creating and marketing transactions which may have been designed solely to enable companies to manipulate revenue streams, obtain loans, or move liabilities off balance sheets without altering the economic and business risks faced by the companies or any other mechanism to obscure a company's financial picture.

(b) REPORT.—The Comptroller General shall report to Congress not later than 180 days after the date of enactment of this Act on the results of the study required by this section. The report shall include a discussion of regulatory or legislative steps that are recommended or that may be necessary to address concerns identified in the study.

TITLE VIII—CORPORATE AND CRIMINAL FRAUD ACCOUNTABILITY

SEC. 801. SHORT TITLE.

This title may be cited as the "Corporate and Criminal Fraud Accountability Act of 2002".

SEC. 802. CRIMINAL PENALTIES FOR ALTERING DOCUMENTS.

(a) IN GENERAL.—Chapter 73 of title 18, United States Code, is amended by adding at the end the following:

"§ 1519. Destruction, alteration, or falsification of records in Federal investigations and bankruptcy

"Whoever knowingly alters, destroys, mutilates, conceals, covers up, falsifies, or makes a false entry in any record, document, or tangible object with the intent to impede, obstruct, or influence the investigation or proper administration of any matter within the jurisdiction of any department or agency of the United States or any case filed under title 11, or in relation to or contemplation of any such matter or case, shall be fined under this title, imprisoned not more than 20 years, or both.

"§ 1520. Destruction of corporate audit records

"(a)(1) Any accountant who conducts an audit of an issuer of securities to which section 10A(a) of the Securities Exchange Act of 1934 (15 U.S.C. 78j–1(a)) applies, shall maintain all audit or review workpapers for a period of 5 years from the end of the fiscal period in which the audit or review was concluded.

"(2) The Securities and Exchange Commission shall promulgate, within 180 days, after adequate notice and an opportunity for comment, such rules and regulations, as are reasonably necessary, relating to the retention of relevant records such as workpapers, documents that form the basis of an audit or review, memoranda, correspondence, communications, other documents, and records (including electronic records) which are created, sent, or received in connection with an audit or review and contain conclusions, opinions, analyses, or financial data relating to such an audit or review, which is conducted by any accountant who conducts an audit of an issuer of securities to which section 10A(a) of the Securities Exchange Act of 1934 (15 U.S.C. 78j–1(a)) applies. The Commission may, from time to time, amend or supplement the rules and regulations that it is required to promulgate under this section, after adequate notice and an opportunity for comment, in order to ensure that such rules and regulations adequately comport with the purposes of this section.

"(b) Whoever knowingly and willfully violates subsection (a)(1), or any rule or regulation promulgated by the Securities and Exchange Commission under subsection (a)(2), shall be fined under this title, imprisoned not more than 10 years, or both.

"(c) Nothing in this section shall be deemed to diminish or relieve any person of any other duty or obligation imposed by Federal or State law or regulation to maintain, or refrain from destroying, any document.".

APPENDIX A: SARBANES-OXLEY ACT OF 2002

(b) CLERICAL AMENDMENT.—The table of sections at the beginning of chapter 73 of title 18, United States Code, is amended by adding at the end the following new items:

"1519. Destruction, alteration, or falsification of records in Federal investigations and bankruptcy.
"1520. Destruction of corporate audit records.".

SEC. 803. DEBTS NONDISCHARGEABLE IF INCURRED IN VIOLATION OF SECURITIES FRAUD LAWS.

Section 523(a) of title 11, United States Code, is amended—
  (1) in paragraph (17), by striking "or" after the semicolon;
  (2) in paragraph (18), by striking the period at the end and inserting "; or"; and
  (3) by adding at the end, the following:
  "(19) that—
    "(A) is for—
      "(i) the violation of any of the Federal securities laws (as that term is defined in section 3(a)(47) of the Securities Exchange Act of 1934), any of the State securities laws, or any regulation or order issued under such Federal or State securities laws; or
      "(ii) common law fraud, deceit, or manipulation in connection with the purchase or sale of any security; and
    "(B) results from—
      "(i) any judgment, order, consent order, or decree entered in any Federal or State judicial or administrative proceeding;
      "(ii) any settlement agreement entered into by the debtor; or
      "(iii) any court or administrative order for any damages, fine, penalty, citation, restitutionary payment, disgorgement payment, attorney fee, cost, or other payment owed by the debtor.".

SEC. 804. STATUTE OF LIMITATIONS FOR SECURITIES FRAUD.

(a) IN GENERAL.—Section 1658 of title 28, United States Code, is amended—
  (1) by inserting "(a)" before "Except"; and
  (2) by adding at the end the following:
"(b) Notwithstanding subsection (a), a private right of action that involves a claim of fraud, deceit, manipulation, or contrivance in contravention of a regulatory requirement concerning the securities laws, as defined in section 3(a)(47) of the Securities Exchange Act of 1934 (15 U.S.C. 78c(a)(47)), may be brought not later than the earlier of—
  "(1) 2 years after the discovery of the facts constituting the violation; or
  "(2) 5 years after such violation.".
(b) EFFECTIVE DATE.—The limitations period provided by section 1658(b) of title 28, United States Code, as added by this section, shall apply to all proceedings addressed by this section that are commenced on or after the date of enactment of this Act.
(c) NO CREATION OF ACTIONS.—Nothing in this section shall create a new, private right of action.

SEC. 805. REVIEW OF FEDERAL SENTENCING GUIDELINES FOR OBSTRUCTION OF JUSTICE AND EXTENSIVE CRIMINAL FRAUD.

(a) ENHANCEMENT OF FRAUD AND OBSTRUCTION OF JUSTICE SENTENCES.—Pursuant to section 994 of title 28, United States Code, and in accordance with this section, the United States Sentencing Commission shall review and amend, as appropriate, the Federal Sentencing Guidelines and related policy statements to ensure that—
    (1) the base offense level and existing enhancements contained in United States Sentencing Guideline 2J1.2 relating to obstruction of justice are sufficient to deter and punish that activity;
    (2) the enhancements and specific offense characteristics relating to obstruction of justice are adequate in cases where—
        (A) the destruction, alteration, or fabrication of evidence involves—
            (i) a large amount of evidence, a large number of participants, or is otherwise extensive;
            (ii) the selection of evidence that is particularly probative or essential to the investigation; or
            (iii) more than minimal planning; or
        (B) the offense involved abuse of a special skill or a position of trust;
    (3) the guideline offense levels and enhancements for violations of section 1519 or 1520 of title 18, United States Code, as added by this title, are sufficient to deter and punish that activity;
    (4) a specific offense characteristic enhancing sentencing is provided under United States Sentencing Guideline 2B1.1 (as in effect on the date of enactment of this Act) for a fraud offense that endangers the solvency or financial security of a substantial number of victims; and
    (5) the guidelines that apply to organizations in United States Sentencing Guidelines, chapter 8, are sufficient to deter and punish organizational criminal misconduct.

(b) EMERGENCY AUTHORITY AND DEADLINE FOR COMMISSION ACTION.—The United States Sentencing Commission is requested to promulgate the guidelines or amendments provided for under this section as soon as practicable, and in any event not later than 180 days after the date of enactment of this Act, in accordance with the procedures set forth in section 219(a) of the Sentencing Reform Act of 1987, as though the authority under that Act had not expired.

SEC. 806. PROTECTION FOR EMPLOYEES OF PUBLICLY TRADED COMPANIES WHO PROVIDE EVIDENCE OF FRAUD.

(a) IN GENERAL.—Chapter 73 of title 18, United States Code, is amended by inserting after section 1514 the following:

"§ 1514A. Civil action to protect against retaliation in fraud cases

"(a) WHISTLEBLOWER PROTECTION FOR EMPLOYEES OF PUBLICLY TRADED COMPANIES.—No company with a class of securities registered under section 12 of the Securities Exchange Act of 1934 (15 U.S.C. 78l), or that is required to file reports under section 15(d) of the Securities Exchange Act of 1934 (15 U.S.C. 78o(d)),

APPENDIX A: SARBANES-OXLEY ACT OF 2002

or any officer, employee, contractor, subcontractor, or agent of such company, may discharge, demote, suspend, threaten, harass, or in any other manner discriminate against an employee in the terms and conditions of employment because of any lawful act done by the employee—

"(1) to provide information, cause information to be provided, or otherwise assist in an investigation regarding any conduct which the employee reasonably believes constitutes a violation of section 1341, 1343, 1344, or 1348, any rule or regulation of the Securities and Exchange Commission, or any provision of Federal law relating to fraud against shareholders, when the information or assistance is provided to or the investigation is conducted by—

"(A) a Federal regulatory or law enforcement agency;
"(B) any Member of Congress or any committee of Congress; or
"(C) a person with supervisory authority over the employee (or such other person working for the employer who has the authority to investigate, discover, or terminate misconduct); or

"(2) to file, cause to be filed, testify, participate in, or otherwise assist in a proceeding filed or about to be filed (with any knowledge of the employer) relating to an alleged violation of section 1341, 1343, 1344, or 1348, any rule or regulation of the Securities and Exchange Commission, or any provision of Federal law relating to fraud against shareholders.

"(b) ENFORCEMENT ACTION.—

"(1) IN GENERAL.—A person who alleges discharge or other discrimination by any person in violation of subsection (a) may seek relief under subsection (c), by—

"(A) filing a complaint with the Secretary of Labor; or
"(B) if the Secretary has not issued a final decision within 180 days of the filing of the complaint and there is no showing that such delay is due to the bad faith of the claimant, bringing an action at law or equity for de novo review in the appropriate district court of the United States, which shall have jurisdiction over such an action without regard to the amount in controversy.

"(2) PROCEDURE.—

"(A) IN GENERAL.—An action under paragraph (1)(A) shall be governed under the rules and procedures set forth in section 42121(b) of title 49, United States Code.
"(B) EXCEPTION.—Notification made under section 42121(b)(1) of title 49, United States Code, shall be made to the person named in the complaint and to the employer.
"(C) BURDENS OF PROOF.—An action brought under paragraph (1)(B) shall be governed by the legal burdens of proof set forth in section 42121(b) of title 49, United States Code.
"(D) STATUTE OF LIMITATIONS.—An action under paragraph (1) shall be commenced not later than 90 days after the date on which the violation occurs.

"(c) REMEDIES.—

"(1) IN GENERAL.—An employee prevailing in any action under subsection (b)(1) shall be entitled to all relief necessary to make the employee whole.

"(2) COMPENSATORY DAMAGES.—Relief for any action under paragraph (1) shall include—
"(A) reinstatement with the same seniority status that the employee would have had, but for the discrimination;
"(B) the amount of back pay, with interest; and
"(C) compensation for any special damages sustained as a result of the discrimination, including litigation costs, expert witness fees, and reasonable attorney fees.".
"(d) RIGHTS RETAINED BY EMPLOYEE.—Nothing in this section shall be deemed to diminish the rights, privileges, or remedies of any employee under any Federal or State law, or under any collective bargaining agreement.".

(b) CLERICAL AMENDMENT.—The table of sections at the beginning of chapter 73 of title 18, United States Code, is amended by inserting after the item relating to section 1514 the following new item:

"1514A. Civil action to protect against retaliation in fraud cases.".

SEC. 807. CRIMINAL PENALTIES FOR DEFRAUDING SHAREHOLDERS OF PUBLICLY TRADED COMPANIES.

(a) IN GENERAL.—Chapter 63 of title 18, United States Code, is amended by adding at the end the following:

"§ 1348. Securities fraud

"Whoever knowingly executes, or attempts to execute, a scheme or artifice—
"(1) to defraud any person in connection with any security of an issuer with a class of securities registered under section 12 of the Securities Exchange Act of 1934 (15 U.S.C. 78l) or that is required to file reports under section 15(d) of the Securities Exchange Act of 1934 (15 U.S.C. 78o(d)); or
"(2) to obtain, by means of false or fraudulent pretenses, representations, or promises, any money or property in connection with the purchase or sale of any security of an issuer with a class of securities registered under section 12 of the Securities Exchange Act of 1934 (15 U.S.C. 78l) or that is required to file reports under section 15(d) of the Securities Exchange Act of 1934 (15 U.S.C. 78o(d));
shall be fined under this title, or imprisoned not more than 25 years, or both.".

(b) CLERICAL AMENDMENT.—The table of sections at the beginning of chapter 63 of title 18, United States Code, is amended by adding at the end the following new item:

"1348. Securities fraud.".

TITLE IX—WHITE-COLLAR CRIME PENALTY ENHANCEMENTS

SEC. 901. SHORT TITLE.

This title may be cited as the "White-Collar Crime Penalty Enhancement Act of 2002".

APPENDIX A: SARBANES-OXLEY ACT OF 2002

SEC. 902. ATTEMPTS AND CONSPIRACIES TO COMMIT CRIMINAL FRAUD OFFENSES.

(a) IN GENERAL.—Chapter 63 of title 18, United States Code, is amended by inserting after section 1348 as added by this Act the following:

"§ 1349. Attempt and conspiracy

"Any person who attempts or conspires to commit any offense under this chapter shall be subject to the same penalties as those prescribed for the offense, the commission of which was the object of the attempt or conspiracy.

(b) CLERICAL AMENDMENT.—The table of sections at the beginning of chapter 63 of title 18, United States Code, is amended by adding at the end the following new item:

"1349. Attempt and conspiracy.".

SEC. 903. CRIMINAL PENALTIES FOR MAIL AND WIRE FRAUD.

(a) MAIL FRAUD.—Section 1341 of title 18, United States Code, is amended by striking "five" and inserting "20".

(b) WIRE FRAUD.—Section 1343 of title 18, United States Code, is amended by striking "five" and inserting "20".

SEC. 904. CRIMINAL PENALTIES FOR VIOLATIONS OF THE EMPLOYEE RETIREMENT INCOME SECURITY ACT OF 1974.

Section 501 of the Employee Retirement Income Security Act of 1974 (29 U.S.C. 1131) is amended—
  (1) by striking "$5,000" and inserting "$100,000";
  (2) by striking "one year" and inserting "10 years"; and
  (3) by striking "$100,000" and inserting "$500,000".

SEC. 905. AMENDMENT TO SENTENCING GUIDELINES RELATING TO CERTAIN WHITE-COLLAR OFFENSES.

(a) DIRECTIVE TO THE UNITED STATES SENTENCING COMMISSION.—Pursuant to its authority under section 994(p) of title 18, United States Code, and in accordance with this section, the United States Sentencing Commission shall review and, as appropriate, amend the Federal Sentencing Guidelines and related policy statements to implement the provisions of this Act.

(b) REQUIREMENTS.—In carrying out this section, the Sentencing Commission shall—
  (1) ensure that the sentencing guidelines and policy statements reflect the serious nature of the offenses and the penalties set forth in this Act, the growing incidence of serious fraud offenses which are identified above, and the need to modify the sentencing guidelines and policy statements to deter, prevent, and punish such offenses;
  (2) consider the extent to which the guidelines and policy statements adequately address whether the guideline offense levels and enhancements for violations of the sections amended by this Act are sufficient to deter and punish such offenses, and specifically, are adequate in view of the statutory increases in penalties contained in this Act;
  (3) assure reasonable consistency with other relevant directives and sentencing guidelines;
  (4) account for any additional aggravating or mitigating circumstances that might justify exceptions to the generally applicable sentencing ranges;

(5) make any necessary conforming changes to the sentencing guidelines; and

(6) assure that the guidelines adequately meet the purposes of sentencing, as set forth in section 3553(a)(2) of title 18, United States Code.

(c) EMERGENCY AUTHORITY AND DEADLINE FOR COMMISSION ACTION.—The United States Sentencing Commission is requested to promulgate the guidelines or amendments provided for under this section as soon as practicable, and in any event not later than 180 days after the date of enactment of this Act, in accordance with the procedures set forth in section 219(a) of the Sentencing Reform Act of 1987, as though the authority under that Act had not expired.

SEC. 906. CORPORATE RESPONSIBILITY FOR FINANCIAL REPORTS.

(a) IN GENERAL.—Chapter 63 of title 18, United States Code, is amended by inserting after section 1349, as created by this Act, the following:

"§ 1350. Failure of corporate officers to certify financial reports

(a) CERTIFICATION OF PERIODIC FINANCIAL REPORTS.—Each periodic report containing financial statements filed by an issuer with the Securities Exchange Commission pursuant to section 13(a) or 15(d) of the Securities Exchange Act of 1934 (15 U.S.C. 78m(a) or 78o(d)) shall be accompanied by a written statement by the chief executive officer and chief financial officer (or equivalent thereof) of the issuer.

"(b) CONTENT.—The statement required under subsection (a) shall certify that the periodic report containing the financial statements fully complies with the requirements of section 13(a) or 15(d) of the Securities Exchange Act of 1934 (15 U.S.C. 78m or 78o(d)) and that information contained in the periodic report fairly presents, in all material respects, the financial condition and results of operations of the issuer.

"(c) CRIMINAL PENALTIES.—Whoever—

"(1) certifies any statement as set forth in subsections (a) and (b) of this section knowing that the periodic report accompanying the statement does not comport with all the requirements set forth in this section shall be fined not more than $1,000,000 or imprisoned not more than 10 years, or both; or

"(2) willfully certifies any statement as set forth in subsections (a) and (b) of this section knowing that the periodic report accompanying the statement does not comport with all the requirements set forth in this section shall be fined not more than $5,000,000, or imprisoned not more than 20 years, or both.".

(b) CLERICAL AMENDMENT.—The table of sections at the beginning of chapter 63 of title 18, United States Code, is amended by adding at the end the following:

"1350. Failure of corporate officers to certify financial reports.".

TITLE X—CORPORATE TAX RETURNS

SEC. 1001. SENSE OF THE SENATE REGARDING THE SIGNING OF CORPORATE TAX RETURNS BY CHIEF EXECUTIVE OFFICERS.

It is the sense of the Senate that the Federal income tax return of a corporation should be signed by the chief executive officer of such corporation.

TITLE XI—CORPORATE FRAUD ACCOUNTABILITY

SEC. 1101. SHORT TITLE.

This title may be cited as the "Corporate Fraud Accountability Act of 2002".

SEC. 1102. TAMPERING WITH A RECORD OR OTHERWISE IMPEDING AN OFFICIAL PROCEEDING.

Section 1512 of title 18, United States Code, is amended—
 (1) by redesignating subsections (c) through (i) as subsections (d) through (j), respectively; and
 (2) by inserting after subsection (b) the following new subsection:
"(c) Whoever corruptly—
 "(1) alters, destroys, mutilates, or conceals a record, document, or other object, or attempts to do so, with the intent to impair the object's integrity or availability for use in an official proceeding; or
 "(2) otherwise obstructs, influences, or impedes any official proceeding, or attempts to do so,
shall be fined under this title or imprisoned not more than 20 years, or both.".

SEC. 1103. TEMPORARY FREEZE AUTHORITY FOR THE SECURITIES AND EXCHANGE COMMISSION.

 (a) IN GENERAL.—Section 21C(c) of the Securities Exchange Act of 1934 (15 U.S.C. 78u–3(c)) is amended by adding at the end the following:
 "(3) TEMPORARY FREEZE.—
   "(A) IN GENERAL.—
     "(i) ISSUANCE OF TEMPORARY ORDER.—Whenever, during the course of a lawful investigation involving possible violations of the Federal securities laws by an issuer of publicly traded securities or any of its directors, officers, partners, controlling persons, agents, or employees, it shall appear to the Commission that it is likely that the issuer will make extraordinary payments (whether compensation or otherwise) to any of the foregoing persons, the Commission may petition a Federal district court for a temporary order requiring the issuer to escrow, subject to court supervision, those payments in an interest-bearing account for 45 days.
     "(ii) STANDARD.—A temporary order shall be entered under clause (i), only after notice and opportunity for a hearing, unless the court determines that

notice and hearing prior to entry of the order would be impracticable or contrary to the public interest.

"(iii) EFFECTIVE PERIOD.—A temporary order issued under clause (i) shall—

"(I) become effective immediately;

"(II) be served upon the parties subject to it; and

"(III) unless set aside, limited or suspended by a court of competent jurisdiction, shall remain effective and enforceable for 45 days.

"(iv) EXTENSIONS AUTHORIZED.—The effective period of an order under this subparagraph may be extended by the court upon good cause shown for not longer than 45 additional days, provided that the combined period of the order shall not exceed 90 days.

"(B) PROCESS ON DETERMINATION OF VIOLATIONS.—

"(i) VIOLATIONS CHARGED.—If the issuer or other person described in subparagraph (A) is charged with any violation of the Federal securities laws before the expiration of the effective period of a temporary order under subparagraph (A) (including any applicable extension period), the order shall remain in effect, subject to court approval, until the conclusion of any legal proceedings related thereto, and the affected issuer or other person, shall have the right to petition the court for review of the order.

"(ii) VIOLATIONS NOT CHARGED.—If the issuer or other person described in subparagraph (A) is not charged with any violation of the Federal securities laws before the expiration of the effective period of a temporary order under subparagraph (A) (including any applicable extension period), the escrow shall terminate at the expiration of the 45-day effective period (or the expiration of any extension period, as applicable), and the disputed payments (with accrued interest) shall be returned to the issuer or other affected person.".

(b) TECHNICAL AMENDMENT.—Section 21C(c)(2) of the Securities Exchange Act of 1934 (15 U.S.C. 78u–3(c)(2)) is amended by striking "This" and inserting "paragraph (1)".

SEC. 1104. AMENDMENT TO THE FEDERAL SENTENCING GUIDELINES.

(a) REQUEST FOR IMMEDIATE CONSIDERATION BY THE UNITED STATES SENTENCING COMMISSION.—Pursuant to its authority under section 994(p) of title 28, United States Code, and in accordance with this section, the United States Sentencing Commission is requested to—

(1) promptly review the sentencing guidelines applicable to securities and accounting fraud and related offenses;

(2) expeditiously consider the promulgation of new sentencing guidelines or amendments to existing sentencing guidelines to provide an enhancement for officers or directors of publicly traded corporations who commit fraud and related offenses; and

(3) submit to Congress an explanation of actions taken by the Sentencing Commission pursuant to paragraph (2) and

any additional policy recommendations the Sentencing Commission may have for combating offenses described in paragraph (1).

(b) CONSIDERATIONS IN REVIEW.—In carrying out this section, the Sentencing Commission is requested to—

(1) ensure that the sentencing guidelines and policy statements reflect the serious nature of securities, pension, and accounting fraud and the need for aggressive and appropriate law enforcement action to prevent such offenses;

(2) assure reasonable consistency with other relevant directives and with other guidelines;

(3) account for any aggravating or mitigating circumstances that might justify exceptions, including circumstances for which the sentencing guidelines currently provide sentencing enhancements;

(4) ensure that guideline offense levels and enhancements for an obstruction of justice offense are adequate in cases where documents or other physical evidence are actually destroyed or fabricated;

(5) ensure that the guideline offense levels and enhancements under United States Sentencing Guideline 2B1.1 (as in effect on the date of enactment of this Act) are sufficient for a fraud offense when the number of victims adversely involved is significantly greater than 50;

(6) make any necessary conforming changes to the sentencing guidelines; and

(7) assure that the guidelines adequately meet the purposes of sentencing as set forth in section 3553 (a)(2) of title 18, United States Code.

(c) EMERGENCY AUTHORITY AND DEADLINE FOR COMMISSION ACTION.—The United States Sentencing Commission is requested to promulgate the guidelines or amendments provided for under this section as soon as practicable, and in any event not later than the 180 days after the date of enactment of this Act, in accordance with the procedures sent forth in section 21(a) of the Sentencing Reform Act of 1987, as though the authority under that Act had not expired.

SEC. 1105. AUTHORITY OF THE COMMISSION TO PROHIBIT PERSONS FROM SERVING AS OFFICERS OR DIRECTORS.

(a) SECURITIES EXCHANGE ACT OF 1934.—Section 21C of the Securities Exchange Act of 1934 (15 U.S.C. 78u–3) is amended by adding at the end the following:

"(f) AUTHORITY OF THE COMMISSION TO PROHIBIT PERSONS FROM SERVING AS OFFICERS OR DIRECTORS.—In any cease-and-desist proceeding under subsection (a), the Commission may issue an order to prohibit, conditionally or unconditionally, and permanently or for such period of time as it shall determine, any person who has violated section 10(b) or the rules or regulations thereunder, from acting as an officer or director of any issuer that has a class of securities registered pursuant to section 12, or that is required to file reports pursuant to section 15(d), if the conduct of that person demonstrates unfitness to serve as an officer or director of any such issuer.".

(b) SECURITIES ACT OF 1933.—Section 8A of the Securities Act of 1933 (15 U.S.C. 77h–1) is amended by adding at the end of the following:

"(f) AUTHORITY OF THE COMMISSION TO PROHIBIT PERSONS FROM SERVING AS OFFICERS OR DIRECTORS.—In any cease-and-desist proceeding under subsection (a), the Commission may issue an order to prohibit, conditionally or unconditionally, and permanently or for such period of time as it shall determine, any person who has violated section 17(a)(1) or the rules or regulations thereunder, from acting as an officer or director of any issuer that has a class of securities registered pursuant to section 12 of the Securities Exchange Act of 1934, or that is required to file reports pursuant to section 15(d) of that Act, if the conduct of that person demonstrates unfitness to serve as an officer or director of any such issuer.".

SEC. 1106. INCREASED CRIMINAL PENALTIES UNDER SECURITIES EXCHANGE ACT OF 1934.

Section 32(a) of the Securities Exchange Act of 1934 (15 U.S.C. 78ff(a)) is amended—

(1) by striking "$1,000,000, or imprisoned not more than 10 years" and inserting "$5,000,000, or imprisoned not more than 20 years"; and

(2) by striking "$2,500,000" and inserting "$25,000,000".

SEC. 1107. RETALIATION AGAINST INFORMANTS.

(a) IN GENERAL.—Section 1513 of title 18, United States Code, is amended by adding at the end the following:

"(e) Whoever knowingly, with the intent to retaliate, takes any action harmful to any person, including interference with the lawful employment or livelihood of any person, for providing to a law enforcement officer any truthful information relating to the commission or possible commission of any Federal offense, shall be fined under this title or imprisoned not more than 10 years, or both.".

Speaker of the House of Representatives.

Vice President of the United States and President of the Senate.

Appendix B
SUMMARY OF NEW DISCLOSURE REQUIREMENTS

The following chart summarizes the principal rules and guidance adopted or proposed by the SEC relating to the preparation of SEC periodic and other reports.

Currently Applicable Rules and Guidance

Topic & Rules/Release	Disclosure Item	10-K	Annual Proxy	10-Q	20-F
Critical Accounting Policies (*Cautionary Advice Regarding Disclosure About Critical Accounting Policies*, No. 33-8040 (Dec. 12, 2001) http://www.sec.gov/rules/other/33-8040.htm)	• Explanations of "critical accounting policies," related judgments and uncertainties and the likelihood of materially different amounts under different conditions or assumptions; audit committee review recommended.	Part II, Item 7 (MD&A)	N/A	Part I, Item 2 (MD&A)	Item 5 (MD&A)
Equity Compensation Plans (*Final Rule: Disclosure of Equity Compensation Plan Information*, No. 33-8048 (Dec. 21, 2001) http://www.sec.gov/rules/final/33-8048.htm)	• Tabular presentation of equity compensation plan information; break-out of information for plans not approved by security holders (S-K Item 201(d)).	Part III, Item 12 (incorporation by reference from proxy permitted)	Item 10	N/A	N/A
	• Exhibit filing of equity compensation plans not approved by security holders (S-K Item 601(b)(10) (iii)(B)).	Part III, Item 15 (Exhibits)	N/A	Part II, Item 6 (Exhibits)	N/A
Related Party Transactions (*Commission Statement about Management's Discussion*	• Disclosure about related party and similar transactions to the extent necessary for an	Part II, Item 7 (MD&A)	N/A	Part I, Item 2 (MD&A)	Item 5 (MD&A)

APPENDIX B: DISCLOSURE REQUIREMENTS

Topic & Rules/Release	Disclosure Item	10-K	Annual Proxy	10-Q	20-F
and Analysis of Financial Condition and Results of Operations, No. 33-8056 (Jan. 22, 2002) http://www.sec.gov/rules/other/33-8056.htm	understanding of the company's current and prospective financial position and operating results.				
Liquidity Items (*Commission Statement about Management's Discussion and Analysis of Financial Condition and Results of Operations, No. 33-8056 (Jan. 22, 2002)*) http://www.sec.gov/rules/other/33-8056.htm	• Disclosures concerning certain off-balance sheet transactions, arrangements and other relationships with unconsolidated entities. (Superseded by SEC's final rules on disclosure in MD&A of information about off-balance sheet obligations). • Tabular disclosure of certain contractual obligations aggregated by category. (Superseded by SEC's final rules on disclosure in MD&A of information about contractual obligations).	Part II, Item 7 (MD&A) Part II, Item 7 (MD&A)	N/A N/A	Part I, Item 2 (MD&A) Part I, Item 2 (MD&A)	Item 5 (MD&A) Item 5 (MD&A)

THE SARBANES-OXLEY ACT: ANALYSIS AND PRACTICE

Topic & Rules/Release	Disclosure Item	Location			
		10-K	Annual Proxy	10-Q	20-F
	• Tabular disclosure of lines of credit, guarantees and certain other contingent commercial commitments aggregated by category. (Not superseded)	Part II, Item 7 (MD&A)	N/A	Part I, Item 2 (MD&A)	Item 5 (MD&A)
Foreign Private Issuer Filings (*Final Rule: Mandated EDGAR Filing for Foreign Issuers, No. 33-8099 (May 14, 2002)* http://www.sec.gov/rules/final/33-8099.htm)	• Foreign private issuers are now subject to mandatory EDGAR filing, including Forms 20-F and 6-K.	N/A	N/A	N/A	EDGAR filing
	• Full translations required for certain foreign language documents; an English summary permitted for others.	N/A	N/A	N/A	Item 19 (Exhibits)
CEO/CFO Certifications Sarbanes-Oxley Section 302 (*Final Rules: Certification of Disclosure in Companies' Quarterly and Annual Reports, No. 33-8124 (Aug. 29, 2002)* http://www.sec.gov/rules/final/33-8124.htm; and *Management's Reports on Internal Control over Financial Reporting and Certification of Disclosure in Exchange Act Periodic Reports, No. 33-8238 (June 5, 2003)* http://www.sec.gov/rules/final/33-8238.htm)	• CEO and CFO certifications regarding disclosure in periodic reports, disclosure controls and procedures and other matters (Exchange Act Rules 13a-14, 15d-14).	Immediately following signature page, before exhibits. On and after August 14, 2003 as an exhibit.	N/A	Immediately following signature page, before exhibits. On and after August 14, 2003 as an exhibit.	Immediately following signature page, before exhibits. On and after August 14, 2003 as an exhibit.

262

APPENDIX B: DISCLOSURE REQUIREMENTS

Topic & Rules/Release	Disclosure Item	Location				
		10-K	Annual Proxy	10-Q	20-F	
CEO/CFO Certifications Sarbanes-Oxley Section 906	• CEO and CFO certifications regarding disclosure in periodic report.	Accompanies report. On and after August 14, 2003 as an exhibit.	N/A	Accompanies report. On and after August 14, 2003 as an exhibit.	Accompanies report. On and after August 14, 2003 as an exhibit.	
Disclosure Controls Sarbanes-Oxley Section 302 (*Final Rule: Certification of Disclosure in Companies' Quarterly and Annual Reports*, No. 33-8124 (*Aug. 28, 2002*) http://www.sec.gov/rules/final/33-8124.htm)	• Disclosure regarding conclusions of evaluation of disclosure controls and procedures, significant changes in internal control over financial reporting.	Part III, Item 14	N/A	Part I, Item 4	Item 15	
Website Access to Reports (*Final Rule: Acceleration of Periodic Report Filing Dates and Disclosure Concerning Website Access to Reports*, No. 33-8128 (*Sept. 5, 2002*) http://www.sec.gov/rules/final/33-8128.htm)	• Accelerated filers must disclose their website address if they have one, and whether, during the period covered by the report, they made their Forms 10-K, 10-Q and 8-K available on their website free of charge as soon as reasonably practicable after electronic filing with the SEC.	Part I, Item 1	N/A	N/A	N/A	

Topic & Rules/Release	Disclosure Item	Location			
		10-K	Annual Proxy	10-Q	20-F
Non-GAAP Financial Measures Sarbanes-Oxley Section 401(b) *(Final Rule: Conditions for Use of Non-GAAP Financial Measures, No. 33-8176 (Jan. 22, 2003)* http://www.sec.gov/rules/final/33-8176.htm)	• All public disclosures (not just filings, which for these purposes also include Form 8-K) of non-GAAP financial information generally required to be accompanied by most directly comparable measure and quantitative reconciliation (Regulation G).	Wherever non-GAAP financial measure presented	Wherever non-GAAP financial measure presented	Wherever non-GAAP financial measure presented	Wherever non-GAAP financial measure presented
	• Conditions applicable to use of non-GAAP financial information in SEC filings (S-K, Item 10(e)).	Wherever non-GAAP financial measure presented	Wherever non-GAAP financial measure presented	Wherever non-GAAP financial measure presented	Wherever non-GAAP financial measure presented
Furnishing of Earnings Releases on Form 8-K *(Final Rule: Conditions for Use of Non-GAAP Financial Measures, No. 33-8176 (Jan. 22, 2003)* http://www.sec.gov/rules/final/33-8176.htm)	• Announcements or releases of material non-public information regarding results of operations or financial condition for a completed quarterly or fiscal period must be furnished on a Form 8-K within five business days of the announcement or release.	N/A	N/A	Item 12 of Form 8-K	N/A

APPENDIX B: DISCLOSURE REQUIREMENTS

Topic & Rules/Release	Disclosure Item	Location			
		10-K	Annual Proxy	10-Q	20-F
Items Highlighted in Review of Fortune 500 Companies (*Summary by the Division of Corporation Finance of Significant Issues Addressed in the Review of the Periodic Reports of the Fortune 500 Companies (Feb. 27, 2003)* http://www.sec.gov/divisions/corpfin/fortune500rep.htm)	• Provide more meaningful critical accounting policy disclosure. • Restrictions on use of non-GAAP financial information. • Expanded disclosure regarding: — revenue recognition policies; — restructuring charges; — impairment charges; — pension plans; — securitized financial assets and off-balance sheet arrangements; and — contingent liabilities relating to product liability or environmental issues. • Comply with segment reporting rules.	Part II, Item 7 (MD&A)	N/A	Part I, Item 2 (MD&A)	Item 5 (MD&A)

265

Adopted Rules and Guidance with Transition Periods

Topic & Rules/Release	Disclosure Item	Applies to Reports For Periods Ending	Location 10-K	Location Annual Proxy	Location 10-Q	Location 20-F
Liquidity Items Sarbanes-Oxley Section 401(a) *(Final Rule: Disclosure in Management's Discussion and Analysis about Off-Balance Sheet Arrangements and Aggregate Contractual Obligations, No. 33-8182 (Jan. 28, 2003)* http://www.sec.gov/rules/final/33-8182.htm)	• Specific disclosures about certain off-balance sheet arrangements (S-K Item 303(a)(4)). (Supersedes guidance provided in January 2002 SEC Statement about MD&A).	Annual reports for periods ending after June 15, 2003 and quarterly reports thereafter.	Part II, Item 7 (MD&A)	N/A	Part I, Item 2 (MD&A)	Item 5 (MD&A)
	• Tabular disclosure concerning specified categories of contractual obligations (S-K Item 303(a)(5)). (Supersedes guidance provided in January 2002 SEC Statement about MD&A).	Annual reports for periods ending after December 15, 2003 and quarterly reports thereafter.	Part II, Item 7 (MD&A)	N/A	Part I, Item 2 (MD&A)	Item 5 (MD&A)
Auditor Independence Sarbanes-Oxley Section 208 *(Final Rule: Strengthening the Commission's Requirements Regarding Auditor Independence, No. 33-8183 (Jan. 28, 2003)* http://www.sec.gov/rules/final/33-8183.htm) (rev. No. 33-8183A (Mar. 26, 2003) http://www.sec.gov/rules/final/33-8183a.htm)	• Disclosure of breakdown of audit fees, audit-related fees, tax fees, and other fees billed by the principal accountant during the past two fiscal years.	After December 15, 2003.	Part II, Item 16 (incorporation by reference from proxy permitted)	Item 9(e)	N/A	Item 16C

APPENDIX B: DISCLOSURE REQUIREMENTS

Topic & Rules/Release	Disclosure Item	Applies to Reports For Periods Ending	Location			
			10-K	Annual Proxy	10-Q	20-F
	• Disclosure of audit committee pre-approval policies and procedures.	After December 15, 2003. Pre-approval required starting May 6, 2003.	Part II, Item 16 (incorporation by reference from proxy permitted)	Item 9(e)	N/A	Item 16C
	• Specific disclosures on use of *de minimis* exception.	After December 15, 2003.	Part II, Item 16 (incorporation by reference from proxy permitted)	Item 9(e)	N/A	Item 16C
Financial Expert Sarbanes-Oxley Section 407 *(Final Rule: Disclosure Required by Sections 406 and 407 of the Sarbanes-Oxley Act of 2002, No. 33-8177 (Jan. 23, 2003)*	• Disclosure of whether or not company has an audit committee financial expert (as defined); if yes, identify, state if independent and describe experience; if not, explain why not (S-K Item 401(h)).	July 15, 2003 (independence disclosure required for foreign private issuers beginning July 31, 2005).	Part III, Item 10 (incorporation by reference from proxy permitted)	Item 7 (inclusion in proxy not required, but permitted to enable	N/A	Item 16A

Topic & Rules/Release	Disclosure Item	Applies to Reports For Periods Ending	10-K	Annual Proxy	10-Q	20-F
http://www.sec.gov/rules/final/33-8177.htm) (rev. No. 33-8177A (Mar. 26, 2003) http://www.sec.gov/rules/final/33-8177a.htm)				incorporation by reference into 10-K)		
Code of Ethics Sarbanes-Oxley Section 406 (*Final Rule: Disclosure Required by Sections 406 and 407 of the Sarbanes-Oxley Act of 2002, No. 33-8177* (Jan. 23, 2003) http://www.sec.gov/rules/final/33-8177.htm)	• Disclosure of whether or not the company has adopted a written code of ethics for CEO and senior financial officers meeting specified criteria; if not, explain why not.	July 15, 2003	Part III, Item 10 (incorporation by reference from proxy permitted)	Item 7 (inclusion in proxy not required, but permitted to enable incorporation by reference into 10-K)	N/A	Item 16B
	• Exhibit filing of code of ethics. OR	July 15, 2003	Part III, Item 15 (Exhibits)	N/A	N/A	Item 19 (Exhibits)
	• Website posting or availability, free of charge, of code of ethics, with disclosure.		Part III, Item 10 (incorporation by reference	Item 7 (inclusion in proxy not required, but	N/A	Item 16B

APPENDIX B: DISCLOSURE REQUIREMENTS

Topic & Rules/Release	Disclosure Item	Applies to Reports For Periods Ending	Location			
			10-K	Annual Proxy	10-Q	20-F
			from proxy permitted)	permitted to enable incorporation by reference into 10-K)		
	• Disclosure of amendments to code of ethics and any waivers granted.	Reports filed following first filing of above disclosure.	If website posting, Part III, Item 10 (incorporation by reference from proxy permitted)	Item 7 (inclusion in proxy not required, but permitted to enable incorporation by reference into 10-K)	Form 8-K w/in 5 business days OR website posting	Item 16B OR website posting
Accelerated Filing Deadlines (*Final Rule: Acceleration of Periodic Report Filing Dates and Disclosure Concerning Website Access to Reports*, No. 33-8128 (Sept. 5, 2002) http://www.sec.gov/rules/final/33-8128.htm) (rev. No. 33-8128A (Apr. 8, 2003) http://www.sec.gov/rules/final/33-8128a.htm)	• Accelerated filers must file Form 10-K for the first fiscal year ending on or after December 15, 2003 within 75 days of the fiscal year end.	First fiscal year ending on or after December 15, 2003.	Filing date	N/A	N/A	N/A
	• Accelerated filers must file Form 10-K for fiscal years ending on or after December 15, 2004 within 60 days of the fiscal year end.	Fiscal years ending on or after December 15, 2004.	Filing date	N/A	N/A	N/A

Topic & Rules/Release	Disclosure Item	Applies to Reports For Periods Ending	10-K	Annual Proxy	10-Q	20-F
	• During the first fiscal year ending on or after December 15, 2004, accelerated filers must file Form 10-Q within 40 days of the fiscal quarter end.	Beginning Q1 2004 for calendar year filers.	N/A	N/A	Filing date	N/A
	• During all fiscal years ending on or after December 15, 2005, accelerated filers must file Form 10-Q within 35 days of the fiscal quarter end.	Beginning Q1 2005 for calendar year filers.	N/A	N/A	Filing date	N/A
Audit Committee Sarbanes-Oxley Section 301 *(Final Rule: Standards Relating to Listed Company Audit Committees, No. 33-8220* (April 9, 2003) http://www.sec.gov/rules/final/33-8220.htm)	• Disclosure about audit committee and its members (including independence).	Compliance with new listing requirements required by earlier of first annual meeting after January 15, 2004, or October 31, 2004.	Part III, Item 10 (S-K Item 401) (incorporation by reference from proxy permitted)	Item 7(d)	N/A	Item 6

APPENDIX B: DISCLOSURE REQUIREMENTS

Topic & Rules/Release	Disclosure Item	Applies to Reports For Periods Ending	Location			
			10-K	Annual Proxy	10-Q	20-F
	• Disclosure of exemptions from listing standards used.	Foreign private issuers have until July 31, 2005 to comply.	Part III, Item 10 (incorporation by reference from proxy permitted)	Item 7 (inclusion in proxy not required, but permitted to enable incorporation by reference into 10-K)	N/A	Item 16D
CEO/CFO Certifications Sarbanes-Oxley Section 302 (*Final Rule: Management's Reports on Internal Control Over Financial Reporting and Certification of Disclosure in Exchange Act Periodic Reports*, No. 33-8238 (*June 5, 2003*) http://www.sec.gov/rules/final/33-8238.htm)	• Modifications relating to internal control over financial reporting. • Other modifications as to timing of evaluation of disclosure controls and procedures.	Would not apply until the first annual report in which the company provides management's internal control report (see below).	Exhibit 31	N/A	Exhibit 31	Exhibit 31

271

Topic & Rules/Release	Disclosure Item	Applies to Reports For Periods Ending	Location			
			10-K	Annual Proxy	10-Q	20-F
Internal Control Over Financial Reporting Sarbanes-Oxley Section 404 (Final Rule: *Management's Report on Internal Control Over Financial Reporting and Certification of Disclosure in Exchange Act Periodic Reports*, No. 33-8238 (June 5, 2003) http://www.sec.gov/rules/final/33-8238.htm)	• Management report on internal control over financial reporting; auditor attestation to and report on management report.	On and after August 14, 2003 Will apply to fiscal years of U.S. "accelerated filers" ending on or after June 15, 2004 and to fiscal years of other U.S. issuers and foreign private issuers ending on or after April 15, 2005.	Part II, Item 9A	N/A	Part I, Item 4	Item 15

APPENDIX B: DISCLOSURE REQUIREMENTS

	Pending Rulemaking		Location				
Topic & Rules/Release	Disclosure Item	Status	10-K	Annual Proxy	10-Q	20-F
---	---	---	---	---	---	---
Share Repurchases *(Proposed Rule: Rule 10b-18 and Purchases of Certain Equity Securities by the Issuer and Others, No. 33-8160 (Dec. 10, 2002)* http://www.sec.gov/rules/proposed/33-8160.htm)	• Specified tabular disclosure, with footnotes, must be provided relating to share repurchases by the company and affiliated purchasers.	Timing of further action unclear.	Part I, Item 5(c)	N/A	Part II, Item 2(b)	Item 15(e)
Listing Standards *(NYSE: Corporate Governance Rule Proposals (amended proposals filed with SEC Apr. 9, 2003)* http://www.nyse.com/pdfs/amend1-04-09-03.pdf) *(Nasdaq: Summary of Nasdaq Corporate Governance Proposals (February 26, 2003)* http://www.nasdaq.com/about/Web_Corp_Gov_Summary_%20Feb-revised.pdf)	• Existing disclosure about corporate governance and board committees (including audit committee and independence) may be affected.	Proposals have been published for comment by SEC. Comments due by May 8, 2003 on the NYSE proposal and by April 15, 2003 on the most recent Nasdaq proposal.	Part III, Item 10 (incorporation by reference from proxy permitted)	Item 7(d)	N/A	Item 6 Nasdaq: disclose in 20-F (location not specified)
	• Disclosure by foreign private issuers of: — exemptions from listing requirements and alternative practices (Nasdaq); and		N/A	N/A	N/A	NYSE: disclose on website or in annual report to shareholders

273

			Location			
Topic & Rules/Release	Disclosure Item	Status	10-K	Annual Proxy	10-Q	20-F
	— significant ways in which their corporate governance practices differ from those required of domestic issuers (NYSE).					
	• Annual CEO certification that he or she is not aware of any violation of listing standards (NYSE).		Include if company does not publish a separate annual report to shareholders.	N/A	N/A	N/A
	• Availability of corporate governance guidelines, committee charters, code of business conduct, code of ethics on website; disclosure of availability in annual report to shareholders (NYSE).		N/A	N/A	N/A	N/A

APPENDIX B: DISCLOSURE REQUIREMENTS

Topic & Rules/Release	Disclosure Item	Status	Location			
			10-K	Annual Proxy	10-Q	20-F
Critical Accounting Policies (*Proposed Rule: Disclosure in Management's Discussion and Analysis about the Application of Critical Accounting Policies, No. 33-8098 (May 10, 2002)* http://www.sec.gov/rules/proposed/33-8098.htm)	• Disclosure about critical accounting estimates, including sensitivity analysis, segment analysis and quarterly updates.	Timing of further action unclear.	Part II, Item 7 (MD&A)	N/A	Part I, Item 2 (MD&A)	Item 5 (MD&A)
	• Audit committee report to cover discussion of critical accounting policies.		Part II, Item 7 (MD&A)	N/A	Part I, Item 2 (MD&A)	Item 5 (MD&A)
	• Disclosure about new accounting policies.		Part II, Item 7 (MD&A)	N/A	Part I, Item 2 (MD&A)	Item 5 (MD&A)
New 8-K Items (*Proposed Rule: Additional Form 8-K Disclosure Requirements, No. 33-8106 (June 17, 2002)* http://www.sec.gov/rules/proposed/33-8106.htm)	• Significantly expand items that require disclosure under Form 8-K and shorten filing deadline for most items to 2 business days.	Timing of further action unclear.	N/A	N/A	N/A	N/A

APPENDIX C
ADDITIONAL RESOURCES

The following are additional materials concerning the Sarbanes-Oxley Act and related developments. They may be found on the website of Cleary, Gottlieb, Steen & Hamilton at *www.clearygottlieb.com*.

Topic	Date	Number	Title
Critical Accounting Policies	January 4, 2002	2-2002	SEC Issues Cautionary Advice About the Use of 'Pro Forma' Financial Information in Earnings Releases and Disclosure About Critical Accounting Policies
	June 12, 2002	21-2002	SEC Proposes Disclosure on Critical Accounting Policies
Liquidity Items/ Related Party Transactions	January 31, 2002	6-2002	SEC Issues Statement Regarding Management's Discussion and Analysis of Financial Condition and Results of Operations
Foreign Private Issuer Filings	June 7, 2002	19-2002	SEC Adopts New Rules Requiring Electronic Filing by Foreign Governments and Foreign Private Issuers Including New Translation Requirements for Foreign Language Documents
	September 30, 2002	52-2002	Preparing for Filing via the SEC's EDGAR System: An Overview for Foreign Governments and Foreign Private Issuers
CEO/CFO Certifications & Disclosure/Internal Controls	August 30, 2002	43-2002	SEC Issues Rules Regarding Certification of Annual and Quarterly Reports
	October 28, 2002	60-2002	SEC Proposes Rules to Implement Sections 404, 406, 407 and 303 of the Sarbanes-Oxley Act
Accelerated Filing; Website Access to Reports	September 16, 2002	45-2002	SEC Adopts New Rules Requiring Accelerated Filing of Annual and Quarterly Reports
Off-Balance Sheet Arrangements and Contractual Obligations	February 20, 2003	21-2003	SEC Adopts Rules to Implement Section 401(a) of the Sarbanes-Oxley Act
Non-GAAP Financial Measures; Furnishing of Earnings Releases on Form 8-K	January 30, 2003	13-2003	SEC Adopts Rules to Implement Section 401(b) of the Sarbanes-Oxley Act and to Require Furnishing of Earnings Releases on Form 8-K

THE SARBANES-OXLEY ACT: ANALYSIS AND PRACTICE

Topic	Date	Number	Title
Auditor Independence & Fees	February 28, 2003	25-2003	SEC Adopts Final Rules under the Sarbanes-Oxley Act Regarding Auditor Independence and Retention of Audit Records
Financial Expert; Code of Ethics	February 20, 2003	20-2003	SEC Adopts Final Rules under Sections 406 and 407 of the Sarbanes-Oxley Act
Share Repurchases	January 6, 2003	1-2003	SEC Proposes Amendments to Rule 10b-18 and Disclosure of Issuer Equity Repurchases
Audit Committee	April 18, 2003	37-2003	SEC Adopts Audit Committee Standards Under Sarbanes-Oxley Act Section 301
Improper Influence on Auditor	June 9, 2003	49-2003	SEC Adopts Rules Implementing Section 303 of the Sarbanes-Oxley Act
Management's Internal Control Reports	June 23, 2003	55-2003	SEC Adopts New Rules on CEO/CFO Certification and Internal Controls

Appendix D
FORMS OF OFFICER CERTIFICATION

FORM 1

Original Form of Section 302 Certification for Issuers other than Asset-Backed Issuers and Registered Investment Companies[1]

I, [identify the certifying individual], certify that:

1. I have reviewed this [annual report on Form 10-K] [annual report on Form 20-F] [annual report on Form 40-F] [quarterly report on Form 10-Q] of [identify registrant];

2. Based on my knowledge, this [annual] [quarterly] report does not contain any untrue statement of a material fact or omit to state a material fact necessary to make the statements made, in light of the circumstances under which such statements were made, not misleading with respect to the period covered by this [annual] [quarterly] report;

3. Based on my knowledge, the financial statements, and other financial information included in this [annual] [quarterly] report, fairly present in all material respects the financial condition, results of operations and cash flows of the registrant as of, and for, the periods presented in this [annual] [quarterly] report;

4. The registrant's other certifying officers and I are responsible for establishing and maintaining disclosure controls and procedures (as defined in Exchange Act Rules 13a-14 and 15d-14) for the registrant and have:

a) designed such disclosure controls and procedures to ensure that material information relating to the registrant, including its consolidated subsidiaries, is made known to us by others within those entities, particularly during the period in which this [annual] [quarterly] report is being prepared;

---

[1] Separate certification required for each officer. This form of certification is effective until superseded on August 14, 2003 by Form 2, as described below.

b) evaluated the effectiveness of the registrant's disclosure controls and procedures as of a date within 90 days prior to the filing date of this [annual] [quarterly] report (the "Evaluation Date"); and

c) presented in this [annual] [quarterly] report our conclusions about the effectiveness of the disclosure controls and procedures based on our evaluation as of the Evaluation Date;

5. The registrant's other certifying officers and I have disclosed, based on our most recent evaluation, to the registrant's auditors and the audit committee of registrant's board of directors (or persons performing the equivalent function):

a) all significant deficiencies in the design or operation of internal controls which could adversely affect the registrant's ability to record, process, summarize and report financial data and have identified for the registrant's auditors any material weaknesses in internal controls; and

b) any fraud, whether or not material, that involves management or other employees who have a significant role in the registrant's internal controls; and

6. The registrant's other certifying officers and I have indicated in this [annual] [quarterly] report whether there were significant changes in internal controls or in other factors that could significantly affect internal controls subsequent to the date of our most recent evaluation, including any corrective actions with regard to significant deficiencies and material weaknesses.

Date:……………..

Title: _____

APPENDIX D: FORMS OF OFFICER CERTIFICATION

FORM 2

Amended Form of Section 302 Certification for Issuers other than Asset-Backed Issuers and Registered Investment Companies[2]

I, [identify the certifying individual], certify that:

1. I have reviewed this [specify report] of [identify registrant];

2. Based on my knowledge, this report does not contain any untrue statement of a material fact or omit to state a material fact necessary to make the statements made, in light of the circumstances under which such statements were made, not misleading with respect to the period covered by this report;

3. Based on my knowledge, the financial statements, and other financial information included in this report, fairly present in all material respects the financial condition, results of operations and cash flows of the registrant as of, and for, the periods presented in this report;

4. The registrant's other certifying officer(s) and I are responsible for establishing and maintaining disclosure controls and procedures (as defined in Exchange Act Rules 13a-15(e) and 15d-15(e)) [and internal control over financial reporting (as defined in Exchange Act Rules 13a-15(f) and 15d-15(f)] for the registrant and have:

> (a) Designed such disclosure controls and procedures, or caused such disclosure controls and procedures to be designed under our supervision, to ensure that material information relating to the registrant, including its consolidated subsidiaries, is made known to us by others within those entities, particularly during the period in which this report is being prepared;
>
> [(b) Designed such internal control over financial reporting, or caused such internal control over financial reporting to be designed under our supervision, to provide reasonable assurance regarding the reliability of financial reporting and the preparation of financial statements for external purposes in accordance with generally accepted accounting principles;]

---

[2] Adopted in SEC Release No. 33-8238 (June 5, 2003). The new form of certification will be effective August 14, 2003, except that the bracketed language in paragraph 4 will become effective for U.S. "accelerated filers" beginning with the annual report for their fiscal year ending on or after June 15, 2004 (April 15, 2005 for all other issuers, including foreign private issuers). Although the text of the certification will be introduced by the words "exactly as set forth below," the SEC has stated that "certifying officers may temporarily modify the content of their Section 302 certifications" to eliminate this language pending its effectiveness. SEC Release No. 33-8238 (June 5, 2003), 68 Fed. Reg. 36636, 36653 (June 18, 2003).

(c) Evaluated the effectiveness of the registrant's disclosure controls and procedures and presented in this report our conclusions about the effectiveness of the controls and procedures, as of the end of the period covered by this report based on such evaluation; and

(d) Disclosed in this report any change in the registrant's internal control over financial reporting that occurred during the registrant's most recent fiscal quarter (the registrant's fourth fiscal quarter in the case of an annual report) that has materially affected, or is reasonably likely to materially affect, the registrant's internal control over financial reporting;[3] and

5. The registrant's other certifying officer(s) and I have disclosed, based on our most recent evaluation of internal control over financial reporting, to the registrant's auditors and the audit committee of the registrant's board of directors (or persons performing the equivalent functions):

(a) All significant deficiencies and material weaknesses in the design or operation of internal control over financial reporting which are reasonably likely to adversely affect the registrant's ability to record, process, summarize and report financial information; and

(b) Any fraud, whether or not material, that involves management or other employees who have a significant role in the registrant's internal control over financial reporting.

Date: ....

Title: _____

---

[3] For foreign private issuers and Canadian issuers that report under the MJDS, this paragraph will clarify that the disclosure relates to changes during the period covered by the annual report.

APPENDIX D: FORMS OF OFFICER CERTIFICATION

FORM 3

Form of Section 906 Certification[4]

Pursuant to Section 906 of the Sarbanes-Oxley Act of 2002 (subsections (a) and (b) of Section 1350, Chapter 63 of Title 18, United States Code), each of the undersigned officers of [identify issuer] (the "Company"), does hereby certify, [to such officer's knowledge,][5] that:

The [Quarterly Report on Form 10-Q for the quarter ended [specify]] [Annual Report on Form [10-K] [20-F] [40-F] for the year ended [specify]] of the Company fully complies with the requirements of Section 13(a) or 15(d) of the Securities Exchange Act of 1934 and information contained in the Form [10-Q] [10-K] [20-F] [40-F] fairly presents, in all material respects, the financial condition and results of operations of the Company.

Dated:……………..   _____
                                    Name:
                                    Title: Chief Executive Officer

Dated:……………..   _____
                                    Name:
                                    Title: Chief Financial Officer

---

[4] The SEC has recommended that issuers include the following legend after the text of each Section 906 certification:

> A signed original of this written statement required by Section 906, or other document authenticating, acknowledging, or otherwise adopting the signature that appears in typed form within the electronic version of this written statement required by Section 906, has been provided to [name of issuer] and will be retained by [name of issuer] and furnished to the Securities and Exchange Commission or its staff upon request.

SEC Release No. 33-8238 (June 5, 2003), 68 Fed. Reg. 36636, 36653, n. 157 (June 18, 2003).

[5] Although this language does not appear in Section 906 of the Sarbanes-Oxley Act, it would appear appropriate in light of the fact that Section 906 imposes criminal liability for inaccurate certifications that are knowingly or willfully furnished by an officer.

FORM 4

Form of Section 302 Certification for Asset-Backed Issuers[6]

I, [identify the certifying individual], certify that:

1. I have reviewed this annual report on Form 10-K, and all reports on Form 8-K containing distribution or servicing reports filed in respect of periods included in the year covered by this annual report, of [identify issuer];

2. Based on my knowledge, the information in these reports, taken as a whole, does not contain any untrue statement of a material fact or omit to state a material fact necessary to make the statements made, in light of the circumstances under which such statements were made, not misleading as of the last day of the period covered by this annual report;

3. Based on my knowledge, the distribution or servicing information required to be provided to the trustee by the servicer under the pooling and servicing, or similar, agreement, for inclusion in these reports is included in these reports;

4. [Alternative 1: I am responsible for reviewing the activities performed by the servicer under the pooling and servicing, or similar, agreement and based upon my knowledge and the annual compliance review required under that agreement, and except as disclosed in the reports, the servicer has fulfilled its obligations under the servicing agreement; and]

[Alternative 2: Based on my knowledge and upon the annual compliance statement included in the report and required to be delivered to the trustee in accordance with the terms of the pooling and servicing, or similar, agreement, and except as disclosed in the reports, the servicer has fulfilled its obligations under the servicing agreement; and][7]

5. The reports disclose all significant deficiencies relating to the servicer's compliance with the minimum servicing standards based upon the report provided by an independent public accountant, after conducting a review in compliance with the Uniform Single Attestation Program for Mortgage Bankers or similar proce-

---

[6] To be executed by the trustee of the trust (if the trustee signs the annual report) or the senior officer in charge of securitization of the depositor (if the depositor signs the annual report). Alternatively, the senior officer in charge of the servicing function for the master servicer (or entity performing the equivalent functions) may sign the certification.

[7] Alternative 1 should be used by all servicers that file and sign periodic reports, while Alternative 2 should be used by trustees or depositors that file or sign periodic reports.

APPENDIX D: FORMS OF OFFICER CERTIFICATION

dure, as set forth in the pooling and servicing, or similar, agreement, that is included in these reports.

[In giving the certifications above, I have reasonably relied on information provided to me by the following unaffiliated parties; [name of the servicer, sub-servicer, co-servicer, depositor or trustee].]

Date: ....

Title:

FORM 5

Section 302 Certification for Registered Investment Companies[8]

I, [Identify the certifying individual], certify that:

1. I have reviewed this report on Form N-CSR of [identify registrant];

2. Based on my knowledge, this report does not contain any untrue statement of a material fact or omit to state a material fact necessary to make the statements made, in light of the circumstances under which such statements were made, not misleading with respect to the period covered by this report;

3. Based on my knowledge, the financial statements, and other financial information included in this report, fairly present in all material respects the financial condition, results of operations, changes in net assets, and cash flows (if the financial statements are required to include a statement of cash flows) of the registrant as of, and for, the periods presented in this report;

4. The registrant's other certifying officer(s) and I are responsible for establishing and maintaining disclosure controls and procedures (as defined in Rule 30a-3(c) under the Investment Company Act of 1940) [and internal control over financial reporting (as defined in Rule 30a-3(d) under the Investment Company Act of 1940)] for the registrant and have:

> (a) Designed such disclosure controls and procedures, or caused such disclosure controls and procedures to be designed under our supervision, to ensure that material information relating to the registrant, including its consolidated subsidiaries, is made known to us by others within those entities, particularly during the period in which this report is being prepared;

> [(b) Designed such internal control over financial reporting, or caused such internal control over financial reporting to be designed under our supervision, to provide reasonable assurance regarding the reliability of financial reporting and the preparation of financial statements for external purposes in accordance with generally accepted accounting principles;]

> (c) Evaluated the effectiveness of the registrant's disclosure controls and procedures and presented in this report our conclusions about the effectiveness of the disclosure controls and procedures, as of a date within 90 days prior to the filing date of this report based on such evaluation; and

---

[8] Effective August 14, 2003, except that the bracketed language in paragraph 4 will become effective beginning with the annual report for the registrant's first fiscal year ending on or after June 15, 2004.

APPENDIX D: FORMS OF OFFICER CERTIFICATION

(d) Disclosed in this report any change in the registrant's internal control over financial reporting that occurred during the registrant's most recent fiscal half-year (the registrant's second fiscal half-year in the case of an annual report) that has materially affected, or is reasonably likely to materially affect, the registrant's internal control over financial reporting; and

5. The registrant's other certifying officer(s) and I have disclosed to the registrant's auditors and the audit committee of the registrant's board of directors (or persons performing the equivalent functions):

(a) All significant deficiencies and material weaknesses in the design or operation of internal control over financial reporting which are reasonably likely to adversely affect the registrant's ability to record, process, summarize, and report financial information; and

(b) Any fraud, whether or not material, that involves management or other employees who have a significant role in the registrant's internal control over financial reporting.

Date: ....

Title: _____